SCIENCE EDUCATION HEALTH AND CONSCIOUSNESS

SCIENCE EDUCATION HEALTH AND CONSCIOUSNESS

Sampooran Singh

Dr. (Mrs.) Kanwaljit Kaur

Publications

KALPAZ PUBLICATIONS

DELHI-110 052

Science Education Health and Consciousness

Rs. 875

ISBN : 81-7835-443-8

Published in 2005 in India by
Kalpaz Publications,
C-30, Satyawati Nagar,
Delhi-110 052
Email : kalpaz@hotmail.com

Lasertype Setting by: Tact Computer Graphics, Delhi
Printed at: Salasar Imaging System, Delhi

Contents

Part III
Health Technology

Preface

Humanity is in supreme peril, not from another species, not from outer space, but from within its own conditioned psyche. During the last 400 years, science has made accelerative progress and has added immensely to material comfort. But during the last 10,000 years, or more, it has slowly added to human psychological imbalances, ecological crisis and other challenges. The worst is that these conditionings have now travelled from the conscious level to sub-conscious level and all human efforts to end this paradox have proved to be futile. Federico Mayor Zaragoza, in his address to seventy-four Nobel laureates in January 1988, said, "Never before, until now, has the tension between science and the human conscience, between technology and ethics, reached a point where it has become a threat to the world as a whole". Many eminent philosophers-mystics, politicians, Secretaries-General of the United Nations, and so on, have echoed that we are heading towards self-annihilation, self-destruction.

We are transiting into a global society. Politics have become global. Economics has become global. Now the growth of globalization has taken place, but not the development of global consciousness. Globalization is taking place as the result of science and technology and the thrust of evolution, but global consciousness is not keeping pace with the globalization. Now the transition is happening almost every five to seven years, for all practical purposes, there is a new technological generation. So time has encapsulated, but our conditioned mind is still functioning in the old rhythms, which is repetitive and mechanical and depends upon inheritance of the past. Globalization has put a severe restraint on the freedom of economically weak and smaller nations. Man is losing sensitivity at an accelerative pace.

Robert Muller in the Foreword to the SourceBook for the Parliament of Religions, Chicago, 1993, wrote, "Nevertheless, one dimension has been missing from this extraordinary journey; a dimension lamented by Secretaries-General Dag Hammarskjold, U Thant and Javier Perez de Cuellar: the spiritual dimension, the highest, deepest, most common, universal and binding dimension of all .... The common heritages and their spirituality can be the greatest single contribution to a better world".

What we need in the final analysis is a transmutation of consciousness. Jonas Salk, an eminent scientist, wrote, "Will man become a package of pathology or remain a package of potential. It would seem more worthwhile to learn and devote one's life to the development of potential rather than of nursing pathology". We have to end the epidemic of disorders (conditionings) of the mind, and enhance our living in a higher quantum energy potential of consciousness.

Present Living : Our Shared Responsibility

Without being aware of it and without being rigorously systematic about it; the mind, in order to see itself, it first cuts itself up into one state which sees (the subject-of-cognizance) and another state which is seen (the objective world). In this severed and mutilated condition whatever is seen is *only partially* itself. There is energy exchange between the subject and the object, which leads to distortion of both and both are recorded as a single channel computer. The way of seeing things – the old paradigm – has aptly been called "the hypnosis of social conditioning", an induced fiction in which we have collectively agreed to participate. It is our conditioning, our current world view that we were taught by our parents, teachers and society. The whole mankind has programmed itself to live out of that collective conditioning; the present way of living is our shared worldview or social conditioning – by our parents, teachers and society – is leading us to self-destruction or self-annihilation.

An exploration of the cause of the emergence of human challenges and the cause to resolve them so far is as under:

(a) ***The Challenges Facing Mankind :* 1900-1950:** Albert Einstein – in an essay "Out of Later Years" – wrote, "The confidence in the stability, even the very basis of existence, of human society has largely vanished. One senses not only a threat to man's cultural heritage but also that a lower value is placed upon all that one will like to see defended at all costs .... Life in human society meant dangers of all sorts .... even standards of virtue, aspiration and practical truth were taken for granted as an inviolable heritage, common to all civilised humanity .... The sanctity of life vanished .... The lie was raised to the dignity of a political instrument. It was a manifestation of weakness of character and lack of responsibility on the part of the leaders in the affected countries". This presents evidence that the human psyche during the first five decades of twentieth century got heavily conditioned leading to lowering of its sensitivity.

(b) ***The Challenges Facing Mankind : 1950 – to date:*** The recent challenges – global terrorism, hijacking, religious fundamentalism, ethnic conflicts, organised crime, drug-trafficking, corruption, and so on – have emerged in the last five decades of the twentieth century. All these challenges are constructs of the human mind, and forms the root of intellection and is therefore next to impossible to uproot by intellection. Einstein stated, "The significant problems we face cannot be solved at the same level of thinking we used when we created them".

(c) The cause is that (i) the human psyche during the twentieth century has got heavily conditioned and has lost its sensitivity; (ii) this loss of sensitivity is leading to self-destruction and self-annihilation; (iii) intellect or logical reason cannot transform the conditioned psyche, which implies that one has to transcend the partial experience and fragmentary knowledge (information) – a symbolic-dualistic frame of reference of mind spectrum; (iv) one is driven to objective observing and understanding; (v) all discoveries are the result of common intuition and faith, and not cold logic; (vi) we have to enhance our awareness which is observation without identification, without condemnation, without denial and acceptance; (vii) we need moral education where morals emerge from the deepest dimension (subjective) of Consciousness; and (viii) this leads to a quantum jump from symbolic-dualistic frame of reference to non-dual and non-conceptual frame of reference of Mind Continuum.

(d) The accelerative conditioning of the human psyche during the twentieth century has led to a serious crisis – which is that knowledge (information) proliferates but wisdom atrophies. The crisis cannot be resolved at socio-economic-political level or by "United Nations Security Council (UNSC)". The answer is embedded in Albert Einstein's prophetic words, that mankind needs "objective observing and understanding" to attain "peace and serenity", or in other words, "Symbiosis of Science and Spirituality". In common parlance, the aspirations of mankind (and that of UNSC) is: "Creativity in Science!", or "Generation of Innovations for Freedom and Peace".

Resolution of Human Paradox or Mutation of the Human Psyche

Although each person seems separate and independent, all of us are connected to patterns of intelligence that governs the whole cosmos. Our bodies are part of a universal body, our minds are aspects of a universal mind.

Nature is benevolent, she has been releasing Her Truth, bit by bit, in the minds of eminent scientists for the past one century, and now it has brought man on the control panel of conditioned human psyche. Many eminent scientists – Einstein, Schrodinger, Heisenberg, Eddington, and so on – have stumbled upon another mode of knowing, called intimate, or insight, or intuition, or non-dual knowledge, or understanding of life directly, instead of in the abstract, linear terms of representational thinking. The non-dual and integral state (Sri Aurobindo called it the Supermind or Supramental state) is a relaxation into a sacred state of non-action, non-knowing, non-experiencing. It is leading man to oneness of life, or the wholeness of life, which is free from all conflicts. This leads man to discover a life without conflict, to live peacefully, to live with a great abundance of love. It is the all integral dimension of Consciousness that heals. This is the consummation of human life.

We need restructuring of science-education-health to *observe* truthfully and sincerely the conditioned and the Unconditioned Energy, and this will flow to mutation of the psyche. The different steps in observation, which are expressed to understand and learn, are as under:

(a) ***Ending of I-consciousness:*** If a thought coupled with volitions encounters the true-subject, the I-consciousness is knocked off because it is at the lowest quantum energy potential. This suggests that: (i) the movement of thought-time is independent of I-consciousness; (ii) it is the movement of collective human effort; (iii) both the I-consciousness and thought-structure have a conceptual reality.

(b) ***Ending of Thought-Time:*** When thought-time comes in the realm of true-subject, the photons meet an 'impregnable wall', or "event-horizon", or "frequency-barrier", and are dissipated, which implies that thought-time goes to abeyance and what is left behind is the *fact*, the *true*, the *present*, the *what is*!

(c) **Ending of the Fact:** If we continue observing or listening to the *fact*, without justification, or condemnation, or motivation, we observe that there is only the *fact* and nothing else. The fact itself is the operator and not you operating on the fact. If you leave the fact alone, it has no time. The fact is free from fear. The fact grows, which implies that there is release of tremendous energy and the fact moves to higher quantum energy potential. This is expressed as Pure Consciousness → Fact.

(d) **Dialogue from within nature:** *We have to initiate a dialogue with nature from within nature, and nature responds to this experimental interrogation. If a scientist, who is aware of "restructured science-education-health" and lives in that awareness, asks questions addressed to nature, he invariably succeeds in receiving answers directly from nature. Nature is an "open-book" to him.*

(e) ***Understanding:*** The observation flows to understanding and learning. Understanding and learning are born in non-duality. Intuition (insight) is perception without any doubt. ***Understanding, learning and action are a cyclic process, which results in a spiral going upwards in the vertical dimension; it is a growth in the vertical dimension.*** The higher the understanding, the higher the expression of the Consciousness in the human brain-body system.

Education

We want a revolution, psychological revolution, in which the whole human race has to participate and every man is an equal partner. This revolution will regenerate or rejuvenate human mind so that it perceives the new dimension of an integral and all-inclusive consciousness, that can guarantee human survival along with all fauna and flora.

We need a quantum jump from symbolic-dualistic frame of reference of mind spectrum to non-symbolic, non-dualistic, non-conceptual frame of reference of Mind Continuum. All education is to resolve the crisis of perception. To understand this whole movement of life requires intelligence, not the intelligence of thought, or books, or knowledge, but the intelligence of love and compassion with its sensitivity.

All education is freedom of mind. Freedom means to have no conflict, psychologically, inwardly. And with freedom, the brain becomes holistic, not fragmented in itself. Freedom also means love and compassion. Intelligence is inherent in compassion.

All present education is defined in terms of rupture between man and nature. This has to be rectified as all arts are leading to 'direct perception' and science must bring in harmony with laws of nature. Science is part of human relations and modern science must involve him. This has been echoed by Niels Bohr, a Nobel laureate in Physics, in words, "We are both spectators and actors in the great drama of existence". We must realize that man's power to resist nature is hopelessly puny. The task of turning the age-old tide of violence, fear, competition, ambition have to be jettisoned because these lead to "indirect perception". One is deeply touched by the large gap between the superhuman task and the frailties of human endeavours.

We have to jettison the horizontal dimension of consciousness, which is basically pathological, and imbibe the vertical dimension of consciousness, which is fundamentally non-dual and non-conceptual. This will add timelessness, eternity of creation to the infinity of existence, the Unmanifest releases the spiritual energy raising the quantum energy potential of the whole existence. In philosophical language, it is called the manifestation of the Divine in human life. The Divine realm is free of all psychological imbalances, ecological crisis, conflict, chaos, disorder, violence, terrorism and other human challenges. The manifestation of the Divine blossoms into a new Being, a new World, and a new Creation. The Divine Mother (Madame Mirra Alfasa) in 1963 wrote, "The only hope for the future is a change in man's consciousness and the change is bound to come". The message in 1967 read, "Men, countries, continents! The choice is imperative: Truth, or the abyss". The Mother had once observed, "Three-fourth of humanity is obsolete".

Education is the basis of the mutation of the human psyche. As the children are taught various disciplines and skills, they are given the capability to observe the conditioned psyche and the Unconditioned Energy. This observation tends to make them self-aware which flows to Intelligence/Wisdom. This fosters a right relationship with other fellow beings, with nature, with the universe itself.

Aims and Objects of Education

Albert Einstein, the greatest scientist of all time, wrote that man is here for the sake of other man, for the sake of whole mankind; and indeed for the sake of all human beings. **The fundamental research into the manifestation of ever greater potential and newer dimensions of Consciousness would be our core commitment, action and responsibility.** We are here on this planet to share our findings with all human beings.

Teilhard de Chardin concluded that humanity would enter a new age of evolution and metamorphose itself into a higher, peaceful, more responsible, super conscious, and spiritual global species. Many other eminent scientists and philosophers-mystics share this view. This is possible if we ***"educate the instruments of pure perception"*** which Nature has endowed us with. Such education will energise the ***"understanding and learning of life directly"***, which blossoms to intuition, spontaneity and right action. When "understanding is stabilized, the mind-brain-body system makes a quantum jump to higher awareness, or higher Consciousness. In the state of higher quantum energy potential of Consciousness, all pain, misery, fragmentation, psychological imbalances, go to abeyance, and it ushers a new era of order, harmony, interrelatedness, freedom, non-violence, peace and bliss. This is the consummation of human life. It is the greatest vocation in the world.

Introduction

Man had an evolutionary origin, the *Homo Homonid* appeared at about 4.5 million years ago, and *Homo sapiens* at about 2.5 million years ago. For 2,000 years, or more, he had been observing, comparing, and seeking to classify his observations. Julian Huxley in 1959 wrote, "Man's evolution is not biological but psychosocial, it operates by the mechanism of cultural tradition, which involves the cumulative self-reproduction and self-variation of mental activities and their products".

Man is an amphibian who lives simultaneously in two worlds – (a) the '*known*', time-space-causation matrices, the successive consciousness, the symbolic-dualistic world; and (b) the *Unknown*, timelessness, the Simultaneous Consciousness, the non-dual and non-conceptual world. The known constructs neurological tension and chemical pressure; it constructs conflict, chaos and duality; and it is leading to self-destruction or self-annihilation. But it offers no guidance in regard to the much more fundamental problem of the relationship of man and the timelessness, or to the still, tranquil and equipoised Mind.

Modern physics has confirmed: (a) all the concepts we use to describe nature are limited, and creations of the mind, the conditioned psyche; parts of the map, not of the territory; (b) in order to see itself, it cuts itself up into at least one state which sees, and at least one other state which is seen; in this severed and mutilated condition whatever it sees is *only partially* itself; (c) the interaction between the seer (subject) and the seen (object) introduces duality; (d) it constructs space-time matrices in quick succession, and man has started living in the synthetic world and divorced the Reality, the Universal Consciousness, and (e) this has resulted in constructing innumerable psychological imbalances which is leading man to self-annihilation.

Man's psychosocial evolution, over uncountable aeons, has led to: (a) the mind perceives the object (time-space-causation matrices) as direct perception; (b) it then recalls or retrieves the past corresponding memory; (c) there is coherent superpositions of recalled memory on direct perception leading to sharing of energy and resulting in distorted perception and modified memory; (d) it implies grafting the past concepts on the present (direct perception) leading to transforming a perceptual model to a conceptual model; and (e) the conceptual model or symbolic-dualistic frame of reference of mind spectrum expresses itself as neurological tension and chemical pressures, conflict and chaos. Man started living in a conceptual world – man-made social cosmos, and rejected the Reality, the Consciousness. The whole world is unknowingly caught in a crisis of perception, barring a few individuals. The conflict, fragmentation, chaos and duality is leading to self-destruction or self-annihilation.

During the last 10,000 years, man has been trying to end this conflict, violence, fear through ideals, concepts, thought-structures, but all this has fallen on the deaf ears of mankind. At all levels, there is a growing realisation that the existing models of education, both in the East and West, have failed, and there is total lack of relevance between the human being and the complex contemporary society.

The accelerative growth of science and technology has given us the capacity to resolve our psychological imbalances, ecological crisis, and other challenges. But the materialistic approach and competition has landed us to that knowledge proliferates, but wisdom languishes. It is evident that this yawning chasm will need to be bridged; and perhaps some benign turn of destiny enables us to stave off disaster.

Where is Science Going?

Max Planck, Nobel laureate in physics, in an article entitled, "Where is Science Going?" wrote:

> It is a fact that there is a point, one single point in the immeasurable expanse of mind and matter, where science and therefore every causal method of research is inapplicable, not only on practical grounds, but also on logical grounds, and will always remain inapplicable. This is the point of [our] individual awareness.

George Wald, Nobel prize in medicine, 1967, wrote:

> Our society has taken a wrong turn. In our thirst for knowledge, we have cut ourselves off from wisdom. In our pride in science, we have come to despise and reject intuitive and instinctual perceptions that have heretofore animated and given perspective and hope and meaning to human existence. By now the problem is not transcendence, but survival. If we are to survive there must be fundamental changes in direction, not only organizational, but in our ways of thinking. We have to think different thoughts and to want different things.
>
> We who know where we are going, are now heading rapidly toward self-extinction, toward removing humankind from the cosmic scene, and for the most trivial of reasons: profit, the rivalry of the United States and the Soviet Union, the momentum

> of the military-industrial complex in both nations. The cosmic drama will go on elsewhere, ignorant of our demise, caring nothing; but we will have no further part in it .... Does that matter? It matters to us.

Seeing – the event in consciousness – seems to be in another universe, unapproachable by science

Jacques Monod, Nobel-prize-winning biologist, wrote, "What we see opening before us today is an abyss of darkness". Hideki Yukawa, a Japanese Nobel laureate, wrote:

> The development of science, far from encouraging the formation and development of an integrated view of man in his many different aspects, has tended rather to split and destroy that view.... The danger that all these trends will combine to destroy the unity of man's various aspects and lead eventually to the loss even of his humanity cannot be denied. It is equally undeniable, I believe, that such a split would deprive man of his happiness.

P. Krishna, an eminent physicist, in a lecture in USA, said, "We are going today towards self-annihilation and not much time is left now".

The objective science is leading mankind to self-annihilation. Man knows precisely the methodology of mutation of human psyche, but his ignorance and arrogance is not permitting him to act.

Nature of Human Crisis

Humanity's ethical and spiritual development has not kept pace with the accelerative progress of material technology, and this imbalance threatens to destabilize and even destroy human civilization. Public life today is dominated by ephemeral values, psychological imbalances (violence, fear, greed, acquisition, competition, motive, desire, and so on) to the almost utter neglect of abiding spiritual principles. Indeed, there appears to be a fundamental crisis of perception, response, values which aggravates current economic, social and political tensions. Accompanied by raging ecological problems, religious fundamentalism, terrorism, corruption, poverty, hunger, and so on, these tensions tend to push the world ever closer to self-destruction.

Today, after billions of years of prebiological evolution and metabiological evolution, mankind is at an evolutionary crossroads. We stand at a juncture wherein we are in supreme peril – not a peril from another species, not a peril from outer space, but a peril from ourselves. From deep within the human psyche, there has developed this terrible power that threatens not only our generation but generations yet to be born, and not only our race, but all species of life on this planet.

There are two fundamental questions – (a) ***Has humanity taken a wrong turn which has created this chaos in the world?; and*** (b) ***What needs to be done within the consciousness of man to preserve our very existence and bring about a new culture?"*** *We must explore these challenges through observation with a view to understand the happenings within us which will resolve this paradox.*

The Western scientific approach to knowledge is based on variability of the objective means of observation. The Eastern approach to knowledge is based on the non-variability of the subjective means of observation. Nature has been benevolent to release 'Her Truths' bit by bit in the minds of eminent scientists, perhaps due to systematic, rigorous and consistent approach of science. Some of the latest discoveries are as under:

(a) The nature of consciousness was the subject of two scientific conferences in 1996, one at Moscow and the other at Cambridge University. At Moscow, the Russian scientists put forward the idea of a Life Field beyond our physical concepts of time, space and the known electromagnetic and gravitational fields. At Cambridge, a new scientific approach was discussed "which would include subjective experience as valid information and address all forms of human experience – including intuition, spirituality and mystical encounters". The Life Field and *Brahman* are synonymous.

(b) Ervin Laszlo wrote, "We are not just observing it, we are not even just immersed in it, we are integral part of it .... the space time field is a sea of potential energy – a plenum, not a vacuum". This is synonymous to our ancient view of 'void', 'nothingness' and so on. It also suggests oneness of life.

(c) Many eminent neuro-physiologists, neuro-surgeons, scientists – such as Karl Pribram, Roger Sperry, John Eccles – have opined, "Brain science could no longer afford to shut out that part of the world which we call subjective", and we have to recognise "the importance of a neglected area of science, namely the study of human subjective experience".

(d) Science has provided irrefutable evidence that modern science and pure religion are identical and are complementary. The combination today of the spiritual energies of these two complementary disciplines in the life of man will produce fully integrated human beings, and thus help to evolve a complete human civilisation for which the world is ripe and waiting.

(e) The Council for a Parliament of World's Religions (CPWR), Chicago, held International Summits at Delhi on December 7-10, 2003 and at Barcelona (Spain) on July 7-13, 2004.

(f) The United Nations Foundations, Secretary-General Mr Kofi Annan, on September 23, 2003 appointed 16 Eminent Personalities for the future of United Nations to "examine the current challenges to peace and security" [www.unfoundation.org]. This is a major initiative in support of the High Level Panel and will be meeting shortly. A report entitled, UNDP Human Development Report, 2004, was released on July 15, 2004.

(g) According to one estimate, twenty thousand scientists around the globe are currently engaged in the exploration of consciousness. Never before, so many subjective scientists, in addition to philosophers-mystics, were investigating consciousness.

There is an urgency to disseminate the exploration of "Symbiosis of Science and Spirituality", or "Science and Technology – New Challenges". The aims and objects of the monograph is "to initiate a dialogue with an open mind". There is considerable repetition in different articles, because these have been penned as independent so that the reader may read any chapter he is interested in. The truth of each article has emerged as intuition or insight during the last 28 years. The intuition blossoms to mutation, which happens in the brain through insight, not through knowledge, not through accumulation. The insight is the ability to see a truth directly, a direct perception of the truth, and education must foster that. There is an urgency to share this with every scientist on the globe and to call for their response. Perhaps after these discussions, a second model may emerge which will be a beacon light to mankind.

The Union of Concerned Scientists – over 1670 scientists, including 104 Nobel laureates – have issued "***World Scientists' Warning to Humanity***" in April 1993, reads as:

A new ethic is required .... This ethic must motivate a great movement, convincing reluctant leaders and reluctant governments and reluctant peoples themselves to effect the needed changes.

Many eminent politicians, scientists, philosophers-mystics, and lovers of mankind have proclaimed that "we are going towards self-annihilation and not much time is left now". J. Krishnamurti, in prophetic words in 1954, wrote, "There must be a radical revolution. The world crisis demand it. Our lives demand it". Our search is for the truth, we urgently need a perception of a boundless energy of infinite existence, infinite movement, infinite activity pouring itself out in limitless Space, in eternal Time.

The Resolution of Human Paradox

Nature is benevolent, she has been releasing her truth, bit by bit, in the minds of eminent scientists for the last one century, perhaps due to the rigorous, consistent and persistent enquiry, or observation. Some of the important scientific discoveries are as under:

(a) Many eminent scientists – including Albert Einstein, Werner Heisenberg, Erwin Schrodinger, Arthur Eddington, and so on – have stumbled upon another mode of knowing, called direct or intimate, or insight, or intuition, or "the understanding of life directly, instead of in the abstract, linear terms of representational thinking". The symbolic-dualistic frame of reference of mind spectrum makes a quantum jump to non-dual and non-conceptual frame of reference of Mind Continuum. It had run its course to that of annihilating edge of dualism, or dualism between subject and object.

(b) Albert Einstein warned us of nuclear threats in words:

> Science can denature plutonium but science cannot denature evil in the heart of man.... The splitting of the atom has changed everything except our mode of thinking and thus we drift towards unparalleled catastrophe. If you wish to avert disaster, we must first be aware of the dangers.

We have to be aware of the dangers and limitations of the conditioned psyche and how. its dynamics is leading us to self-destruction or self-annihilation. The answer to this paradox is to enhance our level of awareness to achieve mutation in the human psyche; or in other words, a quantum jump from psychosocial evolution to spiritual evolution.

(c) Many eminent scientists – say, Karl Pribram, John Eccles, Roger Sperry – "spoke of the importance of a neglected area of science, namely the study of human subjective experience". The exchange of energy between the subjective (inner) and the objective (outer) takes place in about few millionth of a second. "The outer and the inner" is a single dynamic movement and cannot be treated as two movements. The inner is called the true-subject, which is non-variable attentivity, or reaction-free attentivity, or objectless attention. The non-variable attentivity understands the wholeness of life. At the moment of attention, all the conditioning goes to abeyance, all the image-building comes to an end, and it is only when you are not attentive that the whole cycle of the recall of the past inheritance starts.

(d) When thought coupled with volitions, motives, desires encounters true-subject, the I-consciousness first goes to abeyance and then the thought-structure is knocked off. Ilya

Prigogine, Nobel Prize, 1977, wrote, "It is physics that presupposes an observer situated within the observed world. Our dialogue with nature will be successful only if carried on from within nature". This implies that the observer and the observed are "in here", and not the observed is "out there".

(e) Albert Einstein stated, ***"Without radically transforming ourselves, there can be no transformation of the individual and the society. A system cannot transform man. Transformation comes through self-knowledge and not through belief".***

Action Plan

The present book entitled **Science, Education, Health and Consciousness** is divided in three parts, which are not separate from each other. This is done as an exegetical convenience, a device to make the complex story of the generation of the spectrum of the consciousness a little easier to tell. In each section, copious references are given as we feel that the general public is not aware of the scientific progress in this field because the subject is neither taught in schools/colleges, nor the parents, nor the society deals with this. But this is vital for our survival and excellence. If man escapes the responsibility of understanding, learning and living this perennial knowledge, he does so at his own peril, and that of India and mankind.

Part I : Science and Technology – Man Self-Unfolding

The fundamental challenge facing mankind is "not wars or nuclear war", but the conditioned psyche which has emerged from the psychosocial evolution of man over uncountable aeons. Every activity of I-consciousness and thought structure leads to enhancing entropy – nervous tension and chemical pressure – of the system. Evidently the only answer to human paradox is transcending I-consciousness and thought structure. Karan Singh wrote, "We stand at a juncture wherein we are in supreme peril – not a peril from another species, not a peril from outer space, but a peril from ourselves. From deep within the human psyche, there has developed the terrible power that threatens not only our generation but generations yet to be born, and not only our race, but all species of life on this planet".

(a) ***The Cause of Human Failure:*** For the last 10,000 years, or more, man has been trying to end psychological imbalances and live in order, non-violence and peace; but all techniques, beliefs, percepts and thought structures have proved to be sterile to transform the psyche. To resolve our challenges we have to enhance our level of awareness and live in that quantum energy potential of Consciousness. We urgently need to enquire, or observe, or experimental interrogation of the conditioned psyche and the Unconditioned Energy and this will flow into mutation or radically transformation of the psyche.

(b) ***The Subjective and the Objective Dimensions:*** Man is an amphibian who lives simultaneously in two dimensions – the given (inner, subjective) and the home-made (outer, objective). Many eminent neuro-scientists, neuro-physiologists, neuro-surgeons have echoed that "Brain science cannot afford to shut out that part of the world which we call subjective". The exchange of energy between the subjective (inner) and the objective (outer) takes place in about few millionth of a second. The outer and the inner are one, a unitary movement, not separate, but whole. It is a single dynamic movement.

(c) ***Restructuring of Science:*** We have to restructure our objective science so that it takes in its ambient both the outer and the inner dimensions of life. This deals with the wholeness of life and we call the inner as the true-subject.

(d) ***Restructuring of Education:*** We have to restructure education so that it deals with the sensual world and the trans-sensual world.

(e) **Restructuring of Medical Education:** We have to restructure medical education so that it deals with the sensual and trans-sensual dimensions of life, or the wholeness of life.

Part II : Project Launched by United Nations on 23 September 2003

The UN Foundation, along with partners from around the globe, has launched a major initiative in support of the High-Level Panel appointed by UN Secretary-General Kofi Annan, to assess 21st Century threats to international peace and security. The High-Level Panel will recommend ways in which the international community can reform to effectively address modern-day challenges. [www.unfoundation.org/].

This acted as a catalyst for exploration and the findings were submitted as three papers to the UN on April 16, 2004; and one paper on April 26, 2004. We penned four papers during the last four months, which are published as the present monograph.

If thought-structure coupled with volitions (I-consciousness) encounters the higher quantum energy potential of Consciousness (restructured science-education), the thought-structure and I-consciousness go to abeyance. The true-subject has now the awareness of the whole, the fact, the true, the present, the what is! It bestows understanding and learning. These flower to intuition (insight), spontaneity and right action. The Intelligence is activised and ends the current evolutionary crisis. It leads to transcend the psychic age and be a harbinger to the spiritual age.

The aims and objects of this monograph is to "initiate a global dialogue with an open mind". This "open sharing" may lead to a modified technology to "global peace and security".

Part III : Health Technology

The theme of Indian Science Congress – 2005 is Health Technology. All diseases are maladjustment of the human mind-brain-body system, or conditioned human psyche, or crisis of perception. Health is a complete physical, mental, psychological and social well-being; it is a dynamic state which is equipoised and balanced. A living in the *present*, the now heals; and living in the past and duality suppresses man's sensitivity and enhances disease. There is an urgency to restructure medical education which takes in its ambient the psychodynamics of the mind-brain-body system and the Unconditioned Energy; or in other words, the wholeness of life. The curricula of medical education has got to be restructured which implies the wholeness of life. We have to restructure the bio-medical model and adopt the holistic ecological model. The restructured medical education takes in its ambient the wholeness of life.

We have to understand, learn and live the art of observation of the conditioned psyche which bestows freedom. Freedom blossoms to transcend I-consciousness and thought structure. This gives insight which is a timeless perception. It is insight alone that can decondition the brain. Insight is complete and from that completeness there can be logical, sane, rational action. Only then there can be flowering of the brain. Only then can you have a complete relationship with the mind.

Healing is alive, complex and holistic. All human illness basically results from the interplay of mind, body and environment, so the bio-medical model will have to be integrated with ending the psychic pandemic.

Healing implies ending the crisis of perception. Healing implies to transcend I-consciousness, thought-structures and other psychological imbalances. Healing implies to end all pathological approaches and enhance potentials of consciousness. To sum up, we have to "restructure science-education-health". We have to arrange special courses for the existing doctors.

We have to work for ***restructuring of science, restructuring of education, restructuring of health (medical science), awareness of human perennial values, and live that understanding at every moment.*** *This is a super-historic breakthrough of releasing a new principle of integral* *consciousness (spirituality), which has got the potentiality of transforming the entire planetary life and ushering a New Age.*

Symbiosis of Science and Spirituality: Many eminent scientists during the last 5-7 decades have started exploration of Cosmic Consciousness or Life Field, and have concluded that consciousness expresses itself in two dominant dimensions – (a) ***successive consciousness***, which is time, or time-space matrices, and (b) ***Simultaneous Consciousness***, which is timeless.

Spirituality is the science of life and living. It has the potential to rectify "the inner structural crisis" or "the crisis of perception". We need urgently symbiosis of science and spirituality. This is a pointer to grow into the dimensions of non-violence, fearlessness, love and peace.

Spirituality is an experimental science and as precise as mathematics. Its dimensions are homogeneous, undifferentiated and non-dimensional. It is verifiable by another explorer, but this wisdom *and* truth *cannot be passed from one experimentor to another (non-communicable truth). So every body is all alone to undertake this exploration. Man is only a conduit for expression of nature's evolutionary impulse.*

Spirituality has the potential to rectify the inner structural crisis, and understand and live according to the immutable laws of nature. This is a pointer to persuade the human beings to grow into the maturity of love, friendship and peace. In the art of living spirituality, the human survival and excellence is embedded.

Summary

The deepest exploration by eminent men of science are as under:

(a) The Consciousness is fundamental and rational thought is a derivative. Fritjof Capra stated, "The rational part of research would, in fact, be useless if it were not accompanied by the intuition that gives scientists new insights and make them creative". Max Born, a Nobel laureate in physics, stated, "Clever, rational ways of thinking are not enough. The danger of mass slaughter .... can only be overcome by moral conviction, by a determination to replace national prides and prejudices with human love".

(b) Hideki Yukawa wrote, "Abstraction cannot work by itself, but has to be accompanied by intuition".

(c) Intuition (insight) is fundamental and reason is a derivative. Man has to base himself on Consciousness, the wholeness of life. He has to explore himself, the infinite hierarchical quantum energy potential of Consciousness.

(d) Man has to resolve the crisis of perception. We need to regenerate or rejuvenate a new "instrument of perception", which is a free gift to every human being and is embedded deep in our mind-brain-body system.

(e) The future of mankind is embedded in rejuvenating the "instrument of perception" – it is embedded in direct perception.

The Wholeness of Life

(a) Observation (seeing), listening (hearing), understanding and learning, action and nature's expressions are direct, so these are in communion with immutable laws of nature. The direct is in the timeless realm, so it bestows the truth. Thinking, thought, memory and inheritance are indirect; these are in the symbolic-dualistic world, or conceptual world. In worshipping a symbol, you will lose the real, the truth. This leads us to a fundamental truth: (a) the arts of observation/listening leads to ending I-consciousness and thought-structure; and (b) the art (observation/listening) leads us to rejuvenation of a creative and compassionate global Consciousness.

(b) The Truth self-expresses Itself in a non-symbolic, non-dualistic and non-conceptual frame of reference of Mind Continuum; it revels in freedom (thought coupled with volition goes to abeyance); it leads toa silent and tranquil Mind; it lives in the feeling of the Now.

(c) There are two instruments available to man: (a) The instrument of knowledge, the known, the time-space-causation matrices, the successive consciousness; it is an intellectual process, the observer operating on the thing observed, it is analysis, the altering and the adding, it is called *non-fact*, the *false*, the past, the *what should be*?; and (b) the instrument of direct perception, the Unknown, the Simultaneous Consciousness, it is in the timeless realm, there is neither the observer nor the observed, the thought-structure blossoms and dies, it is born of observation and self-awareness, it is called the *fact*, the *true*, the *present*, the *what is*!, it blossoms to Intelligence.

(d) Transformation is not in the future, can never be in the future. It can only be in the *fact*, the *true*, the *now*, the *present*, the *what is*! It is the pure perception, the *timeless perception*. It is seeing the false as the false and the true as the true, because when you see something very clearly as the truth, that truth liberates. When you see something is false, that false thing drops away. We see that the symbolic-dualistic world (perceptual world) is false, so when truth is seen, the false drops away. The direct perception bestows truth, and the mind is completely still. A still Mind resolves all the challenges. Truth expresses Itself as '*direct perception*', '*timeless perception*', *thought-free perception*, the *Now*, the Present.

(e) Man has to understand, learn and live in the wholeness of life, it is simply a flowering, an unfolding of the Divine (to live in direct perception of the highest quantum energy potential of Cosmic Consciousness, the Life Field). The 'direct perception' is a pointer to ending all duality, all conflict, all violence and fear, and man revels in order, harmony, non-violence and peace. The fulfilment of human life is embedded in 'direct perception'; it implies there is no path to follow, there is no authority, no systems, no goals – no past, present or future.

(f) This establishes the true relationship between man and man, between man and nature, where all conflicts vanish. This also ends all conflicts in society and a sane society emerges. This bestows a higher creativity to non-symbolic and non-dualistic frame of reference of Mind Continuum. Sri Aurobndo wrote, "(this) must lead to the ultimate discovery that man is inwardly a soul and a conscious power of the Divine and that the evocation of this real man within is the right object of education and indeed of all human life if it would find and live according tot he hidden Truth and deepest law of its own Being". This is called flowering of "symbiosis of science and spirituality". This is the consummation of human life.

(g) We have to initiate "an open dialogue with an open mind", and perhaps this sharing of the perennial knowledge may lead to a new model of mutation of human psyche and realm of Unconditioned Energy. This flows to order, harmony, non-violence and peace. In case man escapes his responsibility today, he will be forced to initiate the plan tomorrow after some catastrophe as discussed by Sri Aurobindo. Nature's laws are eternal, infinite and immutable. This is the consummation of human life. This is the only vocation of man.

Sampooran Singh
Dr (Mrs) Kanwaljit Kaur

Part I
Science and Technology : Man Self-Unfolding

The aims and objects of this monograph is "to open a dialogue with an open mind" especially with scientists, philosophers and social-activists. This sharing leads to self-knowledge of the mind-brain-body system. It flowers to self-awareness of the whole system. The self-awareness or attentivity – in the words of Albert Einstein – opens to "objective observation and understanding", which flows to transcending thought-structure coupled with volitions, and this blossoms to "peace and serenity". This energises Intelligence which resolves all challenges, and man revels in order, harmony, non-violence and peace. This is the only vocation of human life.

It is the moral responsibility of awakened men and Governments to submit this as Agenda for the United Nations. If man escapes his responsibility, he will do so at his own peril and that of India and mankind.

1

The Limitations of Science and Technology

The Principles of Objectivation and Understanding of Scientific Research

Abstract

Modern science has propounded that there exists Life Field (Cosmic Consciousness)–"a holistic frequency realm" that "transcends spatial and temporal boundaries". The world extended in space and time is but our representation–man-made social cosmos. The material world has been constructed by excluding the Subject of Cognizance from the domain of nature that we endeavour to understand; "obviously, therefore, it can neither act on it nor be acted on by any of its parts".

Science aims at making true and adequate statements about its object. Science and technology mainly focusses attention on the material progress of life and on technical solution to human challenges; it explores a modified use of the known–and this is called invention (not discovery). Although science is a human activity, yet all values are missing and quite particularly meaning and end are missing.

Science is an intellectual endeavour, and it rejects all intuition (insight). Intellect is repetitive and mechanical; and cannot give direct understanding of life. Science gathers experience and knowledge (information); it rejects pure perception which is always now, the present. Science rejects the creative processes in life.

Science makes progress largely by a combination of two aspects: open-mindedness and the following of abstract concepts. Abstract concepts produce narrow-mindedness, so the whole question of moral, spiritual and other dimensions is pushed out of science.

Scientists behave as though the intellect, analytical processes and objectivity (ignoring subjectivity) were the whole basis of human life. Science is silent about the real nature of human beings. This leads to entropy which is death or self-annihilation.

We have to explore how science is developed through educational institutions and through institutionalized science. Erwin Schrodinger wrote, "Scientific attitudes would have to be rebuilt, science must be made anew. Care is needed".

Many eminent scientists–neuro-physiologists, neuro-surgeons, neuro-scientists–have opined, "Brain science could no longer afford to shut out that part of the world which we call subjective". We have to "restructure science-education", which takes in its ambient both the objective and the subjective dimension of life and is called the "true-subject"; it observes the whole conditioned and unconditioned psyche which leads to I-consciousness and thought-time going to abeyance; the pure Consciousness (Life Field) bathes the purified brain (neurones) and expresses Itself as order, harmony, nonviolence and peace.

Man (*Homo sapiens*) has an evolutionary origin at about 2.5 million years ago. The psychological imbalances, ecological crisis, pollution challenges, a rising wave of violence and crime, terrorism, religious fundamentalism, ethnic conflicts, corruption, increasing unemployment, poverty, hunger, malnutrition, health crisis, are forcing man inevitably to face the realities of the human situation. All appeals to achieve full disarmament and permanent peace; all declarations by Nobel laureates; all appeals by Pugwash Conferences (since 1957); all appeals by the International Physicians for the Prevention of Nuclear War (IPPNW); by Secretaries-General of the United Nations; all proclamations of a manifesto by eminent scientists, philosophers, mystics have fallen on the deaf ears of mankind. During the last 10,000 years, or more, man invented innumerable techniques, systems, beliefs, concepts, thought-structures, but all have proved to be sterile in mutation of his psyche, and man has miserably failed. Nature's evolutionary impulse over uncountable aeons, his way of living in the 'external' field of time-space-causation matrices, and his total jettisoning of Life Field or Quantum Field Consciousness (QFC) are directing him to self-destruction, or self-annihilation, or death.

The principle of objectivation and the principle of the understandability of nature were put forward in 1947 by Erwin Schrodinger form the basis of scientific method.[1] Science aims at nothing but making true and adequate statements about its object. The scientist only implies two things, namely truth and sincerity, imposes them upon himself and upon other scientists. Schrodinger wrote, "the object is science itself, as it has developed and has become and at present is, not as it *ought* to be or *ought* to develop in nature".[2] He added, "Scientific attitudes have to be rebuilt, science must be made anew. Care is needed". Ilya Prigogine discussed the paradox of classical science in words:

> It revealed to men a dead, passive nature, a nature that behaves as an automaton which, once programmed, continues to follow the rules inscribed in the program. In this sense the dialogue with nature isolated man from nature instead of bringing him closer to it. A triumph of human reason turned into a sad truth. It seemed that science debased everything it touched.[3]

P. Krishna, an eminent physicist, summarised the dialogue between J. Krishnamurti and David Bohm in words, "Has humanity taken a wrong turn which has created this chaos in the world?" and "What needs to be done within the consciousness of man to preserve our very existence and bring about a new culture?"[4]

We explored the basis of scientific research in the light of mind-brain system and published it in 1997 in Prabuddha Bharata.[5] The science is progressing at a fantastic rate. This article is a revision of the technology of mutation of the human psyche in the light of discoveries of science during the last decade.

It also explores the fundamental questions–"Where have we erred and whither we are going" and "Can we create a mutation in consciousness and bring about a new culture?" It explores the "wholeness" of life, which regenerates Intelligence or Wisdom, and this expresses itself as order, harmony, nonviolence and peace.

The Principle of Objectivation

Modern physics has confirmed most dramatically that "while the stuff from which our world picture is built is yielded exclusively from the sense organs as organs of the mind, so that every man's world picture is and always remains a construct of his mind and cannot be proved to have any other existence, yet the conscious mind itself remains a stranger within that construct, it has no living space in it, you can spot it nowhere in space.... The scientific views of natural processes formed in this way lack all sensual qualities and therefore cannot account for the latter" The time-space-causation construct, or man-made social cosmos, is invariably dualistic, and its activity is materialistic. Schrodinger added, "The values are missing, and quite particularly meaning and end are missing".[6] This living in the conditioned psyche is leading man to self-destruction and self-annihilation.

Science is the search for truth. The practical value of science has been astonishingly too great, beyond all expectations. A selfless unfaltering devotion to truth and the use of knowledge for man's upliftment are the ideals of a scientist. Truth is what all earnest scientists seek. The aim of science is to investigate nature and human experience objectively. Objectivity and precision, in respect of both thought and its verbal formulation, are two important characteristics of the scientific methods. Maurice H. Wilkins, Nobel Prize in Medicine, 1962, wrote:

> Science makes progress largely by a combination of two aspects: open-mindedness and the following of abstract concepts. Abstraction involves excluding and narrowing down, which is the very opposite of open-mindedness. Science always puts the most emphasis on this abstracting and narrowing down, on analytical procedures and on the role of the intellect as distinct from intuition and feelings.... The whole question of moral, spiritual, and other dimensions is normally pushed out of science. So, something in the nature of science often does lead people towards destruction. Abstraction can be regarded as a form of violence and, as various poets have remarked, science often does violence to nature.[7]

It is the violence or aggression embedded in the human psyche, or mind-brain-body system which leads science to destruction. They lose their capacity to be broad-minded, open-minded and sensitive, and this leads science to destruction. Science focusses attention on the material aspect of life and on technical or rational solution of human problems. The material prosperity and rationality leads to psychological imbalances.

Hideki Yukawa, a Japanese N.L. in physics wrote, "The development of science, far from encouraging the formation and development of an integrated view of man in his many different aspects, has tended rather to split and destroy that view .... The danger that all these trends will destroy the unity of man's various aspects and lead eventually to loss even of his humanity cannot be denied".[8]

About 1600 Kepler and Galileo, simultaneously and independently, formulated the principle that the laws of nature are to be discovered by measurement. All propositions were to be confined to that which was objectively measurable and verifiable. We call the objective measurement, verification, recording it as memory, and recall of memory in our daily life is called the principle of objectivity.

Wrong Turn Taken by Mankind

Hideki Yukawa concluded:

> The human emotions have their origins deep in the human heart. In most cases, their beginnings lie in regions beyond the reach of human consciousness and moral reflection. As I have already said, man has things in him that are unknown even to himself. He still retains within him many things that he possessed before man became man. He has them whether he

> realizes it or not. The human emotions are closely related to these.... Every individual has in him things that cannot be simply defined. Thus human emotions, and human happiness in turn, are closely bound up with these indefinables.

Aldous Huxley discussed the symbols in two domains–the domain of science and the domain of politics and religion. He wrote:

> Thinking in terms of, and acting in response to, one set of symbols (in the domain of science), we have come, in some small measure, to understand and control the elementary forces of nature. Thinking in terms of, and acting in response to, another set of symbols (in the domain of politics and religion), we use these forces as instruments of mass murder and collective suicide.... In the second case symbols originally ill-chosen were never subjected to thorough-going analysis and never re-formulated so as to harmonize with the emergent facts of human existence.[9]

It is the ill-chosen symbols of politics and religion which lead to violence, aggression and psychological imbalances. Again the symbols of objective science–divorcing subjective dimension, measurement, comparison and verification of objective field that have added to human misery.

The capability of abstract thought, "presupposed the presence of intuition .... The important point would appear to be the balance of cooperation between intuition and abstraction".[10] Fritjof Capra wrote, "Rational knowledge and rational activities would certainly constitute the major part of scientific research.... The rational part of research would, in fact, be useless if it were not complemented by the intuition that gives scientists new insights and makes them creative".[11] As no measurement and verification of intuition (insight) is possible, hence scientists rejected the presence of the power of intuition. There seems to exist a general feeling of estrangement of science from intuition (insight).

Maurice H. Wilkins wrote, "Science being a human activity (cannot be), separated from all human virtues and values".[12] Max Born (N.L.) wrote, "clever, rational ways of thinking are not enough. The danger of mass slaughter .... can only be overcome by moral convictions, by a determination to replace national prides and prejudices with human love".[13]

In Victor F. Weisskopf words, Yukawa was of the opinion that "the present-day physicists have lost the gift of foresight from their forerunners .... science is a part of human relations and that modern scientific work involves him and other scientists with society to an even greater extent than other people. .... demonstrate how difficult is the task of turning the age-old tide of human motivation and aggression, ... was concerned about the large gap between the superhuman task and frailties of human endeavours".[14]

According to one estimate, twenty thousand scientists around the globe are currently engaged in the exploration of consciousness. Never before, so many subjective scientists, in addition to philosophers-mystics, were investigating consciousness.[15]

Over 1670 scientists, including 104 Nobel laureates issued a "World Scientists' Warning to Humanity" in April 1993.

> Human beings and the natural world are on a collision course. Human activities inflict harsh and often irreversible damage on the environment and on critical resources.
>
> A new ethic is required–a new attitude towards discharging our responsibility for caring for ourselves and for the earth. We must recognize the earth's limited capacity to provide for us. We must recognize its fragility. We must no longer allow it to be ravaged. This ethic must motivate a great movement, convincing reluctant leaders and reluctant governments and reluctant peoples themselves to effect the needed changes.[16]

Will the scientists of the world wake up from deep slumber to explore the wholeness of life. To save mankind from impending catastrophe, we have to explore the conditioned psyche and Unconditioned Energy *here* and *now*.

Where is Science Leading Mankind?

Jacques Monod (N.L.) wrote, "What we see opening before us today is an abyss of darkness".[17] George Wald (N.L.), in prophetic words, wrote:

> We who know where we are going, are now heading rapidly toward self-extinction, toward removing humankind from the cosmic scene, and for the most trivial of reasons: profit, the rivalry of the United States and the Soviet Union, the momentum of the military-industrial complex in both nations. The cosmic drama will go on elsewhere, ignorant of our demise, caring nothing; but we will have no further part in it.... Does that matter? It matters to us.[18]

P. Krishna wrote, "We are going towards self-annihilation and not much time is left now".[19] The human survival is at stake. We must– through observation, understanding, learning and art of living– end the disorder, the violence, in our consciousness.

It is evident that we have to explore the new global consciousness in the light of the recent discoveries in science. In our own lives, each one of us must move towards a realisation of the truth at the core of our being, the glowing higher consciousness that is the birthright of each individual born on this planet, because in the ultimate analysis it is the crucible of our individual selves alone that the poison of conditioning the psyche can be contained and transformed into the new consciousness that we seek. In this lies the faith for individual freedom as well as the survival of our planet earth. We intuitively see that even at this late hour, we can marshal our inner (spirituality) and outer (science) dimensions and we succeed in making the vital transition to the new consciousness? It is this most crucial of all decisions that it is the privilege and responsibility of our generation to make, because it is this, in the ultimate analysis, that will prove whether there is really new perception (not reason) for mutation in the new global society that is so rapidly emerging before us.

Today after billions of years of prebiological evolution and metabiological evolution, mankind is at an evolutionary crossroads. One road is leading to Buddha (Intelligence, Wisdom) and the other to self-destruction, self-annihilation. The self-annihilation is basically due to our conditioned psyche.

J. Krishnamurti stated, "The truth can be discovered only through self-observation and the mirror of relationships.... We can get beyond our destructive conditionings. It urges us to begin to change our patterns of ego-centred activity now, so that humanity will be diverted from its present malevolent course".[20] We concluded, "The future of mankind is open: either we continue the present way of life and destroy ourselves, or we learn to watch the mind in action and resolve the crisis of perception. Let mankind undertake a collective experiment for the mutation of the human psyche, which is the only global prescription to save mankind from annihilation, to heal our diseased mind-brain-body system, and to heal our planet. We shall surely survive if we understand the prove that we are worthy of survival".[21]

Observation

D.S. Kothari wrote, "In dealing with atomic phenomena we have to recognise that the act of observation is accompanied by an inevitable disturbance which alters the state of the observed system in an unpredictable manner. What is observed is different from what it was before the act of observation. This is inherent in the nature of things. It cannot be eliminated".[22] As Sullivan put it, "We cannot observe the course of nature without disturbing it",[23] or Andrade, "Observation means interference with what we are observing .... observation disturbs reality".[24] It was abundantly clear to those physicists that objective measurement and verification could no longer be the mark of absolute reality.

The scientific mode of mind will invariably lead to objective values, and it does not have the capacity to bestow subjective values. Many eminent scientists–Werner Heisenberg, Edwin Hubble, Max Planck, Bertrand Russell, Lincoln Barnett, Max Born, and so on–have concluded that we cannot impart value education at reason or intellect level.[25]

Scientific (Objective) Research

Schrodinger wrote, "Mind has erected the objective outside world of the natural philosopher out of its own stuff. Mind could not cope with this gigantic task otherwise than by the simplifying device of excluding itself–withdrawing from its conceptual creation. Hence the latter does not contain its creator".[26] Charles Sherrington wrote, "The material world has only been constructed at the price of taking the self, that is, mind, out of it, removing it; mind is not part of it; obviously, therefore, it can neither act on it nor be acted on by any of its parts".[27] Spinoza and C.J. Jung hold the same opinion. This leads us to a fundamental proposition that: (a) the Subject of Cognizance is at the immanent quantum energy potential of Consciousness; (b) the objective world excludes the Subject from the domain of nature that we endeavour to understand; (c) the objective world is at the lowest quantum energy potential of consciousness; (d) there is no energy exchange between the subject and the object; (e) the subject is "in-here" and the object is "out-there"; (f) the object bestows the *fact*, the objective values; (g) it leads to an awareness of non-dual and non-conceptual frame of reference of mind spectrum; and (h) this leads to invention (and not discovery).

Invention, which means to modify the known with the help of the known, is based on past knowledge. Knowledge is a movement under limitation; so invention is also limited. All objective research is often called an invention.

In the modern world, there is technical advancement at an accelerated pace, but this is neither accompanied by inward growth nor by psychological flowering. This has resulted in an imbalance. We have yet to know how to live together in cooperation and harmony. We have cultivated the intellect and are yet to cultivate the heart. We are superficial, intellectually brilliant, capable of great inventions, producing the most destructive means for liquidating each other, creating more and more dissension amongst ourselves. We create a world that is utterly confused and miserable, and our interpersonal relations are flimsy and superficial.

The Principle of Understandability of Nature

The symbolic-dualistic frame of reference of mind spectrum is repetitive and mechanical, so it has no newness and no creativity. The scientific mode of mind moves from fact to fact, so it gives objective-truth which leads to invention.

Arthur Eddington wrote:

> We have two kinds of knowledge which I call symbolic knowledge and intimate knowledge .... [The] more customary forms of reasoning have been developed for symbolic knowledge only. The intimate knowledge will not submit to codification and analysis; or, rather, when we attempt to analyze it the *intimacy is lost and it is replaced by symbolism*".[28]

Alan W. Watts discussed the "unconventional knowledge (aimed at) the understanding of life directly, instead of in the abstract, linear terms of representational thinking".[29] The direct understanding of life is also termed as intimate, or direct, or intuition, or insight, or non-dual knowledge. It is the creative or silent or equipoised mind that bestows direct understanding of life.

Many eminent scientists–including Albert Einstein, Werner Heisenberg, Erwin Schrodinger, Arthur Eddington, and so on–have stumbled upon another mode of perception (knowing), which is "understanding of life directly, instead of in the abstract, linear terms of representational thinking". This implies "understanding the wholeness of life". Understanding expresses itself in the non-dual and non-conceptual frame of reference of Mind Continuum. ***Understanding is a movement in the non-duality, a movement of the whole being***. Understanding comes only when the mind is very quiet, tranquil, silenced. Understanding leads to a perception of the whole. Perception has nothing to do with knowledge (information). ***The perceptions are born of non-duality and responses are born of spontaneity***. It awakens the awareness, the intelligence, which arises out of observation, self-knowing and compassion.

Creativity, however, is not born of knowledge or past experience and so does not involve time. When the mind is attentive, the Absolute energy bathes the brain cells and intuition results. Learning in the true sense takes place in the state of attention. Intuition is fundamental while logic or intellect is a derivative. Intuition happens in the timeless domain and flows into creativity. What we need now is an extraordinary inward richness and that richness can only come when we understand Truth, when we are capable of perceiving Truth. There can be no transformation in the external world without a transformation in the inner world. The basic need is to transform the human psyche. This transformation means to see the false as false and the true as true. Only Truth can liberate the mind from its own preconditioned state. It is Truth that liberates, not your striving to be free.

> J. Krishnamurti, in prophetic words, discussed the direct understanding of life:

> Understanding comes into being from the now, the present, which is always timeless .... To perceive truth needs no preparation; preparation implies time and time is not the means of understanding truth. Time is continuity and truth is timeless, non-continuous. Understanding is non-continuous, it is from moment to moment, unresidual.[30]

> Understanding comes only when the mind is very quiet .... Only the truth can liberate the mind from its own ideation; to see the truth, the mind must realize the fact that as long as it is agitated it can have no understanding.[31]

> Seeing the false as the false and the true as the true is transformation, because when you see something very clearly as the truth, the truth liberates. When you see that something is false, that false thing drops .... Truth is not cumulative. It is from moment to moment.[32]

The truth is defined as perception of the innermost Self, the expression of the Cosmic Consciousness, or Active Reality. Love is not different from truth. Love is that state in which the thought process has completely ceased.

This suggests that the outer (objective) and the inner (subjective) are not two separate movements, but one dynamic whole. And this we call as "restructured science" which takes in its ambient both the objective and the subjective dimensions of life. Similarly the restructured education deals with the sensual and trans-sensual world. The dialogue with nature is carried on by "restructured science-education".

Consciousness, Life Field, Quantum Field Consciousness (QFC)

Karl Pribram (N.L.) said, "We are here in celebration of the paradigm shift. Brain science must deal with the awareness of awareness. It could no longer afford to shut out that part of the world which we call subjective".[33] Roger Sperry (N.L.) spoke of the importance of a neglected area of science, namely the study of human subjective experience. He wrote, "Instead of renouncing or ignoring consciousness, the new interpretation gives full recognition to the primacy of inner conscious awareness as a causal reality".[34] John Eccles (N.L.) also emphasized the importance of the phenomenon of "conscious experience".[35] Wilder Penfield (N.L., Neurosurgeon) concluded that "our mind and our brains are not at all the same .... It is the mind which experiences and it is the brain that records that experience".[36]

The outer (objective) and the inner (subjective) are not two separate movements. It is a unitary movement, not separate, but one whole. Man has now to work to treat the outer and the inner as one. We call it "restructured science-education". The restructured science takes in its ambient both the subjective and the objective dimensions of life. The restructured education deals with the sensual and the trans-sensual world. It deals with the observer situated within the observed world. The dialogue with nature is carried on from within nature. It sees the wholeness of life. The subject now is non-variable attentivity, or reaction-free attentivity, or objectless attention. The "restructured science-education" deals with the wholeness of life, so it is at the transcendent aspect of the absolute, or Cosmic Consciousness. The Consciousness is Eternal, Infinite and Immutable.

When thought-structure coupled with volitions (I-consciousness) encounters the realm of the transcendent Consciousness, the thought-structure or thought-time goes to abeyance. Due to shortage of space, it is not discussed.[37]

When true-subject observes the conditioned psyche, one perceives that–(a) thought-time is independent of I-consciousness; (b) it is the product of collective human effort through centuries; (c) it (photons) cannot cross the "event horizon"; (d) it goes to abeyance and leads to non-dual and non-conceptual frame of reference of Mind Continuum; and if the observation is sustained, it leads to order, harmony, nonviolence and peace.

The brain and the mind are independent and are shared by mankind. The successive consciousness and Simultaneous Consciousness are shared by mankind. The "restructured science-education" deals with the wholeness of life, so the subject and the object are within nature, or in other words, both are "in-here". The universe beyond the "event horizon" is a new universe with intelligent life in it.

The happenings in nature are very fast–say the time between the subjective and the objective may be about a few millionths of a second; the photons are devoured by a black hole in less than a hundred microseconds,[38] and same order of time may be there when photons are absorbed by a mind; the time taken for a signal to move from a cell to muscle is of the order of about five thousandths of a second,[39] which corresponds to something moving to and fro two hundred times a second. It appears that the brain does not have the capacity to record time of this order of magnitude.

We are beginning a new age of awareness, the age of quantum consciousness, the age of the conscious atom. By observing within ourselves, we may be able to solve the problems facing us on the final frontier–the frontier of Cosmic Consciousness.[40]

Restructured Science-Education

The "restructured science-education" deals with the wholeness of life, so it is at the transcendent aspect of the absolute, or Cosmic Consciousness. In other words, it is at the transcendent quantum energy potential of Consciousness, or the highest frequency of the Consciousness. The observer is situated within the observed world, or both the observer and the observed are "in-here". The dialogue between the observer and the observed is within nature.

Ending of I-consciousness: If a thought coupled with volitions encounters the true-subject, the I-consciousness is knocked off because it is at the lowest quantum energy potential. This suggests that: (a) the movement of thought-time is independent of I-consciousness; (b) it is the movement of collective human effort; (c) both the I-consciousness and thought-structure have a conceptual reality.

Ending of Thought-Time: When thought-time comes in the realm of true-subject, the photons meet an 'impregnable wall', or "event-horizon", or "frequency-barrier", and are dissipated, which implies that thought-time goes to abeyance and what is left behind is the *fact*, the *true*, the *present*, the *what is*!

Ending of the Fact: If we continue observing or listening to the *fact*, without justification, or condemnation, or motivation, we observe that there is only the *fact* and nothing else. The fact itself is the operator and not you operating on the fact. If you leave the fact alone, it has no time. The fact is free from fear. The fact grows, which implies that there is release of tremendous energy and the fact moves to higher quantum energy potential. This is expressed as Pure Consciousness Fact. It helps the fact to make a quantum jump in the vertical dimension of Consciousness. When the fact is left alone, it is operating and you do not have to do a thing about it, it matures and blossoms. Immediacy of perception dissolves the fact, and one revels in Pure Consciousness or Intelligence. Only in Intelligence there is complete security. Intelligence sees the false as the false and ends the false. Mutation happens in the timelessness. To understand Consciousness or an enquiry into the subject is the perception of that immeasurable state.

Understanding and learning are born in non-duality. Intuition (insight) is perception without any doubt. ***Understanding, learning and action are a cyclic process, which results in a spiral going upwards in the vertical dimension; it is a growth in the vertical dimension.*** The higher the understanding, the higher the expression of the Consciousness in the human brain-body system.

A Critique on the Mysterious Mind-Brain-Body System

(a) ***Psychological Mode of Mind:*** The mind splits itself into the subject and the object and there is energy interaction between them. The subject is "in-here" and the object "out-there". Both are continuities of change, and it constructs psychological imbalances, ecological crisis, and other challenges.

(b) ***Scientific Mode of Mind:*** There is no energy exchange between the subject and the object. The subject is at the immanent quantum energy potential, while the object is at the lowest quantum energy potential of consciousness. The subject is "in-here" and the object "out-there". It bestows perception of the objective fact. It moves from fact to fact.

(c) ***Restructured Science-Education:*** Both the subject and the object are "in-here", so the dialogue is carried on from within nature. The fact also goes to abeyance. The true-subject observes itself. There is perception of order, harmony, nonviolence and peace.

Resolution of Objective Science Paradox

We want to find, *here* and *now*, a new vision of science as part of an active and creative culture developing in peace, and some aspects are discussed as under:

(a) Science deals with objective enquiry, precision and pursuit of truth. It makes progress largely by a combination of two aspects: open-mindedness and the following of abstract concepts. Science always puts the most emphasis on this abstraction and narrowing down, on analytical procedures and on the role of the intellect. Its characteristics are: (i) all moral, spiritual and other dimensions are pushed out of science; (ii) the present-day scientists have lost the gift of intuition; (iii) science is a human activity, but all values are transcended; (iv) it focuses attention on material aspects of life and on technical solution to human problems; (v) it permeates competition, acquisition, and helps growth of psychological imbalances, ecological crisis and cause and effect; (vi) science as it is today does not tell us very much about the real nature of man; (vii) man divorced from nature could never be happy and man's power to resist nature is hopelessly puny; and (viii) we have to rebuild scientific attitudes, but care, intuition and perception of the wholeness of life is needed.

(b) All knowledge is structured in consciousness. The creative process involves a quantum jump from logical and scientific reason to philosophic reason or non-dual and non-conceptual frame of reference of Mind Continuum; in other words, from a relative frame of reference to an absolute rest frame of mind. Knowledge emanates from it as quantas depending on the frame of reference of mind. D.S. Kothari, an eminent physicist, in prophetic words, wrote:

> The new theorems, unless trivial, are of course first "discovered" and then proved. Discovery is an inspired guess, a flash of insight. It is not a step by step process, but a sort of quantum jump.... A rational account of a discovery, the proof, follows and not precedes the discovery.[41]

Fundamental discoveries which go deep into the nature of things are the result of uncommon intuition and faith, not cold logic.[42]

The discovery presupposes a systematic interaction between theoretical concepts (deductive, intellectual approach) and observation (inductive, experimental results). Intuition, or insight, or discovery is a timeless perception. Intuition results in the discovery of truth in nature hitherto unknown in man. Intuition is fundamental and rationality is a derivative.

(c) We have to initiate a dialogue with nature from within nature, and nature responds to this experimental interrogation. If a scientist, who is aware of "restructured science-education" and lives in that awareness, asks questions addressed to nature, he invariably succeeds in receiving answers directly from nature. Nature is an "open-book" to him.

(d) When the paradox is resolved, the Pure Consciousness expresses Itself in a pure Mind as order, harmony, nonviolence and peace. This guarantees our survival and excellence.

Concluding Comment

Mankind is caught in a great delusion. It thinks it can solve its problems through legislation, through political and social reform, through scientific and technological progress, through greater knowledge, greater wealth, greater power and greater control. It may solve some problems with all these; but those are all trivial problems and temporary cures. We shall go on creating new problems on the one hand and trying to solve them on the other to maintain the illusion of 'progress'. And not much time is left now, because the conditioning is leading mankind to insanity, irrationality, and annihilation.

Man is an amphibian who lives simultaneously in three dimensions of consciousness or Life Field –(a) successive consciousness, or time-space-causation world, or symbolic-dualistic world; (b) scientific mode of mind, or non-dual and non-conceptual frame of reference of mind spectrum; and (c) a hidden dimension of the highest quantum energy potential of Cosmic Consciousness or Life Field.

The wrong turns taken by present objective science are–(a) science mainly focusses attention on the material progress of life and on technical solution to human challenges. It does not touch the subjective realm of life; (b) It has divorced intuition (insight) and mainly deals with reason and intellect; (c) It is divorced from all virtues and values of life; (d) Science is a human activity. It makes progress largely by a combination of two aspects–open-mindedness and the following of abstract concepts. The scientific education we have now has produced a narrow-minded way of thinking among scientists, so that they give no proper attention tot he moral and psychological dimensions; (e) It is leading to self-destruction and self-annihilation; and (f) It deals with small part of life and ignores the wholeness of life.

The mutation in Consciousness happens when the "restructured science-education" observes the conditioned psyche and the Unconditioned Energy, or in other words, the wholeness of life. This resolves the age-old tide of I-consciousness, thought-structures, psychological imbalances, ecological crisis, and other human challenges. This guarantees human survival and excellence.

An exploration of the mutation in consciousness is the only consummation of life. This is the only vocation of mankind. If we escape our responsibility, it will jeopardize the future of India and of mankind.

References

1. Erwin Schrodinger, *What is Life? & Mind and Matter*, Cambridge University Press, 1967, pp. 110-137
2. *Ibid.*, pp. 126-27, 132
3. Ilya Prigogine and Isabelle Stengers, *Order Out of Chaos*, Bantam Books, 1984, p. 6
4. P. Krishna, *Education, Science and Spirituality*, The University of California, 1993, cover jacket
5. Sampooran Singh, *Truth in the Light of Mind-Brain System*, Prabuddha Bharata, October 1997, Vol. 102, pp. 690-699
6. Erwin Schrodinger, *op. cit.*, pp. 132, 177, 149
7. Maurice H. Wilkins, in *Synthesis of Science and Religion*, Mumbai: Bhaktivedanta Institute, June 1988, pp. 29, 30
8. Hideki Yukawa, *Creativity and Intuition*, Tokyo: Kodansha International Ltd., 1973, pp. 204, 205, 206
9. Julian Huxley, in J. Krishnamurti, *The First and Last Freedom*, London: Victor Gollancz Ltd., 1977, Foreword, p. 9
10. Hideki Yukawa, *op. cit.*, pp. 101-102
11. Fritjof Capra, *The Tao of Physics*, Bantam Books (Second Edition), 1988, p. 18

12. Maurice H. Wilkins, *op. cit.*, p. 37
13. Max Born, in Hideki Yukawa, *op. cit.*, pp. 189-190
14. Victor F. Weisskopf, in Hideki Yukawa, *ibid.*, Introduction, pp. 10, 12, 13
15. in Sampooran Singh, *Dilip*, July/September, 2003, p. 13
16. The Union of Concerned Scientists, *World Scientists' Warning to Humanity*, USA: Church Street, Cambridge, April 1993
17. Jacques Monod, in *Synthesis of Science and Religion*, *op. cit.*, p. 127
18. George Wald, in *The Evolution of Consciousness*, New Delhi: National Publishing House, 1983, p. 13
19. P. Krishna, *op. cit.*, p. 12
20. J. Krishnamurti and David Bohm, *op. cit.*, Back Cover
21. Sampooran Singh, in *The Odyssey of Science, Culture and Consciousness*, New Delhi: Abhinav Publications, 1990., p. 170
22. D.S. Kothari, *Some Thoughts on Science and Religion*, The University of Delhi, 31.10.1977 and 3.11.1977, p. 25
23. J.W.N. Sullivan, *The Limitations of Science*, New York: Mentor Books, 1949, p. 140
24. E.N. da C. Andrade, *An Approach to Modern Physics*, New York: Doubleday Anchor Books, 1957, p. 255
25. Sampooran Singh, Dr. (Mrs.) Kanwaljit Kaur and Paramjit Singh, *Global Education and Human Survival*, New Delhi: Sanbun Publishers, March 2002, pp. 35-36, 46
26. Erwin Schrodinger, *op. cit.*, p. 131
27. Charles Sherrington, in Erwin Schrodinger, *ibid.*, p. 128
28. Arthur Eddington, in Commins and Linscott, *Man and the Universe*, p. 453
29. Alan W. Watts, *The Ways of Zen*, New York: Vintage Books, 1957, p. 10
30. J. Krishnamurti, *The First and Last Freedom*, *op. cit.*, p. 269
31. *Ibid.*, pp. 277-278
32. *Ibid.*, p. 286
33. Karl Pribram, in Ken Wilber, *The Holographic Paradigm and Other Paradoxes*, Boulder: Shambhala, 1982, p. 17
34. Roger Sperry, in *Synthesis of Science and Religion*, Mumbai: The Bhaktivedanta Institute, June 1988, p. 199
35. John Eccles, in *ibid.*, p. 200
36. Wilder Penfield, in Deepak Chopra, *How to Know God*, Rider, 2000, pp. 215, 217
37. Sampooran Singh and Dr (Mrs) Kanwaljit Kaur, *Peace, Security and Survival?* : *A Scientific Quest*, July 5, 2004, pp. 1-40
38. Deepak Chopra, *op. cit.*, p. 271
39. Fred Alan Wolf, *Taking the Quantum Leap*, San Francisco: Harper and Row, 1981, p. 236
40. *Ibid.*, p. 248
41. D.S. Kothari, in *The Odyssey of Science, Culture and Consciousness*, New Delhi: Abhinav Publications, 1990, pp. 48-49
42. *Ibid.*, in *The Evolution of Consciousness*, New Delhi: National Publishing House, 1983, p. 227

2
The Spectrum of Consciousness

Abstract

Many eminent physicists, neuro-physiologists, neuro-surgeons have opined that every existence/event, including man, is basically a participant of an energy field–called Cosmic Consciousness, or Life Field, or Quantum Field of Consciousness (QFC)–of very high frequency. Man needs a paradigm shift from successive consciousness (self-interacting dynamic state) to Cosmic Consciousness (a self-referral state).

This article explores The Spectrum of Consciousness which heals the psychic disease. The Consciousness expresses itself in three dominant modes–(a) the successive consciousness, (b) the Simultaneous Consciousness, and (c) the "restructured science-education" (true-subject). Man has to learn to move from experience to perception, from intellect to intuition, and from fragmentary living to the wholeness of life.

Our symbolic and dualistic mind is independent of the brain. The symbolic-dualistic mind and non-dual and non-conceptual Mind are shared by the whole mankind. If true-subject observes the conditioned psyche, one perceives that–(a) the movement of thought-time is independent of I-consciousness; (b) it is the movement of collective human effort through centuries; (c) thought (photons) cannot cross the "event horizon"; (d) when thought goes to abeyance, it leads to non-dual and non-conceptual frame of reference of Mind Continuum; and (e) if the observation is sustained, one perceives the order, harmony, non-violence and peace.

It is the Life Field that can end all challenges and lead to survival and excellence of mankind. And if man escapes his responsibility, he does so at his own peril and that of mankind.

Many eminent physicists, neuro-scientists, neuro-surgeons–say, Karl Pribram, Roger Sperry, J.C. Eccles, Wilder Penfield, Erwin Schrodinger, E.P. Wigner, Hideki Yukawa, Albert Einstein and so on–have advocated that it is the consciousness that sustains every existence in this universe including man. The Cosmic Consciousness expresses itself in three dominant potentials–(a) the psychological mode (successive consciousness); (b) the scientific mode (Simultaneous Consciousness); and (c) the "restructured science-education" mode, which deals with the wholeness of life.

Every human being carries hidden within him the highest potential of Consciousness or the highest frequency of Consciousness, which goes beyond the bounds of his present life and enables him to share in a higher life. Cosmic Consciousness governs their lives and organises circumstances of their existence and their individual reactions to these circumstances. We are looking at ourselves. It is this process which we call the universe. We are not just observing it, we are not even just immersed in it: we are an integral part of it. Consciousness plays a dual role in the universe. In the world of the quantum, it is both the awareness and the creation of experience. It is the *being* and the *knowing* of experience. With the stroke of the twentieth-century quantum eraser, the dividing line between ontology (theory of being) and epistemology (theory of knowing) is rubbed out. The fusion of ontology, epistemology and psychology is beginning to emerge.

The United Nations Foundation, along with partners from around the globe, has launched a major initiative to assess 21st century threats to international peace and security on 23 Sept 2003 *(WWW.UNFOUNDATION.ORG)*. We published a monograph in July 2004.[1] The urgency for radical transformation of human psyche has been discussed on pages 9 and 10 of the above referred monograph.

This article explores the conditioned consciousness and the Unconditioned Consciousness, the wholeness of life. We have to educate our physical organism and psychological structure to move into non-action gracefully, voluntarily. This leads us to a state of non-action–the non-dual and non-conceptual frame of reference of mind spectrum–and this observation blossoms to "direct understanding of life", the perception of the *fact*, the *true*, the *present*, the *what is*! If the observation is systematically and rigorously continued, we touch another state of mind called "restructured science-education", or true-subject; which leads to a quantum jump of the objective state of mind. This energises Intelligence which bestows order, harmony, non-violence, peace and security.

Psychological Mode of Conditioned Mind

Measurement means comparison. The becoming, the acquisition is a form of measurement. When there is comparison there is hurt. The word '*better*' is measurement. The word '*more*' is measurement. The word '*progress*' is measurement. *Self-improvement* is measurement. In every psychological activity there is measurement. It is a repetitive and mechanical process, hence there is no newness and creativity.

The mind cuts itself into the subject and the object; there is energy interaction between the subject and the object resulting into distortion of both; the distorted subject sees the distorted object; the distorted object gets recorded as the modified memory; and then this process gets repeated.

Thought is the result of a response, neurological or psychological. Idea is the outcome of a thought process. Thought process is the response of memory. The actor (subject), action (energy exchange) and end or result (object) is a unitary process, which comes into being when action has an end in view. Action towards a result is will. The desire to achieve an end brings out will, which is an actor.

Memory is always the past, and that memory is given life in the present by a challenge. Memory has no life in itself; it comes to life in the present when confronted by a challenge.

Objective Scientific Mode

The scientific mind is very factual. Discovery is its mission, its perception. It sees things through a microscope, through a telescope; everything to be seen actually as it is; from that perception, science draws conclusions, builds up theories. Such a mind moves from fact to fact. Scientific discoveries are shared by the whole world. A scientific mind is precise, clear, prejudiced, which does not condemn, which observes, which sees. A scientific theory is always provisional. It is a guide to further development, to its own replacement.

About 1600, Kepler and Galileo, simultaneously and independently, formulated the principle that the laws of nature are to be discovered by measurement. All propositions were to be confined to that which was objectively measurable and verifiable.

D.S. Kothari wrote, "In dealing with atomic phenomena we have to recognise that the act of observation is accompanied by an inevitable disturbance which alters the state of the observed system in an unpredictable manner. What is observed is different from what it was before the act of observation. This is inherent in the nature of things. It cannot be eliminated".[2] As Sullivan put it, "We cannot observe the course of nature without disturbing it",[3] or Andrade, "Observation means interference with what we are observing .... observation disturbs reality".[4] It was abundantly clear to these physicists that *objective measurement and verification could no longer be the mark of absolute reality, because the measured object could never be completely separated from the measuring subject–the measured and the measurer, the verified and the verifier, at this level, are one and the same.* Quantum physicists discovered that every act of observation made of an atom by a physicist disturbed the atom.

A trapped ion blinks on and off and each blink is a quantum jump. It is a striking illustration that things occur discontinuously in nature.[5] By the first decades of the 20th century, the objective science had run its course to that annihilating edge.

Schrodinger wrote, "Mind has erected the objective outside world of the natural philosopher out of its own stuff. Mind could not cope with this gigantic task otherwise than by the simplifying device of excluding itself–withdrawing from its conceptual creation. Hence the latter does not contain its creator".[6] C.J. Jung and B. Spinoza hold the same opinion. Charles Sherrington wrote, "The material world has only been constructed at the price of taking the self, that is, mind, out of it, removing it; mind is not part of it; obviously, therefore, it can neither act on it nor be acted on by any of its parts".[7] The subject is "in-here" while the object is "out-there". There is no energy exchange between the objective scientific world and the subjective scientific world. It implies that the subject is at the immanent quantum energy potential while the object is at the lowest quantum energy potential. The true-subject is non-variable attentivity, or reaction-free attentivity or objectless attention. The object gives the objective *fact*, the *true*, the *present*, the *what is*!

All experience, everything without exception, is fundamentally a personal, subjective experience. The objective communicable statements become possible about *pairs* of sense impressions and never about single sense impressions. It is this which eliminates subjectivity from science, eliminates "I", and is the basis of the objectivity of science. Max Born stated, "The fact that by comparing pairs communicable, objective statements are possible, has an immense importance because it is the root of speaking, and writing, and of the most powerful instrument of thinking, of mathematics".[8] Objective science by excluding subjectivity cannot, even in principle, deal with our thoughts, feelings, emotions, with subjective experience of any kind. It excludes "I". The exclusion is total.

Brain is a part of the objective world. It can be investigated objectively. On the other hand, mind is subjective. When, for instance, sound wave impinge on our ears, the pressure changes produce electric currents in the nerve fibres which from the ear reach the hearing sensorium of the brain. How do these electric currents in the brain transform into sensations of sound–into music?; and obviously it is the mind that is responsible for this transformation. The same implies to other sensations. Science provides no answer to this riddle. Because of its very objectivity, science can give no answer to this riddle of all riddles.

Arthur Eddington wrote, "The physiologist can trace the nerve mechanism up to the brain (inner sensorium); but ultimately there is a hiatus which no one professes to fill up. Symbolically we can follow the influence of the physical world up to the door of the mind; they ring the bell and then depart".[9] It suggests that the external organs perceive the discontinuity, it then transmits the message through nerve fibres to the internal organs, and the mind analyses and interprets the message as a continuity. Mind perceives a screen of continuity thrown on something that is fundamentally discontinuous. Charles Sherrington wrote, "Thoughts, feelings, and so on are amenable to energy (matter) concept. They lie outside it. Therefore they lie outside *Natural* science .... Mind, for anything perception can compass, goes therefore in our spatial world more ghostly than a ghost. Invisible, intangible, it is a 'thing' not even of outline, it is not a 'thing'. It remains without sensual confirmation, and remains without it for ever".[10]

Wilder Penfield has recorded that in some striking cases of brain surgery when the patient was asked not to move the arm when the corresponding area of the cerebral cortex was electrically stimulated, the patient invariably responded by using the other arm to hold it down. What the electrode did to one arm, the patient's will did to the other".[11] The mind can survive brain traumas and function under anesthesia points very strongly to the separate existence of the mind. Wilder Penfield concluded that "our minds and our brains are not at all the same .... It is the mind which experiences and it is the brain which records the experience". He concluded that the "mind must be a kind of invisible energy that includes the brain, perhaps even controls it".[12] The brain is an "information field", because the brain clearly processes information (as memory) that is flowing and related to all that exists.

The Mind perceives the intuition or insight, and expresses it in the brain (the material structure). Nature invariably works through intuition, so the Mind expresses itself at the highest quantum energy potential of Universal Consciousness, or Life Field, or Quantum Field Consciousness (QFC). It is the Mind that is responsible for intuition, insight and creativity. It suggests that the mind is independent of the brain.

John Eccles made the famous statement that "God is in the gap",[12] where gap implies emptiness, void, silent Mind. Deepak Chopra explained this in words, "The empty spaces of the brain, the tiny synapses between two nerve endings, must be the home of higher mind because it could not be found in the material stuff of the brain".[13]

Restructured Science-Education Mode

Man is an amphibian who lives simultaneously in two worlds– the given (inner) and the home-made (outer time-space matrices, the world of matter). Karl Pribram wrote, "Brain science must deal with the awareness of awareness. It could no longer afford to shut out that part of the world which we call subjective".[14] Roger Sperry spoke of the importance of a neglected area of science, namely the study of the human subjective experience".[15] Similarly many other neuro-scientists, neuro-surgeons, and physicists have spoken that we should treat the subjective and the objective dimensions of human life as a single dynamic movement. Similarly we have to take education as sensual and trans-sensual dimensions of life. There is an urgency to recognise "restructuring of science-education". The energy transduction between the subjective and the objective happens in about few millionth of a second (subjective→objective). The "restructuring of science-education" deals with the wholeness of life.[16] This is called the true-subject. George Wald wrote, "The very crux of twentieth-century physics is the recognition that the observer cannot be excluded from his observations; he is an intrinsic participant in them".[17] Ilya Prigogine wrote, "It is physics that presupposes an observer situated within the observed world. Our dialogue with nature will be successful only if it is carried on from within nature".[18] Erwin Schrodinger wrote, "The world is given to me only once, not one existing and one perceived. Subject and object are only one. The barrier between them cannot be said to have broken down as a result of recent experience in the physical sciences, for this barrier does not exist .... The world is given but once. Nothing is reflected. The original and the mirror-image are identical. The world extended in space and time is but our representation".[19]

The true-subject is at the highest quantum energy potential of Cosmic Consciousness. If the true-subject observes the conditioned psyche, then all volitions, which are at the lowest quantum energy potential, are knocked off. You allow the mind to relax into non-action, your body will be free of tensions and pressures. It implies that all identification with functional roles go to abeyance. The mind becomes silent. Silence is a tension and pressure free state of your being. It implies that being in the silence is in the wholeness of life. It implies that the subject and the object coalesce and duality ends.

I-consciousness: The 'I-consciousness', or the 'me', or the 'self' is the movement of time, put together by the conditioned psyche. It is a mechanical and repetitive process, so it has no growth (evolution), no freedom, no creativeness. The cerebral movement, the psychological movement, the movement of the mind is absolutely irrelevant to discovery of an alternative way of living, discovery of an action that is free of thought, discovery of a way of living where acquisitiveness, the urge for security or the fear of tomorrow has no place at all. It has no factual reality at all. It has a conceptual reality. It has an ideational reality and it has a relevance in our lives. It is the product of an idea. In our civilisation, the concepts are grafted over the perception.

Ending of I-consciousness: If a thought coupled with volition comes in the field of true-subject (restructured science-education), the I-consciousness is knocked off because it is at the lowest quantum energy potential. It implies that Unconditioned Energy from true-subject flows into the conceptual structure and dissipates it. It points out that: (a) What I call my thoughts, my feelings, my memory have a movement and momentum independent of me, or the mental movement has a momentum independent of myself; (b) there is nothing like an individual mind, there is nothing like an individual I-consciousness; (c) thought is the product of collective human effort through centuries; and (d) the racial consciousness and racial momentum of knowledge, experience and thought are shared by mankind. The successive consciousness and Simultaneous Consciousness are shared by mankind.[20]

Ending of Thought Structure: When thought structure comes in the field of restructured science-education, the 'photons' meet an impregnable wall, called 'event horizon', or 'frequency barrier', or 'time barrier'. Deepak Chopra, on the basis of relativistic physics stated, "The speed of light is absolute, it is like a wall that no object can crash through. As we approach the wall, time slows down, mass increases and space becomes curved".[21] He added, "Any place where knowledge stops there is an event horizon". Thought (or photons) cannot cross the 'event horizon', it is bombarded by the non-variable attentivity, and the thought gets annihilated.

At the moment of crossing the 'frequency barrier', the subject-object energy interaction ends, because the photons are knocked down by the energy of attentivity, which is at a higher potential. The object goes to abeyance and dualism ends. The time-space matrices also go to abeyance. The experience and knowledge also stops. All this happens in less than a hundred microseconds.

Deepak Chopra discusses an analogy of black holes. The light passes too near a black hole gets pulled into the field of gravity. Black holes are the remnants of old stars that collapsed onto themselves when they ran out of fuel. The photon falls into the black hole forever, frozen in time. Inside the black hole, however, the photon has already been devoured, in less than a hundred microseconds.

Any place where knowledge stops there is also an event horizon. The brain cannot explore beyond where photons go. There is no perception without juggling photons around. Beyond event horizon, it is a universe with intelligent life in it.

The observation by "restructured science-education" leads to a quantum jump of the Mind Continuum to order, harmony, non-violence and peace, which is a dimension of the wholeness of life. The boundaries of psychological imbalances, ecological crisis and other human challenges, beliefs, concepts are true event horizon, because the mind cannot go beyond them.

We are beginning a new age of consciousness, the age of quantum consciousness, the age of conscious atom. By looking within ourselves, we may be able to solve the problems facing us on the final frontier–the frontier of the Cosmic Consciousness.

Vimala Thakar calls the awareness of the outward and the inward movement of life as meditation. If I am simultaneously aware of the objective challenge, the subject reactions and the causes of the reactions, then it results in freedom. Then the momentum of reaction will not carry me over with it, but I will be ahead of the reaction.[22] I will be aware of the objective challenge only. Thought goes to abeyance and there is perception of the *fact*, the *true*, the *present*, the *non-dual*, the *what is*!

Ending of the Fact: If we continue observing or listening to the *fact*, without justification or condemnation or motivation, we observe there is only the fact and nothing else. The fact itself is the operator, not you operating on the fact. If you leave the fact alone, it has no time. The fact is free from fear. The fact grows, which implies that there is release of tremendous energy[23] and the fact moves to higher quantum energy potential. This is expressed as Pure Consciousness→Fact. It helps the fact to make a quantum jump in the vertical dimension of Consciousness. When the fact is left alone, it is operating and you do not have to do a thing about it, it matures and blossoms. Immediacy of perception dissolves the fact, and one revels in Pure Consciousness or Intelligence. Only in Intelligence there is complete security. Intelligence sees the false as the false and ends the false. Mutation happens in the timelessness. The "restructured science-education" deals with the wholeness of life, so the subject and the object are within nature, or in other words, both are "in-here". The universe beyond the event-horizon is a new universe with intelligent life in it. To understand Consciousness or an enquiry into the subject is the perception of that immeasurable state.

Understanding and learning are born in non-duality. Intuition (insight) is perception without any doubt. ***Understanding, learning and action are a cyclic process, which results in a spiral going upwards in the vertical dimension; it is a growth in the vertical dimension***. The higher the understanding, the higher the expression of the Consciousness in the human brain-body system.

Concluding Comment

A trapped ion blinks on and off and each blink is a quantum jump. You have the ultimate unit doing the dance by itself. It is a striking illustration that things occur discontinuously in nature.

Every inner movement is the movement of the inheritance, the past, every inner movement is conditioned by the past and there is no freedom in the dimension of that movement. Thought-structure knows no freedom.

The I-consciousness, the ego, the "me", the self has no factual reality at all. It has a conceptual reality. It has an ideational reality and it has a relevance in our lives. In our civilisation, the concepts are grafted on the perception. Thought-structure has no factual content. So thought or the word has no reality outside the brain.

The brain and the mind are independent and are shared by mankind. The successive consciousness and Simultaneous Consciousness are shared by mankind. There is nothing in this world which is a construct by an individual man.

Appearing in time-space and causality, this Being is man, as we know him, but behind all appearance is the One Reality --the Cosmic Consciousness, or Quantum Field Consciousness (QFC). Our activities in the waking state are based on successive (or sequential) consciousness, and the results are determined by Simultaneous Consciousness, or the One Reality. It guides to "unifying order, but it is not causality; it is purpose, and not the purpose of the universe and of man, but the purpose *in* the universe and *in* man. The order of the universe may be the order of our mind.

References

1. Sampooran Singh and Dr (Mrs) Kanwaljit Kaur, *Peace, Security and Survival? : A Scientific Quest*, July 5, 2004, pp. 1-40.
2. D.S. Kothari, *Some Thoughts on Science and Religion*, The University of Delhi, 31.10.1977 and 03.11.1977, p. 25.
3. J.W.N. Sullivan, *The Limitations of Science*, New York: Mentor Books, 1949, p. 140.
4. E.N. da C. Andrade, *An Approach to Modern Physics*, New York: Doubleday Anchor Books, 1957, p. 255.
5. New York Times, in *The Invincible*, Nov.-Dec. 1987, Vol. IV, No. 6, pp. 6-10.
6. Erwin Schrodinger, *What is Life*? & *Mind and Matter*, Cambridge University Press, 1967, p. 131.
7. Charles Sherrington, in Erwin Schrodinger, *ibid.*, p. 128.
8. Max Born, *My Life and My Views*, 1968, p. 174; in D.S. Kothari, *Some Thoughts on Science and Religion*, *op. cit.*, p. 44.
9. Arthur Eddington, *The Nature of the Physical World*, 1928, in Sampooran Singh, *The Holistic Education*, New Delhi: Siddharth Publications, 1987, p. 41.
10. Charles Sherrington, in D.S. Kothari, *op. cit.*, p. 46.

11. Wilder Penfield, in D.S. Kothari, *op. cit.*, p. 46.
12. *Ibid.*, in Deepak Chopra, *How to Know God*, Rider, 2000, pp. 215, 217.
13. J.C. Eccles, in Deepak Chopra, *ibid.*, p. 218.
14. Karl Pribram, in Ken Wilber (Ed.), *The Holographic Paradigm and Other Paradoxes*, Shambhala, 1982, p. 17.
15. Roger Sperry, in *Synthesis of Science and Religion*, Mumbai: The Bhaktivedanta Institute, June 1988, p. 199.
16. Sampooran Singh, Dr (Mrs) Kanwaljit Kaur, Paramjit Singh and Amarjit Singh, *March to Peace: The Wisdom of Observatión, Listening and the Power of Commitment*, Chandigarh: Faith Publishers, 20.01.2004, pp. 1-24.
17. George Wald, in *Synthesis of Science and Religion, op. cit.*, p. 19.
18. Ilya Prigogine and Isabelle Stengers, *Order Out of Chaos*, Bantam Books, 1984, p. 218.
19. Erwin Schrodinger, *op. cit.*, pp. 137, 146.
20. Vimala Thakar, (a) *Through Silence to Meditation*, Ahmedabad: Vimal Prakashan Trust, 1998, pp. 22-27; (b) *ibid.*, *Silence*, Holland: Bookfund, 1989, p. 6; and (c) *ibid.*, *The Invincible*, July-August 1987, Vol. IV, No. 4, p. 14.
21. Deepak Chopra, *op. cit.*, pp. 270, 271.
22. Vimala Thakar, *Mutation of Mind*, Ahmedabad: New Order Book Co., 1972, pp. 122, 171.
23. J. Krishnamurti, *Krishnamurti on Education*, Orient Longman, KFI, 1974, pp. 69, 87, 90.

3
The Challenge of Thought

Abstract

We have built a society which is violent, aggressive, acquisitive, money-minded. These have been stored as frequency and amplitude information, called memory or cultural belief structure. Memory is meta-stable and the by-product is called thought-structure or thought-time. Thought has brought about tremendous conflict between human beings–not only between individuals, but also collectively.

Thought is the result of a response, neurological or psychological. Thought being the past has the influence of race, group, family, tradition and so on. Thought is the past and not the future, but it can project itself into the future. Thought or intellect is invariably dualistic and constructs all psychological imbalances, ecological crisis and other human challenges. We have developed intellectually, scientifically, technologically at an accelerative pace, but psychologically we are primitive. The systematic and rigorous observation by the "restructured science-education" ends all I-consciousness and thought-structure. We have to move from experience to perception, from intellect to intuition, from symbolic-dualistic frame of mind spectrum to non-dual and non-conceptual frame of reference of Mind Continuum. It is the Cosmic Consciousness that brings in mutation of human psyche.

One has to rediscover the truth by oneself through observation and relationships with the whole for oneself. Truth is in 'what is'. The ending of I-consciousness and thought-structure blossoms to understanding and learning. This ends all conflict, between individuals and within individuals. It bestows order, harmony, nonviolence, peace and survival. This is the only vocation of life.

The ancient seers of India, about 10,000 years ago, perceived a state of true illumination. There is One Reality, the Unmanifest-Manifested. The nature of the Unmanifest is 'Deep-Silence', 'Inactivity (Non-Vibration)', 'Passivity', 'Immutability', 'Eternal'; and also Activity (Vibration), dynamism and illimitable potency to manifest as many. Activity (Active Reality) expresses which is self-hidden in the Silence (Passive Reality); both are different states of the Supreme Reality, the obverse and converse affirmations; both are Pure Existence and conscious Force, or Self-Existent Bliss and Supreme Intelligence, and are One. The Active Reality is a powerful, highly directional, monochromatic (same frequency) and coherent (the wave is in one phase) beam of energy; or a state of highest frequency (higher frequency means higher energy), or high quantum energy potential.

The Active Reality expresses itself in two dominant modes: (a) the *known*, the successive consciousness, the time-space-causation matrices; and (b) the *Unknown*, the Simultaneous Consciousness, the Absolute, the Life Field, the Quantum Field of Consciousness (QFC). The successive consciousness is at the *lowest* quantum energy potential of consciousness, it is scattered vibrations; while the Simultaneous Consciousness is at the *highest* quantum energy potential of Consciousness, the Life Field. As a symbol we may compare the *known* to a drop of water and the *Unknown* to a fathomless and boundless ocean. The *known* is in the field of time, so it is limited and transient. The Unknown is in the realm of the timeless, so it is Eternal, Infinite and Immutable.

The known is a creation of the mind, the memory, the cultural belief structure, the man-made social cosmos; because thought is the creation of the past. The conditioned psyche (the past) is posing a great threat of the worst possible humanitarian disaster, the worst the world has seen. There is an urgency to prevent a humanitarian catastrophe of this magnitude as it poses a threat to the global stability. The Unknown is hidden and mysterious. Nature, due to its benediction, has embedded in man "a direct understanding of life", which requires a greater intelligence, greater awareness, than merely to accept or give yourself over to an idea, to a concept. This understanding leads to order, harmony, non-violence, peace and security.

We have tried for the last 10,000 years or more, to transform the human psyche through techniques, through systems, beliefs, concepts, thought-structure, positive thoughts, and so on, but we have miserably failed. We have constructed a violent and aggressive world.

This article discusses ending the challenge of thought and I-consciousness, and to be aware of "*What is*!", "the direct understanding of life". The *technology* is extremely difficult because of our distraction– of prejudice, of condemnation, of identification. We have to understand and learn the *fact*, the *true*, the *present*, the *what is*! Only the truth can liberate the mind from its own ideation.

A Critique on Mind-Brain-Body System

What we call mind (with a lower case 'm') is a conditioned energy, moving through the body, monitored by the brain, operating through the senses. We have been busy in nourishing reason or intellect, which is a marvellous instrument. Intellect has been misused because it has emphasised only the activity of thought. Thought has dominated the whole existence of mankind. Intellect, being dualistic, has the capacity to construct a verbal structure as an idea, a conclusion, something to be achieved. Ideas, concepts, thought are not truth. We live in verbal structure. Our social structure is very intellectual; we are cultivating the intellect at the expense of every other factor of our being and therefore are suffocated with ideas or concepts or thought structures.

Thought is the result of a response, neurological or psychological. It is the immediate response of the senses to a sensation, or it is psychological, the response of stored up memory. Memory has no life in itself; it comes to life in the present when confronted by a challenge.

Thinking is a playback of thought coupled with feeling and response of memory–cultural, racial, religious, communal–which is called willing. Willing flows to reaction. These conditionings have been organised and standardized. We are conditioned cerebrally, neurologically, chemically to react to situations in a specific way. To be aware of the dynamics, conditioning and limitations of the conditioned psyche is called self-knowledge.

What we call Mind (with upper case 'M') is the non-dual and non-conceptual frame of reference of Mind Continuum. The Universal Consciousness expresses Itself as intuition (insight), spontaneity and right action, love and compassion, order and harmony. It is the first-hand personal acquaintance of the quantum jump of the conditioned energy consciousness to Universal Consciousness; or in other words, a quantum jump from fragmentary perception to the perception of the Wholeness. The true social action is free from any duality, obeys quantum logic and constructs an ordered, harmonious, nonviolent and peaceful society. The paradigm shift and sane society leads to the integral dimension of Consciousness that can resolve the challenges facing mankind. This is the only guarantee for human survival and excellence.

The Challenge of Thought

The Sympathetic Nervous System: In animals, the response to a challenge comes through fear. This sympathetic activity leads to an increase in heart rate and breathing, and more blood is pumped to the muscles so that the animal can either run or fight. The regulation of the sympathetic nervous system and thus of fight-or-flight mechanism is brought about on the instinctual level. After the challenge is met, the nervous system comes to normal. Instinct is degenerative experience, it is stored in the sub-conscious, and it is useful in case of emergency.

In man, fear is usually related to thinking, not to an actual threat to survival–and therefore the sympathetic nervous system has become unsympathetic to human survival. Man has lost the instinctual level and thought has become the greatest challenge. The challenge of thought cannot be met by suppressing it, or encouraging it, or by changing it into positive thought. The challenge constructs duality, pain, misery and travails. Fritjof Capra wrote, "Among all the species, we are the only one that kill their own kind in pursuit of religion, free markets, patriotism, and other abstract ideas".[1]

Thought is a Construct of the Brain: Thought is a cerebral function–it is the function of brain cells to generate thought out of memory cells. It comes as a response to a challenge–when any challenge arises, the intellect starts thinking. Thought is a function of the brain which points you to the need of security. It shows you that something remains unresolved, incomplete. Even when it creates fear or violence by thinking of the past or future, it compels you to observe fear, violence, so that fear or violence is ended.

Thought divides itself into the thinker and thought, the mischief is brought about by the thinker, not by thought. Thought is innocuous. The thinker creates the mischief by coming into conflict with thought. When thought becomes silent, and all the brain cells are quiet, a transformation or mutation happens in the psyche and intelligence takes over. Perception is always new. Only the new can be limitless and boundless.

Everything created by thought is only the reflection of the past, of limitation. All knowledge (information), thought structures, ideas, beliefs, concepts are sterile in transforming the psyche of man, or in other words, to bring radical transformation or mutation in the human psyche. And no technique, no system can transform thought.

Fritjof Capra wrote, "Neuroscientists have associated peptides with emotions". Candance Pert put it, "White blood cells are bits of the brain floating in the body",[2] so nervous system is not hierarchically structured. Ultimately, this implies that cognition is a phenomenon that expands throughout the organism, operating through an intricate chemical network of peptides that integrates our mental, emotional, and biological activities.

An Ethical Basis of Life

Today the majority of people live in accumulation of bank balance, property, acquisition of material goods, acquiring prestige, power, competition, psychological imbalances, and so on. All these are subtle matter and gets stored as memory or cultural belief structures. Accepting these imbalances and trying to change them are one and the same thing–both imply violence, aggression to thought, words and deeds. Basically there is no order or ethical base in life.

If the "restructured science-education" observes (or enquires) the whole content of violence without effort or struggle or interfering in the flow of violent thought, then the very perception brings a shift from *what should be*?, the *past*, to *what is*!, the *present*; and violent thought-structure goes to abeyance. Only a mind which has become ethical through perception is capable of probing deeper into the mysteries of life, which are called God or love or truth.

Wave-Particle Duality

The new physics tells us that an observer cannot observe without altering what he sees. Observer and observed are interrelated in a real and fundamental sense. What one observes appears to depend upon what one chooses to observe. It appears that the distinction between the "in here" and "out there" is an illusion. What we experience is not external reality, but our interaction with them.

Complementarity is the concept developed by Niels Bohr to explain the wave-particle duality of light. We can demonstrate that light is particle-like with the photo-electric effect, that it is wave-like with the double-slit experiment, and that it is both particle-like and wave-like with Compton scattering. According to Planck rule–higher frequency means higher energy–the wave-aspect is synergistic to the particle-aspect. Similarly X-rays also showed particle-like and wave-like characteristics.

The symbolic-dualistic frame of reference of mind spectrum is aware of the particle-like aspect of thought. If this is observed by "restructured science-education" frame of reference of Mind Continuum, there is transference of energy from the observer to the observed, and we are aware of the wave-like aspect of thought. Our activity introduces discontinuities in whatever we are observing. *To Bohr, discontinuity was a fundamental truth.*[3] If one state of mind is supplied energy, the mind will make a quantum jump to the next higher state–like a staircase and not like a ramp.

D.S. Kothari wrote, "In dealing with atomic phenomena we have to recognise that the act of observation is accompanied by an inevitable disturbance which alters the state of the observed system in an unpredictable manner. What is observed is different from what it was before the act of observation. This is inherent in the nature of things. It cannot be eliminated or allowed for.[4] The act of observation with its accompanying disturbance has profound influence on the atomic objects under observation. Ilya Prigogine wrote, "When an atom is excited, the electron jumps from one orbit to another. At this very instant the atom emits or absorbs a photon the frequency of which corresponds to the difference between the energies characterizing the electron's motion in each of the two orbits. This difference is calculated in terms of Einstein's formula relating energy to frequency".[5]

Physicists call the boundary between psychological frame of reference (successive consciousness) and non-dual frame of reference (Simultaneous Consciousness) as "the event horizon",[6] or "the time barrier", or "the frequency barrier"–on the psychological side lies anything that remains within the speed of light, and on the side of the non-dual frame is anything faster than the speed of light. This speed of light is absolute, it is like what no object can crash through. As we approach the wall, time slows down, mass increases, and space becomes curved.

As an analogy, any light that passes too near a black hole gets pulled into its field. Black holes are the remnants of old stars that collapsed into themselves when they ran out of fuel. If a photon of light tries to go around a black hole, it will start to curve in the hole's direction until it falls in.

Brain Cells and Mind

Experience, knowledge and memories are stored up in the brain. The brain has evolved in time. The brain cells in the process of seeing, either respond in old terms, or held back in abeyance without the past. In perception the old brain does not respond. Perception is not an experience to be stored up and remembered and therefore to become knowledge. When the brain is inattentive, it functions as playback of memory, the experience; but when it is attentive, it transcends experience and is aware of perception. The state of attention is perception. The attention is also called the silence, the emptiness, or the highest quantum energy potential of Consciousness. The brain undergoes mutation, which means the observer and the observed have gone to abeyance.

Wilder Penfield, an eminent brain surgeon, led him to conclude that our minds and our brains are not at all the same. The fact that the mind can survive brain trauma and function under anesthesia points very strongly to the separate existence of the mind. Penfield wrote that "it is the mind which experiences and it is the brain which records that experience".[7] He concluded that the mind must be a kind of invisible energy field that includes the brain, perhaps even controls it.

The human brain did not evolve until 6 million years ago, but the cosmos is 13 billion years old. The brain is degenerate with regard to mind. The brain is basically the biophysical substrate for logical and symbolic processes.

Thought and Time: Cause-effect and effect-cause are within the field of time. Memory, experience, knowledge are within time and thought is the response of all that. Thinking is within the field of time. J. Krishnamurti wrote, "There is a gap between two thoughts. In that interval there might be a different perception and the translation of that perception in time, but the perception itself is not of time".[8]

D.S. Kothari wrote, "As we think–in any sequence of thoughts–there is always a sudden discontinuous jump from one thought to the next. We are not aware of any intermediate stages.... *Quantum jump for thought appears to be as much a necessity for the conscious self as those are for the atom".*[9] Krishnamurti wrote, "We have lost in India, a sense of sensitivity to the world outside of us .... we have lost the sensitive perception".[10]

You give a boy, a small child, a toy. The toy absorbs him, takes him over. Or, you see a great marvelous snow peaked mountain, the grandeur, the magnificence, the glory of it, takes you over. That means that a great thing has absorbed your worries, your concerns, your challenges; and the mind becomes quiet. Similarly if a Mind with a higher quantum energy potential of Consciousness observes a mind with a low quantum energy potential, the lower goes to abeyance. The mind makes a quantum jump to a higher quantum energy potential of Consciousness.

You cannot teach a student to be aware. But you can help him to become sensitive and observe the psychodynamics of the conditioned psyche, and this will flow to transcendence of time and imbibe the *fact*, the *true*, the *present*, the *what is*!

Entropy and Consciousness

The symbolic-dualistic frame of reference of mind spectrum is governed by the "successive consciousness". Its content is past memory, so it offers resistance or friction to the movement of consciousness and thus the organism continually increases its entropy, and tends to approach the dangerous state of maximum entropy, which is death or self-annihilation. Thought is the measure of entropy, it leads to decay, it leads to wastage of energy. A formula is an abstraction created by thought and therefore it is the cause of conflict. The symbolic-dualistic frame of reference moves from *order to disorder*.

The non-dual and non-conceptual frame of reference of Mind Continuum is governed by "Simultaneous Consciousness" or highest quantum energy potential of Consciousness. As thought is absent, so there is no cause of conflict. It is perception. As the non-dual frame is free from any matter content, so it does not offer any resistance, it draws energy from the Absolute, Life Field, it is a movement from *order to higher order*.

Krishnamurti, in prophetic words, wrote:

> The mind which is the vessel of movement, when that movement has no form, no "me", no vision, no image, it is completely quiet .... In it there is no memory. Then the brain-cells undergo a change .... The brain-cells are used to movement in time.

> They are the residue of time and time is movement; a movement within the space which it creates as it moves .... When there is no movement, there is tremendous focus of energy .... So mutation is the understanding of movement, and the ending of movement in the brain-cells themselves.[11]

Ending of Thought-Time

The challenge of thought was explored by ancient sages/seers since the time of Vedas and Upanisads. Swami Vivekananda said, "By the Vedas no books are meant; they mean the accumulated treasury of spiritual laws discovered by different persons in different times".[12]

R.P. Kaushik wrote that, "the first stage prior to recognition and naming is the state of non-verbal or thought-free perception (*nirvikalpa jnana* or pure perception). From this pure perception we proceed to thought, recognition and naming (*savikalpa jnana*, distorted perception)".[13] There is always an interval, however small, between the perception of an object and its recognition and naming. The concepts of thought and naming are grafted on the perception which reduces a perception to a concept. In other words, we are not aware of pure perception but aware of mutilated (distorted) perception, and there is time-gap between perception and mutilated perception, which we call psychological time or I-time, or I-consciousness. It appears that there is no observation but only distortion. The space between the observer and the observed in which self-projection takes place is the psychological space.

Kaushik quoted, "A mind which is dyed with the fusion of the observer and the observed is full of all the riches". He again quoted, "One who sees with the art of pure observation in him ego disappears".[14] The Indian tradition of 'observation' to end I-consciousness is identical to that of modern science.

We extend Patanjal Yoga's concepts to the objective and subjective dimensions of life. The first stage is "pure perception" which is then reduced to 'distorted perception'; similarly it is possible that in the scientific mode of mind, the first stage is a perception of 'the subjective and the objective world', then it is bombarded by thought that "I am a scientist and science deals with measurement of the object". It knocks down the *subjective* and what is left behind is the *objective* (material values), and we are aware of the *material values* only. There is also awareness of the modified use of the *known*, which is often called *invention*. This is known as "the conceptual crisis of the modern West", or of scientific pursuit; and is basically due to the eclipse in transcendence, that encompasses but surpasses our quotidian affairs. The material values express themselves as psychological imbalances and the whole game continues infinitely.

The psychological space is full of desires, aversions and knowledge. If the I-consciousness encounters "restructured science-education", the I-consciousness is knocked off, or it goes to abeyance. The observed ends or there is an intimate contact between the observed and the observer. The psychological fusion of the observer and the observed is observation.

Society: It is what you and I, in our relationship, have created; it is the outward projection of all our own inward psychological states. Society by itself is non-existent. So if you and I do not understand ourselves, merely transforming the outer, which is the projection of the inner, then this action is sterile in transformation of society.

Understanding: There is understanding of 'what is', the fact, when we recognize it without condemnation, without justification, without identification. 'What is' is not static, it is dynamic and changing every moment. We need a very swift mind and a pliable heart. Understanding requires a mind in which there is direct perception. The objective scientific world bestows on us direct perception, which leads to understanding. There is no direct perception in the psychological state of mind because there is resistance. Understanding is *here* and *now*, not tomorrow. It is instantaneously and there is immediate transformation. The revolution is now, not tomorrow. In understanding, all psychological challenges, all thought-structures end, and you are beyond the wave of destruction.

We are the world, and our problems are the world's problems. To transform the world, we must begin with ourselves. We have to understand the psychodynamics of the conditioned psyche and learn to live according to the immutable laws of nature. Self-knowledge is the beginning of wisdom, and therefore the beginning of transformation or regeneration. If we can understand ourselves from moment to moment without the process of accumulation, then the mind becomes tranquil and there can be creativeness.

Einstein concluded, "The experiences of an individual appear to us arranged in a series of events; in this series the single events which we remember appear to be ordered according to the criterion of 'earlier' and 'later'. There exists, therefore, for the individual, an I-time, or subjective time. This in itself is not measurable".[15] The I-time or psychological time is essentially past as it is based on memory and thought. The word 'earlier' by Einstein appears to be pure perception, and the word 'later' to be distorted perception. There is always a time gap or psychological time between the 'earlier' and the 'later'. The thought process operates in psychological time, not in physical time, which is the present. Past never dies. Psychological time revives it. There is chaotic moment from past to future and future to past in quick succession. This chaotic movement of psychological time is a source of conflict, misery and sorrow. In the psychological time and space, he imprisons himself and destroys his freedom.

Mankind has lived for uncountable aeons with sorrow, pain, anxiety, loneliness, despair, violence, fear, and the pursuit of wandering desires, motives and acquisition. We are conditioned to the idea, or the concept, or to the illusion that time is necessary to change from '*what should be*?' to '*what is*!'. Time is the cause of conflict. The psychological time and space imprisons man and this destroys his freedom.

We have to learn how to listen, how to observe–not accumulate how to listen, but just listen, just observe without all the memory. If the observer (the violence) is attentive, the observed (the non-violence, the invented opposite) goes to abeyance.

We have to explore the nature and how desire is born, or nature of fear and birth of fear. We have to observe desire, fear and other psychological imbalances, without control, without suppression, just see how thought is acting on sensations. Observation is only possible when the observer is at a higher quantum energy potential than the observed. In observation, there is ending of thought-time.

The Genesis of Consciousness

Man is an amphibian who lives simultaneously in two worlds–the given (inner, subjective) and the home-made (outer, objective), the world of matter, life and consciousness and the world of symbols.[16] We quote some eminent scientists who advocated that science must take in its fold the objective and the subjective dimensions of life.

Karl Pribram wrote, "Brain science must deal with the awareness of awareness. It could no longer afford to shut out that part of the world which we call subjective".[17] Roger Sperry spoke of the importance of a neglected area of science, namely the study of the human subjective experience. He wrote, "Instead of renouncing or ignoring Consciousness, the new interpretation gives full recognition to the primacy of inner conscious awareness as a causal reality".[18] John Eccles wrote, "We have to assume that our self-conscious mind has some coherence with the neuronal operations of the brain, but we have furthermore to recognize that it is not in a passive relationship"–which is another way of affirming "the primacy of inner conscious awareness as a causal reality".[19] Wilder Penfield concluded that our minds and our brains are not at all the same. He stated that, "It is the mind that experiences and it is the brain that records that experience"

In the oft-quoted words of E.P. Wigner, "The measurement is not completed until its result enters our consciousness .... (this) last step is, at the present state of our knowledge, shrouded in the mystery and no explantion has been given for it so far in terms of quantum mechanics, or in terms of any other theory".[20] Hideki Yukawa wrote, "It is obvious that unless something rises into the consciousness it cannot become an object of rational thought, of rational consideration. At the same time, everyone will surely agree on the importance of an awareness that living in a world open towards both the exterior and the interior is a special characteristic of man's lot".[21] Fritjof Capra wrote, "In modern physics, the question of consciousness has arisen in connection with the observation of atomic phenomena. Quantum theory has made it clear that these phenomena can be understood only as links in a chain of the human observer. In the words of Eugene Wigner, "It was not possible to formulate the laws of [quantum theory] in a fully consistent way without reference to consciousness".[22]

Charles Sherrington wrote, "The material world has only been constructed at the price of taking the self, that is, mind, out of it, removing it; mind is not part of it; obviously, therefore, it can neither act on it nor be acted on by any of its parts".[23] Erwin Schrodinger wrote, "Mind has erected the objective outside world of the natural philosopher out of its own stuff. Mind could not cope with this gigantic task otherwise than by the simplifying device of excluding itself–withdrawing from its conceptual creation. Hence the latter does not contain its creator".[24] Albert Einstein, on 20 Nov. 1950, wrote:

> The most important human endeavor is the striving for morality in our actions. Our inner balance and even our very existence depend on it. Only morality in our actions can give beauty and dignity to life.... To make this a living force and bring it to clear consciousness is perhaps the foremost task of education.[25]

Eugene Wigner observed, "There are two kinds of reality or existence– the existence of my consciousness and the reality or existence of everything. This latter reality is not absolute but only relative".[26] And to quote Cyril Hinshelwood from his presidential address (1962) to the Royal Society (London), "To deny the reality of the inner world is a flat negation of all that is immediate in existence; to minimise its significance is to depreciate the very purpose of living, and to explain it away as a product of natural selection is a plain fallacy".[27]

We have to restructure science so that it takes in its fold both objective and subjective dimensions of life. Similarly education must deal with the sensual world and trans-sensual world. This leads to a new technology of "restructuring science-education", which we call as the true subject. It deals with the wholeness of life. The "restructured science-education" has the potential to end all psychological imbalance and to guarantee human survival.

Man has to learn to move from experience to perception, from intellect to intuition, from fragmentary concepts to the wholeness of life. His survival depends largely on his understanding of himself. He now faces himself.

It is the Cosmic Consciousness that brings mutation in the human psyche, it heals the mind-brain-body system, or the psychic pandemic; it bestows order, harmony, non-violence and peace.

Quantum Jump from Symbolic-Dualistic Mode to Restructured Science-Education Mode

To an experimental physicist, a photon is a quantum of light. A nervous system is just a machine for sensing photons. The Life Field expresses itself dominantly in three modes: (a) the symbolic-dualistic frame, or expression of successive consciousness, or the lowest quantum energy potential of consciousness; (b) the non-dual frame, or expression of Simultaneous Consciousness, or the highest quantum energy potential of Consciousness, or Quantum Field Consciousness (QFC), and (c) the restructured science-education which deals with the wholeness of life.

In a symbolic-dualistic frame of reference, there is exchange of photons (energy transduction) between the subject and the object, so both are continuities of change, and hence invariably gives a mutilated perception, which is the *non-fact*, the *false*, the *past*, the *what should be*? The energy exchange happens in about a few millionth of a second.

If we observe a photon (object) by the scientific mode of mind, we see that photon approaches the velocity of light and it is devoured by the mind. It implies that a photon cannot cross the "event horizon", or the "frequency barrier", or the "boundary wall". In the non-dual frame of reference, the subject is 'in-here' and the object is 'out-there'. There is no exchange of photons between the subject and the object, hence we are aware of the 'objective fact', which is the *fact*, the *true*, the *present*, the *what is*! The "restructured science-education" deals with the wholeness of life, so the subject and the object are within nature; or in other words, both are 'in-here'. The universe beyond the "event horizon" is a new universe with intelligent life in it.

In the non-dual frame of reference, there is self-awareness, but no content, no rush of thoughts in the brain. In the "restructured science-education", you are wholly attentive and the fact also dissolves. What remains behind is the Life Field bathing the neurons of the brain, the Divine Energy expresses itself as order, harmony, non-violence and peace.

Globalisation

We are transiting into a global society. Politics have become global, there is no such thing as a bi-lateral political dispute any longer, any dispute can attain international dimensions. Economics has become global, as is well known. The theory that every country can have its own economic policy is a myth, because economic factors are dictated by forces and countries far away from the growers of primary material. Technologically, we have become globalised, specially with the satellite technology, television itself. The fact that in television you can switch on a set and millions of people throughout the world can simultaneously participate in an event has never happened before in human history.

Now the growth of globalisation has taken place, but not the development of global consciousness. Globalisation is taking place as the result of science and technology, and the thrust of evolution, but global consciousness is not keeping pace with this globalisation. In five years, for all practical purposes, there is a new technological generation. So time has encapsulated.

Globalisation has put a severe restraint on the freedom of nations and of individuals. It has enhanced conditioning of mankind. Man is losing sensitivity at an accelerative pace. He is dehumanizing himself. There is a danger of a loss of, or a split in, our humanity in the world of the future.

The globalisation is a happening due to the accelerative progress of materialism and intellectual development, which is called growth of science and technology. But this has no relation to the manifestation of higher potential of consciousness. We need a creative mutation in consciousness. We have to understand and learn, and to live in that understanding through *observation* of the conditioned and the Unconditioned Energy. Mutation happens in the brain through insight, not through knowledge, not through accumulation. The global Consciousness will self-express itself. In Sri Aurobindo's words, "All will change if man once consents to be spiritualized"; the Divine Mother (Madame Mirra Alfasa) stated, "No human organisation can change radically unless human consciousness itself changes".[28] President Vaclav Havel, Czech Republic, addressing the US Congress in 1990 said, "Without a global revolution in the sphere of human consciousness, nothing will change for the better in our being as human".[29] It is the highest manifestation of the quantum energy potential of Cosmic Consciousness that will lead to the global Consciousness. It is the "restructured science-education" dimension that has the potential of expression of global Consciousness.

Global Ethic

The Union of Concerned Scientists–over 1670 scientists, including 104 Nobel laureates–have issued "*World Scientists' Warning to Humanity*" in April 1993, reads as:

A new ethic is required .... This ethic must motivate a great movement, convincing reluctant leaders and reluctant governments and reluctant peoples themselves to effect the needed changes.[30]

About 12 years have passed, and there seems to be no New Ethic or an Action Plan. The aims and objects of this monograph is to bring awakening to this truth at all levels with a view to avert nature's catastrophe and ensure human survival.

Global ethic is defined as the perception in a non-dual and non-conceptual frame of reference of the Mind Continuum. It is the foundation of all ethical and spiritual values. The universal declaration leading to the emergence of global ethic constitutes a call to mankind that human mind must make a quantum jump from dualistic frame to non-dual frame of reference of Mind Continuum. And one who is wholly consecrated to Truth, who wants to live the Truth, serve the Truth, would know at each moment the ethical values; it would be a kind of intuition or revelation or insight which would make you know the truth, the global ethic at every moment. To perceive the ethical values or global ethic, man has to make a quantum jump from psychosocial evolution to spiritual evolution.[31]

When the conditioned psyche encounters the true-subject (restructured science-education), the thought-structure goes to abeyance and it bestows values which are universal or global. The new ethic resolves all human challenges.

Concluding Comment

Every activity of the symbolic-dualistic state of mind is constructing man-made social cosmos, and this is leading to psychological imbalances– violence, anger, fear, acquisition, and storing these in the psyche. And all this is time. Psychological fragmentation is destroying the beauty of survival. The content of successive consciousness is conflict, pain; and this is in the direction of self-annihilation, self-destruction.

The symbolic-dualistic frame is inattentive, so there is confusion and pain. The non-dual and non-conceptual frame is attentive, so it bestows order, harmony, non-violence and peace. Attentiveness is invariably synergistic to inattentiveness. It is the attentiveness, which is at a higher quantum energy potential of consciousness than inattentiveness, and this heals the diseased psyche. It is the Life Field or Quantum Field of Consciousness (QFC) that ends all challenges of thought coupled with I-consciousness.

Many eminent scientists–including Albert Einstein, Werner Heisenberg, Erwin Schrodinger, Arthur Eddington, and so on–have stumbled upon another "mode of perception (knowing), which is 'direct understanding of life', instead of in the abstract, linear terms of representational thinking". *Understanding is a movement in the non-duality. The perceptions are born of non-duality and responses are born of spontaneity.* It bestows true objective nature. It leads to *invention*, which is a modified use of the known. It leads to fantastic progress of technology.

The systematic and rigorous observations have led some eminent scientists to "restructuring of science-education" which deals with the wholeness of life. The subject and the object are "in-here". So the Cosmic Energy flows to the object. It basically awakens the awareness, the intelligence, which arises out of observation, self-knowing and compassion. There is freedom and non-identification. This bestows order, harmony, non-violence, peace and survival. It leads to important *discoveries*, which is a movement from truth to truth. This is the basis of all sciences. It explores the physics of Consciousness that permeates the whole existence.

The thought-time is the enemy of man. Man has to understand and learn, through observation, the quantum jump from symbolic-dualistic frame of reference of mind spectrum to non-dual and non-conceptual frame of reference of Mind Continuum; from experience to perception; from intellect to intuition; and from fragmentary concepts to the wholeness of life. It is the Cosmic Consciousness that brings in mutation in the human psyche. It bestows order, harmony, non-violence and peace. Man's survival depends largely on his understanding of himself. He now faces himself.

References

1. Fritjof Capra, *The Web of Life*, Flamingo, 1996, p. 286.
2. *Ibid.*, p. 277.
3. Niels Bohr, in Fred Alan Wolf, *Taking the Quantum Leap*, Harper and Row, 1981, p. 85.
4. D.S. Kothari, *Some Thoughts on Science and Religion*, The University of Delhi, 31.10.1977 and 03.11.1977, p. 25.
5. Ilya Prigogine and Isabelle Stengers, *Order Out of Chaos*, Bantam Books, 1984, p. 220.
6. Deepak Chopra, *How to Know God*, Rider, 2000, pp. 270, 271.
7. Wilder Penfield, in Deepak Chopra, *ibid.*, pp. 215, 218.
8. J. Krishnamurti, *Tradition and Revolution*, Madras: Sangam Books, 1974, p. 86.
9. D.S. Kothari, *Atom and Self*, in *The Evolution of Consciousness*, New Delhi: National Publishing House, 1983, p. 212.
10. J. Krishnamurti, *Within the Mind: On J. Krishnamurti*, KFI: B.I. Publication, 1982, p. 147.
11. *ibid.*, *Tradition and Revolution*, *op. cit.*, Preface, pp. viii–ix.
12. Swami Vivekananda, *Chicago Parliament of Religions, 1893, Complete Works*, Vol. I, pp. 6-7.

13. R.P. Kaushik, *Towards a New Consciousness*, New Delhi: Darshan Yoga Sansthan, 1974, p. 63.
14. *ibid.*, in *Kaivalyapada 23*, *Patanjal Yoga*, p. 65; and *25*, *Patanjal Yoga*, p. 66.
15. Albert Einstein, in Lincoln Barnett, *The Universe and Dr. Einstein*, London: Victor Gollancz Ltd., 1949, pp. 39-40.
16. Aldous Huxley, in J. Krishnamurti, *The First and Last Freedom*, London: Victor Gollancz Ltd., 1977, Foreword.
17. Karl Pribram, in Ken Wilber (Ed.), *The Holographic Paradigm and Other Paradoxes*, Shambhala, 1982, p. 17.
18. Roger Sperry, in *Synthesis of Science and Religion*, Mumbai: The Bhaktivedanta Institute, June 1988, p. 199.
19. John Eccles, in *ibid.*, p. 200.
20. E.P. Wigner, in D.S. Kothari, *Some Thoughts on Science and Religion*, *op. cit.*, p. 26.
21. Hideki Yukawa, *Creativity and Intuition*, Tokyo: Kodansha International Ltd., 1973, p. 203.
22. Fritjof Capra, *The Tao of Physics* (*Second Edition*), Bantam Books, 1988, p. 291.
23. Charles Sherrington, in Erwin Schrodinger, *What is Life*? & *Mind and Matter*, Cambridge University Press, 1967, p. 128.
24. Erwin Schrodinger, *ibid.*, p. 131.
25. Albert Einstein, in D.S. Kothari, *Role of Science in Promoting Social and Moral Values*, New Delhi: The Indian Institute of Technology, 1983, Back Cover.
26. E.P. Wigner, in D.S. Kothari, *Some Thoughts on Science and Religion*, *op. cit.*, p. 3.
27. Cyril Hinshelwood, in D.S. Kothari, *ibid.*, p. 3.
28. Sampooran Singh, Dr (Mrs) Kanwaljit Kaur and Paramjit Singh, *The Masterplan Paradigm for Human Survival and Excellence*, Chandigarh: Faith Publishers, February 1998, p. 246.
29. Vaclav Havel, in *Our Global Neighbourhood*, *The Report of the Commission of Global Governance*, New York: Oxford University Press, 1995, pp. 353-54.
30. The Union of Concerned Scientists, *World Scientists' Warning to Humanity*, USA: Church Street, Cambridge, April 1993.
31. Sampooran Singh, *Science, Human Values, Value Education and Peace*, New Delhi: NM&NWM (India), 1993, pp. 84-85.

4
An Exploration of Science and Consciousness

Abstract

Science is the search for truth in the objective world. The aim of science is to study nature and gather human experience and knowledge (information) objectively. All experience and knowledge, everything without exception, is fundamentally personal and subjective. Knowledge is always limited whether now or in the future, and where there is limitation, there is conflict. Knowledge can never be creative, though knowledge can bring about a better physical world. Science is the movement of knowledge gathering more and more. The more is measurement and leads to competition, acquisition, motivation, which are pointers to conflict. Science mainly is the pursuit of materialism, so it leads to invention in the field of the known and can never lead to discovery.

Science is divorced from all human perennial values. Science, being a human activity, can never be separated from all values. Similarly science mainly deals with intellectual pursuit and has jettisoned intuition (insight).

The brain and mind are independent and shared by mankind. The successive consciousness and Simultaneous Consciousness are also shared by mankind. The "restructured science-education" deals with the wholeness of life, so the subject (true-subject) and the object are within nature; in other words, both are 'in-here'. When thought-structure coupled with volitions encounters the true-subject, the I-consciousness is first knocked off, and then the thought-structure goes to abeyance. If this observation is continued for a long chronological time, the fact also goes to abeyance, and Cosmic Consciousness expresses Itself as order, harmony, nonviolence and peace.

Globalisation is taking place as the result of science and technology, and the thrust of evolution, but global Consciousness is not keeping pace with the (material) globalisation. The "restructured science-

education" has the potential of manifestation of global Consciousness. A global ethic is also discussed.

Voltaire wrote, "Everything is governed by immutable laws .... everything is prearranged .... everything is necessary effect .... both (you and I) are toys in the hands of destiny". There is nothing in this cosmos which man can claim as his construct, or as his own. We are much like puppets with someone else (Consciousness) holding the strings.

Science is the search for truth in the objective world, the 'without'. A selfless, unfaltering devotion to truth and the use of knowledge for man's upliftment are the ideals of a scientist. Truth is what all earnest scientists seek. Free enquiry, objectivity, precision, autonomy, freedom, experience are the pillars of the inductive (experimental data) and deductive (theoretical) logic. Discovery is its mission, its perception. It is precise, clear, unprejudiced, which does not condemn, which observes, which sees. It moves from fact to fact.

There is a growing realisation that the basic postulates of the educational structure and its various systems in India and in the rest of the world have failed and that there is total lack of relevance between the human being and the complex contemporary society. The present education trains the mind in the continuation of the past. We are being educated to conform, to fit into a society and their culture, to fit into the stream of social and economic activity, and to fit into the existing political system. Understanding comes only when self-knowledge through self-observation makes a quantum jump to self-awareness. It is awareness of one's total psychological process. Education in the true sense is helping the individual to be mature and free, to flower greatly in love and goodness. The highest function of education is to bring about an integrated individual who is capable of dealing with life as a whole. Education is a way of discovering our true relationship to things, to other human beings, and to nature. Education encourages us to think freely without fear, that helps us to enquire and understand.

The UN was successful in postponing major wars and to achieve transient peace, but was unsuccessful in ending war and violence and achieve sustainable peace. Toward the end of his mandate, Dag Hammarskjold declared, "I see no hope for permanent world peace. We have tried but failed miserably. Unless the world has a spiritual rebirth, civilization is doomed". We have to ask ourselves the question, "Whither are we going?".

President Vaclav Havel, Czech Republic, addressing the US Congress in 1990 said, "Without a global revolution in the sphere of human consciousness, nothing will change for the better in our being as human".[1]

The racial conditioning and our present way of living is leading us to self-destruction, or self-annihilation.

Erwin Schrodinger states, "While the stuff from which our world picture is built is yielded exclusively from the sense organs as organs of the mind, so that every man's world picture is and always remains a construct of the mind and cannot be proved to have any other existence".[2] Arthur Eddington wrote:

The stuff of the world is mind-stuff .... The mind-stuff is not spread in space and time .... Recognizing that the physical world is entirely abstract and without "actuality" apart from its linkage to consciousness, we restore consciousness to the fundamental position.[3]

The world is us and we are the world. The world extended in space and time is but our representation. Our consciousness has two capacities– the *known*, the successive consciousness, the time-space matrices, and the other is the *Unknown*, the Simultaneous Consciousness.

This article discusses the psychological mode of mind, the scientific mode of mind, and technology of mutation in the Consciousness. The mutation will bring about a new culture. This leads to order, harmony, non-violence, peace and survival.

Psychological Mode of Mind

Homo Homonid had an evolutionary origin at about 4.5 million years ago, and *Homo sapien* at about 2.5 million years ago. Julian Huxley stated, "Man's evolution is not biological but psychosocial, it operates by the mechanism of cultural tradition, which involves the cumulative and self-reproduction and self-variation of mental activities and their products.[4]

Man's psychosocial evolution, over uncounted aeons, has led to storing of subtle matter content as frequency and amplitude information, and this is called the cultural belief structure, or conditioning of the human psyche, or psychic pandemic, or memory. It is unstable and spontaneously disintegrates to thought coupled with its volitions or motives. Thought-time constructs the time-space matrices in quick succession, or the sensual world. Man has started living in the sensual world, man-made social cosmos, or a synthetic world. His mode of living is divorced from the Reality, the Universal Consciousness, the Truth. He is aware of the *non-fact*, the *false*, the *past*, the *what should be*?; or in other words, he has started living in a set of illusions. The whole mankind is caught unknowingly in a crisis of perception. The thought-time constructs all psychological imbalances–violence, greed, fear, anger and so on. The *Homo sapiens* have emerged as a violent species. We have built a society which is violent, and we, as human beings, are violent. Every activity of the conditioned human psyche is dualistic, so it adds to entropy of the mind-brain-body system which is a pointer towards self-annihilation or self-destruction.

Genesis of Psychological Imbalances: Modern physics has confirmed: (a) all the concepts we use to describe nature are limited, and creations of the mind, the conditioned psyche; parts of the map, not of the territory; (b) in order to see itself, it cuts itself up into at least one state which sees, and at least one other state which is seen; in this severed and mutilated condition whatever it sees is *only partially* itself; (c) the interaction between the seer (subject) and the seen (object) happens in about few millionth of a second and this results in self-awareness of the distorted subject and the object; (d) both the subject and the object are continuities of change and can never give perception of the *fact*, the *true*, the *present*, the *what is*!; and (e) the distorted perception leads to duality and gives pain, misery, fragmentation and strife.

Resolution of the Present Human Paradox: We have to educate our physical organism and psychological structure through observation by the scientific mode of mind. This results in a movement from self-knowledge to understanding of life directly (self-awareness), it flows to a quantum jump from symbolic-dualistic frame of mind spectrum to non-dual frame of reference of Mind Continuum; and from intellect to intuition (insight). So one moves from activity to non-action, from speech to verbal silence, from movement to non-motion gracefully and voluntarily. It energises the Cosmic Intelligence that takes charge of one's being.

Scientific Mode of Mind

Science is the search for truth. The aim of science is to study nature and human experience objectively. Objectivity and precision, both as to thought and its verbal formulation, are two important characteristics of the scientific method. The advance of knowledge is at present reduced to what Einstein described as "extracting one incomprehensible from another incomprehensible". Maurice H. Wilkins, Nobel Prize in Medicine, 1962, wrote, "Science makes progress largely by a combination of two aspects: open-mindedness and the following of abstract concepts. Abstraction involves excluding and narrowing down, which is very opposite to open-mindedness .... Science is a human activity .... The whole question of moral, spiritual and other dimensions is normally pushed out of science".[5]

All experience, every thing without exception, is fundamentally a personal, subjective experience. Max Born wrote, "The fact that by comparing pairs communicable, objective statements are possible, has an immense importance because it is the root of speaking and writing, and of the most powerful instrument of thinking, of mathematics".[6]

The scientific mode of mind is synergistic to the psychological mode of mind, which implies that the scientific mode is at a higher quantum energy potential of Consciousness, or in other words, it is at the immanent aspect of Consciousness, or the absolute. The objective world has the following attributes:

(a) Schrodinger wrote, "Without being aware of it and without being rigorously systematic about it, we exclude the Subject of Cognizance from the domain of nature that we endeavour to understand .... Mind has erected the objective outside world of the natural philosopher out of its own stuff. Mind could not cope with this gigantic task otherwise than by the simplifying device of excluding itself–withdrawing from its conceptual creation. Hence the latter does not contain its creator".[7] Charles Sherrington wrote, "The material world has only been constructed at the price of taking the self, that is, mind, out of it, removing it; mind is not part of it; obviously, therefore, it can neither act on it nor be acted on by any of its parts".[8] C.J. Jung and B. Spinoza have identical perception. This also suggests that there is no energy interaction between the subject and the object. The self-observation bestows perception of the fact, the objective truth.

(b) The objective world picture is 'colourless, cold, mute'. Schrodinger wrote, "Colour and sound, hot and cold are our immediate sensations; small wonder that they are lacking in a world model from which we have removed our own mental person .... The physical world picture lacks all the sensual qualities that go to make up the Subject of Cognizance. The model is colourless and soundless and unpalpable .... The scientific views of natural processes formed in this way lack all sensual qualities and therefore cannot account for the latter".[9]

(c) Eddington wrote, "The frank realization that physical science is concerned with a world of shadows is one of the most significant of recent advances".[10] Schrodinger wrote, "Democritus of Abdera was aware of this in fifth century B.C.".

(d) Schrodinger wrote, "The world of science lacks, or is deprived of, everything that has a meaning only in relation to the consciously contemplating, perceiving and feeling subject. I mean in the first place the ethical and aesthetical values, any values of any kind, everything relating to the meaning and scope of the whole display .... The values are missing, and quite particularly meaning and end are missing".[11]

The Genesis of Creativity in Science: Mind has a very wide spectrum. It has the capacity to make quantum jumps to different frames of reference in that spectrum. A creative process involves many frame of reference, and the different frames are shown diagrammatically.[12-14] Duc to shortage of space, these steps are not discussed in this paper.

Rational knowledge and rational activities certainly constitute the major part of scientific research, but it must be complemented by the intuitive insights that makes a scientist creative. Albert Einstein, in almost the last interview that he gave to the international magazine LIFE said as follows:

> The mind can proceed only so far upon what it knows and can prove. There comes a point where the mind takes a leap–call it intuition or what you will–and comes out upon a higher plane of knowledge, but can never prove how it got there. All great discoveries have involved such a leap.
>
> Physics is essentially an intuitive and concrete science. Mathematics is only a means for expressing the laws that govern phenomena.[15]

The mind follows logical and scientific reason as far as it can guide, but when reason or intellect realises its limitations, then the conscious-mind makes a quantum jump to a higher plane and intuition tends to come suddenly, and characteristically, not when sitting at a desk working out the equations, but when relaxing in the bath, during a walk in the woods, on the beach, etc. During these periods of relaxation after concentrated intellectual activity, the intuitive mind seems to take over and can produce the sudden clarifying insights which add creativeness to scientific research. The intuition is not through external sensory organs and the internal sensorium in the brain, but through another set of neurones, which is often called in literature as the 'heart', the centre of inspiration; so it is obtainable through means other than reason and it is not irrational but extra-rational or beyond-rational.

All knowledge is structured in consciousness. The creative process involves a quantum jump from logical and scientific reason to philosophic reason or non-dual and non-conceptual frame of reference of Mind Continuum; in other words, from a relative frame of reference to an absolute rest frame of mind. Knowledge emanates from it as quantas depending on the frame of reference of mind.

D.S. Kothari, in prophetic words, wrote:

> The new theorems, unless trivial, are of course first "discovered" and then proved. Discovery is an inspired guess, a flash of insight. It is not a step by step process, but a sort of quantum jump.... A rational account of a discovery, the proof, follows and not precedes the discovery.[16]

> Fundamental discoveries which go deep into the nature of things are the result of uncommon intuition and faith, not cold logic.[17]

Education and Values

The core of the natural science is the outer world and the core of values is the inner world. The outer world, "the flood of external objects of cognizance has made the subject of cognizance withdraw to the background", and "obviously it can neither act on it (subject) nor be acted on by any of its parts". Science by itself cannot supply us any ethic.

Recently, many eminent scientists–Werner Heisenberg, Edwin Hubble, Max Planck, G.F. Chew, Bertrand Russell, Lincoln Barnett, Max Born, and so on–have concluded that we cannot impart value education at reason or intellect level.[18]

All ethical/spiritual values proceed from the trans-sensual dimension of human personality, the Life Field, these self-emerge from the dimension of the wholeness of life, the restructured science-education dimension of life. The values express themselves in the non-dual frame of reference of Mind Continuum.

Wrong Turn Taken by Mankind

The insight by Sri Aurobindo is as under:

> The evolution of mind working upon life has developed an organization and use of matter which can no longer be supported by human capacity without an inner change. The problem is fundamental and in putting its evolutionary Nature is confronting man with a critical choice which must one day be solved in the true sense if the race is to arrive or even to survive.[19]

George Wald, Nobel Prize in Medicine, 1967, in prophetic words, wrote:

> We who know where we are going, are now heading rapidly toward self-extinction, toward removing humankind from the cosmic scene, and for the most trivial of reasons: profit, the rivalry of the United States and the Soviet Union, the momentum of the military-industrial complex in both nations. The cosmic drama will go on elsewhere, ignorant of our demise, caring nothing; but we will have no further part in it.... Does that matter? It matters to us.[20]

David Bohm, an eminent physicist, and J. Krishnamurti, the philosopher-mystic discussed "The Future of Humanity", and they raised two fundamental questions as, "***Has humanity taken a wrong turn which has created the chaos***

in the world?*" and "*What needs to be done within the consciousness of man to preserve our very existence and bring about a new culture?". Mankind took a wrong direction and thereafter they are just continuing that direction.[21] We are going towards self-annihilation and not much time is left now.

Hideki Yukawa, a Japanese Nobel Laureate in Physics, concluded:

> The danger that all these trends (psychological, social, ecological, violence, and so on) will combine to destroy the unity of man's various aspects and lead eventually to the loss even of his humanity cannot be denied. It is equally undeniable, I believe, that such a split would deprive man of his happiness.

To save ourselves, by such efforts, from the danger of a loss of, or a split in, our humanity in the world of the future–this, I believe, is the course that man must take from now on. This, it is my personal conviction, is true wisdom for modern man.[22]

There is the large gap between the superhuman task and the frailties of human endeavours. Hideki Yukawa quotes Max Born–a Nobel Prize winner: "Clever, rational ways of thinking are not enough. The danger of mass slaughter .... can only be overcome by moral conviction, by a determination to replace national prides and prejudices with human love".[23]

Objective Scientific Mode of Mind

It is evident that we have to explore the new global consciousness in the light of the recent discoveries in science. In our own lives, each one of us must move towards a realisation of the truth at the core of our being, the glowing higher consciousness that is the birthright of each individual born on this planet, because in the ultimate analysis it is the crucible of our individual selves alone that the poison of conditioning the psyche can be contained and transformed into the new consciousness that we seek. In this lies the faith for individual freedom as well as the survival of our planet earth. We intuitively see that even at this late hour, we can marshal our inner (spirituality) and outer (science) dimensions and we succeed in making the vital transition to the new consciousness? It is this most crucial of all decisions that it is the privilege and responsibility of our generation to make, because it is this, in the ultimate analysis, that will prove whether there is really new perception (not reason) for mutation in the new global society that is so rapidly emerging before us.

You cannot impose the order on top of disorder. You cannot impose non-violence on a consciousness which is violent because that violence has deep-rooted causes in the psyche. Unless these causes are eliminated there is no ending of violence. We cannot survive unless all psychological imbalances are dissolved through observation by higher quantum energy potential of consciousness.

Mutation is possible in the brain through insight, not through knowledge, not through accumulation. That insight is the ability to see a truth directly, a direct perception of the truth, and education must foster that. "The restructured science-education", which observes the wholeness of life, is the only panacea for human survival.

The "objectivity" of science was discussed by Erwin Schrodinger, Charles Sherrington, B. Spinoza and C.J. Jung. It appears that the subject of the mind spectrum is at the immanent quantum energy potential and is divorced from the ultimate or transcendent quantum energy potential of the Consciousness. The subject is non-variable attentivity, or reaction-free attentivity, or objectless attention. The object of the mind is the only reality which has the lowest quantum energy potential; or in other words, the immanent quantum energy potential has gone to abeyance and its only linkage is the lowest quantum energy potential of consciousness. It represents the relative field of consciousness. The objective material world can neither act on the subject nor be acted on by any of the parts.

The subject is "in-here" while the object is "out-there". There is no energy exchange between the objective and the subjective. So the objective world gets recorded as the *fact*. The object gives the objective *fact*, which is a partial objective truth. It gives invention, which is a modified use of the known. It cannot give us a discovery, which is an entirely new principle or a theorem.

Restructured Science-Education

Karl Pribram wrote, "Brain science must deal with the awareness of awareness. It could no longer afford to shut out that part of the world which we call subjective".[24] Roger Sperry spoke of the importance of a neglected area of science, namely the study of human subjective experience. He wrote, "Instead of renouncing or ignoring consciousness, the new interpretation gives full recognition to the primacy of inner conscious awareness as a causal reality".[25] John Eccles also emphasized the importance of the phenomenon of "conscious experience".[26]

The outer (objective) and the inner (subjective) are not two separate movements. It is a unitary movement, not separate, but one whole. Man has now to work to treat the outer and the inner as one. We call it "restructured science-education". The restructured science takes in its ambient both the subjective and the objective dimensions of life. The restructured education deals with the sensual and the trans-sensual world. It deals with the observer situated within the observed world. The dialogue with nature is carried on from within nature. It sees the wholeness of life. The subject now is non-variable attentivity, or reaction-free attentivity, or objectless attention. The "restructured science-education" deals with the wholeness of life, so it is at the transcendent aspect of the absolute, or Cosmic Consciousness. The Consciousness is Eternal, Infinite and Immutable.

When thought-structure coupled with volitions (I-consciousness) encounters the realm of the transcendent Consciousness, the thought-structure or thought-time goes to abeyance. Due to shortage of space, it is not discussed.[27]

When true-subject observes the conditioned psyche, one perceives that–(a) thought-time is independent of I-consciousness; (b) it is the product of collective human effort through centuries; (c) it (photons) cannot cross the "event horizon"; (d) it goes to abeyance and leads to non-dual and non-conceptual frame of reference of Mind Continuum; and if the observation is sustained, it leads to order, harmony, nonviolence and peace.

The brain and the mind are independent and are shared by mankind. The successive consciousness and Simultaneous Consciousness are shared by mankind. The "restructured science-education" deals with the wholeness of life, so the subject and the object are within nature, or in other words, both are "in-here". The universe beyond the "event horizon" is a new universe with intelligent life in it.

The happenings in nature are very fast–say the time between the subjective and the objective may be about a few millionths of a second; the photons are devoured by a black hole in less than a hundred microseconds,[28] and same order of time may be there when photons are absorbed by a mind; the time taken for a signal to move from a cell to muscle is of the order of about five thousandths of a second,[29] which corresponds to something moving to and fro two hundred times a second. It appears that the brain does not have the capacity to record time of this order of magnitude.

We are beginning a new age of awareness, the age of quantum consciousness, the age of the conscious atom. By observing within ourselves, we may be able to solve the problems facing us on the final frontier–the frontier of Cosmic Consciousness.[30]

What is Consciousness?

Sri Aurobindo wrote:

> The Supreme is Pure Being, Absolute Existence, *sat*. He is Existence because He alone *Is*, there being nothing else which has any ultimate reality or any being independent of His self-manifestation .... The Supreme is also pure awareness, Absolute Consciousness, *cit* .... The Supreme is, finally, Pure Ecstasy,

Absolute Bliss, *ananda* .... God is Satchidananda .... Consciousness is a reality inherent in existence.[31]

The dimensions of Consciousness are Homogeneous, Undifferentiated and Dimensionless.

Consciousness performs a dual role in the universe. In the world of quantum, it is both the awareness and the creation of experience. It is the *being* and the *knowing* of experience. With the stroke of the twentieth-century quantum eraser, the dividing line between ontology (theory of being) and epistemology (theory of knowing) is rubbed out. The fusion of ontology, epistemology and psychology is beginning to emerge. Consciousness is the quantum connection between the numerous layers making up the quantum machine. In other words, we are quantum conscious "golems". We are beginning a new age of awareness, the age of quantum consciousness, the age of the conscious atom.[32]

The Consciousness expresses Itself in a material structure, the brain. The human bring did not evolve until 6 billion years ago, but the cosmos is 13 billion years old. Brain is a part of the objective world. It can be investigated objectively. The brain is basically the biophysical substrate for the mental processes, for logical and symbolic processes. The brain maps out the degenerate relationships between mind-body system. Each higher stage (expression of quantum energy potential of consciousness) is synergistic to its junior components, it includes them but is more than them. Mind is subjective. The brain is degenerate to mind.

Concluding Comment

Schrodinger wrote, "A moderately satisfying picture has only been reached at the high price of taking ourselves out of the picture, stepping back into the role of a non-concerned observer .... Subject and the object are only one.... The original (subject) and the image (object) are identical".[33]

Ilya Prigogine wrote, "The behaviour of reality (is) unrelated to our beliefs, our ambitions or our hopes". He again wrote, "It is physics that presupposes an observer situated within the observed world. Our dialogue with nature will be successful only if carried on from within nature".[34]

The two blatant antinomies are resolved as under :

(a) The dimensions of "restructured science-education" are subjective realm and objective field–where the subjective realm is the true-subject of cognizance, the true-observer, and the objective field is that is observed. The self-observation of the conditioned psyche (object, observed) are within the observed world; or in other words, it opens a dialogue with nature when this is carried on from within nature. Both subjective and objective are "in-here", that is participators in nature. The principle enunciated by Ilya Prigogine is identical at a deeper level to self-observation by restructured science-education.

(b) The observation by restructured science-education considers subject and object are only one, and results into ending the duality, which implies ending of all psychological imbalances, ecological crises and so on.

This leads to ending all thought-structures coupled with volitions and pure Consciousness bathes the brain cells. This bestows a mind that lives with love, compassion and humility. The expression of pure Consciousness is Oneness, Order, Harmony, Rhythm, Non-violence, Peace and Security.

David Bohm, in the Preface to "The Future of Humanity" wrote, "(Krishnamurti) emphasizes that mind is essentially free of the distorting bias that is inherent in the conditioning in the brain, and that through insight arising in proper undirected attention without a center, it can change the cells of the brain and remove the destructive conditioning".[35] We intuit that the "*proper undirected attention*" is the "restructured science-education" and this is the dimension of the wholeness of life. This bestows intuition (insight) that can create a mutation in Consciousness and bring about a New Culture.

The mutation in Consciousness happens when the "restructured science-education" observes the conditioned psyche and both the '*inner*' and the '*outer*' are within the field of the transcendent aspect of the Absolute, the Life Field–this is the essence of the technology of a mutation in Consciousness which has the capacity to end all psychological imbalances and ecological crisis, and also the capacity to bring about a ***New Culture***. This blossoms to peace, security and survival of mankind. This is the only vocation of mankind and is the consummation of life.

When "restructured science-education" takes hold as the Subject of Cognizance, the path lies open to a world of continuing realisation and enrichment of liberty, justice, prosperity and joy for all. Towards this great end India with its unique heritage and culture has an especial opportunity and obligation. This is the only vocation of man. At a deeper level, this is governed by our survival.

Mankind can survive only if the disorder, or violence, or psychological imbalances end in our consciousness. And this happens when "restructured science-education" takes over as the true subject. It is the Life Field or Quantum Field Consciousness (QFC) that can lead to survival of mankind.

India was once the "Light of Asia". She has now to fulfil her historic role of being the Light of the World. India has been called upon *here* and *now* to save Life in the world from extinction. Will she wake up from deep slumber and "***Lead Kindly Light Amid the Encircling Gloom***". We share the privilege and the responsibility.

References

1. President Vaclav Havel, in *Our Global Neighbourhood : The Report of the Commission on Global Governance*, New York: Oxford University Press, 1995, pp. 353-54.
2. Erwin Schrodinger, *What is Life*? & *Mind and Matter*, Cambridge University Press, 1967, p. 132.
3. Arthur Eddington, *Nature of the Physical World*, Cambridge University Press, 1928, pp. 276-77; in George Wald, in *Synthesis of Science and Religion*, Mumbai: Bhaktivedanta Institute, June 1988, p. 20.
4. Julian Huxley, *Evolution after Darwin*, Chicago: University Press, 1959, Vol. III, pp. 251-52.
5. Maurice H. Wilkins, in *Synthesis of Science and Religion*, *op. cit.*, p. 30.
6. Max Born, *My Life and My Views*, Chapter Five, "*Symbol and Reality*", 1968, p. 174; in D.S. Kothari, *Some Thoughts on Science and Religion*, Delhi University, 31.10.1977 & 3.11.1977, p. 44.
7. Erwin Schrodinger, *op. cit.*, pp. 127, 131.
8. Charles Sherrington, in Erwin Schrodinger, *ibid.*, p. 128.
9. Erwin Schrodinger, *op. cit.*, pp. 128, 148, 177.
10. Arthur Eddington, in Erwin Schrodinger, *ibid.*, pp. 130, 177.
11. Erwin Schrodinger, *ibid.*, pp. 148, 149.
12. Sampooran Singh, *The Epistemology of Scientific Knowledge, Science and Culture*, April 1982, Vol. 48, No. 4, pp. 119-25; and *Creativity in Science*, Gandhi Marg, May 1985, Vol. 7, No. 2, pp. 104-19.
13. *Ibid.*, *The Art of Creativity in Education*, in *The Holistic Education*, New Delhi: Siddharth Publications, 1987, pp. 145-70.
14. *Ibid.*, *The Survival of Mankind and Quantum Jump from Violence to Peace*, New Delhi: Books India International, 1999, pp. 142-59.
15. Albert Einstein, in *Nature*, Vol. 278, March 15, 1979.
16. D.S. Kothari, in *The Odyssey of Science, Culture and Consciousness*, New Delhi: Abhinav Publications, 1990, pp. 48-49.
17. *ibid.*, in *The Evolution of Consciousness*, New Delhi: National Publishing House, 1983, p. 227.
18. Sampooran Singh, in *Global Education and Human Survival: A Scientific Appraisal*, New Delhi: Sanbun Publishers, March 2002, pp. 46, 35-36.
19. Sri Aurobindo, in *The Odyssey of Science, Culture and Consciousness*, New Delhi: Abhinav Publications, 1990, p. 41.
20. George Wald, in *The Evolution of Consciousness*, New Delhi: National Publishing House, 1983, p. 13.
21. J. Krishnamurti and David Bohm, *The Future of Humanity*, in P. Krishna, *Education, Science and Spirituality*, USA: Institute for Higher Education, Research and Dialogue, 1993, pp. 13 & Back Cover.

22. Hideki Yukawa, *Creativity and Intuition*, Tokyo: Kodansha International Ltd., 1973, pp. 205, 206.
23. Max Born, in Hideki Yukawa, *ibid*., pp. 189-190.
24. Karl Pribram, in Ken Wilber, *The Holographic Paradigm and Other Paradoxes*, Boulder: Shambhala, 1982, p. 17.
25. Roger Sperry, in *Synthesis of Science and Religion*, Mumbai: The Bhaktivedanta Institute, June 1988, p. 199.
26. John Eccles, in ibid., p. 200.
27. Sampooran Singh and Dr (Mrs) Kanwaljit Kaur, *Peace, Security and Survival : A Scientific Quest*, Chandigarh: July 5, 2004, pp. 16-17.
28. Deepak Chopra, *How to Know God*, Rider, 2000, p. 271.
29. Fred Alan Wolf, *Taking the Quantum Leap*, San Francisco: Harper and Row, 1981, p. 236.
30. *Ibid*., p. 248.
31. Sri Aurobindo, *What is Consciousness*?, Pondicherry: Sri Aurobindo Society, All India Magazine, July 1999, pp. 11, 15.
32. Fred Alan Wolf, *Taking the Quantum Leap*, San Francisco: Harper & Row, 1981, pp. 229, 211, 248.
33. Erwin Schrodinger, *op. cit*., pp. 128, 137, 146.
34. Ilya Prigogine and Isabelle Stengers, *Order Out of Chaos*, New York: Bantam Books, 1984, pp. 8, 218.
35. J. Krishnamurti and David Bohm, *The Future of Humanity*, KFI, 1987, Preface, pp. 2-3.

5
An Exploration of Science and Education

Abstract

Sri Aurobindo wrote, "The true teaching is that nothing can be taught". The secret of teaching is "the understanding of life directly". The self-unfoldment and the higher quantum energy potential of Consciousness are the means and the process.

Education must be concerned with the cultivation of the total human being. The whole world is within us and we are the world. We have to introduce the science of mind-brain-body system in the science curriculum and transpersonal psychology in the arts. We have to teach the child to learn to read the book of life through the art of listening, the art of observing, the art of learning, and the art of living the wholeness of life.

The instrument of observation must be non-variable and should not construct the observed, so it is free from any evaluation, judgement, conclusion. Such a living fosters the perennial human values through the enhancement of awareness. We must learn to view the world holistically.

The subject is non-variable attentivity, or reaction-free attentivity, or objectless attention. This flows to a quantum jump from reason to intuition. We urgently need a symbiosis of science and spirituality.

The experimental interrogation or observation of conditioned psyche by "restructured science-education" mode of mind leads to transcendence of I-consciousness and thought-structure. If the observation is continued over a long chronological time, the fact also goes to abeyance and Intelligence is regenerated, which expresses Itself as order, harmony, nonviolence and peace, which guarantees human survival and excellence.

Man (*Homo sapien*) has been engaged for a million years or more, in making symbols, concepts and images of fragmentary experience and partial knowledge (information), which are recorded as frequency and amplitude information in the mind-brain-body system, and called memory (subjective dimension), or cultural belief structure. The mind splits itself as subject and object; there is coherent superpositions of different webs of the subject on the object which leads to mutilated perception and modified memory. We do not see things as they are–we see them as we are. The world is seen not as it is, but in its various relationships to the 'me' (I-consciousness) of the memory. The past is the 'me'. There is no 'me' in the present. As long as the mind is operating in the past, there is the 'me', and the mind is the past. The cultural belief structures or past thought-structures are called conditionings and lead to conflict, violence, aggression, fear and other psychological imbalances.

Man has been trying to end violence (conflict) in the psyche for the last 10,000 years or so, but all intellectual approaches, thought-structures, beliefs, have proved to be sterile in transforming the human psyche; rather these have added to the conditionings.

The accelerative progress of science and technology, and thrust of evolution have led to globalization, but global consciousness is not keeping pace with the globalization. The rapid information technology has led to a point where the time has encapsulated. The planet has been reduced to a 'global village', or a 'global cottage'. This is leading to further conditioning the psyche. Many eminent scientists, philosophers-mystics, educationists, politicians have echoed that we are heading towards self-annihilation or self-destruction.

During the last five decades, Nature is releasing Its hidden secrets in the minds of eminent scientists, perhaps due to persistent and consistent research. The scientific discoveries touch the fringes of the ancient "Indian Perennial wisdom". Modern science has brought man on the control panel of mutation or transformation of the human psyche. There is an urgency to share this with scientists, philosophers-mystics and other lovers of mankind.[1-6]

There is an urgency to heal the human psyche. Healing is only possible when we jointly and individually explore the human challenges at their roots through the arts of listening and observation. We have to move from self-knowledge through self-observation to self-awareness.

The United Nations Organisation has recently embarked on teaching of "resolution of conflict" and "peace education for kids at Kindergarten level". The UN has written to the Universities in at least ten countries to include the model in their curriculum.[7] The details of the model have not been published.

This article discusses, 'peace education' in the light of the recent discoveries of science. It explores restructuring of science, restructuring of education, the instrument of perception. It discusses the arts of listening and observation of the conditioned psyche and these lead to I-consciousness and thought-structure going to abeyance. The symbiosis of science and spirituality is also discussed. It presents an action plan or paradigm shift from psychosocial evolution to spiritual evolution. The aims and objects of this research paper is to initiate a 'global dialogue with an open mind' for peace education.

Restructuring of Science

Scientific research involves the observer as a participator and this involves the consciousness of the human observer. Hence there are no objective properties of nature, independent of the observer. Eddington wrote, "The frank realization that physical science is concerned with a world of shadows is one of the most significant of recent advances".[8] Schrodinger remarked that Democritus in the fifth century B.C. was aware of it, but we ignored and kept on exploring the 'world of shadows'.[9]

Many eminent physicists–including Albert Einstein, Werner Heisenberg, Erwin Schrodinger, Arthur Eddington, and so on–have stumbled upon another mode of knowing, called intimate, or direct, or intuition (insight), or non-dual knowledge. This is the culminating insight of 400 years of persistent and consistent scientific research. Arthur Eddington wrote:

> We have two kinds of knowledge which I call symbolic knowledge and intimate knowledge.... [The] more customary forms of reasoning have been developed for symbolic knowledge only. The intimate knowledge will not submit to codification and analysis; or, rather, when we attempt to analyze it the *intimacy is lost and it is replaced by symbolism.*[10]

Eddington added, "The intimate knowledge of the reality (is) behind the symbols of science". Alan W. Watts wrote it leads to "the understanding of life directly, instead of in the abstract terms of representational thinking".[11] This suggests that man is an amphibian who lives simultaneously in two worlds–the objective (time-space-causation matrices) and the subjective, the timelessness, the higher quantum energy potential of Consciousness. There is an urgency to restructure science so that restructured science takes in its ambient both the objective and the subjective dimensions of life. The restructured science is synergistic to thought-structures and I-consciousness.

Roger Sperry, Nobel laureate in physiology and medicine, 1981, wrote, "Once science modifies its traditional materialist-behaviorist stance and begins to accept in theory and to encompass in principle within its causal domain the whole world of inner conscious, subjective experience (the world of the humanities), then the very nature of science itself is changed".[12]

Maurice H. Wilkins, Nobel prize in medicine, 1962, wrote:

> The open-minded enquiry of the scientist is not something peculiar to science itself but is characteristic of the good way of living for human being in general.... To say that the essence of science is that you are always enquiring and open-minded is to say that you are in fact living a virtuous life.[13]

B. D. Josephson, Nobel prize in physics, 1973, wrote:

> All the different levels are open to exploration if we develop our nervous systems so that they tune in. One can imagine that this would be a part of the scientific training of the future; scientists working in this field would try to develop their nervous systems so that they could explore these regions.... We would say really the whole structure of science, once we get to the quantum level (where the unmanifest order makes observable order), would be directly the result of God's presence and works.[14]

The integration of subject and object in science is true science. True science explores all coordinate systems of the Mind Continuum. It implies the investigation of the unity of perception, the dimensions of inner space, and the transcendence of psychological imbalances. Science must include in its purview the field of human self-awareness, the field of human consciousness, and the human ego, which sees itself as a subject divided from the objective world. Scientific research must include the dimensions of "subjective" research and bring about the restructuring of "objective" science, thereby bestowing a perception of wholeness. This has been the cardinal aim of psychoscience. The particular must be seen in the light of the general, and the general in the light of the overall subtext of reality.[15]

Restructuring of Education

Education must be concerned with the cultivation of the total human being, the nurturing of the mind-brain-body system. It should have two aims. The primary aim is to give the child the capacity to be and to remain awake to the dynamics of his or her own mind. The secondary aim is to teach the child the various skills and disciplines. We have to introduce the science of the mind-brain-body system in the science curriculum and transpersonal psychology in the arts. We have to teach the child to learn to read the book of life through the art of listening, the art of observing, the art of learning, and the art of living in a way that he or she is meaningfully connected to the context of the social and biological nexus and of the overall subtext of Reality. The educational structure must help generate human values through the enhancement of such awareness. We must learn to view the world holistically. This leads to the awakening of Intelligence which arises out of observation, self-knowledge, and compassion or Love. Intelligence, Truth, or Love, which are expressions of the same feelingful or intuitively felt Reality, alone has the capacity to resolve all human psychological problems.[16]

In the words of Ramana Maharishi, "Illiteracy is ignorance and education is learned ignorance. Both are ignorant of the true Aim".[17] Ken Wilber wrote, "The 'true Aim' is the non-dual mode of knowing, while being literate or illiterate concerns the dualistic and symbolic mode of knowing. Ignorance, in other words, is ignorance of the non-dual and non-conceptual mode of knowing, which would instantly reveal the universe to be Mind-only".[18]

Education must encourage the right kind of self-observation, which flows to scientific temper. It is to perceive the wholeness of life at every moment, which is not to give significance to the '*part*', to the '*me*' and the '*mine*', but to help the mind-brain-body system to go above the psychological mode and to understand the *real*, the *fact*.[19]

Education deals with the sensual dimension and trans-sensual dimension of life. The sensual dimension is often called the objective field and the trans-sensual dimension as subjective realm. The restructured science and restructured education are a single dynamic flow, one unitary movement, and we call it "restructured science-education".

Recently, many eminent scientists–Werner Heisenberg, Edwin Hubble, Max Planck, G.F. Chew, Bertrand Russell, Lincoln Barnett, Max Born, and so on–have concluded that we cannot impart value education at reason or intellect level.[20,21]

The Instrument of Perception

The whole world is within us and we are the world. The revolution must take place at the very root of our being and that it can take place only when we know how to observe what we are. The instrument of observation must be non-variable and should not construct the observed, so it is free from any evaluation, judgement, conclusions. Such an instrument observes the *fact*, the *what is*! It observes the whole movement of living. It is always fresh, new and creative. It has the capacity for a radical revolution, or a transformation, or a mutation of human psyche. Nature, in its benediction, has embedded this instrument, which we call the scientific mode of mind–it implies both the objective and the subjective dimensions of life. The subject is non-variable attentivity, or reaction-free attentivity, or objectless attention. The mind is aware of the *fact*. The very perceiving is the action, so perception and action can never be separated. Perception-understanding-learning-action is a single dynamic flow, a unitary movement.

The perception is without decision, without an idea, and this bestows freedom. The perception is of the actuality, not something in relation to 'what should be'.

Spirituality

Spirituality bestows perception of the wholeness, it leads to emergence of human values, a global ethic, a new ethical outlook. It bestows tranquility of mind, which leads to freedom and peace. The ethical/spiritual values, which emerge from the trans-sensual dimension of the human personality, are universal, which implies that these transcend economic, ethnic, national, religious, and social divisions.

Spirituality teaches you the art of living. It bestows intuition, creativity and spontaneity at every moment. Both objective research and subjective research use the same tool–direct perception (intuition), and to communicate that intuition by verbal cognition (words are drawn from factual memory) and draw rational inference. Both exclude the I-consciousness. It implies to have understanding of life directly, which is to live intuitively at every moment, and then put that intuition in words which is called communicable intuition. It is nature's law that non-dualistic thought and spontaneous action do not leave any mark on the human psyche, because non-dualistic thought is at a higher quantum energy potential than the conditioned psyche. It teaches to live without any psychological debris. It is living according to the laws of nature.

Spirituality is understanding the conditioned mind, the matter content of the consciousness, and also to perceive the unconditioned energy; so it is the science of the wholeness of life. It aims at self-actualisation of the hidden human potential. Spirituality is fundamental and objective science is a derivative. A symbiosis of science and spirituality is the key to the survival of mankind. It jettisons all pain, misery and travails, and ushers a new era of freedom, peace and bliss. This is the only vocation of the human race.[22]

Principles of True Teachings

All intelligence/wisdom is structured in the Cosmic Consciousness. So all teaching is revealing, all becoming is an unfolding. Self-attainment is the secret. We have to make a quantum jump from self-knowledge through self-observation to self-awareness. So self-awareness and higher hierarchical level of consciousness are the means. The principles of true teaching, as enunciated by Sri Aurobindo are as under:

(a) Nothing can be taught. The teacher is not an instructor or task-master, for he is a helper and a guide. His business is to suggest and not to impose. He does not impart knowledge to him, he shows him how to acquire knowledge for himself.

(b) The mind has to be consulted in its own growth. It is he himself who must be induced to expand according with his own nature. The chief aim of education should be to help the growing soul to draw out that in itself which is best and make it perfect for a noble use.

(c) A free and natural growth is the condition of genuine development.

(d) The teacher will not seek to impose himself or his opinion on the passive acceptance of the receptive mind. The teacher has to guard against any turning of the means into a limitation, against the mechanising of process. His whole business is to awaken the divine light and set working the divine force.

(e) Every child is an enquirer, an investigator, analyser, a merciless anatomist. Appeal to those qualities in him and let him acquire without knowing is the right temper and the necessary fundamental knowledge of the scientist.

(f) The child must understand and learn to live according to the immutable laws of nature. It is to bring home to the child that all activities in terms of rupture between man and nature must go to abeyance. The art of living is a dialogue with nature when carried on from within nature. It is by allowing Nature to work that we get the benefit of the gifts she has bestowed on us.[23]

(g) J. Krishnamurti, in prophetic words, wrote, "What I am interested in is to awaken the mind. We say that the mind of the child can be kept alive through knowledge and therefore we pour in knowledge which only dulls the mind. A mind that functions in knowledge is a limited mind. But a mind that is extraordinarily alert, tremendously alive, not only learning from books, memorising some facts, but also learning how to look; how to listen, such a mind will impart its aliveness to a mind which is still seeking, enquiring, innocent. Therefore knowledge will not destroy".[24] A scientific mode of mind which takes in its ambient both the objective and the subjective dimension of life, is rooted in the wholeness of life, so it is alert and alive.

To sum up, the student must deeply understand the dynamics of his instruments–say the instrument of experience, knowledge and memory, the instrument of perception, the understanding of the fact, and transcendence of the fact. The student has to culture intuition (insight), spontaneity and right action. The true education blossoms to bathing the mind-brain-body system at every moment of living.

Peace Education

(a) As long as the mind is agitated or psychological mode of mind, it can have no understanding. Understanding comes when the frame of reference of mind makes a quantum jump from self-knowledge through self-observation to self-awareness. Each student has to unravel and understand himself the confusion and disorder of his own nature.

(b) The *outer* and the *inner* are one, a unitary harmonious dynamic movement. Education implies awareness of the *outer* sensual world and the *inner* trans-sensual world. It is awareness of the wholeness of life at every moment. But the whole cannot be understood through the part. It can only be understood through non-dual and non-conceptual frame of reference of Mind Continuum.

(c) Education, in the true sense, is to awaken intelligence/wisdom, and love and compassion. It is intelligence that brings order and harmony, non-violence and peace in the system.

(d) Education must help the child to educate himself. Teach him to look at himself. The child can draw out the truth in himself. This gives him the freedom which flowers to natural growth. He must develop the right scientific temper and then work for understanding of life.[25]

(e) The old paradigm is the Cartesian, Newtonian world view, the mechanistic world view, which is a construct by the relative frame of reference, the psychological mode of mind, the symbolic-dualistic frame of reference of mind spectrum. The new paradigm is the wholistic, ecological world view, and is a construct by the absolute rest frame, non-dual frame, non-conceptual frame of reference by Mind Continuum. The traditional educational structure is the old paradigm and the proposed educational structure is the new paradigm, and we are at present in the midst of a paradigm shift. We urgently need the shift.

(f) The present objective science is map maker. The restructured science is often called the non-dual and non-conceptual state, and is a part of the territory. When the non-dual state is sustained for a long chronological time, it bestows intuition (insight), spontaneity and right action, and some philosophers call it mystical insight of the perennial philosophy. Intuition is fundamental and reason (intellect) is a derivative.

(g) ***The foundation of renaissance of education is to regenerate the unexplored and hidden dimension of Universal Consciousness, so Silence is the gateway and the only way. In Silence, the mind relaxes into non-action. When the mind-brain-body system is equipoised the intuition and spontaneity blossoms. Intuition bestows value-oriented education or holistic education.***[26]

Global Ethics

Global ethics is defined as the perception in a non-dual frame of reference of the mind spectrum. It is the foundation of all ethical and spiritual values. The universal declaration leading to the emergence of global ethics constitutes a call to mankind that human mind must make a quantum jump from dualistic frame to non-dual frame of reference of mind spectrum. And one who is wholly consecrated to Truth, who wants to live the Truth, serve the Truth, would know at each moment the ethical values; it would be a kind of intuition or revelation or insight which would make you know the truth, the global ethics at every moment. To perceive the ethical values or global ethics, man has to make a quantum jump from psychosocial evolution to spiritual evolution.[27]

St. Paul says, "I may speak in tongues of men or of angels, but if I am without love, I am a sounding gong or a clanging cymbal".[28] We must love one another or die. And love is the foundation of peace.[29]

Quantum Jump from Reasson to Intuition

We are living in one of the critical periods of human history when all the intellectual and emotional currents of the people of the world converge upon one and the same point–what are the causes of our failure to construct a non-violent and peaceful world, to bring about radical transformation or mutation of the human psyche, and to guarantee human survival. And even a hundred years ago, there was an intimation thrown to the whole world that man will have to transcend reason, to go beyond the cerebral activity, discover a movement of Unconditioned Energy, the Cosmic Consciousness; but all attempts for such a transcendence have fallen on the deaf ears of mankind.

Fritjof Capra wrote, "Einstein experienced relativity theory before he formulated it. Bohr experienced quantum mechanics before he formulated them. Feynman experienced quantum field theory and Chew experienced S-matrix theory before their formulation.... Feynman has his physics in his bones.... Geoffrey Chew has the theory in his bones".[30] D.S. Kothari wrote, "The new theorems, unless trivial, are of course first "discovered" and then proved. Discovery is an inspired guess (intuition), a flash of insight. It is not a step by step process, but a sort of quantum jump.... A rational account of a discovery, the proof, follows and not precedes the discovery".[31]

All great discoveries have arisen from the realm of the timelessness, so scientific enquiry is not a cerebral activity and gathering information but a quest of the Timelessness, the Divinity, the Life Field. A selfless, unfaltering devotion to truth and use of knowledge for man's uplift– higher hierarchical expression of Consciousness–are the only vocation of a scientist. It is the quantum jump from reason to intuition, from intellect to Intelligence that makes life fulfilling and bestows non-violence, peace and guarantee survival.

A generation is coming up determined to explore the dimension of consciousness, a form of energy that is entirely independent of cerebral energy, and radically different from the brain and its product –thought, knowledge or experiences.

Quantum Jump from Psychosocial Evolution to Spiritual Evolution

During the past few decades, many eminent men–especially physicists–have realised that we are moving from crisis to crisis, and that these are different facets of one and the same crisis; and that this crisis is essentially a crisis of perception. What we need, then, is a new 'paradigm'–a new vision of reality; a fundamental change (a quantum jump) in our thoughts, perceptions and values. The beginnings of this change, of the shift from the mechanistic to the holistic conception of reality, are already visible in all fields and likely to dominate in the next few decades.

Philosophical Approach: Madame Mirra Alfassa wrote, "We are at precisely such a turning-point in the world's history.... A great luminous consciousness broods over the earth, creating a kind of stir in its atmosphere. All who are open receive a ripple from this eddy, a ray of this light and seek to give form to it, each according to his capacity....".[32] She added, "We are here .... to prepare ourselves for the blossoming of a new consciousness and a new life.... we want to become instruments that are as perfect as possible, instruments that express the divine will in the world. And if the instruments are to be perfect, they must be cultivated, educated, trained".[32] Sri Aurobindo wrote, "This *direct working* effects a conversion of the whole being which is the indispensable condition of our real perfection.... a living of man in the Divine and a divine living of the Spirit in humanity–will therefore be the principle and the whole object of an integral Yoga of self-perfection".[33]

Vimala Thakar, an eminent philosopher-mystic, wrote:

> I do hope that all over the world there will be entirely new systems of education, not only new orientations to education, but the very approach to education will have to go through a radical revolution where the acquaintance with the biological and the psychological organism, the rhythm in which the body and the mind moves, will be incorporated in the syllabus of the students. We are teaching physics, chemistry, biology and traveling in space, but nobody talks about the inner space and how to travel there, how to take the inward journey. Those of

> us who have not had the privilege of going through such education will have to educate ourselves.[34]
>
> As we teach the science of physics and chemistry, we will have to teach the science of mind, stripping it of all unessential and superfluous associations .... So, there must be a reorientation of the whole educational system–education as the medium of helping the children to understand their minds much better.[35]
>
> The time has become ripe for the next phase of mutation, in which the quality and content of consciousness will become unconditionally free.... from psychological structure .... The pilgrimage from animality to spirituality will therefore include a revolution in our relationship to and cooperation with the planet on which we are living .... Life would provide the field for discovering the Truth and the stream of relationships would provide the instrument for purification and unfoldment of liberation or enlightenment.... The process of self-education (radical transformation or mutation of mind-brain-body system) through purification has remained unacknowledged and unattended up to now.[36]

Scientific Approach: Erwin Schrodinger raised a very baffling question, "Who are we really? Where have I come from and where I am going".[37] He again wrote, "Our skill is truly nothing when held against the life and the emotions of the soul.... If you have to face the body of a deceased friend whom you sorely miss, is it not soothing to realize that this body was never really the seat of his personality but only symbolically for practical reference".[38] He himself provided answer to this paradox in words, "I think that I-I (the Self), in the widest meaning of the word, that is to say, every conscious mind that has said or felt 'I'–am the person, if any, who controls the 'motion of the atoms' according to the Laws of Nature".[39] Eugene Wigner also provided an answer to this paradox in words, "Self-identity demands consciousness. You would not have identity without consciousness. Consciousness creates identity. I know that I am I. And it is my consciousness which knows, which tells me that".[40]

David Bohm discussed "Unbroken Wholeness in flowing movement". He added, "Whatever part, element, or aspect we may abstract in thought, this still enfolds the whole and is therefore intrinsically related to the reality, from which it has been abstracted".[41] The cultural belief structure or the matter content of consciousness or successive consciousness has two potentials–the immanent potential, the known, which is dominant, and the transcendent potential, the *Unknown*, which is latent or hidden or unmanifest. Man lives simultaneously in two dimensions–the known and the Unknown. The Unknown is the 'I-I', the *Self*, the *Brahman*, the *Void*, the *Life Field*, the *Fundamental Vibration*, the *Active Reality*. The Fundamental Vibration is self existing, self-consistent, the ground of *being*, the ground of existence, self-perpetuating conscious energy.

Modern science (especially physics) has provided experimental evidence to the ancient Indian 'Wisdom' that the cosmos (and beyond cosmos) is permeated with Eternal, Infinite, Immutable, Conscious Energy with very high frequency (higher frequency means higher energy); it is called Universal Consciousness, or *Brahman*; its dimensions are homogeneous-undifferentiated-dimensionless; and it is one continuum. It has the capacity to express itself as harmony, order, nonviolence and peace. It hierarchically expresses itself as different existences, the individuated particularized expression of that wholeness, which is oneness to manyness. Its dimensions are heterogeneous-differentiated-multidimensional. There is the play of a cycle forever present in the creation: the expression of the whole as many, or into its diverse existences, and then the reintegration of the many into one whole. In common parlance the individuated particularized expression of that wholeness (*Brahman*) is called the *Atman* or the *Soul*. Atman is individuated intelligence, the immanent quantum energy potential of Consciousness (the successive consciousness); and *Brahman* is non-individuated supreme Intelligence (Simultaneous Consciousness). When *Atman* transcends thought-time coupled with its volitions and limitations, then *Atman* = *Brahman*–the successive consciousness goes to abeyance and Simultaneous Consciousness (ultimate quantum energy potential of consciousness) takes over.

Expressions of Intelligence/Wisdom

(a) Mind has the power to create illusions in the psychological mode of mind. The craving for sensation, gratification, acquisition add to illusions and strife. To end these illusions, one has to make a quantum jump from psychosocial evolution through self-observation to spiritual evolution.

(b) It is only when we are aware of every movement of our own thought and feelings in our relationship with people, with things and with nature that the mind is open, pliable, not tethered to self-productive demands and pursuits; and only then there is sensitivity or creativeness.

(c) Discovery is the beginning of creativeness; and without creativeness there can be no sustainable peace or joy for man.

(d) Creativeness comes into being when there is constant awareness of the ways of mind, and the hindrances it has built for itself.

Creativeness comes into being when there is non-dual and non-conceptual frame of reference of Mind Continuum.

(e) Creativeness is a state of being in which conflict and sorrow of the self (memory or successive consciousness) go to abeyance.

(f) Creativeness is a state in which truth can come into being. Truth comes into being when there is complete cessation of thought; and thought ceases only when the self is absent. The silence is a state of no-mind, so truth comes into being when there is total silence.[42]

(g) ***World Peace:*** Modern civilisation is based on violence, and is therefore courting death. In a competitive society, we cannot have brotherhood. All psychological imbalances are antagonistic to the immutable laws of nature. It is the inward strife which, projected outwardly, becomes the world conflict.

Peace is not achieved through any ideology, or thought-structure; it does not depend on legislation; it comes only when we as individuals begin to understand our own psychological process. We must become aware of our own actions, thoughts and feelings in every day life. World Peace is an expression of Intelligence/Wisdom.

J. Krishnamurti, in a most spectacular passage, wrote:

> ***Peace is not to be achieved by patchwork reform, nor by a mere rearrangement of old ideas and superstitions. There can be peace only when we understand what lies beyond the superficial, and thereby stop this wave of destruction which has been unleashed by our own aggressiveness and fears; and only then will there be hope for our children and salvation for the world.... Without a change of heart, without goodwill, without the inward transformation which is born of self-awareness, there can be no peace, no happiness for men.***[43]

The right education of the mind-brain-body system is central to the transformation or mutation of the human conditioned mind and the creation of a new culture. The new culture will blossom to world peace, human survival and excellence.

An Experimental Interrogation of Mind-Brain-Body System

(a) *Psychological Mode of Mind:* The psychosocial evolution of man for a million years or more has led to storing of experience and knowledge (information), and this is called conditioned inheritance. In order to *see* itself, the mind cuts itself up into at least one state that sees (subject), and at least one other state which is seen (object); in this severed and mutilated condition, whatever it sees is only *partially itself*; there is energy interaction between subject and the object, resulting into mutilation of both; the mutilated object is recorded as modified memory and the mutilated object is seen; and this results in the crisis of perception or psychic pandemic. The crisis of perception is defined as unawareness of the *fact*, the *true*, the *present*, the *what is*!; and awareness of the *non-fact*, the *false*, the *past*, the *what should be*? This process is antagonistic to the laws of nature, so it constructs pain, misery and strife. Every activity of this process adds to conflict. This process breaks down any experimental dialogue or experimental interrogation with nature.

(b) ***Scientific Mode of Mind:*** Man is an amphibian who lives simultaneously in two dimensions–the inner, the subjective and the outer, the objective. The outer and the inner are one, a unitary movement, a dynamic whole. The interaction between the outer and the inner takes less than one millionth of a second. It embraces the wholeness of life. It is synergistic to thought-structures coupled with volitions.

To be psychologically free and original can only come about when you are aware of your own inward activities. Observe what you are thinking, and never let a single thought escape without the nature of it, the source of it. When you begin to see that which is false, then there is the beginning of awareness, of intelligence. You have to be a light to yourself.

Only the truth can liberate the mind from its own ideation; to see the truth, the mind must realize the fact that as long as it is agitated it can have no understanding. It is the non-dual frame of reference that can bestow understanding.

(c) ***Ending of I-Consciousness or Ego:*** The restructured science (subjective dimension) takes up the role of true-subject. It sees the I-consciousness without interfering in its flow. It observes the I-consciousness from within nature; in other words, the subjective dimension observes the objective dimension.

If a thought coupled with volition comes in the field of true-subject (restructured science-education), the I-consciousness is knocked off because it is at the lowest quantum energy potential. It implies that the movement of thought structure is independent of my volition, it is independent of the movement of the ego. It is a tremendous discovery that: (a) what I call my volition (I-consciousness) is at a lower quantum energy potential than thought structure; (b) the mental movement has a momentum independent of *me* so the vanity that these are my thoughts disappears; (c) thought has an independent existence of *me*, which implies a realisation of the limitations of the activity of volition and the immensity of the thought structure and its movement; or there is nothing like '*I*' or '*me*' in the movement of thought; and (d) I do not act upon my thoughts, or I do not jump to evaluate or judge them, so this establishes a new relationship of thought structure and myself (I-consciousness).

It is objective approach to subjective reactions, subjective feelings. It wakes up in the heart, or the wholeness of life, or the restructured science-education. The true-subject observes the subjective reactions as objects. This observation knocks down the concept that there is a thinker and movement of thought as two separate entities. There is nothing like an independent mind and there is nothing like an independent I-consciousness, and this bestows a sense of great freedom within. Every perception and understanding results in growth. A simple perception can result in an objective approach to all the subjective world; this objectivation of the subjective world is a tremendous natural law.

Such a perception enhances the attention of the true-subject, and the motiveless exposure of the object knocks the object. The creativity embedded in the system enhances the sensitivity and self-expression of the Intelligence. The mind-brain-body relaxes itself; it implies that you move out of the enclosure of culture, enclosure of time-space and conditionings.

(d) ***Ending of Thought Structure:*** The thought-structure coupled with volition is a conceptual reality, man-made world, man-made social cosmos. Life inside us (subjective dimension) is free of the man-made world and thought-structure and ego has no relevance. The true-subject (restructured science-education) is non-variable attentivity, or reaction-free attentivity, or objectless attention. One moves from the doer and the experience to the observer and the witnesser. In this state one does not jump to evaluate, or to compare. If one continues in this state of observation, the consciousness that "I am observing melts away". If the state of observation is sustained and you go back to it, time and again in your daily life, so that state of observation becomes a normal state of consciousness–now called the attention–then there is no more the feeling that I am observing.

When thought structure comes in the field of restructured science, the 'photons' meet an impregnable wall, called 'event horizon', or 'frequency barrier', or 'time barrier'. Deepak Chopra, on the basis of relativistic physics stated, "The speed of light is absolute, it is like a wall that no object can crash through. As we approach the wall, time slows down, mass increases and space becomes curved". He added, "Any place where knowledge stops there is an event horizon". Thought (or photons) cannot cross the 'event horizon', it is bombarded by the non-variable attentivity, and the thought gets annihilated.

At the moment of crossing the 'frequency barrier', the subject-object energy interaction ends, because the photons are knocked down by the energy of attentivity, which is at a higher potential. The object goes to abeyance and dualism ends. The time-space matrices also go to abeyance. The experience and knowledge also stops. All this happens in less than a hundred microseconds.

Vimala Thakar calls the awareness of the outward and the inward movement of life as meditation. If I am simultaneously aware of the objective challenge, the subject reactions and the causes of the reactions, then it results in freedom. Then the momentum of reaction will not carry me over with it, but I will be ahead of the reaction. I will be aware of the objective challenge only. Thought goes to abeyance and there is perception of the *fact*, the *true*, the *present*, the *non-dual*, the *what is*!

(e) ***Ending of the Fact:*** If we continue observing or listening to the *fact*, without justification or condemnation or motivation, we observe there is only the fact and nothing else. The fact itself is the operator, not you operating on the fact. If you leave the fact alone, it has no time. The fact is free from fear. The fact grows, which implies that there is release of tremendous energy and the fact moves to higher quantum energy potential. This is expressed as Pure Consciousness → Fact. It helps the fact to make a quantum jump in the vertical dimension of Consciousness. When the fact is left alone, it is operating and you do not have to do a thing about it, it matures and blossoms. Immediacy of perception dissolves the fact, and one revels in Pure Consciousness or Intelligence. Only in Intelligence there is complete security. Intelligence sees the false as the false and ends the false. Mutation happens in the timelessness. To understand Consciousness or an enquiry into the subject is the perception of that immeasurable state.

Understanding and learning are born in non-duality. Intuition (insight) is perception without any doubt. ***Understanding, learning and action are a cyclic process, which results in a spiral going upwards in the vertical dimension; it is a growth in the vertical dimension***. The higher the understanding, the higher the expression of the Consciousness in the human brain-body system.[44]

To sum up, mental movement or thought-structure has tremendous momentum; it cannot lead to non-duality; it cannot bestow direct understanding of life; so cerebral movement is irrelevant in direct understanding of life. Understanding is the perfume of a communion, it happens in a non-dual frame of reference of Mind Continuum.

To understand the false as false is the beginning of wisdom. To understand the content of bondage, to understand the bondage as the bondage, is the beginning of freedom. To know the conditionings and the relative field where they have to be used, is already the beginning of being free of the conditionings. The aim of human life is to be free from the conditionings and the bondage, and to imbibe the realm of intelligence, which bestows intuition, spontaneity and right action.

The experimental interrogation of the conditioned psyche will blossom to freedom, equality and fraternity. People will meet one another in love and friendship. When the awareness of unity moves in relationship you call it love, you call it vulnerability, openness, humility. Love is its own protection and truth is its own certainty and security. All other securities created by man's mind are hollow. There will be non-violence and sustainable peace. This will guarantee the human survival.

An Action Plan or A Paradigm Shift

The holistic education is a new experiment at a collective level which is bound to unify, to coalesce to a new movement, to a new understanding, that is bound to result in total transformation of our society into a new culture, a new civilisation. The rising of a new culture is basically a higher perception at a higher quantum energy potential of consciousness, or a new dimension of consciousness. It is a quantum jump in consciousness–from intellect to intuition, from logical and scientific reason to philosophical reason. The problem facing mankind is to become aware with a new dimension of consciousness which will generate a new dimension of relationship.

The Action Plan or a Paradigm Shift is as under:

(a) To educate the educator is to have him understand himself. This is one of the most difficult undertakings, because most of us are already crystallized within a system of thought or a pattern of action. The teachers training programme is *how to think* and not *what to think*.

(b) We have to introduce psychodynamics of mind-brain-body system in science faculty and transpersonal psychology in art faculty as a part of educational curriculum at University/College/School level.

(c) The principle governing restructuring of education is fundamentally based to assist nature for an evolution of life. The evolution of mankind can only happen when there is understanding and spontaneity; dynamic interplay of intuition and action; and awareness of the transcendent dimension of life.[45]

(d) The first priority of holistic education programme is to "to educate the educator". It is then extended to university, to colleges and then to schools, and not the other way from school to college to university.

(e) The action plan has to be multifaceted and multidimensional. It is a stupendous task. We envisage the following levels:[46]

School Level: It is advisable to divide school education in two sub-levels–age 4 to 10 and age 10 to 16. The conditioning in children is in two modes–hereditary which manifests progressively between age 3 to 12, and social conditionings due to external environments (including parents, neighbours and friends). The aim in both cases is to decrease the conditionings at both levels.[47]

College Level: The aim is to help each individual to discover all these psychological hindrances and not merely impose upon him new patterns and conduct, new modes of thought. The programme is at national level and also at international level. We suggest that *workshops* be fundamentally based on symbiosis of modern science and spirituality. A tentative programme of a workshop is: Restructuring of Science and Education; Psychodynamics of Mind-Brain-Body System; Transpersonal Psychology of Human Psyche; Fundamental Revolution or Radical Transformation of Human Psyche; Intuition and Learning; Depth Introspection of Life, and so on.

Post-graduate and Doctoral Levels: This bestows understanding and learning as this gives deep understanding and learning the wholeness of life. The scientific mode of mind is sustained over long chronological time and it dissolves the old conditionings and prevents new formation of patterns. Of course, the approaches are slightly variant at each level.

Parents' Level: This has to be confined to general seminars or open sharing conducted at different levels.

(f) ***Aims and Objects of Education:*** The teacher-student, at all levels, is aware of the psychodynamics and limitations of our mind-brain-body system in all our relationships, which blossoms to understanding and learning and to live in the light of that feelingful understanding. In common parlance, this is called higher awareness; in other words, it implies being alert and observant in all relationships and this blossoms into integrated human beings. Only right education–and not ideologies, or reforms in socio-political-economic system, or leaders or intellectual approaches–can provide a lasting solution for our psychological problems and miseries; and bestow on us a non-violent and peaceful society.

(g) There will be need to create some infrastructure for conducting courses. There is need to write books for guidance of teachers and students, and for different levels. This is possible if Government of India approves of the basic programme. Without Government active support, any action plan will prove to be a failure. And if Government escapes its responsibility, it will jeopardize the future of India and mankind.

Concluding Comment

The whole mankind is caught in a crisis of perception, or psychic pandemic. All experience, knowledge (information), thought-structures, beliefs, concepts, patterns of value education are sterile in transforming (mutation) the human psyche. So all present education has no significance to living, and is absolutely irrelevant to understanding the wholeness of life.

We have to educate physical organism and psychological structure to understand and live in the scientific temper. In a scientific mode of mind, there is no I-consciousness, no thought-structure, no psychological imbalances, but observe what is–which actually is the fact. It is not produced by thought, it is the outcome of awareness which is meditation, when the meditator is absent.

We have to introduce the psychodynamics of mind-brain-body system in science faculty and transpersonal psychology or deep ecology in art faculty as a part of the educational curricula at University/College/School levels and in technical institutions. Man has to learn himself to perceive higher perceptive sensitivity, or higher quantum energy potential of Consciousness, of Life Field. This energises the Intelligence, which blossoms to order, harmony, non-violence and peace.

Attention implies the scientific mode of mind or restructured science-education, and inattentiveness implies the psychological mode of mind. At the moment of attention all the conditionings go to abeyance, and it is only when you are inattentive, the construction of space-time-causation matrices begin. Nature's law appears to be that if any entity or event at a lower frequency (thought-structure and I-consciousness) comes in the field of higher frequency (restructured science-education), then the event at lower frequency explodes and gets annihilated. Man has to understand and live in the realm of attentivenss/awareness.

The key to radical transformation or mutation of the mind-brain-body system is the level of expression of Consciousness. Transformation can only be *here* and *now*, and not in the future. It can only be *now*, from moment to moment. Only the truth can liberate the mind from its own ideation. In other words, it is only the higher hierarchical expression of Consciousness that can resolve all human challenges. Human destiny is embedded in a higher level of Awareness/Consciousness. It is the Unmanifest, the Cosmic Consciousness that governs the destiny of the whole human race, including all animate and inanimate life. The Intelligence expresses itself in a pure Mind as order, harmony, non-violence and peace. The Intelligence guarantees human survival and excellence.[48]

References

1. Sampooran Singh, *The Holistic Education*, New Delhi: Siddharth Publications, 1987, pp. i - xlvi, 1-230.
2. Sampooran Singh, Dr (Mrs) Kanwaljit Kaur, and Paramjit Singh, *Global Value Education : A Scientific Appraisal*, Chandigarh: Faith Publishers, January 2001, pp. i - xii, 1-116.
3. Sampooran Singh, *Atam Science, Education for a Global Society*, 7.10.2001, pp. i - viii, 1-39; & *A Review of Symbiosis of Science and Spirituality*, 7.10.2002, pp. xvi - xx, 1-36, Dagshai Cantt: The Atam Science Trust.
4. Sampooran Singh, Dr (Mrs) Kanwaljit Kaur, and Paramjit Singh, *Global Education and Human Survival: A Scientific Appraisal*, New Delhi: Sanbun Publishers, March 2002, pp. i–xiv, 1-88.
5. Sampooran Singh, *A Scientific Vision of Education for a Global Society*, in *Education for a Global Society : Interfaith Dimensions*, The Temple of Understanding, Shipra, 2003, pp. 86-107.
6. Sampooran Singh, *A New Vision of Education and Peace*, Chandigarh: Faith Publishers, April 2003, pp. 1-32.
7. Ms Gay A. Rosenblum Kumar, *UN Launches Peace Education for Kids*, The Tribune, April 9, 2004.
8. Arthur Eddington, *The Nature of the Physical World*, Cambridge University Press, 1928, Introduction; in Erwin Schrodinger, *What is Life*? & *Mind and Matter*, Cambridge University Press, 1967, p. 130
9. Erwin Schrodinger, *ibid.*, p. 177.
10. Arthur Eddington, in A. Commins and R.N. Linscott, Ed., *Man and the Universe, The Philosophers of Science*, New York: Washington Square Press, 1969, pp. 453, 468.

11. Alan W. Watts, *The Ways of Zen*, New York: Vintage Boks, 1967, p. 10.
12. Roger Sperry, in Erdmann, and D. Stover, *Beyond a World Divided: Human Values and the Brain-Mind Science of Roger Sperry*, Boston: Shambhala, 1991.
13. Maurice H. Wilkins, in *Synthesis of Science and Religion*, Mumbai: The Bhaktivedanta Institute, June 1988, p. 29.
14. B.D. Josephson, in *ibid.*, pp. 44, 47.
15. J. Krishnamurti and David Bohm, *The Transformation of Man*, 1980, Videocassette # 10.
16. Sampooran Singh, in USA: *PsychoScience*, Supplement, Fall/Winter 1994; Reprinted USA: *PsychoScience*, Spring-Summer 1995, Vol. 2, No. 1, pp. 41-49; and Reprinted *The Masterplan Paradigm for Human Survival and Excellence*, Chandigarh: Faith Publishers, 1998, pp. 228-41.
17. Ramana Maharishi, in Ken Wilber, *The Spectrum of Consciousness*, USA: The Theosophical Publishing House, 1982 (Third Quest Book), p. 110.
18. Ken Wilber, *ibid.*, p. 110.
19. Sampooran Singh, et. al., in (see *Reference 4 above*), p. 26.
20. *ibid.*, pp. 35-36, 46.
21. Sampooran Singh, in (see *Reference 5 above*), pp. 91-92.
22. Sampooran Singh, et. al., in (see *Reference 2 above*), pp. 34-35.
23. *Words of Sri Aurobindo and the Mother, The Right Object of Education and India's National Education*, All India Magazine, June 2001.
24. *Krishnamurti on Education*, Orient and Longman, Krishnamurti Foundation India, 1974, Cover Page.
25. Sampooran Singh, in (see *Reference 5 above*), pp. 103-105.
26. Sampooran Singh, et. al., in (see *Reference 2 above*), p. 68.
27. ib*id*., p. 46.
28. St. Paul (1 Cor. 13.1), *World Goodwill Newsletter*, 2004, No. 1.
29. Sampooran Singh, et. al., in (see *Reference 2 above*), p. 20.
30. Fritjof Capra, in Ken Wilber, *The Holographic Paradigm and Other Paradoxes*, Shambhala, 1982, pp. 220-221.
31. D.S. Kothari, in *Odyssey of Science, Culture and Consciousness*, New Delhi: Abhinav Publications, 1990, pp. 48-49.
32. *Words of Sri Aurobindo and the Divine Mother, op. cit.*, pp. 44, 45
33. Sri Aurobindo, *ibid.*, p. 46.
34. Vimala Thakar, *Towards Total Transformation*, Ahmedabad: New Order Publishing Co., 1970, p. 79.
35. *ibid.*, *Mutation of Mind*, Ahmedabad: New Order Book Co., 1972, pp. 145-146.
36. *ibid.*, November 2, 2000
37. Erwin Schrodinger, NP, *What is Life*? & *Mind and Matter*, Cambridge: University Press, 1967, p. 152.

38. *ibid.*, p. 134.

39. *ibid.*, p. 93.

40. Eugene Wigner, in *Synthesis of Science and Religion*, Mumbai: The Bhaktivedanta Institute, 1988, p. 262.

41. David Bohm, *Wholeness and the Implicate Order*, London: ARK Paperbacks, 1983, p. 172.

42. J. Krishnamurti, *Education and the Significance of Life*, Delhi: B.I. Publications, 1978, pp. 124-128.

43. J. Krishnamurti, *ibid.*, pp. 84, 68.

44. Sampooran Singh and Dr (Mrs) Kanwaljit Kaur, *Challenges to Peace and Security: A Scientific Quest and Symbiosis of Science and Spirituality*, unpublished.

45. Sampooran Singh, et. al., in (see *Reference 4 above*), pp. 68, 69.

46. Sampooran Singh, in (see *Reference 3 above*), 7.10.2001, pp. 38, 39.

47. Roland Fischer, an eminent pharmacologist, says, "Most children's artistic impulses start disappearing around the age of 9 because they are '*brainwashed*' from the age of 6 onward to use their left hemisphere. The left hemisphere is essentially the rational, linear thinking, verbally oriented half, and that this hemisphere is cultivated by experience and education at the expense of the right hemisphere which is the seat of creative, visual and artistic impulses that govern a different–subjective, non-temporal–consciousness". It implies that the creativity goes on decreasing and intellect is being nourished as the child grows from the age of 6 to 9, or 4 to 10. [*Altered States of Consciousness: Mind Researchers Meet*, Science, 9 March 1973, Vol. 179, No. 4077, p. 982]. Houston says, "We are perhaps on the verge of a golden age of brain and mind research".

48. Sampooran Singh, et. al., *Pathways to Peace : The Wisdom of Listening and Power of Commitment*, Chandigarh: Faith Publishers, January 1, 2004, pp. 1-42; and *ibid.*, *March to Peace : The Wisdom of Observation, Listening and the Power of Commitment*, *ibid.*, January 20, 2004, pp. 1-24.

6

A Scientific Exploration of the Nature's Evolutionary Impulse? : Man Unfolding

Abstract

This article explores, "Where Nature's evolutionary impulse is leading mankind?" Nature's self-dynamics is unfoldment of man, so that at every moment, he presents a higher quantum energy potential or higher frequency of Cosmic Consciousness. It presents a technology for a quantum jump from psychosocial evolution to spiritual evolution.

Man's evolution is not biological but psychosocial; and this led him to the emergence of subjective dimension in addition to the objective dimension. There is coherent superpositions of different webs of subjectivity over objectivity, and this led him to I-consciousness and thought-structure.

Many eminent philosophers-mystics and scientists have discussed that there is an "action without idea". It implies a quality of mind where there is no fragmentation at all. It is active present all the time. It is called the non-dual mind, or intuition, or insight. It leads to direct understanding of life. In technical parlance we call it the "Third Breakthrough".

Many eminent neuro-physiologists, neuro-surgeons, and so on– say Karl Pribram, Roger Sperry, John Eccles–have opined that "brain science can no longer afford to shut out that part of the world which we call subjective". It implies that modern science advocates to "restructure science-education", which takes in its ambient both the objective and the subjective dimension of life, and we call it the "Fourth Breakthrough". This is a guide to a quantum jump from rationality to intuition, from experience and knowledge (information) to perception, from intellect to understanding of life direct, to symbiosis of science and spirituality, which are basically unfoldment of Cosmic Consciousness in a pure Mind.

An Action Plan has also been discussed. It blossoms to new relationship, peace, security.

Every scientist, every philosopher-mystic, every saint, every human being, somewhere in his depths, is asking the fundamental question: "Where Nature's evolutionary impulse is leading mankind?", or exploring technologies for manifestation of higher quantum energy potential of Consciousness. William Saroyan puts the same question in simple words:

> In the time of your life, live, so that in that wondrous time you shall not add to the misery and sorrow of the world, but shall smile to the infinite delight and mystery of it.[1]

Humanity's ethical and spiritual development has not kept pace with the progress of material technology, and this imbalance threatens to destabilise and destroy human civilisation. There is a profound imbalance in our culture–in our thoughts and feelings, our values and attitudes and our social-economic-political structures. Indeed, there appears to be a fundamental crisis of human values, and the mankind is suffering a psychic pandemic of the most virulent type. It is also called the 'crisis of perception' which aggravates current economic, social and political tensions. Accompanied by raging ecological problems, these tensions tend to push the world even closer to self-destruction or self-annihilation.

The world is us and we are the world. We have tried for the last 10,000 years to radically transform the conditioned psyche but we have miserably failed. We have constructed a violent and aggressive world. The world presents new dangers, new problems and new challenges. But it also offers the real hope of creating a safer and more equitable era. A new world is taking shape. The future is now in our hands.

This article explores the conditioned human psyche, the Unconditioned, Eternal, Infinite Energy; it explores the manifestation of higher quantum energy potential of Consciousness. It discusses the march of objective science. It is the inner voyage from knowledge to understanding and learning, from rationality to intuition, from confrontation to cooperation, from war and aggression to peace and security. Nature's evolutionary impulse is unfoldment of man, so that at every moment, he presents a higher quantum energy potential or higher frequency of Cosmic Consciousness. It presents a technology for a quantum jump from psychosocial evolution to spiritual evolution.

Nature's Evolutionary Impulse

Teilhard de Chardin, the eminent paleontologist, divided the evolution into four stages–geosphere, biosphere, noosphere and christosphere. Broadly geosphere deals with inorganic (physical) evolution, biosphere with biological (organic) evolution, noosphere with psychosocial evolution and christosphere with spiritual evolution.[2]

The physical evolution over uncountable aeons gave birth to biological evolution with the appearance of the living cell, a *first breakthrough* occurred, and continued steadily onward through a process of internal organic complexity and organic integration, accompanied by an increase of the value of awareness and of the consequent grip of the organism on the external environment. This process has achieved a *second breakthrough*, with the emergence of man. Julian Huxley wrote, "Man's evolution is not biological but psychosocial, it operates by the mechanism of cultural tradition, which involves the cumulative self-reproduction and self-variation of mental activities and their products".[3]

The quantum jump from biological evolution to psychosocial evolution involved the appearance of the subjective dimension, so release of subjectivity comes in as important additional dimension. There is coherent superpositions of different webs of subjectivity on the objectivity. This leads to cultural belief structure or memory picture or symbol system. The subjective memory-picture undergoes disintegration and the product is called thought. Thought is sequential, successive and one dimensional, while the real world represents itself as multidimensional, non-successive, simultaneous patterns of infinite richness and variety.

Thought is the enemy of man. It is basically successive consciousness and constructs time-space-causation matrices. It leads to the emergence of thought patterns and I-consciousness. It is the relative field of consciousness. It leads to duality, pain and suffering.

Erwin Schrodinger, Charles Sherrington, C.J. Jung and B. Spinoza concluded that the object has immanent quantum energy potential and is divorced from the ultimate quantum energy potential. Schrodinger has called it "the principle of objectivation".[4] Further science deals with the "world of shadows".[4] It implies that the subject can never be aware of the true object, as both the subject and the object are continuities of change and the object has immanent quantum energy potential.

Man erred in this process and the double crisis of psychosocial evolution and cultural (art of living) process. Nature is now set to rectify this error, and man is preparing himself for a quantum jump from psychosocial evolution to spiritual evolution, predicted by many eminent scientists and philosopher-mystics.

Third Breakthrough: If a mind sees a sudden danger, or sees something immense (as a snow-covered peak, or a steep precipice, or a deep gorge) the immensity or grandeur possesses the subject momentarily and there is action without an idea. It implies that there is a quality of mind where there is no fragmentation at all. It is active present all the time. It is called the non-dual mind, or intuition or insight. It is a state of awareness, which is an expression of the Unmanifest, the Unknown.

The new theorems, unless trivial, are first "discovered" and then proved. Discovery is a flash of insight, it happens in the non-dual realm, or "discontinuous" field. It is not a step by step process, but a sort of quantum jump arranged by Nature's evolutionary impulse. A rational account of a discovery, the proof follows and not precedes the discovery. Many eminent scientists, who followed persistent and rigorous scientific observation, have experienced the non-dual mode of knowing or discoveries came to them as flashes.[5]

At some appropriate epoch, Nature started expressing itself as a subjective dimension. Eddington wrote, "The intimate knowledge will not submit to codification and analysis; or rather, when we attempt to analyze it, the *intimacy is lost and it is replaced by symbolism*".[6] Alan W. Watts wrote, "The understanding of life directly, instead of in the abstract linear terms of representational thinking".[7] Many eminent scientists–including Albert Einstein, Werner Heisenberg, Erwin Schrodinger, Arthur Eddington, and so on–have stumbled upon the understanding of life directly. Schrodinger called it as "*the principle of understanding*". This is also called the intimate, or direct, or non-dual knowledge.

Fourth Breakthrough: The outer (objective) and the inner (subjective) are not two separate movements. It is a unitary movement, not separate, but one whole. Man has now to work to treat the outer and the inner as one. We call it restructured science-education. The restructured science takes in its ambient both the subjective and the objective dimensions of life.[8] The restructured education deals with the sensual and the trans-sensual world. It deals with the observer situated within the observed world. The dialogue with nature is carried on from within nature. It sees the wholeness of life. The subject now is non-variable attentivity, or reaction-free attentivity, or objectless attention. This is called the true-subject, or *fourth breakthrough*.

When thought-structure and I-consciousness come within the field of restructured science and education, the I-consciousness first goes to abeyance and then thought-structure is annihilated. What is left behind is the *fact*, the *true*, the *present*, the *what is*! If observation is further continued the fact also goes to abeyance and only pure Consciousness remains which bathes the brain cells.

When thought-structure and I-consciousness go to abeyance, the relative frame of reference of symbolic-dualistic frame of mind spectrum make a quantum jump to non-dual and non-conceptual frame of Mind Continuum.

A mind that has set aside seeking in the future, and has denied its past is ethical–this is also called a mind with scientific temper. A non-dual and non-conceptual frame of reference is ethical. The ethical nature is beyond conflict and psychological imbalances. An ethical mind is synergistic to psychological mode of mind.

To sum up, "the principle of objectivation" is the *second breakthrough*, it is called the symbolic, or map, or dualistic knowledge; "the principle of understanding" is the *third breakthrough*, it is called the intimate, or direct, or non-dual knowledge; and "the principle of restructuring of science-education" is the *fourth breakthrough*. These breakthroughs are not water-tight or air-tight compartments, but one flows into the other.

The March of Science

Science is the search for truth. A selfless, unfaltering devotion to truth and the use of knowledge for man's upliftment are the ideals of a scientist. The widespread view of science (objective or Newtonian), as an abstract and abstruse collection of data, a source of technological innovation with little relevance to human values, leaves out of account the fact that scientists not only report on observations and measurements, but also create, and make use of, the corresponding view of the world. Albert Einstein discussed the limitation of science in words:

> Science can denature plutonium but science cannot denature evil in the heart of man.
>
> The splitting of the atom has changed everything except our mode of thinking and thus we drift towards unparalleled catastrophe.[9]
>
> The significant problems we face cannot be solved at the same level of thinking we used when we created them".[10]

Einstein himself provided answer to this paradox, "Our new idea is simple: to build a physics valid for all coordinate systems" or frame of reference of the mind spectrum or wholeness of life.

Ilya Prigogine stated, "A triumph of human reason turned into a sad truth. It seemed that science debased everything it touched.... Present-day research leads us farther and farther from the opposition between man and the natural world".[11] The objective science is leading us to self-annihilation.

Understanding and Learning

The psychological mode of mind is mechanical and repetitive, so there is no newness or creativity. It cannot understand or learn anything. It is only the non-dual and non-conceptual frame of reference of Mind Continuum that has understanding and learning.

Only the truth can liberate the mind from its own ideation; to see the truth, the mind must realize the fact that as long as it is agitated it can have no understanding. Seeing the false as the false and the true as the true is transformation, because when you see something very clearly as the truth, that truth liberates.[12]

Understanding, learning and action are a cyclic process, which results in a spiral going upwards in the vertical dimension; it is a growth in the vertical dimension. The higher the understanding, the higher the expression of the Consciousness in the human mind-brain-body system.

Rationality and Intuition

All knowledge is structured in consciousness. Schrodinger wrote:

> The world is given to me only once, not one existing and one perceived. Subject and object are only one. The barrier between them cannot be said to have broken down as a result of recent experience in the physical sciences, for this barrier does not exist.[13]

> The world is given but once. Nothing is reflected. The original (Absolute) and the mirror-image (pure perception) are identical. The world extended in space and time is but our representation.[13]

Fritjof Capra wrote in prophetic words:

> The rational part of research would, in fact, be useless if it were not complemented by the intuition that gives scientists new insights and makes them creative.[14]

Recently, many eminent scientists–Werner Heisenberg, Edwin Hubble, Max Planck, G.F. Chew, Bertrand Russell, Lincoln Barnett, Max Born, and so on–have concluded that we cannot impart value education at reason or intellect level.[15] This suggests that intuition is fundamental and rationality is a derivative. We have to base ourselves at intuition level, and then explain intuition at reason level. The meaning (non-verbal and metaphysical) behind every intuition is perennial human values, so human values represent the creativeness of human non-dual frame of reference in the Mind Continuum.

Symbiosis of Science and Spirituality

(a) Spirituality is the science of Consciousness, the wholeness of life. It proceeds from the whole and with the awareness of the whole, we observe the parts.

(b) In spirituality, the emphasis is on the act of perception, the quality of the instruments employed for perception, and the quality of consciousness behind the perception. It explores the trans-psychological dimension of consciousness.

(c) We want a revolution, psychological revolution, in which the whole human race has to participate and every man is an equal partner. This revolution will regenerate or rejuvenate human mind so that it perceives the new dimension of an integral and all-inclusive Consciousness that can guarantee human survival along with all fauna and flora.

(d) Both spirituality and science have non-authoritarian approach– an approach not conditioned by the past. Spirituality and "restructured science-education" are entirely different technologies, but both converge at the apex in their search for truth, or Reality sustaining the truth.

Man Unfolding

Man is an amphibian who lives simultaneously in two worlds: immanent quantum energy potential (manifest) and the ultimate quantum energy potential (Unmanifest). Man-unfolding implies release of energy potential, bit by bit, from the Unmanifest to the manifest, from highest frequency of Consciousness to the immanent frequencies of consciousness. Man-unfolding is a happening in the realm of non-duality. Man has to understand and learn to live in harmony with Nature's evolutionary impulse, which implies to transcend psychosocial evolution and imbibe spiritual evolution.

The psychological mode of mind (manifest, continuity) splits itself into the subject and the object; it deals with thought-structure and I-consciousness which are the past habit patterns. It is repetitive and mechanical. The psychological heredity or habitual continuity is the basis of man's conscious life. The alterations at the conscious level will produce only a psychological variation leaving the unconscious factors of heredity unchanged. A variation is only a superficial change, not affecting the constituent factors of heredity.

The history of human growth has indeed been a saga of an increasing quantum energy potential or frequency of consciousness of the subjective over the objective; or in other words, it is (subjective→objective), or progressive mastery of mind over matter. The Unmanifest (Timeless Moment) is the deep silence which pervades the whole manifested universe. We see only the dance of manifestation and never have a glimpse of the calm Unmanifest which provides the ground for the manifest to express itself in a myriad ways. The silence of the mind is at a higher quantum energy potential or higher frequency than that of the manifest. It is only the silent mind that can establish communion with the silence of the universe. It is a quantum jump from symbolic-dualistic frame of reference to non-dual and non-conceptual frame of Mind Continuum. This is the *third breakthrough* in man's unfolding.

When I-consciousness and thought-structure go to abeyance, what is left behind is the *fact*, the *true*, the *present*, the *what is*! If observation is continued, then the quantum energy potential from the Cosmic Consciousness flows to the *fact*, and the fact goes to abeyance.

There is flow of energy from within and man attains higher awareness; this is called "man unfolding". Ervin Laszlo wrote, "We are not just observing it, we are not just immersed in it: we are integral part of it".[16] Obviously we have to understand and live in the wholeness of life, or in other words, we have to live in the highest quantum (transcendent) energy potential of Consciousness–and this happens if man self-unfolds himself at every moment of his life.

A Critique on Nature's Evolutionary Impulse

Nature's Evolutionary Plan: Man has been gifted the faculty of consciousness, which we have used at the lowest quantum energy potential or the lowest frequencies for our material progress. He started living in a man-made social world, and divorced the Reality. Obviously this has resulted in a set of illusions, which are projections of desire, pleasure, fear, violence, and so on. J. Krishnamurti and David Bohm had a dialogue on "*The Ending of Time*" and Krishnamurti concluded the following:

> ***I have a million years of experience, and it has given me a certain capacity. And I realize at the end of it all there is no relationship between me and truth.... Is it a shock to discover that your brain, and your mind, your knowledge, are valueless? All your examinations, all your struggles, all the things that you have gathered through years and years, centuries, are absolutely worthless? .... What you have done or not done is absolutely of no value.... The ground says, whatever you have done 'on earth' has no meaning..... It has given me a tremendous shock to discover the truth, that all the churches, prayers, books, have absolutely no meaning–except how we can build a better society, and so on.... So there is only one thing, and that is to discover that all that I have done is useless–ashes!***[17]

The Resolution of Human Paradox: Krishnamurti and David Bohm had discussions on "*The Future of Humanity*". Bohm summarised Krishnamurti's vision in words:

> Krishnamurti does not, however, regard these limitations as inevitable. Rather, he emphasizes that mind is essentially free of the distorting bias that is inherent in the conditioning of the brain, and that through insight arising in proper undirected attention without a center, it can change the cells of the brain and remove the destructive conditioning.[18]

Pupul Jayakar and Sunanda Patwardhan in the Preface to "*Within The Mind*" wrote:

> The central core is that man has to be a light unto himself. Truth is a process of self-discovery. No one can give the truth to another.[19]

Humanity has taken a wrong turn. This has to be rectified *here* and *now*. If man takes an inner voyage–through listening, observing and enquiring he touches compassion, love and intelligence that originates beyond thought, beyond time, even beyond emptiness. Krishnamurti says, "Love has no cause. Hate has a cause. Insight has no cause. The material process, as thought, has a cause. Where there is love, hate can never exist".[17] A cause can end. This means giving one's mind, one's heart, one's whole being to the observation *here* and *now*. Nature reveals her truth through "self-enquiry in which the movements of mind as thought and action are revealed and the rising of an insight which perceives "what is" without judgement or attempt to change that which is revealed; an enquiry, into man's outer and inner being, that is concerned with the ending of the movement of becoming. Out of this arises action that will transform man and his environment".[19]

An Action Plan: We presented an Action Plan for human survival. Mark Germine wrote, "Singh's plan has been received favourably by others active in the United Nations. It is a plan of great compassion and depth. What Dr. Singh calls for is no less than an epiphany of the human species. Such an "epiphany" of humankind was explicit in the writings of Teilhard de Chardin".[20] This has been modified and the salient points are as under:

(a) The psychological mode of mind is repetitive and mechanical, it is an expression of the past, therefore one participates in a dance of the mind. The dance is repetitive. The mechanistic world-view that seems to dominate contemporary objective science and society has led to state of increasing fragmentation and conflict, both within the experience of individual human beings and in society as a whole.

(b) We have to educate the educator, or conduct teachers training course. To conduct courses at all levels–research scholars at doctoral level or post-graduate level especially in science faculties of different universities, and at lower levels in colleges and schools.

(c) We have to introduce psychodynamics of mind-brain-body system in science faculty and trans-personal psychology in art faculty as a part of educational curriculum at University and College level.

(d) We have to share through open dialogues the psychodynamics of conditioned mind and the dimension of Consciousness. The aim of these dialogues is "exploration of a spiritually inspired understanding of life" and "holistic living".

(e) The principle governing restructuring of education is fundamentally based to assist nature for an evolution of life.

The evolution of mankind can only happen when there is understanding and spontaneity; dynamic interplay of intuition and action; and awareness of the transcendent dimension of life. The real goal for each one of us is: awaken and activise in ourselves perfect spiritual consciousness. A true seeker is the one who with his ideal in view, goes on purifying his feeling, thoughts and actions. We have to learn to empty our mind of all worldly thoughts and wait silently for the vision of the universal consciousness.

(f) The above programme is at national level and also at international level. We suggest that workshops be fundamentally based on symbiosis of modern science and spirituality. a tentative programme of a workshop is: Restructuring of Science and Education; Psychodynamics of Mind-Brain-Body System; Transpersonal Psychology of Human Psyche; Fundamental Revolution or Radical Transformation of Human Psyche; Intuition and Learning; Depth Introspection of Life, and so on.

(g) The Action Plan has to be multifaceted and multidimensional. The fundamentals are "to educate the educator or training of teacher", and writing of books both for the teachers and students; and naturally these are at different levels, and in different languages. This is a stupendous task.

(h) The aim is to initiate "an open dialogue with an open mind", which is the awakening of the process of dialogue itself as a free flow of meaning among all the participants".[21] In a dialogue, each participant is able to put aside his own views (conditionings) and listens to those of others. A genuine dialogue is possible if each participant jettisons his personal symbolic-dualistic frame of reference of mind and adopts a non-dual and non-conceptual frame of reference of Mind Continuum. It unfolds insight, spontaneity and right action. To have genuine dialogue we need to investigate the conditioned psyche and the Unconditioned Energy, or in other words, we need to educate ourselves.

(i) A radical transformation or mutation–from duality to non-duality–absolutely necessary to transform this world politically and economically and socially. In Schrodinger's words, "The original (Absolute, Truth, Reality) and the mirror-image (pure perception) are identical". There is no dichotomy between the subject and the object, or in other words, the mind does not split into the subject and the object. But this transformation must begin with the individual, *here* and *now*. The *thinker* and the *thought*, the *seer* and the *seen*, are one. Schrodinger says, "Subject and object are only one". The dance of the mind (symbolic-dualistic) ends; or in other words, it is a state of *no-mind.* This split of the mind ends when the ultimate quantum energy potential bathes the brain cells.

(j) We have to "restructure science-education", which deals with the wholeness of life; this we call *fourth breakthrough.* When thought-structure and I-consciousness come within the field of restructured science-education, thought-structure with its volitions goes to abeyance. When the brain cells are bathed by the ultimate quantum energy potential of Cosmic Consciousness, there is perfect order and peace.

(k) The man coupled with the earth and its environments is a cancer patient today. And the human world is at death bed. Many eminent scientists, philosophers-mystics share the view that we "***educate the instruments of pure perception***" which Nature has endowed us with. Such education will energise the "***understanding and learning of life directly***", which blossoms to intuition, spontaneity and right action. When "understanding is stabilized, the mind-brain-body system makes a quantum jump to higher awareness, or higher Consciousness. In the state of higher quantum energy potential of Consciousness, all pain, misery, fragmentation, psychological imbalances, go to abeyance, and it ushers a new era of order, harmony, interrelatedness, freedom, non-violence, peace and bliss.

(l) There will be need to create some infrastructure for conducting courses. There is need to write books for guidance of teachers and students, and for different levels. This is possible if Govt. of India approves of the basic programme. Without Government active support, any action plan will prove to be a failure. And if Government escapes its responsibility, it will jeopardize the future of India and mankind.

Blossoming of Spirituality : Flowering of the "Action Plan"

Freedom: In a truly secular and democratic society, freedom of the press, of thought and speech and action are recognised as the highest of all values. But mankind is living in a conditioned psyche, where thought and speech and action are a repetitive processes and as such there is no freedom, newness or creativity. We define freedom as transcendence of thought with its entanglement with volitions, motives and desires. In other words, freedom is "cessation of I-making tendencies", or abeyance of "the machinery of image production". It implies that freedom of thought and speech and action emerge from a non-dual and non-conceptual frame of reference of Mind Continuum.

Freedom is pure observation without direction, without fear of punishment and reward. Freedom is without motive; freedom is not at the end of evolution of man but lies in his first step of his existence. In scientific observation one begins to discover the lack of freedom. Freedom is found in the choice of awareness, in the attentiveness of our daily existence and activity. Freedom comes, when even momentarily, thought or pseudo-subject goes to abeyance and non-variable attentiveness takes over as the true-subject (restructured science-education). Pure observation bestows insight, which is without any shadow of past or time. The timeless insight brings about a deep radical mutation in the conditioned psyche or mind-brain-body system.

Marilyn Ferguson studied the changes in mind-brain-body system in words:

> The subjective accounts have been correlated with concrete evidence of physical change: higher levels of integration in the brain itself, more efficient processing, different 'harmonics' of the brain's electrical rhythms, shifts in perceptual ability.
>
> Meditation, chanting, and similar techniques increase the coherence and harmony in the brainwave patterns; they bring about greater synchrony between the hemispheres, which suggests that higher order is achieved. On occasion it appears that increasing populations of nerve cells are recruited into the rhythm, until all regions of the brain seem to be throbbing, as if choreographed and orchestrated. The usually dissynchronous patterns in the two sides seem to become entrained to each other. Brainwave activity in older, deeper brain structures may also show an unexpected synchrony with the neocortex.[22]

It is evident that radical transformation or mutation in the brain happens when the conditioned psyche is exposed to the higher quantum energy potential of Consciousness. Some meditators have reported that they see 'tiny sparks' in the brain during meditation, which is the explosion of past thought-structure; and they called it *cold fission* of matter.

Order: The mind-brain-body system is accustomed to remembrance, to experience, knowledge and memory, to desire, motive, acquisition, will; and this is time. Human interference produce discontinuities or unnatural movements. There is interaction between the subject (inner) and the object (out there), and this results in distortion of both the subject and the object. Physicists call this way of seeing the *Superposition Principle.*[23] We have to explore our own tranquility–so that the expression of the highest quantum energy potential of Consciousness, or Life Field, or Absolute is not interfered with.

Cosmos is perfect order. Man-made chaos, the world extended in space and time is but our representation, and this is man-made chaos. Krishnamurti said, "To learn is to observe and act". He added, "If you observe, man lacks a sense of beauty–beauty as sensitivity not only physically, but also of the heart and mind. To be sensitive is to be intelligent.... By learning about disorder, there is order".[24] Order is something of immense benediction, an immense timeless incorruptible state, the Life Field.

Fred Alan Wolf, prophetically wrote, "Quantum physics appears to describe a universal order that includes us in a special way .... The thought that atoms may not exist without observers of atoms is, to me, a very exciting thought .... The order of the universe may be the order of our own minds".[25] It is the non-dual and non-conceptual frame of reference of Mind Continuum that has the capacity to construct order.

Ending of Violence: Mind, in order to see itself, evidently it must cut itself up into at least one state which sees (subject, inner), and at least one other state which is seen (object, outer somewhere as time-space-causation matrices). There is energy interaction between the subject and object, resulting into distortion of both. The inner distortion or aggression inside in the consciousness is violence. Psychological violence implies inward anger, hatred, wanting to dominate people, not only physical domination but the domination of ideas. This process leads to fragmentation, strife, and is responsible for violence. So violence is a construct of the psychological mode of mind, or a construct of the conditioned mind-brain-body system, or man-made social cosmos. It is an indication of psychological immaturity. Psychologically he is as primitive as the primitive man.

You cannot impose the order on top of disorder. You cannot impose non-violence on a consciousness which is violent, because that violence has deep-rooted causes in the psyche. Unless these causes are eliminated, there is no ending of violence. It is only when violence ends, there can be non-violence.[26]

Krishnamurti wrote, "My brain is the brain of humanity .... I am humanity, and what humanity has done, I have done? And I see that it does not produce benediction and therefore all that has been done, has no meaning". In 1979, Krishnamurti wrote, "A general destructive violence, a fragmentation at all levels, and a growing lack of sensitivity was permeating the landscape of India". Inwardly there is no duality. There is only 'what is', that is, I am violent. The observer is the past, who has known what violence is. The observer is not different from that which he is observing. The separation of the observer (inner) and the observed (out there) is the root cause of violence.

To learn is to observe and to act. By learning about violence, there is non-violence. ***We have to learn to observe violence by restructured science-education, which is invariably rooted in the wholeness, and is called true-subject.*** When a thought-structure coupled with I-consciousness encounters the true-subject, it explodes and goes to abeyance; it leads to a perception of the *fact*, which is a pointer to non-violence. Violence is at the lower quantum energy potential of consciousness than that of the true-subject; so it is the expression of Universal Consciousness or Life Field that bestows non-violence.

The observation by the true-subject implies ending of all psychological imbalances–say fear, greed, anger, jealousy, acquisition, and so on.

Mutation: It is the psychological load in the psyche that undergoes radical transformation. The transformation is in the whole mutant. To accept the authority of experience and knowledge for relating to Life is to accept the authority of the concept of time and there is duality.

Knowledge is storing memory as frequency and amplitude information. When thought-structure with its volition has an encounter with the true-subject, the thought-structure dissipates and goes to abeyance, and this results in mutation of the psyche. Mutation is a happening.

Mutation is possible in the brain through insight, not through knowledge, not through accumulation. That insight is the ability to see a truth directly, a direct perception of the truth, and education must foster that.[26]

Cause of Our Failure in Religious and Spiritual Realms

Every religion reveals two dimensions–religion as a socio-political expression, and religion as an expression to perceive the attributes of the Universal Consciousness–such as order, rhythm, non-violence, peace and security.

Spirituality is the physics of Consciousness. It is the awareness of the wholeness around you and within you. It explores what the truth is, what the *fact* is. It teaches us to live with the *fact*.

The traditional religion and spirituality is to read some sacred books, go to Church, which is basically a remembrance of the *past*. P. Krishna wrote, "Christ did not become Christ through a Church or a belief. He came upon that through his own understanding, through his own enquiry. Buddha came upon his consciousness, his understanding, through his own meditation, his own enquiry". In spirituality the truth is not cumulative, it is from moment to moment. The traditional spirituality is termed as *static* spirituality and its dynamism is lost. The student is only aware of the past, he has to learn through observation or enquiry the truth in the Consciousness.

Krishnamurti stated, "India has lived all these centuries on ideas. She has to move from a life based on ideas, which are *non-fact*, to seeing the *fact*".[24] The traditional spirituality teaches us about the past, the *non-fact*, and not about the present, the *fact*. We have to jettison the traditional spirituality and learn about the present, the *fact*. Every student has to rediscover the truth for one-self. It is called as the *Fourth Breakthrough* of the evolutionary impulse.

Relationship

Life is relationship. It is relationship of intimacy, of communion. It is lack of understanding of relationship that causes conflict. The psychological mode of mind gives relationship through the past, there is no true relationship in the psychological field. All relationships are illusions, or distortions.

Relationship is possible in a non-dual and non-conceptual frame of reference of the Mind Continuum. A mind free from the *known* revels in freedom. All education is to learn relationship between you and the Absolute (Life Field), between you and me, and so on. Relationships flow to freedom, non-violence and peace, which bestows a healthy society.

Peace

Peace is related to human psychology. As long as there is inherent violence in the individual psyche, the political leaders of the world and heads of the States shall never be able to end war and create peace in the world. The intellect has the capacity to purchase transient peace between two violent points, but it does not have the capacity to end violence and construct sustainable peace.

A quantum jump from the symbolic-dualistic state (the self-interacting state, the successive consciousness) to non-dual and non-conceptual state (the self-referral state, the Simultaneous Consciousness) will bestow lasting global peace and human survival.

Security

The non-dual and non-conceptual frame of reference of Mind Continuum bestows total security, including all psychological challenges of life. Global security also encompasses economic and environmental society. The symphony of life forms are free from all psychological insecurity.

Concluding Comment

If humankind is to have a future : (a) we have to investigate the conditioned psyche; (b) to explore the Unconditioned Energy; and this exploration will enable us to make a quantum jump from symbolic-dualistic frame to non-dual and non-conceptual frame of Mind Continuum. It is an inner journey from psychosocial evolution to spiritual evolution. This blossoms to order, harmony, non-violence and peace. And if we escape our responsibility, we do so at our peril.

George Wald, Nobel Prize in Medicine, 1967, says:

> By now the problem is not transcendence, but survival. If we are to survive there must be fundamental changes in direction, not only organizational, but in our ways of thinking. We have to think different thoughts and to want different things.... All the mystics through the ages have agreed that to achieve wisdom one must quiet the brain, stop using it as a tool, put aside knowledge and learning, try indeed to free one's consciousness, empty one's mind, and in quiet see what enters.[27]

The only assignment for man is to work sincerely to understand the Nature's evolutionary impulse, which results in self-unfoldment of man essential for peace, survival and excellence.

Albert Einstein, in almost the last interview that he gave to the international magazine LIFE said as follows:

> The mind can proceed only so far upon what it knows and can prove. There comes a point where the mind takes a leap–call it intuition or what you will–and comes upon a higher plane of knowledge, but can never prove how it got there. All great discoveries have involved such a leap.[28]

When the mind realises that it cannot resolve the challenge, then energy from the Unmanifest flows to the mind raising its quantum energy potential–called a quantum leap from continuity to discontinuity, from time to timelessness–then the mind perceives the intuition (insight). The quantum leap is called self-unfoldment, so all higher knowledge is structured in Consciousness and Nature self-reveals it.

Vaclav Havel, addressing the US Congress in 1990, said, "Without a global revolution in the sphere of human consciousness, nothing will change for the better in our being as humans".[29] Sri Aurobindo wrote, "All will change if man consents to be spiritualized".[30] The Divine Mother (Madame Mirra Alfassa) declared, "No human organization can change radically unless human consciousness itself changes".

Man unfolding presents the bewildered humanity a holistic and integral Vision for the solution of its thousands of problems–and the solution is lasting and permanent. It is the integral dimension of Consciousness that can resolve the challenges facing mankind. It is to heal the mind-brain-body system, or in other words, it is to end the psychic pandemic. This is the only guarantee for human survival and excellence.

There is an urgency for a radical revolution, or mutation of human psyche–to empty the consciousness of total human past. The duality also goes to abeyance. One operates from a Consciousness that has no centre and no circumference, one that no past, and is unconditioned and unsullied by the touch of thought. This bestows sustainable peace.

The blossoming of spirituality is the manifestation of a new, integral and holistic Consciousness. This Consciousness acting as *Light* and *Force* will lead to the growth of the whole man and the whole world holistically. This would be a historic breakthrough that would end the age-long failures of mankind and end the handicaps and fetters of planetary life. Man revels in order, harmony, non-violence, peace and security.

To sum up, man, in the long history of Nature's evolutionary impulse took a wrong direction and thereafter he is just continuing in that direction. It is deep-rooted patterns of thinking in the mind. There is an urgency *here* and *now* to change the direction towards mutation in the brain cells themselves–otherwise one will go only in that direction and meet a catastrophe.[31] Fritjof Capra wrote, "As the turning point approaches, the realization that evolutionary changes of this magnitude cannot be prevented by short-term political activities provides our strongest hope for the future".[32] To save mankind from the impending catastrophe, we have to explore the conditioned psyche and Unconditioned Energy *here* and *now*. If we escape our responsibility, it will jeopardize the future of India and mankind.

References

1. William Saroyan, in *Noetic Sciences Review*, Summer 1989, Number 11, p. 1.
2. Teilhard de Chardin, in Sampooran Singh, *The Holistic Education*, New Delhi: Siddharth Publications, 1987, p. 109.
3. Julian Huxley, *Evolution After Darwin*, Vol. III, pp. 251-52.
4. Erwin Schrodinger, *What is Life? & Mind and Matter*, Cambridge University Press, 1967, pp. 126-37; & Arthur Eddington, in Erwin Schrodinger, *ibid*., p. 130.
5. D.S. Kothari, in *The Odyssey of Science, Culture and Consciousness*, New Delhi: Abhinav Publication, 1990, pp. 48-49.
6. Arthur Eddington, in Commins and Linscott, ed., *Man and the Universe, The Philosophers of Science*, New York: Washington Square Press, 1969, p. 453.
7. Alan W. Watts, *The Ways of Zen*, New York: Vintage Books, 1957, p. 10.
8. Sampooran Singh and Dr (Mrs) Kanwaljit Kaur, *Peace, Security and Survival? : A Scientific Quest*, July 2004.
9. Albert Einstein, in Ken Keyes Jr, *The Hundredth Monkey*, Vision Books, Ed., February 1984; Sampooran Singh, *The Human Paradox*, Chandigarh: Faith Publishers, 1988, p. 41.
10. *ibid*., in Joel D. Beverslusis, *A SourceBook for the Community of Religions*, Chicago: The Council for a Parliament of the World's Religions, 1993, p. 234.
11. Ilya Prigogine and Isabelle Stengers, *Order out of Chaos*, New York: Bantam Books, 1984, pp. 6, 4.

12. J. Krishnamurti, *The First and Last Freedom*, London: Victor Gollancz Ltd., 1977, pp. 278, 286.
13. Erwin Schrodinger, *What is Life? & Mind and Matter*, *op. cit.*, pp. 137, 146.
14. Fritjof Capra, *The Tao of Physics*, Bantam Books, Second Edition, 1988, p. 18.
15. Sampooran Singh, Dr (Mrs) Kanwaljit Kaur, Paramjit Singh and AVM Manjit Singh, *Global Education and Human Survival*, Delhi: Sanbun Publishers, pp. 46, 35-36.
16. Ervin Laszlo, in *The Odyssey of Science, Culture and Consciousness*, New Delhi: Abhinav Publications, 1990, p. 237.
17. J. Krishnamurti and David Bohm, *The Ending of Time*, San Francisco: Harper and Row, 1985, pp. 105, 107, 110, 123.
18. David Bohm, in *The Future of Humanity*, 1987, Preface, pp. 2, 3.
19. Pupul Jayakar, et. al., in *On J. Krishnamurti, Within The Mind*, KFI, 1982, p. 6.
20. Sampooran Singh, *An Action Plan for Human Survival* (a) Supplement, USA: *PsychoScience*, Fall/Winter 1994; (b) Reprinted *PsychoScience*, Spring-Summer 1995, Vol. 2, No. 1, pp. 41-49; and (c) Reprinted, *The Masterplan Paradigm for Human Survival and Excellence*, Chandigarh: Faith Publishers, February 1998, pp. 228-41.
21. David Bohm, *Unfolding Meaning*, Mickleton and Loveland: Foundation House Publications, 1985, p. 175.
22. Marilyn Ferguson, *The Aquarian Conspiracy*, L.P. Tarcher, 1980, pp. 67, 79.
23. Fred Alan Wolf, *Taking the Quantum Leap*, Harper and Row, 1981, p. 186.
24. Pupul Jayakar, in *A Biography: Krishnamurti*, Harper and Row, 1986, pp. 314, 315, 389, 379, 317.
25. Fred Alan Wolf, *op. cit.*, Introduction, p. 6.
26. P. Krishna, *Education, Science and Spirituality*, USA: Institute for Higher Education, Research and Dialogue, California, April 3, 1993, pp. 15, 10.
27. George Wald, in *The Evolution of Consciousness*, New Delhi: National Publishing House, 1983, p. 14.
28. Albert Einstein, in Sampooran Singh, *The Holistic Education*, New Delhi: Siddharth Publications, 1987, p. 155.
29. Vaclav Havel, in *Our Global Neighbourhood: The Report of the Commission on Global Governance*, New York: Oxford University Press, 1995, pp. 353-54.
30. Sri Aurobindo, in *The Masterplan Paradigm for Human Survival and Excellence*, Chandigarh: Faith Publishers, 1998, p. 246; and Divine Mother, *ibid.*, p. 246.
31. Sampooran Singh and Dr (Mrs) Kanwaljit Kaur, *Peace, Security and Survival: A Scientific Quest*, July 2004, pp. 9, 10.
32. Fritjof Capra, *The Turning Point*, London: Wildwood House, 1982, p. 466.

7

The Human Survival: Challenges of Science and Technology

Abstract

About 1600, scientists formulated the principle that the laws of nature are to be discovered by measurement. Experience and reason are the two pillars on which science is built.

The limitations of science are: (a) Science makes progress by open-mindedness and following of abstract concepts. Abstraction involves excluding and narrowing down, and rejecting intuition (insight) as this is not amendable to measurement; (b) Science rejected all perennial values, as all values emerge from the depth potential of man; and the whole question of moral, spiritual and other dimensions is normally pushed out of science; (c) Science follows the method of induction (experimental) and deduction (theoretical). Kothari wrote, "What we observe is different from what was before the act of observation .... No observation, no measurement is possible without a relevant theoretical frame work"; (d) The present education has produced narrow-minded scientists, and they have lost the gift of foresight inherited from their forerunners; (e) There is realisation that physical science is concerned with a world of shadows; (f) The development of science tended rather to split and destroy the integrated view of man which may ultimately lead to dehumanization of man; (g) Technology is leading to mad-armament race and destructive weapons. The conditioned psyche coupled with destructive weapons is leading mankind to mass murder and collective suicide; and (h) Globalisation is taking place at an accelerative pace, but global consciousness is not keeping pace with material globalisation.

The answer to this paradox is embedded in mutation of human psyche and symbiosis of science and spirituality. Man has emerged on this planet to perceive the highest quantum energy potential of Cosmic Consciousness or Life Field; and to live in order, harmony, nonviolence and peace. Nature, out of its benediction, is bound to help mankind for his survival and excellence.

Science is the search for truth. A selfless, unfaltering devotion to truth and the use of knowledge for man's upliftment are the ideals of a scientist. Truth is what all earnest scientists seek. *Pure science* tries earnestly to understand the truth of nature through a dispassionate inquiry or observation; while the technology is *applied science*, in which the truth discovered by pure science flows as technical inventions for enhancement and enrichment of human life. These two are intimately related.

The Cosmic Consciousness expresses Itself in the field of the *known* and in the realm of the *Unknown*. As a symbol we compare the known to a drop of water, and the Unknown to a fathomless and bottomless ocean. The known is in the field of time, the field of science and technology, so it is limited and transitory. The Unknown is in the realm of the pure Religion, the Life Field, the Quantum Field Consciousness (QFC), so it is eternal, infinite and immutable.

Pure science deals with something *unknown*, which is basically a revelation by nature, and is called discovery of a truth in nature hitherto unknown to man. Technology deals with finding modified use of the *known* and leads to better instruments; and is called invention. Technology is the non-linear tool available to humanity which affected fundamental changes in ground rules of economic competitiveness and better environments; and this brings prosperity in society.

Technology is also associated with mad-armament race, and constructs more destructive weapons for killing man. Man has now the capacity to convert this beautiful globe into a charred-out cinder circling the sun into eternity? The whole human psyche is conditioned, and there has developed a terrible power that threatens not only our generation but generations yet to be born, and not only our own race, but all species of life on this planet.

This article explores the wrong turn taken by mankind and where science and technology, as it is today, leading mankind. It explores the cause, which leads to human extinction. We have to explore our survival. Man divorced from nature could not be happy and man's powers to resist nature is hopelessly puny.

Wrong Turn Taken by Mankind

(a) Galileo Galilei said, "Experience and reason are the two pillars on which science is built". He added that the laws of nature are to be discovered by measurement. He taught us that, "mere acceptance of stimuli which came from the environment and which result in the accumulation of memory in the brain is insufficient for our purpose .... He asked questions addressed to nature and succeeded in receiving answers directly from nature".[1] Galileo expressed two basic truths–intellectual approach based on memory is insufficient, and one has to receive answers directly (direct perception) from nature. It is sad that scientists ignored this truth although 400 years have passed.

(b) There are two methods of thinking in science. One is the method of induction which was advocated by Francis Bacon and effectively used by Galileo Galilei. It starts with the comparison of more or less similar experiences or experimental results. The other is the method of deduction which was consciously employed by Rene Descartes in guiding his own mental activities. D.S. Kothari wrote, "No observation, no measurement, is possible without a relevant theoretical frame work .... A scientific theory is always provisional. It is a guide to further development and replacement".[2] We laid more emphasis on that "the laws of nature are to be discovered by measurement". Kothari wrote, "What we observe is different from what was before the act of observation". Sullivan put it, "We cannot observe the course of nature without disturbing it"; or Andrade, "Observation means interference with what we are observing .... observation disturbs reality". It was clear to those physicists that *objective measurement and verification could no longer be the mark of absolute reality.* In spite of that observation gives a distorted perception, scientists stuck to that "all propositions were to be confined to that which was objectively measurable and verifiable". The error was committed about 400 years ago and thereafter we are just continuing in that direction. We did not stop to explore if that was the right direction. We opine that the errors were: (a) to transform the measurement to the psychological level, and (b) to analyze a small fragment in the field of time and ignore the Unknown, the realm of the timeless, which is immutable, infinite and eternal. In the Unknown realm, the measurement does not apply.

(c) Maurice H. Wilkins wrote, "Science makes progress largely by a combination of two aspects: open-mindedness and the following of abstract concepts. Abstraction involves excluding and narrowing down, which is the very opposite of open-mindedness. Science always puts the most emphasis on this abstracting and narrowing down, on analytical procedures and on the role of the intellect as distinct from intuition and feelings.... The whole question of moral, spiritual and other dimensions is primarily pushed out of science".[3]

(d) Science divorces all human values in spite of the fact that it is a human activity. How therefore can science, being a human activity, be separated from all virtues and values.

(e) The capability of abstract thought presupposed the presence of the power of intuition (insight). The intuition is not amenable to measurement, so it was rejected by scientists. Hideki Yukawa wrote, "The important would appear to be the balance or cooperation between intuition and abstraction .... There seems to be a general feeling of the estrangement of science from other cultural activities such as philosophy and literature". Yukawa "ascribes this split in our culture to the secondary role to which intuition has been relegated".

(f) Yukawa wrote, "The development of science, far from encouraging the formation and development of an integrated view of man in his many different aspects, has tended rather to split and destroy that view .... The danger that all these trends will combine to destroy the unity of man's various aspects and lead eventually to the loss even of his humanity cannot be denied. It is equally undeniable, I believe, that such a split would deprive man of his happiness .... To save ourselves from the danger of a loss of, or a split in, our humanity in the world of the future .... is the course that man must take from now on".[4]

(g) Arthur Eddington wrote, "The frank realisation that physical science is concerned with a world of shadows is one of the most significant of recent advances". This was known to Democritus of Abdera during fifth century B.C., and even before.[5] The physicists thought that they were dealing with the world itself and no attention was paid to Democritus perception.

(h) Globalisation is taking place as the result of science and technology and the thrust of evolution, but global consciousness is not keeping pace with the globalisation. The index of human progress is higher and higher level of expression of global consciousness–and certainly not any material progress.

The Human Survival : Where is Science and Technology Going?

Many eminent politicians, scientists, philosophers-mystics and lovers of mankind (social activists) have opined that the challenge of science and technology have to be resolved *here* and *now*, and not tomorrow, as our survival is at stake. President Vaclav Havel, Czech Republic, on July 4, 1994, wrote, "We are going through a transitional period .... Cultural conflicts are increasing and are understandably more dangerous today than at any other time in history. The end of the era of rationalism has been catastrophic .... The only reliable path .... is self-transcendence. Transcendence as the only alternative to extinction". He added on September 9, 1994, "Modern man has lost his transcendental anchor".[6]

Richard Lamm, Former Governor of Colorado, quoted Stuart Udall, and said, "The whole human enterprise is a machine without brakes, for there are no indications that the world's political leaders will deal with the realities until catastrophes occur .... We have already passed the point of no return, and tragic convulsions are at hand".[7]

George Wald wrote, "We who know where are we going, are now heading rapidly towards self-extinction, towards removing humankind from the cosmic scene .... The cosmic drama will go on elsewhere, ignorant of our demise, caring nothing, but we will have no further part in it".

Here we encounter a curious paradox. George Wald suggested in prophetic words, "All the mystics through the ages have agreed that to achieve wisdom one must quiet the brain, stop using it as a tool, put aside knowledge and learning, try indeed to free one's consciousness, empty one's mind, and in quiet see what enters".[8] Based upon our exploration of the human psyche for the last 25 years, we opine, "A true-scientist lives according to the immutable laws of nature; the brain is in a no-mind state; so his perception is direct. He revels in freedom, order, harmony, nonviolence and peace". We have submitted a monograph entitled **Peace, Security and Survival? : A Scientific Quest** to the United Nations Foundation in July 2004.

Erwin Schrodinger wrote, "Scientific attitude would have to be rebuilt. Science must be made anew. Care is needed".[9] Maurice H. Wilkins wrote, "It is also a question of how science is developed through educational institutions and through institutionalized science. I agree with Einstein that the sort of scientific education we have now has produced a narrow-minded way of thinking amongst scientists, so that they give no proper attention to the moral and psychological dimensions".

We have been exploring the human psyche for more than 25 years and have propounded a *technology* to end I-consciousness, thought-structure and the *fact*. This will lay the foundation for mutation of human psyche and symbiosis of science and spirituality. This will blossom to human survival and excellence.

References

1. Galileo Galilei, in Hideki Yukawa, *Creativity and Intuition*, Tokyo: Kodansha International Ltd., 1973, pp. 111, 143.
2. D.S. Kothari, *Some Thoughts on Science and Religion*, The University of Delhi, 31st Octo. & 3rd Nov. 1977, p. 33.
3. Maurice H. Wilkins, in *Synthesis of Science and Religion*, Mumbai: The Bhaktivedanta Institute, June 1988, pp. 30, 37, 35.
4. Hideki Yukawa, *op. cit.*, pp. 101-102, 10, 204, 205, 206.
5. Arthur Eddington, in Erwin Schrodinger, *What is Life? & Mind and Matter*, Cambridge University Press, 1967, p. 130; and Schrodinger, *ibid.*, p. 177.

6. President Vaclav Havel, *Speeches in USA, July 4, 1994, and September 29, 1994.*
7. Richard Lamm, In Michael Burghley, *My World, My Responsibility*, Canada: Foundation House Publication, 1987, p. 10.
8. George Wald, in Kishore Gandhi (Ed.), *The Evolution of Consciousness*, New Delhi: National Publishing House, 1983, p.13.
9. Erwin Schrodinger, *op. cit.*, p. 132.

8

Challenges of Science and Technology

Abstract

Science and technology have made great breakthroughs in medicine, communication, industry, and agriculture. Today, science and technology, if used with compassion, wisdom, and understanding, can abolish poverty, ignorance, illiteracy, and malnutrition from the face of the earth. And yet, with all our knowledge, all our science, what is reigning technology in a world of today?, we are heading towards Mutually Assured Destruction -- MAD – by nuclear weapons and so on.

In a non-dual and non-conceptual frame of reference of Mind Continuum, the perceptions are born of non-duality, of silence, and responses are born of spontaneity. Perception has nothing to do with knowledge. Intelligence begins to use the human brain and help the human being to look at the world in quite a different way. Intuition or insight is the timeless perception. Understanding, learning and action are a cyclic process, which results in a spiral going upwards in the vertical dimension; it is a growth in the vertical dimension. The higher the understanding, the higher the expression of the Consciousness in the human brain-body system.

A true-scientist is one who lives according to the immutable laws of nature, his perception is direct. The brain is in a "no-mind state", so there is direct input of Cosmic Consciousness in the brain cells (neurons). He is free of subject-object dualism, or conflict, or contradiction. It leads to ending of I-consciousness, thought-structure and the fact. Man revels in freedom, order, harmony, nonviolence and peace.

We have to observe the conditioned psyche from within nature by restructured "science-education-health" which we call the true-subject or non-variable awareness. Such an observation, flows to mutation in the brain through regeneration of Supreme Intelligence – not through knowledge, not through accumulation. It is basically an exploration into the Unknown realm, the timelessness, the Simultaneous Consciousness, the Supreme Intelligence, the Life Field. That intelligence (through intuition) is the ability to see a truth directly, a direct perception of the truth, and education must foster that. The mutation guarantees human survival.

Man is an amphibian who lives simultaneously in two dimensions– (a) the *known*, the time-space-causation matrices, the successive consciousness, and (b) the *Unknown*, the Simultaneous Consciousness, the Life Field, the Absolute, the *Brahman*. As a symbol, we may compare the known to a drop of water and the Unknown to a fathomless and boundless ocean. The known is in the field of time, so it is limited and transitory. The Unknown is in the realm of the timelessness, so it is eternal, infinite and immutable.

Life is a multi-dimensional phenomenon and human beings who are expressions of the phenomenon are themselves multi-dimensional creatures. Life is self-generated. There is not a creator, or a personal god who created the world and remained outside it. It is self-generated, self-sustained, self-controlled and self-regulated phenomenon. Life seems to be an Intelligence, an energy of Intelligence which has been unwinding, uncovering, manifesting for billions of years and yet has remained ever virgin and ever fresh. Life field is homogeneous, undifferentiated and dimensionless. Life is the highest quantum energy potential of Cosmic Consciousness, or the highest frequency of Consciousness. It has the capacity to express itself at many potentials of life–Oneness to manyness. At the lowest potential of life field, or common waking state of consciousness, the mind manifests as heterogeneous, differentiated and multi-dimensional. We observe the play of a cycle forever present in creation; the breakdown of an integrated whole (the subject) into its diverse constituents and then the integrated whole (the image); a passage from Unity through diversity to Unity.

Karan Singh wrote, "Today, after billions of years of prebiological evolution and metabiological evolution, mankind is at an evolutionary crossroads. We stand at a juncture wherein we are in supreme peril–not a peril from another species, not a peril from outer space, but a peril from ourselves. From deep within the human psyche, there has developed this terrible power that threatens not only our generation but generations yet to be born, and not only our race, but all species of life on this planet".[1]

Science and technology have made great breakthroughs in medicine, communication, industry, and agriculture. Today, science and technology, if used with compassion, wisdom, and understanding, can abolish poverty, ignorance, illiteracy, and malnutrition from the face of the earth. And yet, with all our knowledge, all our science, what is reigning technology in a world of today? Mutually Assured Destruction–MAD–by nuclear weapons and so on.

Nature has bestowed two gifts to every human being–first, self-knowledge of his own thoughts and feelings which implies that he is conscious of his own mental faculty, or time-space-causation matrices, and second, a hidden faculty of "understanding of life directly", instead of in the abstract, linear terms of representational thinking. The hidden faculty is called non-dual and non-conceptual frame of reference of Mind Continuum. This implies educating the conditioned psyche, so that it transcends I-consciousness and thought structure, and the mind makes a quantum jump from symbolic-dualistic frame of mind spectrum to non-dual frame of Mind Continuum. Nature expresses itself as intuition in a non-dual frame of reference.

We are living at one of the great turning points of human history. It appears that we are sustaining ourselves due to the benevolence of Nature–not on the intellectual ability of man. The benevolence of nature is often called intuition, or insight, or Divine Grace.

This article explores relationship, intuition, science and values, and loss of humanity in the scientific mode of mind spectrum. It also investigates: "Where is science and technology going?"; role of science in human psyche, violence and latest challenges. It explores the resolution of human paradox.

Relationship: Life is relationship, which is expressed through contact with things, with people, with ideas. It is the lack of understanding of relationship that causes conflict. Relationship means communion without fear, freedom to understand each other, to communicate directly. If you avoid a *fact*, you live in ignorance, which can never produce right relationship. There is no understanding in the symbolic-dualistic frame of reference of mind spectrum because it is repetitive and mechanical, and is engaged in becoming, gratification, acquisition and search for security. Understanding is direct, it flows in a non-dual and non-conceptual frame of reference of Mind Continuum. Relationship is really self-revelation which is process of self-knowledge. In relationship, there is love and not responsibility or duty, there is no isolation. So the challenge facing mankind is a quantum jump from symbolic-dualistic frame to non-dual and non-conceptual frame of reference and to live in love which is communion with the Life Field.

Intuition: Commenting on abstract thought, Hideki Yukawa wrote, "It always presupposed the presence of the power of intuition, with which both Greek and Chinese geniuses in ancient times were richly endowed. The important point would appear to be the balance or cooperation between intuition and abstraction .... (In ancient Greece), there, not only were intuition and abstraction in complete harmony and balance with each other, but there was also no such thing as the estrangement of science from philosophy, literature, and the arts. All these cultural activities were close to the mind and heart of human beings". He added, "Man has to begin with intuition, and then he can proceed with the help of his power of abstraction".[2] Maurice H. Wilkins wrote, "The logical and rational is a very important element in science. But emphasis on that trend to make people not notice the essential role of intuition".[3]

All knowledge is structured in consciousness. This recognizes that consciousness alone can be totally self-referral, so the pure mind or non-dual mind can perceive the consciousness. When non-dual state of mind is presented as an object to pure consciousness, then it reveals itself. In the non-dual mind, the intelligence is born of the inner silence, of the inner space. The intelligence is uncluttered by the movement of thought. The dimension of intelligence, of unconditioned energy, of Fundamental Vibration, has no past, so it is free of all conditioning and divisive loyalties, etc. It bestows intuition and insight. Insight implies something which you perceive without any logic, without any motive. It is called immediate perception. ***The perceptions are born of non-duality, of silence, and responses are born of spontaneity***. Perception has nothing to do with knowledge. Intelligence begins to use the human brain and help the human being to look at the world in quite a different way.[4]

Intuition or insight is the timeless perception. It is insight alone that can decondition the brain. Insight is complete and from that completeness there can be logical, sane and rational action. Only then there can be flowering of the brain. Pure clear insight is perception without any doubt. ***Understanding, learning and action are a cyclic process, which results in a spiral going upwards in the vertical dimension; it is a growth in the vertical dimension.*** The higher the understanding, the higher the expression of the Consciousness in the human brain-body system.

The science and technology, as it is today, rejects intuition because it is not amenable to measurement and logical reason. We have to transform the dimensions of science and technology so that these takes in its fold the intuition.

Science and Values: There is a growing realisation that we have constructed a violent world because all value education systems have failed. All science is objective. As all ethical-spiritual values are embedded in the depth dimensions of life, so all scientific models are free of values. David Bohm, an eminent physicist wrote, "Now, it has been fairly commonly agreed that we are at present faced with the challenge of a breakdown in human values that threatens the stability of society throughout the whole world .... The separation of knowledge from values has no meaning, except as a momentary abstraction made for convenience of discussion. The two are inseparably interwoven in a single undivided process, in which it is impossible to have one without the other".[5] Wilkins wrote, "The question of good or bad, of human value, relates to every human activity. How therefore can science being a human activity, be separated from all values".[3]

Loss of Humanity: Hideki Yukawa wrote, "The development of science, far from encouraging the formation and development of an integrated view in his many different aspects, has tended rather to split and destroy that view .... The danger that all these trends will combine to destroy the unity of man's various aspects and lead eventually to the loss even of his humanity cannot be denied".

Where is Science and Technology Going?

Globalization: It is taking place as the result of science and technology and the thrust of evolution, but global consciousness is not keeping pace with the (material) globalisation. The material progress adds to conditioning of psyche, it leads to lowering sensitivity; and it cannot add to global consciousness.

Role of Science and Human Psyche: Albert Einstein stated:

> Science can denature plutonium, but it cannot denature the evil in the heart of man.
>
> The splitting of the atom has changed everything except our mode of thinking and thus we drift towards the unparalleled catastrophe.[6]
>
> One thing I have learnt in my long life: that all our science, measured against reality, is primitive and childlike–and yet it is the most precious thing we have.[7]
>
> The mind can proceed only so far upon what it knows and can prove. Then comes a point where the mind takes a leap–call it intuition or what you will–and comes upon a higher plane of knowledge but can never prove how it got there. All great discoveries have involved such a leap.[8]

Albert Einstein says, "The most incomprehensible thing about the universe is that it is comprehensible". Thought can never comprehend the universe. When the mind realises its own limitations then the mind makes a quantum jump from a relational frame of reference to absolute rest frame, and the absolute rest frame of reference has the intuitive faculty. The universe is comprehensive to an intuitive mind. Einstein refers to intuitive faculty of mind and says:

Physics is essentially an intuitive and concrete science. Mathematics is only a means for expressing the laws that govern phenomena.[9]

Scientific truth is time dependent and logic dependent. A mathematical truth is timeless, independent of experience or play of the human mind; it is beyond intellect and reason; it is intuitive knowledge. All newness, all originality, all creativeness of science and arts lie in the intuitive faculty of mind.

The objective science, which we have developed, does not touch even the fringes of conditioned human psyche and as such is incapable of bringing radical transformation in the psyche. The basic problem is, in the words of Albert Einstein, "Our new idea is simple: to build a physics valid for all coordinate systems", or frames of reference of the mind spectrum. Obviously all terrorism, fear, envy, anger, etc. have their roots in the human psyche. The psychological imbalances and ecological crises can only be resolved through mutation of the human psyche.[10] We have to explore *here* and *now* that human survival involves the growth of a creative and compassionate global consciousness.

Violence: We have built a society which is violent and we, as human beings, are violent. All psychological imbalances–violence, fear, greed, anger and so on–are constructs of the waking state of mind, or relative frame of reference of mind in the mind spectrum. The socio-economic-political systems, the institutionalised religions, the reforms in the external field have so far failed to transform man.

Violence is an indication of psychological immaturity. Wilkins wrote, "The whole question of moral, spiritual and other dimensions is normally pushed out of science. So something in the nature of science often does lead people towards destruction. Abstraction can be regarded as a form of violence .... science often does violence to nature".

Violence is a construct by symbolic-dualistic frame of reference, and nonviolence is a percept in the non-dual and non-conceptual frame of reference of the Mind Continuum; where the non-dual frame is synergistic or at higher quantum energy potential to symbolic-dualistic frame.

Latest Challenges: It is the symbolic-dualistic frame of reference or the conditioned psyche that constructs all challenges. All psychological imbalances, ecological crisis are constructs of the mind. The conditionings at the conscious level of mind have gone deep to the subconscious level. The latest challenges are global terrorism, one country sending terrorists into a neighbouring country to create disturbances and chaos (cross-border terrorism), ethnic conflicts due to religious fundamentalism, corruption, international crime, drugs and arms trafficking, hijacking of aeroplanes, population transfer and so on. There are many hidden challenges as bonded-labour, economic disparity, poverty and hunger. The worst is that in this massacre, women and children are not even spared. The global or international terrorism is considered as a threat to the sovereignty of states, development, stability, and as well as to international peace and security.

During the past few decades, the United Nations Organisation, many politicians, scientists, social activists have issued appeals but all have fallen on the deaf years of mankind. There have been many suggestions–as world body to tackle terrorism, international legal system to fight terrorism–but all suggestions, so far, have failed mankind. All attempts at the international community level to act at the bilateral, regional and multi-lateral levels have only yielded marginal results.

The basic cause of failures is that all human efforts are at the level of external world, and any pledge cannot transform the conditioned psyche. Recently many eminent scientists–Werner Heisenberg, Edwin Hubble, Max Planck, G.F. Chew, Bertrand Russell, Lincoln Barnett, Max Born and so on–have concluded that we cannot impart value education at reason and intellect level;[11] and further intellectual efforts cannot transform the human conditioned psyche.

Resolution of Human Paradox?

Here we meet a curious paradox! Nature invariably expresses itself as pure perception, or intuition, or insight in a pure mind. Nature reveals HER Truth in the minds of eminent physicists, neuro-physiologists, neuro-surgeons, and so on; perhaps they were engaged in rigorous, persistent and consistent observation, or enquiry, or experimental interrogation of the human psyche. We consider them as "subjective-scientists, mystics, sages, rishis" of the highest order, and mankind for their objective research honoured them as Nobel Laureates. It is a paradox that these eminent scientists are talking about limitations of science and technology that is leading mankind to self-annihilation. Erwin Schrodinger, Nobel Prize in Physics, 1931 wrote, "Scientific attitude would have to be rebuilt, science must be made anew".[12] George Wald, Nobel Prize in Medicine, 1967, wrote:

> By now the problem is not transcendence, but survival.... All the mystics through the ages have agreed that to achieve wisdom one must quiet the brain, stop using it as a tool, put aside knowledge and learning, try indeed to free one's consciousness, empty one's mind, and in quiet see what enters .... We who know where we are going, are now heading rapidly toward self-extinction, toward removing humankind from the cosmic scene, and for the most trivial of reasons: profit, the rivalry of the United States and the Soviet Union, the momentum of the

military-industrial complex in both nations. The cosmic drama will go on elsewhere, ignorant of our demise, caring nothing; but we will have no further part in it .... Does that matter? It matters to us".[13]

Ilya Prigogine, Nobel Laureate, 1977, wrote, "A triumph of human reason turned into a sad truth. It seemed that science debased everything it touched".[14]

Based upon our exploration for more than 25 years we opine:

A true-scientist is one who lives according to the immutable laws of nature, his perception is direct. The brain is in a no-mind state, so there is direct input of Cosmic Consciousness in the brain cells (neurons). He is free of subject-object dualism, or conflict, or contradiction. It leads to ending of I-consciousness, thought-structure and the fact. Man revels in freedom, order, harmony, nonviolence and peace.

We have submitted a monograph entitled ***Peace, Security and Survival: A Scientific Quest*** to the United Nations Organisation in July 2004.[15] When "restructured science-education" observes the conditioned psyche, the I-consciousness, thought-structure and the fact go to abeyance; and pure Consciousness bathes the brain cells, and Consciousness expresses Itself as order, harmony, nonviolence and peace. This is the consummation of human life. Recently we penned another monogram entitled ***Science and Technology–New Challenges***.[16]

Russian scientists, in 1996, have proposed a Life Field, beyond our physical concepts of time, space and the known concepts of electromagnetic and gravitational fields. This was followed by another scientific conference at Cambridge University, which concluded, "A new scientific approach would include subjective experience as valid information and address all forms of human experience–including intuition, spirituality and mystical encounters".[17] The Life Field appears to be synonymous to Universal Consciousness or *Brahman*.

The Hon'ble President A.P.J. Abdul Kalam suggested, "A three-pronged strategy to create a better world imparting value education to youths, transforming religion into spiritualism and removing economic disparity".[18] He added that we need a new world order system to met the challenges.

Concluding Comment

Humanity has taken a wrong turn during the last 500 years–rejecting intuition, rejecting human values, living in isolated relationship, fragmentary view of life, material globalisation–which has created this chaos in the world. And in spite of this realisation man has been continuing in that direction, and this direction is leading man to self-annihilation.

Here we meet a curious paradox in our exploration, we have to observe the conditioned psyche from within nature by "restructured science-education" which we call the true-subject or non-variable awareness. Such an observation, flows to mutation in the brain through regeneration of Supreme Intelligence–not through knowledge, not through accumulation. It is basically an exploration into the Unknown realm, the timelessness, the Simultaneous Consciousness, the Supreme Intelligence, the Life Field. That intelligence (through intuition) is the ability to see a truth directly, a direct perception of the truth, and education must foster that. The mutation guarantees human survival.

We have to take urgent steps *here* and *now* to introduce value education at all levels. We have to introduce "Psychodynamics of Mind-Brain-Body System" in the science faculty and "Transpersonal Psychology" in the arts faculty.

It is the Cosmic Consciousness (Supreme Intelligence) that has the capacity to heal a diseased psyche or psychic pandemic. It resolves the challenges–psychological imbalances, ecological crises–and the recent challenges–terrorism, corruption, ethnic conflicts, and so on. This will lead to human survival and a new culture.

All pain and misery is bound to vanish and every human being revels in order, harmony, nonviolence and peace.

References

1. Karan Singh, in *Synthesis of Science and Religion*, Mumbai: Bhaktivedanta Institute, June 1988, pp. 23, 24.
2. Hideki Yukawa, *Creativity and Intuition*, Tokyo: Kodansha International Ltd., 1973, pp. 101-102, 108, 119, 204-205.
3. Maurice H. Wilkins, in *Synthesis of Science and Religion*, *op. cit.*, pp. 31, 37, 30.
4. Sampooran Singh, *Atam Science*, Dagshai: The Atam Science Trust, 7.10.2002, pp. 7, 15.
5. David Bohm, in J. Krishnamurti, *Within the Mind, On J. Krishnamurti*, KFI, 1982, pp. 42, 57.
6. Albert Einstein, in Sampooran Singh, *The Human Paradox*, 1988, p. 41.
7. *ibid.*, in Hoffman, Banesh, *Albert Einstein: Creator and Rebel*, Viking: New York, 1972, Hart Davies, Mac-Gibbon: London, 1973, Paladin: London, 1977.
8. Sampooran Singh, *The Holistic Education*, New Delhi: Siddharth Publications, 1987, p. 155.
9. *ibid.*, in *Letters*, Maurice Solovine, Gauthier Villars: Paris, 1956.
10. Sampooran Singh, Kanwaljit Kaur and Paramjit Singh, *The Masterplan Paradigm for Human Survival and Excellence*, Chandigarh: Faith Publishers, February 1998, pp. 130-159, 228-254.

11. *ibid.*, *Global Education and Human Survival*, New Delhi: Sanbun Publishers, March 2002, pp. 46, 35-36.
12. Erwin Schrodinger, *What is Life*? & *Mind and Matter*, Cambridge University Press, 1967, p. 132.
13. George Wald, in *The Evolution of Consciousness*, New Delhi: National Publishing House, 1983, pp. 14, 13.
14. Ilya Prigogine and Isabelle Stengers, *Order Out of Chaos*, Bantam Books, 1984, p. 6.
15. Sampooran Singh, Dr (Mrs) Kanwaljit Kaur, *Peace, Security and Survival*: *A Scientific Quest*, July 2004, pp. 1-40.
16. Sampooran Singh, *Science and Technology–New Challenges*, unpublished.
17. Joan Walton, *Scientists Tune into Consciousness*, New Science, Winter 1996.
18. President A.P.J. Abdul Kalam, *The Tribune*, September 14, 2004, August 15, 2004.

9

Reflections on the New-Culture Paradigm

Abstract

The recent discoveries of modern science guides man to transcend all psychological imbalances, ecological crisis, terrorism, corruption, ethnic conflicts, and so on. It explores interaction of mind-brain-body system, art of observation, science and intuition, atom and thought, wave-particle complementarity, global ethic and consciousness. We intuitively see that a quantum leap of transcendence of the past psyche is not only possible, but inevitable, if we are to survive as a species and avoid committing suicide by senseless violence or sheer decadence.

The objective science deals with objective values and does not deal with the subjective dimension. It adds to materialism. It rejects intuition (insight), as intuition is not amenable to reason and measurements.

Global ethic is defined as the perception in a non-dual and non-conceptual frame of reference of the Mind Continuum. It is the foundation of all ethical and spiritual values. The universal declaration leading to the emergence of global ethic constitutes a call to mankind that human mind must make a quantum jump from symbolic-dualistic frame to non-dual frame of reference of Mind Continuum. And one who is wholly consecrated to Truth, who wants to live the Truth, serve the Truth, would know at each moment the ethical values; it would be a kind of intuition or revelation or insight which would make you know the truth, the global ethic at every moment. To perceive the ethical values or global ethic, man has to make a quantum jump from psychosocial evolution to spiritual evolution.

The perennial philosophy of ancient India is that man is an amphibian who lives simultaneously in two dimensions–(a) the *known*, the time-space-causation matrices, the waking state of mind, the lowest quantum energy potential of consciousness, the successive consciousness, and (b) the *Unknown*, the Simultaneous Consciousness, the transcendental essence, the highest quantum energy potential of Consciousness. Maharishi Ramana said, "The world is illusory; *Brahman* alone is real. *Brahman* is the world". The various lines of critique as to how the intellect (march of reason) has constructed a violent world has been discussed earlier.[1]

Culture like love will always elude definition and remain an awareness beyond words and concepts, a precious belonging that is within us and also around, linking us to a whole expanse of life, retaining its own uniqueness in time and space. The traditional culture is our present way of living–constructed by psychological mode and scientific mode of mind. It is repetitive and mechanical, so there is no newness and no creativeness. This expresses itself as pain, misery, conflict and contradiction, and it emphasises materialism. Creativeness or creativity is the power to balance, harmonise and integrate, to be aware of all the parts that make a whole without losing sight of the whole that is far more than its parts, and to be able to live in the intensity of fullness. The new-culture paradigm is the altered states (non-dual and non-conceptual state) of consciousness. It transcends the mental life and is the very foundation of Indian culture; it expresses Itself at the highest quantum energy potential or highest frequency of Cosmic Consciousness.

The ancient seers of India, about 10,000 years ago, perceived a state of true illumination. There is One Reality, the Unmanifest-Manifested. The nature of the Unmanifest is 'Deep-Silence', 'Inactivity (Non-Vibration)', 'Passivity', 'Immutability', 'Eternal'; and also Activity (Vibration), dynamism and illimitable potency to manifest as many. Activity (Active Reality) expresses which is self-hidden in the Silence (Passive Reality); both are different states of the Supreme Reality, the obverse and converse affirmations; both are Pure Existence and conscious Force, or Self-Existent Bliss and Supreme Intelligence, and are One. It is the Active Reality which manifests as the perfect freedom and omnipotence of an eternal divine activity in innumerable galaxies as inanimate world and plant and animal kingdoms.

The Active Reality is a powerful, highly directional, monochromatic (same frequency) and coherent (the wave is in one phase) beam of energy; or a state of highest frequency (higher frequency means higher energy), or high quantum energy potential. The intense energy of insight expresses itself as direct perception of the fact, the Reality.[2]

This article investigates the ways and means of achieving creativity, or fullness of life, or integrating time and timelessness, or intellect and intuition. The recent discoveries of modern science guides man to transcend all psychological imbalances, ecological crisis, terrorism, corruption, ethnic conflicts, and so on. It explores interaction of mind-brain-body system, art of observation, science and intuition, atom and thought, wave-particle complementarity, global ethic and consciousness. We intuitively see that a quantum leap of transcendence of the past psyche is not only possible, but inevitable, if we are to survive as a species and avoid committing suicide by senseless violence or sheer decadence.

Comments of Eminent Scientists on Traditional Culture

The concepts of modern physics often show surprising parallels to the ideas expressed in the religious philosophies of the Far East. These have been noticed by some of the great physicists of our century when they came in contact with Far Eastern culture during their lecture tours to India, China and Japan. The following quotations serve as examples:

The general notions about human understanding .... which are illustrated by discoveries in atomic physics are not in the nature of things wholly unfamiliar, wholly unheard of, or new. Even in our own culture they have a history, and in Buddhist and Hindu thought a more considerable and central place. What we shall find is an exemplification, an encouragement, and a refinement of old wisdom.[3]

> For a parallel to the lesson of atomic theory .... [we must turn] to those kinds of epistemological problems with which already thinkers like the Buddha and Lao Tzu have been confronted, when trying to harmonize our position as spectators and actors in the great drama of existence.[4]
>
> The great scientific contribution in theoretical physics that has come from Japan since the last war may be an indication of a certain relationship between philosophical ideas in the tradition of the Far East and the philosophical substance of quantum theory.[5]
>
> Quantum theory and relativity theory–both force us to see the world very much in the way a Hindu, Buddhist, or Taoist sees it, and how this similarity strengthens when we look at the recent attempts to combine these two theories in order to describe the phenomena of the submicroscopic world: the properties and interactions of the subatomic particles of which all matter is made.[6]

Gary Zukav also discussed mind-stretching mysteries of new physics striking parallels with modern psychology and eastern mysticism.[7]

Russian scientists, in 1996, have proposed a Life Field, beyond our physical concepts of time, space and the known concepts of electromagnetic and gravitational fields. This was followed by another scientific conference at Cambridge University, which concluded, "A new scientific approach would include subjective experience as valid information and address all forms of human experience–including intuition, spirituality and mystical encounters".[8] The Life Field appears to be synonymous to Universal Consciousness or *Brahman.*

Interaction of Mind-Brain-Body System

Modern physics has confirmed that all the concepts we use to describe nature are limited, that they are not features of reality, but creations of the mind; parts of the map, not of the territory. Since space and time are now reduced to the subjective role of the elements of the language a particular observer uses his or her description of natural phenomena. Relativity theory has shown that space is not three dimensional and time is not a separate entity. Both are intimately and inseparably connected and form a four-dimensional continuum, which is called "space-time". Spencer Brown wrote, "In order to see, evidently it must cut itself up into at least one state which sees, and at least one other state which is seen. In this severed and mutilated condition, whatever is sees is only *partially itself*".[9] Arthur Eddington put it succinctly, "Nature thus provides that knowledge of one-half of the world will ensure ignorance of the other half". And Haldane muttered that "the universe is not only queerer than we suppose, but it is queerer than we can suppose".

Nature always expresses itself as pure perception (non-verbal or thought-free perception); from this pure perception we proceed to thought, recognition and naming, which implies coherent superpositioning of different webs, and awareness of the distorted perception, and the modified memory is recorded.[10] The whole process implies an exchange of photons (quanta of light), these are 'gentle quantum events', and these bring in a discontinuity at that moment. At the moment of this exchange the distinction between the subject and the object is lost. One flowing web of frequencies (subject) looks at another flowing web of frequencies (object), and then both intermingle losing their identities. Both the subject and the object become continuities of change, so the subject is the object, the thinker is the thought. The interaction may be shown as:

Fact + Recalled Memory → Mutilated Fact + Modified Memory

This is repetitive and mechanical process. There is no creativeness. The state of creativeness cannot exist where there is conflict, ceaseless strife and pain. The answer to this paradox is embedded in our awareness of every movement of our own thought and feeling in our relationship with people, with things and with nature, that the mind is open, pliable, and only then there is sensitivity.

Brain is a part of the objective world, it can be investigated objectively. Mind is subjective. All experience, everything without exception, is fundamentally a personal subjective experience.

Objective science by excluding subjectivity cannot, even in principle, deal with our thoughts, feelings, emotions, with subjective experience of any kind. It excludes "I". The subject is "in-here" and the object "out-there"; as the object excludes subjectivity, so it deals with a small part of life, and rejects the wholeness of life. No considerations of purpose, divine or human, nothing which implies value judgements, can enter the gateway of objective science.

The Art of Observation

The subject-object interaction puts a limitation on the art of observation. Sullivan put it, "We cannot observe the course of nature without disturbing it",[11] or Andrade, "Observation means interference with what we are observing .... Observation disturbs reality".[12] D.S. Kothari wrote, "What is observed is different from what was before the act of observation".[13] George Wald wrote, "The very crux of twentieth-century physics is the recognition that the observer cannot be excluded from his observations; he is an intrinsic participant in them".[14] It was abundantly clear to those physicists that observation, measurement and verification could no longer be the mark of absolute reality.

A scientific mode of mind takes up "the role of a non-concerned observer" in the words of Erwin Schrodinger,[15] it is "unrelated to our beliefs, our ambitions, our hopes", in the words of Prigogine.[16] It must not construct a pseudo-observer, it must see in the present and reject the past remembrance or future projections.

Science and Intuition (Insight)

The objective science, as we have developed, rejects intuition, as intuition is not amenable to reason and measurements. This is one of the basic errors we have committed.

D.S. Kothari wrote, "The new theorems, unless trivial, are of course first '*discovered*' and then proved. Discovery is a flash of insight. It is not a step by step process, but a sort of quantum leap .... A rational account of a discovery, the proof, follows and not precedes the discovery".[17] He added, "We have to recognize that no observation, no measurement, is possible without a relevant theoretical framework .... A scientific theory is always provisional. It is a guide to further development, to its own replacement".[18] He added in prophetic words, "Fundamental discoveries which go deep into the nature of things are the result of uncommon intuition and faith, not cold logic".[19]

Maurice H. Wilkins wrote, "The logical and rational is a very important element in science. But emphasis on that tends to make people not notice the essential role of intuition".[20] Fritjof Capra wrote, "The rational part of research would, in fact, be useless if it were not accompanied by the intuition".

All knowledge is structured in consciousness. This recognizes that consciousness alone can be totally self-referral, so the pure mind or non-dual frame of reference can perceive the consciousness. When consciousness expresses itself at the lowest quantum energy potential in the symbolic-dualistic state of mind, it expresses itself as intellect. When it expresses at the highest quantum energy potential in a non-dual state of mind, it expresses itself as intuition. In the non-dual state of mind, the intelligence is born in the inner silence, of the inner space. The intelligence is uncluttered by the movement of thought. It bestows intuition (insight) which implies that you perceive without any logic, without motive. ***The perceptions are born of non-duality, of silence, and responses are born of spontaneity***.

Atom and Thought

In 1913, Niels Bohr showed that there exists discrete sequence of electron orbits in an atom. When an atom is excited, the electron jumps from one orbit to another. At this very instance, the atom emits or absorbs a photon the frequency of which corresponds to the difference between the energies characterizing the electron's motion in each of the two orbits. This difference is calculated in terms of Einstein's formula relating energy to frequency.

When an atom makes a transition, or a 'jump', from one stationary state to another, the actual process cannot be visualised or even imagined. There are no intermediate stages. We cannot breakdown the process into its components. The entire process of transition from one state to another is a non-visualisable, unanalysable, unity. *It is indivisible*. Its parts cannot even be imagined. It is a 'quantum jump', as we call it.[21] In dealing with atomic phenomena we have to recognise that the act of observation is accompanied by an inevitable disturbance which alters the state of the observed system in an unpredictable manner. What is observed is different from what it was before the act of observation. This is inherent in the nature of things. It cannot be eliminated.[22] In an attempt to understand the mystery of the world of atoms, quantum physics is of the view that atomic object (the different electron orbits) emerge from an "unmanifest mathematical space", and this is called *Hilbert space*. It implies that between any two consecutive orbits, there is realm of pure Consciousness.

There appears to be an analogous situation for *thought processes*. As we 'think'–in any sequence of thoughts–there is always a sudden, discontinuous jump from one thought to the next. We are not aware at all of any intermediate stages. If we were so aware, no thinking would be possible. There would be an almost infinite sequence of 'sub-thoughts' between two thoughts, like an infinity of points between the two ends of a line. ***Quantum jumps for thought appear to be as much a necessity for the conscious self as these are for the atom.*** As the mind quietens, the space between two thoughts enhances and thought structures become less and less, till the mind is totally quiet, which implies that all thoughts go to abeyance and pure Consciousness expresses itself.

Since atoms with consciousness are looking at atoms with consciousness, we have the same experience of wonder and mystery whenever we look at the universe. We are looking at ourselves. It is this process that we call the universe. Richard Feynman says:

> That is what it means when one discovers how long it takes for the atoms of the brain to be replaced by other atoms, to note that the thing which I call my individuality is only a pattern or dance. The atoms come into my brain, dance a dance, then go out; always new atoms but always doing the same dance, remembering what the dance was yesterday.
>
> It is true that the universe is nothing more than mind looking at itself.

Consciousness performs a dual role in the universe. In the world of the quantum, it is both the awareness and the creation of experience. It is the *being* and the *knowing* of experience. With the stroke of the twentieth-century quantum eraser, the dividing line between ontology (theory of being) and epistemology is rubbed out, and fusion of ontology, epistemology and psychology is beginning to emerge. We are beginning a new age of awareness, the age of quantum consciousness, the age of the conscious atom.[23]

Niels Bohr's Principle of Complementarity

Light is particle-like with the photoelectric effect, that it is wave-like with the double-slit experiments and that is both particle-like and wave-like with Compton scattering. Both of these complementary aspects of light (wave and particle) are necessary to understand the nature of light. Wave-like and particle-like are properties of our interactions.

The mind has an in-built mechanism to make a quantum jump from the 'dimension of measure' to the 'dimension of value' and both are complementary to each other. The dimension of measure (objective information content) expresses itself as particle-like behaviour of thought. The dimension of value (subjective information content) expresses itself as wave-like behaviour, and both are complementary. The dimension of value is at a higher quantum energy potential than the dimension of measure. The wave-aspect is an expression at a higher quantum energy potential than that of particle-aspect. This deep understanding would radically alter the level of expression of consciousness of the observer, reorientating it toward a perception of the 'unbroken' of which everything is a form. An understanding of the psychodynamics of mind-brain-body system results in a journey from intellectual entrenchment to intellectual openness; it leads to a quantum leap beyond rationality and simultaneously activates the unconditioned energy, the Fundamental Vibration. It leads to a quantum jump from symbolic-dualistic mind to non-dual mind.[24]

A Global Ethic

Today we perceive that what exists in time which is irreversible, and that what exists outside of time which is eternal, so the outer and the inner are a unitary movement, a single dynamic flow. Ilya Prigogine wrote, "Today we know that time is a construction and therefore carries an ethical responsibility".

The Union of Concerned Scientists–over 1670 scientists, including 104 Nobel laureates–sent "*World Scientists' Warning to Humanity*" in April 1993; which concluded:

> A new ethic is required–a new attitude towards discharging our responsibility for caring for ourselves and for the earth. We must recognize the earth's limited capacity to provide for us. We must recognize its fragility. We must no longer allow it to be ravaged. This ethic must motivate a great movement, convincing reluctant leaders and reluctant governments and reluctant peoples themselves to effect the needed changes.[25]

The 1993 Parliament of the World's Religions met in Chicago and issued "A Global Ethic", and concluded:

> Earth cannot be changed for the better unless the consciousness of individuals is changed first .... This transformation must also be achieved in the areas of ethics and values![26]

The 1993 Parliament of World's Religions wrote, "An ethic already exists within the religious teachings of the world which can encounter the global distress .... The basis for a global ethic–a minimal fundamental consensus binding values, irrevocable standards, and fundamental moral attitudes .... that rights without morality cannot long endure and that there will be no better global order without a global ethics .... We trust that our often millennia-old religious ethical traditions provide an ethic which is convincing and practicable for all women and men of good will, religious and non-religious". Sri Aurobindo stated, "The assertion of a higher than the mental life is the very foundation of Indian culture as of yoga". His philosophy of culture is not static, past-oriented or other-worldly. On the contrary, it is emphatically futuristic, holistic and evolutionary: "a new power and powers of consciousness would be an inevitable consequence of its evolution passing beyond mind to a superior cognitive and dynamic principle".[27]

The foundation of human values must be independent of repetitive and mechanistic dynamics of the conditioned mind. Love, truth, freedom, peace, and so on are the spiritual values and these express themselves when thought-time is transcended, and intelligence is activised. Thought expresses its true subjective nature as values in a non-dual frame of reference. Values are the implicate order of thought, the subjective nature of thought, the wave-aspect of thought, the true nature of thought, the content of consciousness. The declaration of Global Ethic or the Universal Declaration of Human Values is as under:

> **Global ethic is defined as the perception in a non-dual frame of reference of the mind spectrum. It is the foundation of all ethical and spiritual values. The universal declaration leading to the emergence of global ethic constitutes a call to mankind that human mind must make a quantum jump from dualistic frame to non-dual frame of reference of mind spectrum. And one who is wholly consecrated to Truth, who wants to live the Truth, serve the Truth, would know at each moment the ethical values; it would be a kind of intuition or revelation or insight which would make you know the truth, the global ethic at every moment. To perceive the ethical values or global ethic, man has to make a quantum jump from psychosocial evolution to spiritual evolution.**[28]

The future of mankind is hinged on welding of Eastern Spirituality and Western Science, and out of that will emerge a new dimension of all-inclusive integral Consciousness that leads to ending of all human crisis, pain and misery, and bestows freedom, peace and bliss on human life. This is the only vocation of the human race.

Cosmic Consciousness

The New Dimension of Life: Many eminent physicists, neuro-physiologists, neuro-surgeons have talked of dynamic interplay of the objective and the subjective dimensions of life. Karl Pribram wrote, "Brain science must deal with the awareness of awareness. It could no longer afford to shut out that part of the world which we call subjective".[29] He added, "We are here in celebration of the paradigm shift". Roger Sperry spoke of the importance of a neglected area of science, namely the study of human subjective experience".[30] John Eccles also emphasizes the need to deal scientifically with the neglected area of inner conscious awareness.[31] The "second Copernican revolution" is the paradigm shift–importance of inner, subjective perception which is governed by values and meanings and one's own deep intuition–this immutable law of nature has been more and more openly shared.

We have to restructure science which takes in its realm the dynamic interplay of the subjective and the objective dimensions of science. Similarly we have to restructure education which takes in its fold the sensual and trans-sensual dimension. To sum up, we "restructure science-education", which encompasses the wholeness of life. This we call as the true-subject or non-variable subject, and it is at the highest quantum energy potential or highest frequency of Consciousness.

Here we meet a curious paradigm in our observation.[32] We observe the conditioned psyche from within nature by "restructured science-education"–(a) The I-consciousness is first knocked off because it is at the lowest quantum energy potential; it implies that the movement of thought-structure is independent of my volitions, it is independent of the ego; (b) When thought-structure comes in the field of true-subject, the photons meet an impregnable wall, called 'event horizon', and these photons cannot cross the wall and get annihilated; (c) If observation is continued for a long chronological time, the fact also goes to abeyance and pure Consciousness bathing the neurons is left behind; and (d) The pure Consciousness or Intelligence expresses as order, harmony, non-violence and peace. This is the consummation of human life.

Education: The Hon'ble President Dr A P J Abdul Kalam strongly advocated–on 58th Independence Day on August 15, 2004–a comprehensive overhaul of the education system.[33] We opine that the overhaul of education system implies an ethical responsibility. A mind that has set aside seeking in the future and has denied the past is an ethical mind. It refers to non-dual frame of reference of the Mind Continuum and it arises from the depth dimension of man. An ethical mind perceives the fact, "direct perception of actual fact".[33,34] We penned a paper on "Science and Value Education".[35]

Consciousness: Wigner wrote, "The measurement is not completed until its results enter our consciousness .... (this) last step is, at the present state of our knowledge, shrouded in the mystery and no explanation has been given for it so far in terms of quantum mechanics, or in terms of any other theory".[36] Hideki Yukawa wrote, "It is obvious that unless something rises into the consciousness it cannot become an object of rational thought, of rational consideration. At the same time, everyone will surely agree on the importance of an awareness that living in a world open towards both the exterior and the interior is a special characteristic of man's lot".[37] Herman Weyl wrote, "Scientists would be wrong to ignore the fact that theoretical construction is not the only approach to the phenomena of life; another way, that of understanding from within (interpretation), is open to us .... This inner awareness of myself is the basis for the understanding of my fellowmen".[38]

When "restructured science-education" or "non-variable awareness" observes a conditioned psyche for a long chronological time, one perceives pure Consciousness, and this is called that the perception rises in the Consciousness. David Bohm, an eminent physicist, said in a lecture in USA:

> The ultimate perception does not originate in the brain or any material structure, although a material structure is necessary to manifest it. The subtle mechanism of knowing the truth does not originate in the brain.[39]

The ultimate perception arises when Cosmic Consciousness bathes the brain cells; and the material structure of the brain is required for the expression of Consciousness.

Isidor Rabi wrote in prophetic words:

> I don't think that physics will ever have an end. I think that the novelty of nature is such that its variety will be infinite–not just in changing forms but in the profundity of insight and the newness of ideas.[40]

Stapp wrote in 1971:

> Human inquiry can continue indefinitely to yield important new truths.[41]

Max Planck, the father of quantum physics, wrote:

> Science .... means unresting endeavor and continually progressing development toward an aim which the poetic intuition may apprehend, but which the intellect can never fully grasp.[42]

G.F. Chew wrote:

> Our current struggle with [certain aspects of advanced physics] may thus be only a foretaste of a completely new form of human intellectual endeavor, one that will not only lie outside physics but will not even be describable as *scientific*.[43]

Gary Zukav stated, "We need not make a pilgrimage to India or Tibet. There is much to learn there, but here at home, in the most inconceivable of places, amidst the particle accelerators and computers, our own Path without Form is emerging".[44] The immutable law of nature is that the Dancer (Cosmic Consciousness) and the dance (expressions of Consciousness) are the same, and this is Eternal, Infinite and Immutable.

Concluding Comment

Every man's world picture is and always remains a construct of the mind at the lowest quantum energy potential of consciousness. When I-consciousness and thought-structure–which are conceptual worlds–encounters the "restructured science-education" or "non-variable awareness", or "true-subject", these conceptual structures go to abeyance; and Consciousness expresses Itself as order, harmony, nonviolence and peace.

We want a revolution, psychological revolution, in which the whole human race has to participate and every man is an equal partner. This revolution will regenerate or rejuvenate human mind so that it perceives the new dimension of "restructured science-education", that can guarantee human survival along with all fauna and flora.

Maurice H. Wilkins, Nobel Prize in Medicine, 1962, wrote, "I agree with Einstein that the sort of scientific education we have now has produced a narrow-minded way of thinking amongst scientists, so that they give no proper attention to the normal and psychological dimensions", and that this is leading mankind to self-annihilation.

The challenge is addressed not only to the structure of education but to the nature and quality of man's mind and life. This bestows "an understanding of life directly" and to live in the light of that feelingful understanding. This breaks through frontiers of particular cultures and establishes an entirely new set of values, which can create a new civilisation and a new society.

References

1. Sampooran Singh, Dr (Mrs) Kanwaljit Kaur, *Peace, Security and Survival: A Scientific Quest*, July 5, 2004, pp. 1-40.
2. Sampooran Singh, AVM Manjit Singh, Dr (Mrs) Kanwaljit Kaur & Paramjit Singh, *God in Science*, Chandigarh: Vishvas Publications Pvt. Ltd., July 1999, pp. 1, 2.
3. Julius Robert Oppenheimer, in Fritjof Capra, *The Tao of Physics* (*Second Ed.*), 1988, p. 4.
4. Niels Bohr, in Fritjof Capra, *ibid.*, p. 4.
5. Werner Heisenberg, *ibid.*, p. 4.
6. Fritjof Capra, *op. cit.*, p. 5.
7. Gary Zukav, *The Dancing Wu Li Masters*, Fontana/Collins, 1982.
8. Joan Walton, *Scientists Tune into Consciousness*, New Science, Winter 1996.
9. Spencer Brown, *Laws of Form*, New York: Julian Press, 1972, pp. 104-05.
10. R.P. Kaushik, *Towards a New Consciousness*, Delhi: Darshan Yoga Sansthan, 1974, p. 63.

11. J.W.N. Sullivan, *The Limitations of Science*, New York: Mentor Books, 1949, p. 140.
12. E.N. da C. Andrade, *An Approach to Modern Physics*, New York: Doubleday Anchor Books, 1957, p. 255.
13. D.S. Kothari, *Some Thoughts on Science and Religion*, University of Delhi, 31.10.1977 and 03.11.1977, p. 25.
14. George Wald, in *Synthesis of Science and Religion*, Mumbai: The Bhaktivedanta Institute, June 1988, p. 19.
15. Erwin Schrodinger, *What is Life*? & *Mind and Matter*, London: Cambridge University Press, 1967 (Ed.), p. 128.
16. Ilya Prigogine and Isabelle Stengers, *Order Out of Chaos*, Bantam Books, 1984, pp. 5, 312.
17. D.S. Kothari, *The Perception of Truth in Science and Philosophy*, in *The Odyssey of Science, Culture and Consciousness*, New Delhi: Abhinav Publications, 1990, pp. 48-49.
18. *ibid., Some Thoughts on Science and Religion, op. cit.*, p. 33.
19. *ibid., Atom and Self*, in *Evolution of Consciousness*, New Delhi: National Publishing House, 1983, p. 227.
20. Maurice H. Wilkins, in *Synthesis of Science and Religion, op. cit.*, pp. 31, 35.
21. D.S. Kothari, *Atom and Self, op. cit.*, p. 212.
22. *ibid., Some Thoughts on Science and Religion, op. cit.*, p. 25.
23. Richard Feynman, in Fred Alan Wolf, *Taking the Quantum Leap*, San Francisco: Harper and Row, 1981, pp. 228, 248.
24. Sampooran Singh, *A Renwed Look at the Wave-Particle Complementarity in the Light of Mind-Brain Interactions*, Bulletin of the Theosophy Science Study Group, India, June-August 1988, Vol. 26, Nos. 3 and 4, pp. 35-37; & New Delhi: Books India International, 1999, pp. 82-87.
25. Union of Concerned Scientists, *World Scientists' Warning to Humanity*, USA, April 1993.
26. 1993 Parliament of the World's Religions, Chicago, *A Global Ethic*, August 28-September 5, 1993.
27. Sisirkumar Ghose, *Consciousness and Culture*, in *The Evolution of Consciousness*, *op. cit.*, p. 183.
28. Sampooran Singh, *Science, Human Values, Value Education and Peace*, New Delhi: NM & NWM, 1993, pp. i-xiv, 1-90.
29. Karl Pribram, in Ken Wilber, *The Holographic Paradigm and Other Paradoxes*, Shambhala, 1982, pp. 17, 25.
30. Roger Sperry, in *Synthesis of Science and Religion, op. cit.*, p. 199
31. John Eccles, in *ibid.*, pp. 199-200.
32. Sampooran Singh, Dr (Mrs) Kanwaljit Kaur, *Peace, Security and Survival*? : *A Scientific Quest*, July 5, 2004, pp. 1-40.

33. President Dr Abdul Kalam, *The Tribune*, August 15, 2004.
34. Sampooran Singh, Dr (Mrs) Kanwaljit Kaur & Paramjit Singh, *Global Value Education*, Chandigarh: Faith Publishers, January 2001, pp. i-xii, 1-116.
35. Sampooran Singh, *Science and Value Education*, unpublished.
36. E.P. Wigner, in D.S. Kothari, *Some Thoughts on Science and Consciousness*, *op. cit.*, p. 26.
37. Hideki Yukawa, *Creativity and Intuition*, Tokyo: Kodansha International Ltd., 1973, p. 203.
38. Herman Weyl, in Ilya Prigogine, *op. cit.*, pp. 311, 312.
39. David Bohm, *Lecture on April 6, 1977*, University of California, Berkeley, in Gary Zukav, *op. cit.*, p. 327.
40. Isidor Rabi, *Profiles–Physicist, II*, The New Yorker Magazine, October 20, 1975.
41. H. Stapp, in Gary Zukav, *op. cit.*, p. 329.
42. Max Planck, in Gary Zukav, *ibid.*, p. 331.
43. G.F. Chew, in Gary Zukav, *ibid.*, p. 331.
44. Gary Zukav, *ibid.*, p. 331.

10

A Quantum Jump from Violence to Non-violence

The Ending of Terrorism and Other Challenges

Abstract

Violence is a construct by symbolic-dualistic frame of reference of conditioned psyche. Non-violence is a percept in the non-dual and non-conceptual frame of reference in the Mind Continuum. When the restructured "science-education-health" observes the cause of psychological immaturity, all I-consciousness (ego) and thought-structure go to abeyance; or in other words, the symbolic-dualistic frame makes a quantum jump to non-dual and non-conceptual frame of reference of Mind Continuum.

The root of all human challenges – psychological imbalances, ecological crisis, terrorism, corruption, and so on – is embedded in the conditioned psyche, so it is only higher quantum energy potential of Cosmic Consciousness that can end these challenges. One has to be alert, sensitive and attentive. In attentiveness, the Intelligence is energised which brings in mutation or radical transformation of the human psyche. Intelligence sublimates the human challenges.

Modern physics has confirmed that every man's world picture is and always remains a construct of his mind; or in other words, the world extended in space and time is but our representation. Man started living in the *external* objective world and neglected the *inner* subjective world and this has resulted in our construction of a violent and aggressive world.

Man (*Homo sapiens*) has an evolutionary origin at about 2.5 million years ago. We have built a society which is violent, and we, as human beings, are violent; the environment, the culture, in which we live is the product of our struggle, of our pain, of our appalling brutalities. The psychological imbalances, ecological crisis, pollution challenges, a rising wave of violence and crime, terrorism, religious fundamentalism, ethnic conflicts, corruption, increasing unemployment, poverty, hunger, malnutrition, health crisis, are stored in the neuro-chemical system (frequency and amplitude information) over uncountable aeons; and are forcing man inevitably to face the realities of the human situation. All appeals to achieve full disarmament and permanent peace; all declarations by Nobel laureates; all appeals by Pugwash Conferences (since 1957); all appeals by the International Physicians for the Prevention of Nuclear War (IPPNW); by Secretaries-General of the United Nations (Dag Hammarskjold, U. Thant, Javier Perez de Cuellar); all proclamations of a manifesto by eminent scientists, philosophers, mystics have fallen on the deaf ears of mankind. During the last 10,000 years, or more, man invented innumerable techniques, systems, beliefs, concepts, thought-structures, but all have proved to be sterile in mutation of his psyche, and man has miserably failed.

All intellectual approaches have led to modification of the external world, it is a transient and superficial change. It adds to materialism, acquisition, greed, competition, prestige and power. ***The basic challenge facing mankind is mutation or radical transformation of the psyche***, but so far man has not touched even the fringes of human challenges.

Indu Jain, an eminent philosopher-mystic, published two articles entitled, "A Ministry of Non-Violent Defence" and also emphasized that "Hatred and fear are our true adversaries".[1] The secret of non-violent defence is embedded in Mahatma Gandhi's teaching of Ahimsa, or in Jainism, ahimsa is the supreme principle. Ahimsa is pure selfless love for every human being and indeed for every living creature. Ahimsa is non-violence in thought, word and deed (action). Gandhiji says, "Non-violence is the law of the human race and is infinitely greater than and superior to brute force .... Non-violence affords the fullest protection to one's self-respect and sense of honour". In the hands of Mahatma Gandhi, ahimsa–the sword of self-suffering–became a mighty instrument of large-scale social and political change and colonial emancipation.

We have built a society which is violent and we, as human beings, are violent. This article investigates the emergence of violence in the light of recent discoveries in science. The conditionings of human psyche are leading man to self-destruction. The human survival is at stake. Further, the basic cause of violence is that mind splits itself into the subject and the object, due to energy interaction, man has the awareness of distorted perception, and he thus lives in illusion. This article explores the ending of violence, which is in the direction of survival of man.

The Emergence of Violence

For the last three decades, modern science is investigating violence and non-violence in the human psyche. Violence is a construct by common waking state of mind, the symbolic-dualistic frame of reference of mind spectrum, which is at the lowest quantum energy potential of successive consciousness or the lowest frequency of consciousness. Violence is an indication of psychological immaturity.[2]

Man has lived in conflict from time immemorial. Man's psychosocial evolution, over uncounted aeons, has led to storing of subtle matter content as frequency and amplitude information, and this is called the cultural belief structure, or conditioning of the human psyche, or psychic pandemic, or memory. It is unstable and spontaneously disintegrates to thought coupled with its volitions or motives. Thought-time constructs the time-space matrices in quick succession, or the sensual world. Man has started living in the sensual world, man-made social cosmos, or a synthetic world. His mode of living is divorced from the Reality, the Cosmic Consciousness, the Truth. He is aware of the *non-fact*, the *false*, the *past*, the *what should be*?, or in other words, he has started living in a set of illusions. The whole mankind is caught unknowingly in a crisis of perception. The thought-time constructs all psychological imbalances– violence, greed, fear, anger, and so on.

The symbolic-dualistic frame of reference of mind spectrum is at the lowest quantum energy potential of consciousness (or lower frequency) than the non-dual and non-conceptual frame of reference (higher frequency) of Mind Continuum. The symbolic-dualistic frame records only violence. All records are of disturbance. The silence cannot be recorded as it is a happening in the non-dual frame of reference. Whenever someone becomes really silent, he disappears from all records, he is no more a part of our madness.

Jonas Salk wrote, "While violence may be wholly pathological in origin, it may also be a manifestation of resistance and of an attempt to correct unhealthy extremes of excess or of greed inimical to the health of the species and therefore of individuals as well". He added, "Will man become a package of pathology or remain a package of potentials? It would seem more worthwhile to learn to devote one's life to the development of potential rather than to nursing pathology". He added, "We need to become increasingly conscious of the whole of which we are a part, as a species, so that we may function fully, through individually, and in a more healthier as an element in that whole".[3]

The Recent Challenges

The psychological imbalances, ecological crisis are at least 20,000 to 30,000 years old. The recent challenges are terrorism, corruption, religious fundamentalism, ethnic conflicts, drug trafficking, have erupted during the last few decades.[4] Every world leader talks of tackling (say terrorism) at the international level. We opine that the brute force available with

Governments will temporarily suppress the terrorism, which means that terrorism at the conscious level will be suppressed, but the seeds of terrorism will go from conscious level to deep subconscious level and terrorism may erupt at any time any where in the world. Ending of terrorism and other challenges is only possible by mutation of the human psyche and we have to work *here* and *now*, and not *tomorrow*.

Non-violence is a percept in the non-dual and non-conceptual frame of reference in the Mind Continuum. When the "restructured science-education" observes the cause of psychological immaturity, all I-consciousness (ego) and thought-structure go to abeyance; or in other words, the symbolic-dualistic frame makes a quantum jump to non-dual and non-conceptual frame of reference of Mind Continuum. Due to shortage of space the details are not discussed in this article.

Peace is a total way of living. As long as there is inherent violence in the human psyche, there can never be peace in the world. Order, harmony, non-violence and peace require the mutation, or radical transformation, or holistic revolution. It is only holistic education that helps man to grow from knowledge to understanding, from confrontation to cooperation, from rationality to intuition, from intellect to Intelligence.

The world will have to tackle these challenges at two levels:

(a) The challenges are not political, nor economic, nor social; but are evolutionary in nature. Man is treating the symptoms in the external field through socio-political-economic reforms. These may lead to postponement of crisis, but it has no capacity to end the crisis.

    Expedient measures to meet the present challenges are intellectual constructions. These may partially ameliorate human suffering. These measures will be transient and temporary and ephemeral. The expedient measures are already approved by different countries.

(b) Permanent measures are to heal the diseased human psyche, or to work for radical transformation of human psyche. D.S. Kothari, an eminent physicist, quoted Buddha in words, "What the Buddha proclaimed about the imperative need to ***know*** the mind, to ***shape*** the mind, and to ***liberate*** the mind has never been more true than in the Age of the Atom". Permanent measures bring mutation in the human psyche. These lead to quantum jump from symbolic-dualistic frame to non-dual frame of Mind Continuum; and it bestows intuition and spontaneity.[5]

The root of all human challenges–psychological imbalances, ecological crisis, terrorism, corruption, and so on–is embedded in the conditioned psyche, so it is only higher quantum energy potential of Cosmic

Consciousness that can end these challenges. One has to be alert, sensitive and attentive. In attentiveness, the Intelligence is energised which brings in mutation or radical transformation of the human psyche. Intelligence sublimates the human challenges.

The Human Survival

(a) Many eminent scientists–including Albert Einstein, Werner Heisenberg, Erwin Schrodinger, Arthur Eddington–have stumbled upon another mode of knowing, called direct, or intimate, or insight, or intuition, or "the understanding of life directly, instead of in the abstract, linear terms of representational thinking". The non-variable attentivity, or reaction-free attentivity, or objectless attention takes over as the subject–this is called a Mind with a scientific temper, it is tuned to perceive the *fact*, the *true*, the *present*, the *what is*! This reveals the psychodynamics and limitations of the conditioned psyche, the conditionings go to abeyance, and it bestows a perception of intuition and spontaneity. This leads to "the understanding of life directly, instead of in the abstract, linear terms of representational thinking".

(b) Jonas Salk stated, "There is increasing awareness of the distinction between the relationship of the subjective and the objective, the non-rational and the rational, the unconscious and the conscious .... (There is) a need for the development and use both of the intuitive and the intellectual capacities of the mind in a unified and balanced way .... Man needs to become increasingly conscious of the whole of which we are a part, as a species, so that we may function fully, through individually, and in a more helpful way as an element in that whole".[6]

(c) Max Born wrote, "Clever, rational ways of thinking are not enough. The danger of mass slaughter .... can only be overcome by moral conviction, by a determination to replace national prides and prejudices with human love".[7] Hideki Yukawa wrote, "Abstract thought .... could not work by itself. It always presupposed the presence of the power of intuition".[8] Weisskopf quoted Yukawa in words, "How difficult is the task of turning the age-old tide of human ambition and aggression .... (There is) the large gap between the superhuman task and the frailties of human endeavours, even if they are done with the best of intentions".[9]

(d) Fred Alan Wolf wrote, "We are beginning a new age of awareness, the age of quantum consciousness, the age of the conscious atom. By looking within ourselves, we may be able to solve the problems facing us on the final frontier–the frontier of the human spirit". He added, "Since atoms with consciousness are looking at atoms with consciousness, we have the same experience of wonder and mystery whenever we look at the universe. We are looking at ourselves. It is this process that we call the universe .... It (Consciousness) performs a dual role in the universe. In the world of the quantum, it is both the awareness and the creation of experience. It is the *being* and the *knowing* of experience. With the stroke of the twentieth-century quantum eraser, the dividing line between ontology (theory of being) and epistemology (theory of knowing) is rubbed out".[10] The fusion of ontology, epistemology and psychology is beginning to emerge.

(e) In 1996, Russian scientists postulated the idea of "*A Life Field* beyond our physical concepts of time, space and the known electromagnetic and gravitational fields". In another Conference at Cambridge, scientists stated, "A new scientific approach would include subjective experience as valid information and address all forms of human experience–including intuition, spirituality and mystical encounters".[11] The concept of Life Field is synonymous to that of Universal Consciousness or *Brahman* in "Indian Cultural Heritage". This has brought mankind on the control panel of transformation of human psyche.

(f) Richard Lamm, Former Governor of Colorado, quoted Stuart Udall, and said, "The whole human enterprise is a machine without brakes, for there are no indications that the world's political leaders will deal with the realities until catastrophes occur .... We have already passed the point of no return, and tragic convulsions are at hand".[12]

(g) Recently many eminent scientists--say Karl Pribram, Roger Sperry, John Eccles have opined that "brain science .... could no longer afford to shut out that part of the world which we call subjective". The objective (outer) and the subjective (inner) are one, a unitary movement, not separate, but whole. Similarly education deals with the sensual world and the trans-sensual world. We have to "restructure science-education", which takes in its fold both the objective and the subjective dimensions of life, which we call as true subject. When thought-structure coupled with volitions encounters true subject, the thought structure goes to abeyance. This leads to a quantum jump from violence to non-violence, from intellect to intuition. It resolves all human challenges.

To sum up, man is an amphibian who lives simultaneously in two worlds–(a) the time-space-causation matrices, the objective world, an indirect process, a cerebral process in the field of duality, the successive consciousness, the symbolic-dualistic frame of reference of mind spectrum; and (b) the realm of silence, or no-mind, the subjective world, the Simultaneous Consciousness, the non-dual and non-conceptual frame of reference of Mind Continuum, it has the capacity of direct perception of Reality. The human survival is embedded in a quantum jump from symbolic-dualistic frame of reference of mind spectrum to non-dual and non-conceptual frame of Mind Continuum, or in other words, a quantum jump from indirect process to direct understanding of life. The observation by true subject energises Intelligence, which ends all human challenges, and man revels in order, harmony, non-violence and peace.

Spirituality

Meditation is the essence of spirituality. It is an inner mutation. It is the by-product of being in the dimension of silence. As regards meditation, no techniques, practices, formulae are possible.

We have to educate our physical organism and psychological structure so that we make a quantum jump from action to non-action (silence or stillness)–gradually, voluntarily. It becomes a dance of effort and effortlessness, action and relaxation, relationship and solitude, speech and silence–they get blended into one whole. A new balanced human being, who has no imbalances, and therefore no impurities, but who has a grandeur of inner equipoise and a majesty of outer sensual balance, comes into our life. In the state of silence, it is the Intelligence that takes over the charge of our being. This guarantees human survival.

The Action Plan to End Violence

The Action Plan is discussed in an article entitled "Science and Value Education". The permanent measures, to heal the diseased human psyche, are as under:

(a) To educate the educator is to have him understand himself. This is one of the most difficult undertakings, because most of us are already crystallized within a system of thought or a pattern of action. The teachers training programme is *how to think* and not *what to think*.

(b) We have to introduce psychodynamics of mind-brain-body system in science faculty and transpersonal psychology in art faculty as a part of educational curriculum at University/College level.

(c) We have to share through open dialogues the psychodynamics of conditioned mind and the dimension of Consciousness. The aim of these dialogues is "exploration of a spiritually inspired understanding of life" and "holistic living".

(d) To conduct courses at the level of research scholars at doctoral level or post-graduate level especially in the science faculties of different universities.

(e) We have to publish new books on Wholeness of Life; to share this knowledge and initiate a dialogue with an open mind with every man on the globe; and open a global research institute–say "*Centre for Scientific Research on Human Survival and Excellence*"–preferably under the auspices of the United Nations. This will lead to a global paradigm shift.

Concluding Comment

We want a psychological revolution, in which the whole human race has to participate and every man is an equal partner. This collective psychological experiment will awaken the integral and all-inclusive dimension of Consciousness and that can guarantee human survival along with all fauna and flora.

The essence of the masterplan is: (a) ***Restructuring of Science;*** (b) ***Restructuring of Education;*** (c) ***Awareness of Human Values***; and (d) ***Living in the Light of that Feelingful Understanding.*** The answer to the human challenges or a quantum jump from violence to Non-violence is a "Symbiosis of Science and Spirituality"

The world's awareness of our psyche is appalling–we talk and talk without moving a finger to understand oneself. The Prime Minister Dr Manmohan Singh said very rightly at the United Nations General Assembly on September 23, 2004, "We speak about cooperation but seem hesitant to commit ourselves to a global offensive to root out terrorism" and other global challenges (say, psychological imbalances). The *universal disarmament*, *international security order* and *peace* can only flow from the mutation or psychological transformation of the human psyche. There is an urgency to resolve human challenges. The three-pronged cardinal principles to resolve the paradox are as under:

(a) Let every human being look (observe) himself;

(b) The Order of the universe is order of his own mind!;

(c) The innate intuition is to live in peace!

We have to educate our physical organism and psychological structure–it implies to introduce–the anatomy of mind, the physics of consciousness, the biology of cognition, the chemistry of thought in our educational structure. It is observation of the conditioned psyche by attentivity.

If true subject (*restructured science-education*) observes the conditioned psyche and Unconditioned Energy, the I-consciousness and thought-structure go to abeyance, and pure Consciousness bathing the brain cells (neurons) remains. It implies that the Cosmic Consciousness or Cosmic Intelligence takes over the charge of our being, which expresses itself as order, harmony, non-violence and peace.

Those who hear the voice of sanity, clarity and intuition, they understand the non-authoritative approach of spiritual enquiry–which includes: (a) to educate as the way of causing mutation or radical transformation of the psyche; (b) to investigate the conditioned psyche, (c) to explore the Unconditioned Energy–through observation by "restructured science-education". This energises Intelligence, which resolves all human challenges and survival of mankind. This is the consummation of human life.

If man escapes his responsibility, he does so at his own peril, of India and mankind.

References

1. Indu Jain, *The Times of India*, September 21, 2004.
2. Sampooran Singh, (a) *Non-Violence and Relationship to Meet the Challenges to Mankind*, 1988; (b) *The Ending of Violence and the Beginning of Peace*, 1994; and (c) *The Survival of Mankind and Quantum Jump from Violence to Peace*, 1999, New Delhi: Books India International, 1999, pp. 219-327.
3. Jonas Salk, *Man Unfolding*, New Delhi: Allied Publishers Private Limited, 1972, pp. 117, 111, Cover Jacket.
4. Sampooran Singh, Dr (Mrs) Kanwaljit Kaur and Paramjit Singh, *The Masterplan Paradigm for Human Survival and Excellence*, Chandigarh: Faith Publishers, February 1998, pp. 130-159.
5. *ibid.*, *Global Values Education*, *ibid.*, January 2001, p. 104.
6. Jonas Salk, *op. cit.*, pp. 107, 111, 112, Cover Jacket.
7. Max Born, in Hideki Yukawa, *Creativity and Intuition*, Tokyo: Kodansha International Ltd., 1973, pp. 189-190.
8. Hideki Yukawa, *ibid.*, p. 101.
9. Victor F. Weisskopf, in *Introduction* to Hideki Yukawa, *ibid.*, p. 13.
10. Fred Alan Wolf, *Taking the Quantum Leap*, San Francisco: Harper and Row, 1981, pp. 248, 228, 229.
11. Joan Walton, *Scientists Tune into Consciousness*, New Science, Winter 1996.
12. Richard Lamm, Former Governor of Colorado, in Michael Burghley, *My World, My Responsibility*, Canada: Foundation House Publication, 1987, p. 10.

11

The Resolution of Human Paradox

The Ending of Human Challenges

Abstract

Thinking is the response of memory, which is your accumulated knowledge, experience and background. Thought lives in dualistic field. It is the old and can never bring about freedom. It is indirect, which causes a crisis of perception.

We see that all knowledge (information), thought structures, ideals, beliefs, concepts are sterile in transforming the psyche of man, or in other words, to bring radical transformation or mutation in the human psyche.

Nature has embedded in man a new dimension – called "understanding of life directly", or intuition (insight). We have to renounce – indirect (thinking) – and understand to live in direct communion with nature. We have to transcend I-consciousness and thought-structure, and imbibe to live in the realm of Intelligence.

Nature invariably expresses Itself as *pure perception*, or *mirror-image of Reality*, or the *fact*, or the *true*, or the *present*, or the *what is*! Seeing is direct, hearing is direct, touching is direct; understanding is direct, learning is direct; but thinking is indirect. The quantum logic deals with direct perception.

Thinking is a playback of thought coupled with feeling and response of the memory–cultural, racial, religious, communal–which is called willing. There is coherent superpositions of different webs of thought on the direct perception, and this flows to distorted perception due to exchange of energy between direct perception and the recalled memory. Thinking invariably ends in distorted perception, which is an illusion, a *non-fact*, the *false*, the *past* or *future projection*, the *what should be*! It gives fragmentary experience and partial knowledge, and are amenable to rational logic. Willing flows to reaction. These conditionings have been organised and standardized. We are conditioned cerebrally, neurologically, chemically to react to situations in a specific way. To be aware of the dynamics, conditionings and limitations of the conditioned psyche is called self-knowledge.

Thinking always leads to knowing of experience and knowledge, which are stored in the human psyche as cultural belief structures, or cultural dissipative structures. These are meta-stable structures and disintegrate to thought-structures. Thinking is always indirect. Thinking is always "*about something*". Thinking can never give perception of reality, or in other words, it always misses the reality. "*About*" becomes a barrier between you and the reality, *about* always leads to illusion.

Thinking is not a natural process, it is a man-made construction for his convenience, it constructs time-space-causation matrices and expresses that in words, in language. It is at the lowest quantum energy potential of successive consciousness. All conscious energy dealing with thinking is a waste. Man made an error some 30,000 to 40,000 years ago to introduce thinking–it is double crises of civilization and higher and higher expression of consciousness–man never looked and examined his error, in spite of the fact that this crises has led him to pain, misery, duality, conflict, fragmentation.

The immutable law of nature is to "live in peace" and "survival of human species", and this is creating an inner urge in man to transcend I-consciousness and thought-structure. What is needed is "awareness plus action". The human paradox is to transcend (to renounce) thinking and be aware of "awareness plus action". When thought-structure is transcended, the conscious energy of thought will make a quantum jump to higher quantum energy potential of consciousness; or in other words, thought-energy or energy going into thinking becomes energy of awareness. The non-dual and non-conceptual frame revels in energy of awareness.

When I-consciousness and thought-structure are transcended, the symbolic-dualistic frame of reference of mind spectrum makes a quantum jump to non-dual and non-conceptual frame of reference of Mind Continuum; or in other words, self-knowledge makes a quantum jump to self-awareness, and all action emerge from the state of awareness. It implies that we have to renounce (jettison or transcend) thinking and imbibe action which is free from duality and conflict.

Thinking has to be stopped, but not by becoming unconscious (say by sleep or drugs); but by becoming more conscious, alert, aware, so that the energy that is moving in thinking makes a quantum jump to a higher quantum energy potential of consciousness, and a witnessing arises in you, which bestows intuition or insight. The subject (awareness) witness the object and is aware of the *fact*, the *true*, the *present*, the *what is*!

Perception has nothing to do with knowledge (information). The ultimate perception does not originate in the brain, or any other material structure, although a material structure (brain) is necessary to maintain it. When Cosmic Consciousness bathes the brain cells (neurons), a true perception, which is mirror-image of Reality, is born. The perceptions are born of non-duality and responses are born of spontaneity. It awakens the awareness, the intelligence, which arise out of observation, self-knowing and compassion.

Intuition or insight is the timeless perception. It is insight alone that can decondition the brain. Insight is complete and from that completeness there can be logical, sane and rational action. Only then there can be flowering of the brain. Pure clear insight is perception without any doubt. ***Understanding, learning and action are a cyclic process, which results in a spiral going upwards in the vertical dimension; it is a growth in the vertical dimension.*** The higher the understanding, the higher the expression of the Consciousness in the human brain-body system.

The Resolution of Human Paradox

Many eminent scientists–including Albert Einstein, Werner Heisenberg, Erwin Schrodinger, Arthur Eddington–have stumbled upon another mode of knowing, called direct, or intimate, or intuition or insight, or "the understanding of life directly, instead of in the abstract, linear terms of representational thinking". It is evident that these scientists were revelling in the *wholeness* of life and they perceived the truth as direct perception. The subject was non-variable consciousness, or reaction-free attentivity, or objectless attention and they perceived the object as the *fact*. This reveals the psychodynamics which are limitations of the conditioned psyche; the conditionings go to abeyance and it bestows a perception of intuition and spontaneity. The pure perception bestows non-violence, harmony, human values, truth, love and compassion, as it is in communion with Universal Consciousness, the Life Field.

Karl Pribram, an eminent neuroscientist, wrote, "Brain science must deal with the awareness of awareness. It could no longer afford to shut out that part of the world which we call subjective". Roger Sperry spoke of the importance of a neglected area of science, namely the study of human subjective experience". John Eccles also corroborated Sperry's conclusion. This suggests that the outer (objective) and the inner (subjective) are not two separate movements. The outer and the inner are one, a unitary movement, not separate, but whole. The society we have created is the outer; a signal from the outer goes to the inner for recalling the past memory; the inner responds and goes to the outer where energy interaction happens; and this happens in few millionth of a second. This has been the way of life; a life of constant pain and pleasure. This suggests that we have to restructure science so that it takes in its ambient the objective and the subjective dimensions of life. Similarly, we have to restructure the sensual world so that it takes in its fold the trans-sensual dimension of life. The true-subject is "restructured science-education". This deals with the wholeness of life.

When thought-structure comes in the field of the true-subject, it knocks down the I-consciousness because it is at the lowest quantum energy potential of consciousness. If observation is continued over a long chronological time, the thought structure also goes to abeyance and pure consciousness bathes the brain cells which expresses Itself as order, harmony, non-violence and peace. This also is a sure guarantee for human survival and excellence.

Concluding Comment

We see that all knowledge (information), thought structures, ideals, beliefs, concepts are sterile in transforming the psyche of man, or in other words, to bring radical transformation or mutation in the human psyche.

Many eminent scientists–including Albert Einstein, Werner Heisenberg, Erwin Schrodinger, Arthur Eddington–have stumbled upon another mode of knowing, called direct, or intimate, or insight, or intuition, or "the understanding of life directly, instead of in the abstract, linear terms of representational thinking".

It is the integral dimension of Consciousness that can resolve all challenges facing mankind. It is to heal the diseased mind-brain-body system. It is an open call to express higher hierarchical level of expression of consciousness eloquently through restructured science and restructured education for a global society, rising civilisation and our daily living in freedom, peace and bliss. This is the only guarantee to human survival and excellence.

The "restructured science-education" is fundamental for constructing a sane society and the perception of the highest quantum energy potential of Cosmic Consciousness (Life Field, Absolute Subjectivity, *Brahman*). It resolves all human challenges facing mankind, and ushers in a new era of non-violence, peace and bliss.

The essence of life and living or the resolution of human paradox is summed up in words:

There is nothing in man that is his own!

Nature has embedded in him a new dimension–called "understanding of life directly", or intuition (insight).

We have to renounce–indirect (thinking)–and understand to live in direct communion with nature.

We have to transcend I-consciousness and thought-structure, and imbibe to live in the realm of Intelligence.

Everything is determined by the immutable laws of nature.

Everything is prearranged, everything is a necessary effect!

Man is only a puppet, someone else (Intelligence) pulls the strings.

Man is a toy in the hands of destiny.

Man has the capacity to make a quantum jump from symbolic-dualistic frame to non-dual frame and then live in pure perception. In pure perception, there is order, harmony, non-violence and peace.

12

Science, Education, Peace and Consciousness

Abstract

Consciousness expresses itself at hierarchical quantum energy potentials which are psychological mode of mind, the scientific mode of mind, and technology of mutation in the Consciousness. The mutation will bring about a new culture. This leads to order, harmony, non-violence, peace and survival.

All ethical/spiritual values proceed from the trans-sensual dimension of human personality, the Life Field, these self-emerge from the dimension of the wholeness of life, the restructured science-education dimension of life. The values express themselves in the non-dual frame of reference of Mind Continuum.

The dimensions of "restructured science-education-health" are subjective realm and objective field – where the subjective realm is the true-subject of cognizance, the true-observer, and the objective field is that is observed. The self-observation of the conditioned psyche (object, observed) are within the observed world; or in other words, it opens a dialogue with nature when this is carried on from within nature. Both subjective and objective are "in-here", that is participators in nature.

Mankind can survive only if the disorder, or violence, or psychological imbalances end in our consciousness. And this happens when restructured "science-education-health" takes over as the true subject. It is the Life Field or Quantum Field Consciousness (QFC) that can lead to survival of mankind.

Science is the search for truth in the objective world, the 'without'. A selfless, unfaltering devotion to truth and the use of knowledge for man's upliftment are the ideals of a scientist. Truth is what all earnest scientists seek. Free enquiry, objectivity, precision, autonomy, freedom, experience are the pillars of the inductive (experimental data) and deductive (theoretical) logic. Discovery is its mission, its perception. It is precise, clear, unprejudiced, which does not condemn, which observes, which sees. It moves from fact to fact.

There is a growing realisation that the basic postulates of the educational structure and its various systems in India and in the rest of the world have failed and that there is total lack of relevance between the human being and the complex contemporary society. The present education trains the mind in the continuation of the past. We are being educated to conform, to fit into a society and their culture, to fit into the stream of social and economic activity, and to fit into the existing political system. Understanding comes only when self-knowledge through self-observation makes a quantum jump to self-awareness. It is awareness of one's total psychological process. Education in the true sense is helping the individual to be mature and free, to flower greatly in love and goodness. The highest function of education is to bring about an integrated individual who is capable of dealing with life as a whole. Education is a way of discovering our true relationship to things, to other human beings, and to nature. Education encourages us to think freely without fear, that helps us to enquire and understand.

The UN was successful in postponing major wars and to achieve transient peace, but was unsuccessful in ending war and violence and achieve sustainable peace. Toward the end of his mandate, Dag Hammarskjold declared, "I see no hope for permanent world peace. We have tried but failed miserably. Unless the world has a spiritual rebirth, civilization is doomed". We have to ask ourselves the question, "Whither are we going?".

President Vaclav Havel, Czech Republic, addressing the US Congress in 1990 said, "Without a global revolution in the sphere of human consciousness, nothing will change for the better in our being as human".[1] The racial conditioning and our present way of living is leading us to self-destruction, or self-annihilation.

Erwin Schrodinger states, "While the stuff from which our world picture is built is yielded exclusively from the sense organs as organs of the mind, so that every man's world picture is and always remains a construct of the mind and cannot be proved to have any other existence".[2] Arthur Eddington wrote:

> The stuff of the world is mind-stuff .... The mind-stuff is not spread in space and time .... Recognizing that the physical world is entirely abstract and without "actuality" apart from its linkage to consciousness, we restore consciousness to the fundamental position.[3]

The world is us and we are the world. The world extended in space and time is but our representation. Our consciousness has two capacities– the *known*, the successive consciousness, the time-space matrices, and the other is the *Unknown*, the Simultaneous Consciousness.

This article discusses the psychological mode of mind, the scientific mode of mind, and technology of mutation in the Consciousness. The mutation will bring about a new culture. This leads to order, harmony, non-violence, peace and survival.

Psychological Mode of Mind

Homo Homonid had an evolutionary origin at about 4.5 million years ago, and *Homo sapien* at about 2.5 million years ago. Julian Huxley stated, "Man's evolution is not biological but psychosocial, it operates by the mechanism of cultural tradition, which involves the cumulative and self-reproduction and self-variation of mental activities and their products.[4]

Man's psychosocial evolution, over uncounted aeons, has led to storing of subtle matter content as frequency and amplitude information, and this is called the cultural belief structure, or conditioning of the human psyche, or psychic pandemic, or memory. It is unstable and spontaneously disintegrates to thought coupled with its volitions or motives. Thought-time constructs the time-space matrices in quick succession, or the sensual world. Man has started living in the sensual world, man-made social cosmos, or a synthetic world. His mode of living is divorced from the Reality, the Universal Consciousness, the Truth. He is aware of the *non-fact*, the *false*, the *past*, the *what should be*?; or in other words, he has started living in a set of illusions. The whole mankind is caught unknowingly in a crisis of perception. The thought-time constructs all psychological imbalances–violence, greed, fear, anger and so on. The *Homo sapiens* have emerged as a violent species. We have built a society which is violent, and we, as human beings, are violent. Every activity of the conditioned human psyche is dualistic, so it adds to entropy of the mind-brain-body system which is a pointer towards self-annihilation or self-destruction.

Genesis of Psychological Imbalances: Modern physics has confirmed: (a) all the concepts we use to describe nature are limited, and creations of the mind, the conditioned psyche; parts of the map, not of the territory; (b) in order to see itself, it cuts itself up into at least one state which sees, and at least one other state which is seen; in this severed and mutilated condition whatever it sees is *only partially* itself; (c) the interaction between the seer (subject) and the seen (object) happens in about few millionth of a second and this results in self-awareness of the distorted subject and the object; (d) both the subject and the object are continuities of change and can never give perception of the *fact*, the *true*, the *present*, the *what is*!; and (e) the distorted perception leads to duality and gives pain, misery, fragmentation and strife.

Resolution of the Present Human Paradox: We have to educate our physical organism and psychological structure through observation by the scientific mode of mind. This results in a movement from self-knowledge to understanding of life directly (self-awareness), it flows to a quantum jump from symbolic-dualistic frame of mind spectrum to non-dual frame of reference of Mind Continuum; and from intellect to intuition (insight). So one moves from activity to non-action, from speech to verbal silence, from movement to non-motion gracefully and voluntarily. It energises the Cosmic Intelligence that takes charge of one's being.

Scientific Mode of Mind

Science is the search for truth. The aim of science is to study nature and human experience objectively. Objectivity and precision, both as to thought and its verbal formulation, are two important characteristics of the scientific method. The advance of knowledge is at present reduced to what Einstein described as "extracting one incomprehensible from another incomprehensible". Maurice H. Wilkins, Nobel Prize in Medicine, 1962, wrote, "Science makes progress largely by a combination of two aspects: open-mindedness and the following of abstract concepts. Abstraction involves excluding and narrowing down, which is very opposite to open-mindedness .... Science is a human activity .... The whole question of moral, spiritual and other dimensions is normally pushed out of science".[5]

All experience, every thing without exception, is fundamentally a personal, subjective experience. Max Born wrote, "The fact that by comparing pairs communicable, objective statements are possible, has an immense importance because it is the root of speaking and writing, and of the most powerful instrument of thinking, of mathematics".[6]

The scientific mode of mind is synergistic to the psychological mode of mind, which implies that the scientific mode is at a higher quantum energy potential of Consciousness, or in other words, it is at the immanent aspect of Consciousness, or the absolute. The objective world has the following attributes:

(a) Schrodinger wrote, "Without being aware of it and without being rigorously systematic about it, we exclude the Subject of Cognizance from the domain of nature that we endeavour to understand .... Mind has erected the objective outside world of the natural philosopher out of its own stuff. Mind could not cope with this gigantic task otherwise than by the simplifying device of excluding itself–withdrawing from its conceptual creation. Hence the latter does not contain its creator".[7] Charles Sherrington wrote, "The material world has only been constructed at the price of taking the self, that is, mind, out of it, removing it; mind is not part of it; obviously, therefore, it can neither act on it nor be acted on by any of its parts".[8] C.J. Jung and B. Spinoza have identical perception. This also suggests that there is no energy interaction between the subject and the object. The self-observation bestows perception of the fact, the objective truth.

(b) The objective world picture is 'colourless, cold, mute'. Schrodinger wrote, "Colour and sound, hot and cold are our immediate sensations; small wonder that they are lacking in a world model from which we have removed our own mental person .... The physical world picture lacks all the sensual qualities that go to make up the Subject of Cognizance. The model is colourless and soundless and unpalpable .... The scientific views of natural processes formed in this way lack all sensual qualities and therefore cannot account for the latter".[9]

(c) Eddington wrote, "The frank realization that physical science is concerned with a world of shadows is one of the most significant of recent advances".[10] Schrodinger wrote, "Democritus of Abdera was aware of this in fifth century B.C.".

(d) Schrodinger wrote, "The world of science lacks, or is deprived of, everything that has a meaning only in relation to the consciously contemplating, perceiving and feeling subject. I mean in the first place the ethical and aesthetical values, any values of any kind, everything relating to the meaning and scope of the whole display .... The values are missing, and quite particularly meaning and end are missing".[11]

The Genesis of Creativity in Science: Mind has a very wide spectrum. It has the capacity to make quantum jumps to different frames of reference in that spectrum. A creative process involves many frame of reference, and the different frames are shown diagrammatically.[12-14] Due to shortage of space, these steps are not discussed in this paper.

Rational knowledge and rational activities certainly constitute the major part of scientific research, but it must be complemented by the intuitive insights that makes a scientist creative. Albert Einstein, in almost the last interview that he gave to the international magazine LIFE said as follows:

> The mind can proceed only so far upon what it knows and can prove. There comes a point where the mind takes a leap–call it intuition or what you will–and comes out upon a higher plane of knowledge, but can never prove how it got there. All great discoveries have involved such a leap.

Physics is essentially an intuitive and concrete science. Mathematics is only a means for expressing the laws that govern phenomena.[15]

The mind follows logical and scientific reason as far as it can guide, but when reason or intellect realises its limitations, then the conscious-mind makes a quantum jump to a higher plane and intuition tends to come suddenly, and characteristically, not when sitting at a desk working out the equations, but when relaxing in the bath, during a walk in the woods, on the beach, etc. During these periods of relaxation after concentrated intellectual activity, the intuitive mird seems to take over and can produce the sudden clarifying insights which add creativeness to scientific research. The intuition is not through external sensory organs and the internal sensorium in the brain, but through another set of neurones, which is often called in literature as the 'heart', the centre of inspiration; so it is obtainable through means other than reason and it is not irrational but extra-rational or beyond-rational.

All knowledge is structured in consciousness. The creative process involves a quantum jump from logical and scientific reason to philosophic reason or non-dual and non-conceptual frame of reference of Mind Continuum; in other words, from a relative frame of reference to an absolute rest frame of mind. Knowledge emanates from it as quantas depending on the frame of reference of mind.

D.S. Kothari, in prophetic words, wrote:

> The new theorems, unless trivial, are of course first "discovered" and then proved. Discovery is an inspired guess, a flash of insight. It is not a step by step process, but a sort of quantum jump.... A rational account of a discovery, the proof, follows and not precedes the discovery.[16]
>
> Fundamental discoveries which go deep into the nature of things are the result of uncommon intuition and faith, not cold logic.[17]

Education and Values

The core of the natural science is the outer world and the core of values is the inner world. The outer world, "the flood of external objects of cognizance has made the subject of cognizance withdraw to the background", and "obviously it can neither act on it (subject) nor be acted on by any of its parts". Science by itself cannot supply us any ethic.

Recently, many eminent scientists–Werner Heisenberg, Edwin Hubble, Max Planck, G.F. Chew, Bertrand Russell, Lincoln Barnett, Max Born, and so on–have concluded that we cannot impart value education at reason or intellect level.[18]

All ethical/spiritual values proceed from the trans-sensual dimension of human personality, the Life Field, these self-emerge from the dimension of the wholeness of life, the restructured science-education dimension of life. The values express themselves in the non-dual frame of reference of Mind Continuum.

Wrong Turn Taken by Mankind

The insight by Sri Aurobindo is as under:

> The evolution of mind working upon life has developed an organization and use of matter which can no longer be supported by human capacity without an inner change. The problem is fundamental and in putting its evolutionary Nature is confronting man with a critical choice which must one day be solved in the true sense if the race is to arrive or even to survive.[19]

George Wald, Nobel Prize in Medicine, 1967, in prophetic words, wrote:

> We who know where we are going, are now heading rapidly toward self-extinction, toward removing humankind from the cosmic scene, and for the most trivial of reasons: profit, the rivalry of the United States and the Soviet Union, the momentum of the military-industrial complex in both nations. The cosmic drama will go on elsewhere, ignorant of our demise, caring nothing; but we will have no further part in it.... Does that matter? It matters to us.[20]

David Bohm, an eminent physicist, and J. Krishnamurti, the philosopher-mystic discussed "The Future of Humanity", and they raised two fundamental questions as, "***Has humanity taken a wrong turn which has created the chaos in the world?***" and "***What needs to be done within the consciousness of man to preserve our very existence and bring about a new culture?***". Mankind took a wrong direction and thereafter they are just continuing that direction.[21] We are going towards self-annihilation and not much time is left now.

Hideki Yukawa, a Japanese Nobel Laureate in Physics, concluded:

> The danger that all these trends (psychological, social, ecological, violence, and so on) will combine to destroy the unity of man's various aspects and lead eventually to the loss even of his humanity cannot be denied. It is equally undeniable, I believe, that such a split would deprive man of his happiness.

To save ourselves, by such efforts, from the danger of a loss of, or a split in, our humanity in the world of the future–this, I believe, is the course that man must take from now on. This, it is my personal conviction, is true wisdom for modern man.[22]

There is the large gap between the superhuman task and the frailties of human endeavours. Hideki Yukawa quotes Max Born–a Nobel Prize winner: "Clever, rational ways of thinking are not enough. The danger of mass slaughter .... can only be overcome by moral conviction, by a determination to replace national prides and prejudices with human love".[23]

Objective Scientific Mode of Mind

It is evident that we have to explore the new global consciousness in the light of the recent discoveries in science. In our own lives, each one of us must move towards a realisation of the truth at the core of our being, the glowing higher consciousness that is the birthright of each individual born on this planet, because in the ultimate analysis it is the crucible of our individual selves alone that the poison of conditioning the psyche can be contained and transformed into the new consciousness that we seek. In this lies the faith for individual freedom as well as the survival of our planet earth. We intuitively see that even at this late hour, we can marshal our inner (spirituality) and outer (science) dimensions and we succeed in making the vital transition to the new consciousness? It is this most crucial of all decisions that it is the privilege and responsibility of our generation to make, because it is this, in the ultimate analysis, that will prove whether there is really new perception (not reason) for mutation in the new global society that is so rapidly emerging before us.

You cannot impose the order on top of disorder. You cannot impose non-violence on a consciousness which is violent because that violence has deep-rooted causes in the psyche. Unless these causes are eliminated there is no ending of violence. We cannot survive unless all psychological imbalances are dissolved through observation by higher quantum energy potential of consciousness.

Mutation is possible in the brain through insight, not through knowledge, not through accumulation. That insight is the ability to see a truth directly, a direct perception of the truth, and education must foster that. "The restructured science-education", which observes the wholeness of life, is the only panacea for human survival.

The "objectivity" of science was discussed by Erwin Schrodinger, Charles Sherrington, B. Spinoza and C.J. Jung. It appears that the subject of the mind spectrum is at the immanent quantum energy potential and is divorced from the ultimate or transcendent quantum energy potential of the Consciousness. The subject is non-variable attentivity, or reaction-free attentivity, or objectless attention. The object of the mind is the only reality which has the lowest quantum energy potential; or in other words, the immanent quantum energy potential has gone to abeyance and its only linkage is the lowest quantum energy potential of consciousness. It represents the relative field of consciousness. The objective material world can neither act on the subject nor be acted on by any of the parts.

The subject is "in-here" while the object is "out-there". There is no energy exchange between the objective and the subjective. So the objective world gets recorded as the *fact*. The object gives the objective *fact*, which is a partial objective truth. It gives invention, which is a modified use of the known. It cannot give us a discovery, which is an entirely new principle or a theorem.

Restructured Science-Education

Karl Pribram wrote, "Brain science must deal with the awareness of awareness. It could no longer afford to shut out that part of the world which we call subjective".[24] Roger Sperry spoke of the importance of a neglected area of science, namely the study of human subjective experience. He wrote, "Instead of renouncing or ignoring consciousness, the new interpretation gives full recognition to the primacy of inner conscious awareness as a causal reality".[25] John Eccles also emphasized the importance of the phenomenon of "conscious experience".[26]

The outer (objective) and the inner (subjective) are not two separate movements. It is a unitary movement, not separate, but one whole. Man has now to work to treat the outer and the inner as one. We call it "restructured science-education". The restructured science takes in its ambient both the subjective and the objective dimensions of life. The restructured education deals with the sensual and the trans-sensual world. It deals with the observer situated within the observed world. The dialogue with nature is carried on from within nature. It sees the wholeness of life. The subject now is non-variable attentivity, or reaction-free attentivity, or objectless attention. The "restructured science-education" deals with the wholeness of life, so it is at the transcendent aspect of the absolute, or Cosmic Consciousness. The Consciousness is Eternal, Infinite and Immutable.

When thought-structure coupled with volitions (I-consciousness) encounters the realm of the transcendent Consciousness, the thought-structure or thought-time goes to abeyance.[27]

When true-subject observes the conditioned psyche, one perceives that–(a) thought-time is independent of I-consciousness; (b) it is the product of collective human effort through centuries; (c) it (photons) cannot cross the "event horizon"; (d) it goes to abeyance and leads to non-dual and non-conceptual frame of reference of Mind Continuum; and if the observation is sustained, it leads to order, harmony, nonviolence and peace.

The brain and the mind are independent and are shared by mankind. The successive consciousness and Simultaneous Consciousness are shared by mankind. The "restructured science-education" deals with the wholeness of life, so the subject and the object are within nature, or in other words, both are "in-here". The universe beyond the "event horizon" is a new universe with intelligent life in it.

The happenings in nature are very fast–say the time between the subjective and the objective may be about a few millionths of a second; the photons are devoured by a black hole in less than a hundred microseconds,[28] and same order of time may be there when photons are absorbed by a mind; the time taken for a signal to move [illegible] cell to muscle is of the order of about five thousandths of a second,[29] which corresponds to something moving to and fro two hundred times a second. It appears that the brain does not have the capacity to record time of this order of magnitude.

We are beginning a new age of awareness, the age of quantum consciousness, the age of the conscious atom. By observing within ourselves, we may be able to solve the problems facing us on the final frontier–the frontier of Cosmic Consciousness.[30]

Concluding Comment

Schrodinger wrote, "A moderately satisfying picture has only been reached at the high price of taking ourselves out of the picture, stepping back into the role of a non-concerned observer .... Subject and the object are only one.... The original (subject) and the image (object) are identical".[31]

Ilya Prigogine wrote, "The behaviour of reality (is) unrelated to our beliefs, our ambitions or our hopes". He again wrote, "It is physics that presupposes an observer situated within the observed world. Our dialogue with nature will be successful only if carried on from within nature".[32]

The two blatant antinomies are resolved as under :

(a) The dimensions of "restructured science-education" are subjective realm and objective field–where the subjective realm is the true-subject of cognizance, the true-observer, and the objective field is that is observed. The self-observation of the conditioned psyche (object, observed) are within the observed world; or in other words, it opens a dialogue with nature when this is carried on from within nature. Both subjective and objective are "in-here", that is participators in nature. The principle enunciated by Ilya Prigogine is identical at a deeper level to self-observation by restructured science-education.

(b) The observation by restructured science-education considers subject and object are only one, and results into ending the duality, which implies ending of all psychological imbalances, ecological crises and so on.

This leads to ending all thought-structures coupled with volitions and pure Consciousness bathes the brain cells. This bestows a mind that lives with love, compassion and humility. The expression of pure Consciousness is Oneness, Order, Harmony, Rhythm, Non-violence, Peace and Security.

David Bohm, in the Preface to "The Future of Humanity" wrote, "(Krishnamurti) emphasizes that mind is essentially free of the distorting bias that is inherent in the conditioning in the brain, and that through insight arising in proper undirected attention without a center, it can change the cells of the brain and remove the destructive conditioning".[33] We intuit that the "*proper undirected attention*" is the "restructured science-education" and this is the dimension of the wholeness of life. This bestows intuition (insight) that can create a mutation in Consciousness and bring about a New Culture.

The mutation in Consciousness happens when the "restructured science-education" observes the conditioned psyche and both the '*inner*' and the '*outer*' are within the field of the transcendent aspect of the Absolute, the Life Field–this is the essence of the technology of a mutation in Consciousness which has the capacity to end all psychological imbalances and ecological crisis, and also the capacity to bring about a ***New Culture.*** This blossoms to peace, security and survival of mankind. This is the only vocation of mankind and is the consummation of life.

When "restructured science-education" takes hold as the Subject of Cognizance, the path lies open to a world of continuing realisation and enrichment of liberty, justice, prosperity and joy for all. Towards this great end India with its unique heritage and culture has an especial opportunity and obligation. This is the only vocation of man. At a deeper level, this is governed by our survival.

Mankind can survive only if the disorder, or violence, or psychological imbalances end in our consciousness. And this happens when "restructured science-education" takes over as the true subject. It is the Life Field or Quantum Field Consciousness (QFC) that can lead to survival of mankind.

India was once the "Light of Asia". She has now to fulfil her historic role of being the Light of the World. India has been called upon *here* and *now* to save Life in the world from extinction. Will she wake up from deep slumber and "***Lead Kindly Light Amid the Encircling Gloom***". We share the privilege and the responsibility.

References

1. President Vaclav Havel, in *Our Global Neighbourhood : The Report of the Commission on Global Governance*, New York: Oxford University Press, 1995, pp. 353-54.
2. Erwin Schrodinger, *What is Life? & Mind and Matter*, Cambridge University Press, 1967, p. 132.
3. Arthur Eddington, *Nature of the Physical World*, Cambridge University Press, 1928, pp. 276-77; in George Wald, in *Synthesis of Science and Religion*, Mumbai: Bhaktivedanta Institute, June 1988, p. 20.
4. Julian Huxley, *Evolution after Darwin*, Chicago: University Press, 1959, Vol. III, pp. 251-52.
5. Maurice H. Wilkins, in *Synthesis of Science and Religion*, *op. cit.*, p. 30.
6. Max Born, *My Life and My Views*, Chapter Five, "*Symbol and Reality*", 1968, p. 174; in D.S. Kothari, *Some Thoughts on Science and Religion*, Delhi University, 31.10.1977 & 3.11.1977, p. 44.

7. Erwin Schrodinger, *op. cit.*, pp. 127, 131.
8. Charles Sherrington, in Erwin Schrodinger, *ibid.*, p. 128.
9. Erwin Schrodinger, *op. cit.*, pp. 128, 148, 177.
10. Arthur Eddington, in Erwin Schrodinger, *ibid.*, pp. 130, 177.
11. Erwin Schrodinger, *ibid.*, pp. 148, 149.
12. Sampooran Singh, *The Epistemology of Scientific Knowledge, Science and Culture*, April 1982, Vol. 48, No. 4, pp. 119-25; and *Creativity in Science*, Gandhi Marg, May 1985, Vol. 7, No. 2, pp. 104-19.
13. *ibid.*, *The Art of Creativity in Education*, in *The Holistic Education*, New Delhi: Siddharth Publications, 1987, pp. 145-70.
14. *ibid.*, *The Survival of Mankind and Quantum Jump from Violence to Peace*, New Delhi: Books India International, 1999, pp. 142-59.
15. Albert Einstein, in *Nature*, Vol. 278, March 15, 1979.
16. D.S. Kothari, in *The Odyssey of Science, Culture and Consciousness*, New Delhi: Abhinav Publications, 1990, pp. 48-49.
17. *ibid.*, in *The Evolution of Consciousness*, New Delhi: National Publishing House, 1983, p. 227.
18. Sampooran Singh, in *Global Education and Human Survival: A Scientific Appraisal*, New Delhi: Sanbun Publishers, March 2002, pp. 46, 35-36.
19. Sri Aurobindo, in *The Odyssey of Science, Culture and Consciousness*, New Delhi: Abhinav Publications, 1990, p. 41.
20. George Wald, in *The Evolution of Consciousness*, New Delhi: National Publishing House, 1983, p. 13.
21. J. Krishnamurti and David Bohm, *The Future of Humanity*, in P. Krishna, *Education, Science and Spirituality*, USA: Institute for Higher Education, Research and Dialogue, 1993, pp. 13 & Back Cover.
22. Hideki Yukawa, *Creativity and Intuition*, Tokyo: Kodansha International Ltd., 1973, pp. 205, 206.
23. Max Born, in Hideki Yukawa, *ibid.*, pp. 189-190.
24. Karl Pribram, in Ken Wilber, *The Holographic Paradigm and Other Paradoxes*, Boulder: Shambhala, 1982, p. 17.
25. Roger Sperry, in *Synthesis of Science and Religion*, Mumbai: The Bhaktivedanta Institute, June 1988, p. 199.
26. John Eccles, in ib*id.*, p. 200.
27. Sampooran Singh and Dr (Mrs) Kanwaljit Kaur, *Peace, Security and Survival : A Scientific Quest*, Chandigarh: July 5, 2004, pp. 16-17.
28. Deepak Chopra, *How to Know God*, Rider, 2000, p. 271.
29. Fred Alan Wolf, *Taking the Quantum Leap*, San Francisco: Harper and Row, 1981, p. 236.
30. *ibid.*, p. 248.
31. Erwin Schrodinger, *op. cit.*, pp. 128, 137, 146.
32. Ilya Prigogine and Isabelle Stengers, *Order Out of Chaos*, New York: Bantam Books, 1984, pp. 8, 218.
33. J. Krishnamurti & David Bohm, *The Future of Humanity*, KFI, 1987, Preface, pp. 2-3.

13
The Art of Living

Abstract

Living is a communion with the timeless present, the eternity. We have to learn to be alert and attentive to every activity; it means that we have to anchor ourselves to the scientific mode of mind (the wholeness of life). It is an experimental interrogation to whatever I do. The communion with the fact content of life at any moment gives you sense of fulfilment.

Life means dying to the past, dying to the conditionings. It is important to see things as they are, it is to see the present here and now. We need an alternative dynamics of relationship, not memory as the base of relationship, it requires a new dimension of consciousness, a dynamics of spontaneity and innocency. Living requires fearlessness along with reverence for life. We need awareness of the wholeness of life.

Creativeness comes into being when there is constant awareness of the ways of the mind, and of the hindrances it has built for itself. Creativeness is a state of being in which the conflicts and sorrows of the self have gone to abeyance, a state in which mind is not caught up in the demands and pursuit of desires.

The recent discoveries in science have shown that the subjective (inner) and the objective (outer) are one, a unitary movement, one whole. We have to restructure "science-education-health-values", so that it takes in its fold both the dimensions of life; and this deals with the wholeness of life, and this we call true subject. The art of living implies transcending the I-consciousness and thought structure, which has been constructed over the past uncountable aeons. It is the Cosmic Consciousness that can bring radical transformation or mutation of the human psyche.

Man has equated the act of living with the repetitive and mechanical projection of the stuff of memory by the whole sensory system, the neurological system, the chemical system. He looks at the present through the eyes of the past. The body is alive, the non-rational instinctive processes are going on, the cerebral movement of exposing the stuff of the memory in every sensual movement is going on.

The sensual movement was engaged in gathering fragmentary experience, partial knowledge and stored this as memory (frequency and amplitude) in the psyche. The memory gave the concept of continuity (time), sequence (causation), comparison (identification), measurement and security (acquisition and competition). All these have constructed psychological imbalances, ecological problems and other challenges. This led to conditioning (identification) with the past and future projections of the thought-structure.

Is man left as helpless wreck in an ever-raging, ever-rushing, uncompromising current of conditionings, of the past, the yesterday and its future projection. Nature is benevolent because human being seems to be born with the faculty of self-knowledge (the movement of thought coupled with volitions) and understanding of life directly (called self-awareness). The instrument of understanding (the non-dual perception) is embedded in every man.

This article explores the conditioned psyche and the Unconditioned Energy, or Cosmic Consciousness, or Life Field. It eliminates credulity and beliefs from the field of enquiry, it takes into consideration the discoveries of modern science, it is non-authoritative approach to spiritual enquiry, and it explores the symbiosis of science and spirituality. It explores the act of living, the act of responding, and the act of meeting the challenges of life. It is a pointer to ending of psychological misery and suffering in the midst of socio-economic-political life, and also complete snapping of all psychological enclosures with all belonging, with all sense of identification.

The Emergence of Thought

Physics has shown that the stuff of the Consciousness is experience and knowledge (information), which is the root of thought of the human race; and it conditions the human psyche. The thought-structure is repetitive and mechanistic nature of the cerebral movement, and there is no freedom of the mind. With the help of thought–naming, identifying, mentation and forming concepts and ideas, we built the socio-economic-political structures around us. There is constant interaction going on between the man-made world and ourselves.

The Conditioned Mind: The mind is nothing but amalgamated, organised, standardised conditioning. It is a global human activity that has been going on for untold centuries. The conditionings have their own momentum. There is nothing like an individual mind which has its own identity or entity.[1] The mind is shared by the mankind, but patterns of its expressions are different. There is an individual expression, of the wholeness, of the globe, and the individual has its own idiosyncrasies.

The conditionings express themselves as I-ness, or I-consciousness, or the ego. It has no factual reality. It has a conceptual reality. It has an ideational reality. It has a relevance in our lives. The concepts are grafted on the perception and we are aware of the distorted perception.

The Unconditioned Mind: The non-dual and non-conceptual frame of reference is shared by mankind. So man has nothing in him which is his own construct. This demolishes the sense of all pride. All psychological imbalances represent his psychological immaturity and ignorance. Man has to learn "to understand himself directly", and all pride, ignorance and all challenges will vanish. The understanding bestows perceptive sensitivity which blossoms to perception of the truth.

Aspiration: The conditioned mind does not have the capacity for unconditional freedom as it is invariably in prison of the past. The aspiration for perfection, for purity, for freedom are embedded in the non-dual frame of reference of Mind Continuum; or in other words, in the non-rational, non-cerebral and non-chemical content of our being. The aspiration is undifferentiated, non-individuated feel for truth, for freedom, for love.

Authority: Each religion by virtue of its traditions–the concept of my country–constructs an authority. A sense of authority is accompanied by a sense of superiority. The concept of authority divides us. It distorts our relationship.

A non-authoritarian approach by scientific mode of mind implies that the observation is "unrelated to our beliefs, our ambitions, our hopes"; it sees an object "without any psychological imbalances", or it is "understanding of life directly". It gives a perception of the *fact*, the *true*, the *present*, the *what is*!

In psychological relationships, the memory of words inhibits us from looking at the person. The recalled past coherently superpositions itself on the object, and distorts the object. There is nothing like an individual mind or ego. They are only certain cerebral patterns, neuro-chemical patterns of behaviour fed into the human being getting repeated, getting projected endlessly. These patterns are called *reactions*, so reaction is the movement of past in you. These reactions use you for expressing themselves.

Dynamic Interplay of Unmanifest and Manifest

(a) In 1913, Niels Bohr showed that there exists discrete sequence of electron orbits in an atom. When an atom is excited, the electron jumps from one orbit to another. At this very instance, the atom emits or absorbs a photon the frequency of which corresponds to the difference between the energies characterizing the electron's motion in each of the two orbits. This difference is calculated in terms of Einstein's formula relating energy to frequency.

When an atom makes a transition, or a 'jump', from one stationary state to another, the actual process cannot be visualised or even imagined. There are no intermediate stages. We cannot breakdown the process into its components. The entire process of transition from one state to another is a non-visualisable, unanalysable, unity. *It is indivisible.* Its parts cannot even be imagined. It is a 'quantum jump', as we call it. In dealing with atomic phenomena we have to recognise that the act of observation is accompanied by an inevitable disturbance which alters the state of the observed system in an unpredictable manner. What is observed is different from what it was before the act of observation. This is inherent in the nature of things. It cannot be eliminated. In an attempt to understand the mystery of the world of atoms, quantum physics is of the view that atomic object (the different electron orbits) emerge from an "unmanifest mathematical space", and this is called *Hilbert space*. It implies that between any two consecutive orbits, there is realm of pure Consciousness.

(b) There appears to be an analogous situation for *thought processes*. As we 'think'–in any sequence of thoughts–there is always a sudden, discontinuous jump from one thought to the next. Thought is manifestation of consciousness. Between two consecutive thoughts, there is the Unmanifest (immanent quantum energy potential). We are not aware at all of any intermediate stages. If we were so aware, no thinking would be possible. There would be an almost infinite sequence of 'sub-thoughts' between two thoughts, like an infinity of points between the two ends of a line. ***Quantum jumps for thought appear to be as much a necessity for the conscious self as these are for the atom***. As the mind quietens, the space between two thoughts enhances and thought structures become less and less, till the mind is totally quiet, which implies that all thoughts go to abeyance and pure Consciousness expresses itself.[2]

(c) Life begins with breathing in and death begins with breathing out. Each moment when you breathe in, you are reborn; each moment you breathe out you are dead, because breath is life. There is a moment of Unmanifest between the breath in and breath out.

(d) Love is breathing out, hate is breathing in. Love more–that is breathing out.[3] Love is at the highest quantum energy potential of Consciousness and hate is at the lowest quantum energy potential of consciousness.

(e) Seeing is direct, hearing is direct, touching is direct, but thinking is indirect. Knowledge is always indirect, so it is partial and limited. Thinking or experiencing is a material activity. Thought is matter. It is the response of memory. A response from memory is the past. The past is dead, the present is living.

(f) An exploration is from the indirect field (the psychophysical process in the field of duality, subject-object relationship, thought-structures) and proceed to the direct realm (the non-cerebral and non-psychophysical movement, which is called the no-mind state). A journey of indirect field to the direct realm is the art of dying while living. The total discontinuity of the psychological state is called psychological death.

(g) Unless one learns the "Art of Dying while Living", one cannot live a fuller and meaningful life. "Dying while living" is really transcending of all sense of attachment, belongings and dependency upon things, individuals, situations or circumstances. It is really the death of psychological "I", the "me", the "ego", and not the death of the body, the biological organ.

(h) ***Observation of the Manifest and the Unmanifest:*** The gestalt has to be changed–pay more attention to the background (Unmanifest) and less to the figure (manifest). The habit of the mind is–not to look at the background, but to look to the figure. When the observer (subject) observes the figure, the figure goes to abeyance, the mind stops and the objective world will simply vanish. It implies that the figure and the background are one, although both are at different quantum energy potential; but when observation is continued there is transference of energy from background to figure and both become one. It implies that there is no separate figure from the background, their identities are lost.

In meditation, the observed goes to abeyance and then the observer also vanishes. You are in a state of no-mind; the boundaries of the objective and the subjective coalesce and become one; in the emptiness is the unity; Cosmic Intelligence, the background bathes the neurons; the Intelligence gets energised which expresses itself as order, harmony, non-violence and peace. This leads to ending your suffering, your bondage and you gain the perception of the whole.

Response is born of an awareness of the whole situation. It is born in the space of inner freedom, so response is in the non-dual realm. Life is Divinity itself, and at the core of our being is that Divinity wanting to express itself in the form of unconditional freedom, love and compassion. This expression blossoms to harmony and peace.

The Dynamic Alternative Way of Living

Living is a communion with the timeless present, the eternity. We have to learn to be alert and attentive to every activity; it means that we have to anchor ourselves to the scientific mode of mind (the wholeness of life) and then perform the duty even in the psychological mode of mind. It is an experimental interrogation of whatever I do–there is no question of agreeing or disagreeing to the psychological impulse. You do not listen to your own reactions, emotions, attitudes and approaches. In such a case relationship is not a battlefield.

Albert Schweitzer was once asked, "What is your religion?". He replied, "Reverence for Life is my religion".[4] That gratefulness, that humility, that reverence revolutionises your attitude and approach along with the behaviour. Living requires fearlessness along with reverence of life. Fearlessness is required to meet the challenge, not to dodge it.

If one is alert, sensitive and attentive to whatever one does, then the reference to the past becomes unnecessary; because attentiveness or sensitivity is synergistic to the quantum energy potential of the past. In attentiveness, intelligence begins to work because you are not loaded with the past–with the motivations, comparison, measurement, value structures and so on. The alertness, the attentivity makes you fresh. It is only in that freshness that there is communion with the present. Then the perception sees the *fact* as it is.

The communion with the factual content of life at any moment gives you a sense of fulfilment. It is a benediction to be alive, it is a blessing to have an opportunity to live, to see, to hear and to interact, there is a sense of fulfilment. A sense of fulfilment leaves no residue.

Many eminent scientists–Karl Pribram, Roger Sperry, John Eccles–have opined that "brain science .... could no longer afford to shut out that part of world which we call subjective". The outer and the inner are one, a unitary movement, not separate, but whole. It leads to restructuring of science. Similarly education deals with the sensual dimension and trans-sensual dimensions of life. So we have to "restructure science-education". It implies that one is alert and attentive. One pours all his attentivity and sensitivity and tries to understand the wholeness of life. There is a sense of fulfilment in the very living of it. The act of living, the act of responding, the act of meeting the challenges of life gives a tremendous sense of fulfilment. It is a benediction to be alive, it is a blessing to have an opportunity to live, to see (direct), to hear (direct), and to interact. The sense of fulfilment does not leave any residue. You have lived and you have died completely. The sense of fulfilment is the dying.

The Meaning and Significance of Life

Life is like an ever-flowing river–one bank is time-space-causation matrices, the symbolic-dualistic frame of reference of mind spectrum, and the other bank is the emptiness, or nothingness, or no-mind state, or non-dual and non-conceptual frame of reference of Mind Continuum. The river is infested with crocodiles and sharks which are ready to engulf the swimmer, who wants to cross the river. In technical parlance, the physicists call the river as "the event horizon", "the time-barrier", "the frequency barrier", so the time-space matrices is below the velocity of light, and the 'no-mind state' is above the velocity of light. The velocity of light (the river) is the absolute; it is like a wall that no object can cross through. As we approach the wall, time slows down, mass increases and space becomes curved, and the object is devoured or goes to abeyance. We are left with pure Consciousness bathing the brain cells.

You carry your own Tao, the Life Field within. It is your intrinsic nature. It is not dispensable, you cannot put it aside and forget it. You are already there, *here* and *now*. Because you are asleep, you cannot see yourself. The human vision is blurred, as he has conditioned his psyche by desires, motivations, seeking, acquisition, opinion, distinctions, words and theories, and he is ignorant of the fact.

Life means dying to the past, dying to the conditionings. It is important to see things as they are, it is to see the present *here* and *now*. We need an alternative dynamics of relationship, not memory as the base of relationship, it requires a new dimension of consciousness, a dynamics of spontaneity and innocency. Living requires fearlessness along with reverence for life. We need awareness of the wholeness of life.

Order: Every disorder leads to emotional anarchy and intellectual chaos. There is no rhythm in living. Order is the perfume of understanding. Order has the elegance of spontaneity, effortlessness. So this chaotic, shabby, disorderly living at the sensual level, at the verbal level, at the mental level is bondage.

Freedom: Understanding the nature of bondage is the beginning of freedom. Understanding the content of bondage gets converted into a factual urge for freedom. Freedom is spontaneous equibalance, equipoise.

Understanding: An enquiry (observation, experimental interrogation) blossoms or flowers into understanding. The understanding of bondage does liberate. It is not a personal achievement, it is a consummation of human growth applicable to the whole humanity. Enquiry leads to ending of seeking, becoming, acquisition, storing, it blossoms to ending of all psychological imbalances and human challenges.

Violence: George Wald wrote, "All the mystics through the ages have agreed that to achieve wisdom one must quiet the brain, stop using it as a tool, put aside (experience) and knowledge (information), try indeed to free one's consciousness, empty one's mind and in quiet see what enters".[5] In other words, this is quantum jump from symbolic-dualistic frame of reference of mind spectrum to non-dual and non-conceptual frame of reference of Mind Continuum; or to transcend violence and achieve non-violence. It implies to penetrate a boundary that physicists call "the event horizon",[6] an impregnable wall between violence and non-violence. In violence, every movement of thought is below the speed of light, while in non-violence, the movement of consciousness is faster than the speed of light.

The event horizon is at a certain quantum energy potential of consciousness, or at a certain threshold frequency. The mind has the capacity to record when the event is below that threshold frequency as a single channel tape recorder. If the frequency is more than the threshold frequency, the mind cannot record. History records only violence. History does not record silence–it cannot record it. All records are of disturbance. Whenever someone becomes really silent, he disappears from all records. He is no more a part of this madness, of this mad world.

Meditation: The "Unconditioned Freedom of Consciousness" is called meditation. It is not a personal acquisition, but it is an impersonal global entity, where higher quantum energy potential of Consciousness expresses itself. Meditation is a state where total mental activity ceases to function, where the process of acquiring and becoming goes to abeyance, and one is left with the content of being, the unconditioned, the non-personal, the non-dual, the non-conceptual. Meditative state is denuded of all psychological imbalances. Meditation is harmonizing all the energies without any imbalance. Order is its expression in actual relationship and love is its perfume.

Creativity

Persistent, consistent and rigorous scientific observation (enquiry or scientific interrogation) implies to see an "event/process/happening/object" without interfering in its flow, or to see without any transfer of energy to it, or to observe non-subjectively which means without any evaluatory comparison or judgement creeping in. It is to perceive without naming, identifying, without emotionally reacting. Observation without an observer (recalled memory) is attentivity. The state of attentivity gets energised in the whole being, where there is neither subject nor object; or subject-object dualism ends.

If you want to be with life, with the whole, you have to be choiceless, because when you choose, you divide. There is no liking or disliking, there is no identification, or naming; there is no projection. The Cosmic Consciousness shares the ecstasy with you.

Creativeness comes into being when there is constant awareness of the ways of the mind, and of the hindrances it has built for itself. Creativeness is a state of being in which the conflicts and sorrows of the self have gone to abeyance, a state in which mind is not caught up in the demands and pursuit of desires. Creativeness is a state when the mind is quiet (it implies that the self has gone to abeyance). Creativeness self-expresses itself from the dimension of eternity, infinity and immutability–also called timeless state.[7,8]

When one is born into the realm of Intelligence or the non-personal sensitivity, then that sensitivity, that Intelligence uses the brain as well as the physical structure and you can move into relationship. Movement becomes an extension of peace, and speech becomes an extension of silence.

When there is direct understanding of the transcendental Being, the Life Field, which alone can give fullness to every aspect of life. It has been the misfortune of every great teacher that while he speaks from his level of consciousness, his followers can only receive the message on their level; and the gulf between the teaching and understanding grows wider with time. All knowledge is structured in Consciousness, all knowledge flows from within; you have to be a ***Light*** to yourself. You are the subject and the object, the experiencer and the experienced, you are the seeker and you are the sought, you are the disciple and you are the master.

Cosmic Consciousness

Erwin Schrodinger wrote, "No personal god can form part of a world model that has only become accessible at the cost of removing everything personal from it .... I do not find God anywhere in space and time".[9] God is just a metaphor. There is nobody sitting somewhere in heaven, controlling, managing, engineering. Deep inside a subjectivity (inner) is there. Everything is alive and throbbing (vibrating). And this throbbing is not a fragmented process, it is the whole.

God is Cosmic Consciousness permeating every existence. It is alive and conscious. It has the highest quantum energy potential of Consciousness, it has the highest frequency. It is pure Intelligence, Wisdom. It is the Truth of Life. All pure knowledge is structured in the Consciousness. In pure knowledge, opposites lose boundaries, the silence (timelessness) and the world (time) have become one.

Cosmic Consciousness is never an object. "In objectification there are no primal realities, but only symbols". The successive consciousness is merely a symbol. The Absolute Subjective is realistic while cultural and social life are symbolic. In the object there is never any reality, but only the symbols of reality. The subject alone has reality.

The Absolute Subjectivity is the present moment, which contains all time and is therefore itself timeless, and hence ***this timeless present is Eternity itself***–a moment without date or duration, extension or succession, past or future, before or after, "having the whole of its existence simultaneously, which is the nature of Eternity".[10] Some people call the Eternity as God.

Concluding Comment

The *Homo sapiens* have emerged as a violent species. We have built a society which is violent and we, as human beings, are violent. During the last 10,000 years, or more, man has been trying to transcend violence through knowledge (information), thought structures, ideals, beliefs, concepts, but all have proved to be sterile in transforming the human psyche, or in other words, to bring radical transformation or mutation in the human psyche.

The recent discoveries in science have shown that the subjective (inner) and the objective (outer) are one, a unitary movement, one whole. We have to "restructure science-education", so that it takes in its fold both the dimensions of life; and this deals with the wholeness of life, and this we call true subject. When thought structure coupled with its volitions encounters the true subject, the I-consciousness and thought structure go to abeyance. If this observation is continued for a long chronological time, the fact also goes to abeyance, and Cosmic Consciousness expresses itself as order, harmony, non-violence and peace.

A non-authoritarian approach by true-subject is to observe: (a) the conditioned psyche; (b) the Unconditioned Energy; (c) to see an object without any duality or psychological imbalances; (d) to understand life directly; (e) this cumulatively bestows pure perception; and this blossoms to order, harmony, non-violence and peace. The art of living implies transcending the I-consciousness and thought structure, which has been constructed over the past uncountable aeons. It is the Cosmic Consciousness that can bring radical transformation or mutation of the human psyche.

One has to be alert, sensitive and attentive to whatever one does. In attentiveness, the Intelligence begins to work and there is communion with the present, the Divine. This is the consummation of human life.

If man escapes his responsibility, he does so at his own peril, of India and of mankind.

References

1. Vimala Thakar, *The Art of Dying While Living*, Mumbai: Vimal Parivar, 1996, p. 20.
2. D.S. Kothari, *Atom and Self*, in *Evolution of Consciousness*, New Delhi, National Publishing House, 1983, p. 212.
3. Osho, *The Book of Nothing*, Pune: Rebel Publishing House Pvt. Ltd., 1975, pp. 15, 17.
4. Albert Schweitzer, in Vimala Thakar, *op. cit.*, p. 64.
5. George Wald, in *The Evolution of Consciousness*, *op. cit.*, p. 14.
6. Deepak Chopra, *How to Know God*, London: Rider, 2000, pp. 271-272.
7. Dr (Mrs) Kanwaljit Kaur, Paramjit Singh and Sampooran Singh, *Science with Creativity*, UK: Ramakrishna Vedanta Centre, November-December, 2000, Issue 296, pp. 256-267.
8. *ibid.*, September-October, 2001, Issue 301, pp. 224-231; and November-December, 2001, Issue 302, pp. 261-270.
9. Erwin Schrodinger, *What is Life*? & *Mind and Matter*, Cambridge University Press, 1967, p. 150.
10. Ken Wilber, *The Spectrum of Consciousness*, USA: The Theosophical Publishing House, 1982, pp. 82, 98.

14
Relationship and Society

Abstract

We have built a society–a social-economic-political-religious structure–which we have stored in our mind-brain-body system or psyche. It follows a sophisticated process, which leaves us in conflict, violence, fear, anger, and so on. It gives us false relationships which gives nervous/chemical tensions.

Society cannot be transformed by any reform, legislation, concepts, ideals, thought patterns, and so on. It can only be transformed through observation (seeing) and listening (hearing) by higher awareness. This article explores the true relationship between man and nature, between man and man, and ethical responsibility.

Man has to educate and learn to make a quantum jump from symbolic-dualistic mind to non-dual and non-conceptual Mind; and in this education his survival and true relationship is embedded.

Nature invariably expresses itself as direct in a non-dual and non-conceptual frame of reference of Mind Continuum. Observation is direct, listening is direct, understanding and learning is direct, true action is direct; only thinking is indirect.

Life is experience, and experience is relationship. It is expressed through contact with things, with people and with ideas. The action of relationship between you and another, between you and me, is society; and it is based on social-economic-political system and institutionalized religion. Society is a construct by the mind-brain-body system, or by the symbolic-dualistic frame of reference of mind spectrum, or by successive consciousness. The mind cuts itself up into at least one state that sees (subject) and at least one other state which is seen (object). There is energy transduction (energy exchange) between the subject and the object, resulting into distortion of both the subject of cognizance and the object. In this severed and mutilated condition, whatever it sees is only partially itself. We are not aware of the true fact of society but only aware of the non-fact, the false, the *what should be*! Relationship is the awareness of interconnection between two people. It is interconnected between challenge and response. All relationship in the psychological mode of mind is a distortion, an illusion. It is the lack of understanding of relationship that causes conflict.

Ilya Prigogine, who won the Nobel Prize in 1977, wrote:

> It is quite remarkable that we are at a moment both of profound change in the scientific concept of nature and of the structure of human society as a result of the demographic explosion. As a result, there is a need for new relations between man and nature and between man and man. We can no longer accept the old a priori distinction between scientific and ethical values. This was possible at a time when the external world and our internal world appeared to conflict, to be nearly orthogonal. Today we know that time is a construction and therefore carries an ethical responsibility.[1]

This article explores the true relationship between man and man, between man and nature, and ethical responsibility of man. The aim is how to bring about a fundamental, a radical transformation, a mutation in society with a view to end all conflict, violence, pain and misery. There is an urgency for a constant inward revolution, or a creative psychological transformation, in the individual, which flows to transformation of the static, crystallized society.

Transformation of Society and New Relationship

A galaxy of eminent scientists–say Karl Pribram, Roger Sperry, John Eccles, Wilder Penfield, and so on–have opined, "Brain science could no longer afford to shut out that part of the world which we call subjective".[2] We have to "restructure science-education", which takes in its ambient both the objective and the subjective dimension of life and is called the "true-subject". The time interval between the subjective and the objective is less than a hundred microsecond. The outer (objective) and the inner (subjective) are not two separate movements, but a unitary movement, one whole. The objective science must restructure itself and consider the subjective and the objective as one harmonious movement. The restructured science deals with the wholeness of life. The transformation of the outer (society) cannot take place without inner revolution. Since society is always static, any action, any reform which is accomplished without this inward revolution becomes equally static. It has no life-giving quality, so long as there is not this constant inward revolution. We need a ***creative psychological transformation***.

Relationship means communion without fear, freedom to understand each other, to communicate directly. Relationship is really a process of self-revelation, which is a process of self-knowledge. There can be true relationship only when there is love but love is not the search for gratification. Love exists only when there is self-forgetfulness, when there is complete communion, not between one or two, but communion with the highest (Life Field); and that only happens when the I-consciousness and thought-structure goes to abeyance. Love is not different from truth. Love is that state in which the thought process, as time, has completely ceased. Where love is, there is transformation. Transformation is from moment to moment.

There is the urgent task of the transformation of human consciousness, or in other words, an unprecedented shift in consciousness is indeed happening on our planet. Eckhart Tolle wrote that we have to realize "the urgent need for a radical change in human consciousness if humanity is not to destroy both itself and the planet".[3]

Creative Psychological Transformation

(a) ***Psychological Mode of Mind:*** The cultural belief structure, as well as in most of the social-economic-political structures and the greater part of the media, the successive consciousness, the past inheritance is still deeply entrenched in the stream of involuntary and incessant thinking. Identification with your mind creates an opaque screen of concepts, labels, images, words, judgments and definitions that block all your relationships. It creates the illusion of separateness. Thinking has become a disease. This creates psychological imbalances, ecological crisis and human challenges. It implies enslavement of the conditioned mind, a prison-house with golden bars. It leads to pain, misery and travails.

The conditioned psyche, or symbolic-dualistic frame of reference of mind spectrum, or successive consciousness, is far-from-equilibrium conditions. We observe that very small perturbations or fluctuations can become amplified into gigantic, structure-breaking waves and leads to subject-object duality, violence, fear and psychological imbalances.

(b) ***Creative Psychological Transformation:*** About 1600 Kepler and Galileo simultaneously and independently formulated the principle that the laws of nature are to be discovered by measurement. All propositions were to be confined to that which was objectively measurable and verifiable.

A scientific mind takes up "the role of a non-concerned observer", in the words of Schrodinger.[4] It is unrelated to our beliefs, our ambitions, our hopes", in the words of Prigogine.[5] It must not construct a pseudo-observer, it must see the present and reject the past remembrances or future projections. It implies that there is no transfer of energy between the observer and the observed, the seer and the seen, the subject and the object. The thought (object) is at the "successive consciousness" and it cannot sustain itself, so it goes to abeyance. In addition to "observing the thinker", the observation creates a gap in the mind stream simply by the focus of your attention into the Now, the Present–just become intensely conscious of the present moment. Eckhart Tolle wrote, "When a thought subsides, you experience a discontinuity in the mental stream–a gap of no-mind .... You draw consciousness away from mind activity and create a gap of no-mind in which you are highly alert and aware but not thinking".[6] In other words, the whole mind-brain-body system is at the immanent quantum energy potential, so the 'true-subject' is at the non-variable state of consciousness; and thought (object) is at the successive consciousness, and thought cannot sustain the intense energy of the subject, so it disintegrates.

There is an urgency for a radical shift, a discontinuity in the temporal dimension, or in other words, to go beyond successive consciousness which is governed by time. The chattering conditioned psyche makes a quantum jump to no-mind state, and this quantum jump is called radical transformation or mutation of the psyche. Mutation happens in the brain through insight, not through knowledge, not through accumulation. That insight is the ability to see a truth directly, a direct perception of the truth, and education must foster that.

Objective science is an open system embedded in society (social-economic-political system) and linked to it by very dense feed-back loops. It is powerfully influenced by its external environment, and, in a general way, its development is shaped by cultural receptivity to its dominant ideas. Objective science rejects all constructs of the social-economic-political system. It rejects all psychological imbalances, ecological crisis and other human challenges, so we call it "creative psychological transformation". Science must transcend the psychological mode of mind.

In the psychological state of mind, there is disorder and chaos. In the scientific mode of mind (or the art of observation), order and organisation can actually arise 'spontaneously' through a process of self-organisation and self-renewal. For humans, when the time goes to transcendence, the reality expresses itself.

New Relations Between Man and Man

(a) ***Psychological Relations:*** Every activity in the common waking state of mind is repetitive and mechanical. It is basically a recall of the past memory or past inheritance and coherent superpositions of different webs on the object, which results in distortion of both the subject and the object; and awareness of the distorted perception. All relationships in this field are illusions. The interaction is biochemical or nervous tension, it is a continual dance, it remembers what the dance was yesterday, so it is always doing the same dance. Man has learnt to live in distorted perception of the subject (and the object), and utter abandonment of the reality. These relationships, which are false make his life fragmented and chaotic, there is conflict which gives him pain, misery and travails. Every activity in the psychological field leads to enhancing entropy, which is leading mankind to death, self-annihilation and self-destruction. The whole mankind has programmed the mind-brain-body system as a single channel computer, which is a false process.

(b) ***True Relations Between Man and Man:*** Many eminent scientists–including Albert Einstein, Werner Heisenberg, Erwin Schrodinger, Arthur Eddington, and so on–based on a rigorous, consistent and persistent methodology of objective scientific research, have stumbled upon another mode of perception (knowing), which is "understanding of life directly, instead of in the abstract, linear terms of representational thinking".[7] The new mode of perception bestows "direct understanding of life", non-comparative perception, non-evaluatory perception. It is to observe non-subjectively. The acquisitive culture and psychological aggression goes to abeyance. The symbolic-dualistic frame of reference makes a quantum jump to non-symbolic, non-dualistic and non-conceptual frame of reference of Mind Continuum. The non-dualistic frame bestows understanding of life direct which flowers to learning and intuition (insight). The intuition is fundamental and reasoning is a derivative. The true relationship must be based on intuition. The intuition may be expressed at the level of the *derived* intellect. The insight bestows "true relationship" between man and man. The true relationship flows from direct perception of nature in a non-dual and non-conceptual frame of reference of Mind Continuum.

If the level of perception rises to the highest quantum energy potential of Consciousness, then one is conscious of the Being, which is a happening that Being becomes conscious of itself. When Being becomes conscious of itself, it is often called the Presence. Since being, Consciousness and Life are synonymous, we would say the Presence means Consciousness becoming conscious of Itself, or Life attaining self-consciousness. The true relationship flows to conscious of the Presence. This is the ultimate true relationship of man and man.

(c) ***Love:*** Love is not different from truth. Love is that state in which the thought process as time, has completely ceased. Love alone can transform the present madness and insanity in the world–not systems, not theories. Love cannot be thought about, love cannot be cultivated, love cannot be practised. The practice of love, the practice of brotherhood, is in the field of mind, the intellect, therefore it is not love. When all this has stopped, love comes into Being, so love is a happening when the whole system is purified.

Understanding comes only when the mind is very quiet. Only the truth can liberate the mind from its own ideation; to see the truth, the mind must realize the fact that as long as it is agitated it can have no understanding. Stillness of the mind comes only when there is no process of isolation through accumulation but complete understanding of the whole process of relationship. Understanding comes into being from the *now*, the *present*, which is always timeless.

Truth is not cumulative. It is from moment to moment. Eternity is in the moment. Eternity is only now. Where there is love, there is transformation, revolution, because love is transformation from moment to moment. The true relationship must be based on love.

(d) ***The Oneness of Life:*** Life begins with breathing in and death with breathing out. Each moment when you breathe in you are reborn and each moment when you breathe out you are dead. Harlow Shapley discussed:

> With each breath that we or any other man-sized animal breathes, forty thousand million billion argon atoms are inhaled, and then, without loss, since they do not combine with anything, they are exhaled for rapid and thorough diffusion by the winds throughout the earth's atmosphere. Some of the argon atoms breathed in his first day of Adam (or any early man) are in the next breath of all of us. Some of the argon of our today's breathing will be in the first gasp of all infants a century hence. This argon traffic is obviously rich in suggestion; it implies a droll one-worldness and, like sunshine, recognizes no national boundaries. It links us with the breathing animals of the remote past and distant future in a sort of communal way.[8]

Ervin Laszlo discussed the new concept of the cosmos as "an integrated and self-energising system, a totality that creates itself". He wrote:

> The parts of this totality are not radically separate: they are integral elements of the whole. Every "thing" in the cosmos is a coherent "event" and every event is the summed result of all the other events .... The cosmos is a system of interacting waves: it is a sea where the effect of the smallest perturbation propagates throughout the entire field .... the new physics and the new cosmology do not recognize discrete things and independent events in the universe, only ripples upon ripples, waves upon waves, interpenetrating and propagating in a seamless sea.[9]

The Vedantic viewpoint is identical to that of modern science.

New Relations Between Man and Nature

(a) The process of distortion of observation was well known in Patanjal Yoga. R.P. Kaushik wrote, "The stage prior to recognition and naming is a state of non-verbal or thought-free perception (*nirvikalpa jnana* or pure perception). From this pure perception we proceed to thought, recognition and naming (*savikalpa jnana*)".[10] The concepts are grafted on perception, which reduces a perception to a concept. This suggests that observation (seeing), listening (hearing), touching is direct; but thinking is indirect.

(b) Understanding comes only when the mind is very quiet. The mind is quiet when the thought-structure goes to abeyance, so there is discontinuity in the mental stream–called no-mind state. In the no-mind state, there is flow of Consciousness or in the discontinuity the Unmanifest appears.

(c) The occurrence of observation (seeing) or listening (hearing), smelling or breathing is a movement in the sphere of non-duality. This is expressed in words as:
In the art of observation there is the Unmanifest.
In the art of listening there is the Unmanifest.
In the art of breathing there is the Unmanifest.
In the art of sensual perceptions there is the Unmanifest.[11]

(d) ***Nature invariably expresses itself as direct in a non-dual and non-conceptual frame of reference of Mind Continuum.***

Ethical Responsibility

Recently, many eminent scientists–Werner Heisenberg, Edwin Hubble, Max Planck, G.F. Chew, Bertrand Russell, Lincoln Barnett, Max Born, and so on–have concluded that we cannot impart value education at reason or intellect level.[12]

Value is the implicate order of thought, the subjective nature of thought, the true nature of thought. Modern physics has shown that value education, in essence, implies a quantum jump from symbolic-dualistic frame to non-dual frame, or higher awareness, or higher quantum energy potential, or higher hierarchical expression of consciousness.

Value education is to cultivate capacity for understanding relationship which is life in its wholeness. Any form of education that concerns itself with a part and not with the whole of man inevitably leads to increasing conflict and suffering. The whole cannot be understood through the part; it can only be understood through perception and spontaneous action. At the fundamental level, it implies to understand the dynamics of all frames of reference of the mind-brain spectrum. Understanding comes only through self-knowledge, which is awareness of one's total psychological process. Education in the true sense is helping the individual to be mature and free, to flower greatly in love and goodness. The highest function of education is to bring about an integrated individual who is capable of dealing with life as a whole.

Value education is concerned with the cultivation of the total human being, the nurturing of the heart-mind-brain-body system. It has two aims: the primary aim is to give him the capacity to be awake to the dynamics of his own mind-brain system, or in other words, to be aware of one's total psychological process which bestows understanding through self-knowledge; and the secondary aim is to train the child in various skills and disciplines, or in other words, to learn techniques to earn one's own livelihood. The University/College curricula should incorporate the "Dynamics of Human Mind" in the Science Faculty, and the "Transpersonal Psychology" in the Arts Faculty at the Graduate/Post Graduate levels. Similar courses have to be designed at the school level.

The primary aim of value education is to penetrate into the innermost recesses of the mind; to be aware of the inherited conditionings; to be closed to the environment and open to the Absolute; and to be completely free of the mental movement and thereby enter the dimension of Silence. The art of living is to be entirely free of the psychological suffering in the midst of all relationships.[13]

Value education has the capacity to jettison all psychological problems, including the mad armament race, fear of nuclear holocaust, ecological disasters, violence, poverty and hunger; and usher in an era of peace, freedom and bliss. It can create a new society.

Swami Ranganathananda, President of the Ramakrishna order, in December 1966 stated, "Indian thought has always upheld the view that all values proceed not from matter but from the spirit of man .... All ethical values are essentially spiritual values; they proceed from the trans-sensual dimension of the human personality. This dimension, which stimulates the ethical sense, is beyond the reach of animals and of such humans who, like animals are content to live at the sensate level". S.P. Kanal wrote, "To teach children to value truth in life is to cultivate in them a commitment to scientific temper, that is love for and use of scientific method in understanding and evaluating situations in life".

The Declaration of Global Ethic or The Universal Declaration of Human Values: Love, truth, freedom, peace, and so on are the spiritual values and these express themselves when thought-time is transcended, and intelligence is activised. Thought expresses its true subjective nature as values in a non-dual frame of reference. Values are the implicate order of thought, the subjective nature of thought, the wave-aspect of thought, the true nature of thought, the content of consciousness.

Global ethics is defined as the perception in a non-dual frame of reference of the mind spectrum. It is the foundation of all ethical and spiritual values. The universal declaration leading to the emergence of global ethic constitutes a call to mankind that human mind must make a quantum jump from dualistic frame to non-dual frame of reference of Mind Continuum. And one who is wholly consecrated to Truth, who wants to live the Truth, serve the Truth, would know at each moment the ethical values; it would be a kind of intuition or revelation or insight which would make you know the truth, the global ethics at every moment. To perceive the ethical values or global ethic, man has to make a quantum jump from psychosocial evolution to spiritual evolution.

The future of mankind is hinged on welding of Eastern Spirituality and Western Science, and out of that will emerge a new dimension of all-inclusive integral Consciousness that leads to ending of all human crisis, pain and misery, and bestows freedom, peace and bliss on human life. This is the only vocation of the human race.[14]

The Pilgrimage Within

The aim of human life is to make a quantum jump from symbolic-dualistic frame of reference of mind spectrum to non-dual and non-conceptual frame of reference of Mind Continuum, which is also called as "no-mind" state; from intellect to intuition (insight). It is a journey, a pilgrimage, from the labyrinth of our sophisticated conditioned minds, that constructs illusions of time-space-causation matrices to understanding and seeing the reality. These tremendously powerful words (feelingful understanding) were echoed millions of years ago and are as under:

> ***You are the way, and you are the goal, and there is no distance between you and the goal. You are the seeker and you are sought; there is no distance between the seeker and the sought. You are the worshipper and you are the worshipped. You are the disciple and you are the master. You are the means and you are the end. This is the Great Way.***[15]

This is the pilgrimage within, which blossoms to the emergence of the New Human Being. In simple language, you have to educate your own mind-brain-body system, or you have to prepare yourself for a quantum jump from duality to non-duality, from illusion to truth, from a movement of the past, the inheritance to the Present, the Now; and be aware of the conscious-Presence, the Reality, the Infinite, the Life Field.

As the human race grows into different dimensions of Life, the ethos change, the quality of the spiritual, religious enquiry changes. There is no end to it. There cannot be an absoluteness about any approach to spirituality. Scientific approach means tentativeness. May be the twentyfirst century sees a different quality of approach, of attitude, and the pilgrimage continues, because Life is Infinite.

Concluding Comment

(a) We have constructed a society–social-economic-political system–which is a construct by the conditioned mind and is stored in the human brain. The society (outer) is static, as it has no life-giving quality. The society cannot be changed by any reform, or legislation, or religious formula based on belief, ideals, dogmatism, conformity; as all these reforms are at the same quantum energy potential of consciousness as the society. This change cannot be achieved through any evolution–which is time.

(b) Ilya Prigogine, Nobel Prize winner in 1977, suggested a new relation between man and nature, man and man, and ethical responsibility. This revolution in relationship must be immediate, not in time. It is only the action of I-consciousness and thought-structure that has to be changed; or in other words, the action of will and assertiveness that needs to be changed, because the only mischief in relationship is conflict between individuals or within individuals, and conflict *is* will and assertiveness.

(c) There are arts of observation, listening, understanding, learning, acting, and these are *direct*; but thinking is indirect. Direct implies to live in communion with the immutable laws of nature, and *indirect* means to live antagonistic to the laws of nature. Every *direct* act of living is an act of worship, because it enhances the quantum energy potential of consciousness of the system. In other words, nature invariably expresses itself as direct in a non-dual and non-conceptual frame of reference of Mind Continuum.

(d) In the symbolic-dualistic frame, the direct is superpositioned by the thinker leading to distorted perception, which expresses itself as pain, chaos, conflict and travails.

(e) Man has to educate and learn to make a quantum jump from symbolic-dualistic mind to non-dual and non-conceptual Mind; and in this education his survival and true relationship with nature is embedded. If man escapes his responsibility of constructing true relationship with society, in the symbolic-dualistic frame of reference, he does so at his own peril, of India and mankind.

(f) The transformation of the society (outer) is only possible when man observes and listens to the misery and travails of the society without interfering in their flow. It implies to have no opinion, for or agains, no likes or dislikes, no choosing to accept or reject, and so on. This leads to a quantum jump of symbolic-dualistic frame to non-dual and non-conceptual frame; which is called no-mind state. This bestows a perception of the "objective-truth", the fact.

(g) If we continue observing or listening to the fact (objective truth), without justification, or condemnation, or motivation, the fact itself grows which implies that there is release of tremendous energy and the fact moves in the *vertical dimension* of *Itself.* This permits the fact to go to abeyance and only pure Consciousness is left behind. All societal entropy vanishes and this guarantees human survival and excellence.

(h) It is a gigantic experiment in the laboratory of one's own mind-brain-body system where all human beings are equal partners. This flowers to "an open dialogue with an open mind" where each human being is able to put aside his own views and listens to those of others. There is no 'guru' and no disciple, everybody tries to understand and learn. And every human being has to undertake the experiment in the laboratory of his own mind-brain-body system.

The challenge is to dissolve the old patterns of I-consciousness and thought-structure, rather than to try to contradict it, to control it, or to destroy it by force or will. An understanding and learning through observation flowers to transformation of society (this world politically, economically and socially), but the transformation must begin with the individual.

References

1. Ilya Prigogine and Isabelle Stengers, *Order Out of Chaos*, New York: Bantam Books, 1984, p. 312.
2. Karl Pribram, in Ken Wilber, *The Holographic Paradigm and Other Paradoxes*, Boulder: Shambhala, 1982, p. 17.
3. Eckhart Tolle, *The Power of the NOW*, Australia: 2004, Preface (p. xv).
4. Erwin Schrodinger, *What is Life? & Mind and Matter*, London: Cambridge University Press, Ed 1967, p. 128.
5. Ilya Prigogine, *op. cit.*, p. 5.
6. Eckhart Tolle, *op. cit.*, pp. 17, 19, 20.
7. Allen W. Watts, *The Ways of Zen*, New York: Vintage Books, 1957, p. 10.
8. Harlow Shapley, *Of Stars and Men*, London: Elek Books, 1958, p. 40.
9. Ervin Laszlo, *Emerging Concepts of the Cosmos*, The Scientific and Medical Network, Newsletter No. 49, August 1992, p. 28; in Sampooran Singh, *The Piigrimage to the Third Millennium*, January 1995, p. 31.
10. R. P. Kaushik, *Towards a New Consciousness*, Delhi: Darshan Yoga Sansthan, 1974, pp. 63-71.
11. Sampooran Singh, *Science With Creativity : A Vision on Human Survival and Excellence*, unpublished.
12. Sampooran Singh, Dr (Mrs) Kanwaljit Kaur and Paramjit Singh, *Global Education and Human Survival: A Scientific Appraisal*, New Delhi: Sanbun Publishers, March 2002, pp. i-xiv, 1-88.
13. Sampooran Singh, *Science, Human Values, Value Education and Peace*, New Delhi: New Man and New World Movement (India), September 1993, pp. 39-40, 41, 77-78.
14. *Ibid.*, pp. 84-85.
15. Osho, *The Book of Nothing*, Pune: Rebel Publishing House, 1975, Introduction, p. x.

15

Science with Creativity A Vision on Human Survival and Excellence

Abstract

The Memory or cultural belief structure is the movement of inheritance in the psyche. Our mind is the time, our mind is the past. This article discusses the conceptual crisis, limitations of science and technology. It also discusses the principle of objectivation and the direct understanding of nature by objective science.

Many eminent scientists have advocated that the objective science must restructure itself to take in its ambient both the objective and the subjective dimension of life, or the wholeness of life. Science must restructure itself to take in its fold–science-education-health dimensions; and this is called true subject.

When I-consciousness or thought-structure which are at the successive consciousness come in the field of true-subject, these are annihilated. And pure Consciousness is aware of Itself.

It discusses the states of consciousness and the benediction of the Divine, the Infinite, the Timelessness. It discusses the art of living and an action plan or a Paradigm shift.

The "science with creativity" is an experiment of creating a "New Man"–a human being who lives in harmony with the inner and the outer, with himself and his environment, and who is free from all ideologies and conditionings that now divide humanity. The human survival is embedded in this gigantic experiment. And if man escapes his responsibility, he does so at his own peril, of India and of mankind.

Man has an evolutionary origin. The *Homo Homonid* emerged at about 4.5 million years ago and *Homo sapiens* at about 2.5 million years ago. We are living in one of the critical periods of human history–we stand at a juncture wherein we are in supreme peril–not a peril from another species, not a peril from outer space, but a peril from our conditioned psyche. Every activity of the conditioned psyche enhances entropy which is leading us to self-destruction, self-annihilation.

The Evolutionary Process: Teilhard de Chardin, the eminent paleontologist, divided the evolution into four stages–geosphere, biosphere, noosphere and christosphere. Broadly geosphere deals with inorganic (physical) evolution, biosphere with biological (organic) evolution, noosphere with psychosocial evolution and christosphere with spiritual evolution.[1]

Vedanta views the entire evolutionary process as progressive evolution of structure and form, and as greater and greater manifestation of the entire Self within, or Life Field. The psychosocial evolution over uncountable aeons has led us to "Humanity stands at a critical juncture in history, one that calls for a strong moral and spiritual leadership to help set a new direction for society";[2] in other words, it implies a quantum jump from psychosocial evolution to spiritual evolution.

Physicists have realised that all their theories of natural phenomena, including the 'laws' they describe, are creations of the human mind; properties of our conceptual map of reality, rather than of reality itself; or in other words, parts of the map, not of the territory. The world extended in space and time is but our representation.

Man appeared to be an amphibian who lives simultaneously in two dimensions–the *given* (inner, subjective) and the home-made (outer, objective). The evolutionary impulse in man led to the emergence of an inner dimension–called subjective. Ever since the time of the Vedas and Upanisads, some sages and saints in India explored both the dimensions–the objective and the subjective. As a symbol, we may compare the objective field to a drop of water and the subjective realm to a fathomless and boundless ocean. The objective is in the field of time, so it is limited, transient, ephemeral and finite. The subjective is in the realm of the timelessness, so it is eternal, infinite and immutable. In the scientific parlance, the objective is at the lowest quantum energy potential of consciousness; and is called "successive consciousness". The subjective is at the highest quantum energy potential, or highest frequency, and is called Simultaneous Consciousness.

Rationalism and the March of Reason: The cerebral activity–storing of experience and knowledge (information) coupled with volitions, motives, desires, acquisitions led to the discovery of reason. Reason is a precious value thrown up by evolution and the source of much human progress in culture and civilisation. With the help of reason man could formulate various concepts and ideas; discover the law of causation or cause and effect relationship; the concept of time maturing into sequence and continuity; and with the help of imagination (future projection), he constructed an infinite variety of symbols that helped him to communicate with one another. So out of belief into the faith of reason and rationality grew man the world over: science and technology, industrialization, means of transport and communication, agriculture, medicine and so on. Man pursued the frontiers of reason and rationality over uncountable aeons.

Limitations of Reason: For the last 10,000 years, or more, man has been trying to end psychological imbalances through knowledge (information), thought structures, ideals, beliefs, concepts, but he found all to be sterile in transforming the human psyche; because intellect is at the same quantum energy potential as the conditionings. This highlighted the limitations of experience, knowledge and intellect. Recently many eminent scientists–Werner Heisenberg, Edwin Hubble, Max Planck, G.F. Chew, Bertrand Russell, Lincoln Barnett, Max Born, and so on–have concluded that we cannot impart value education at reason or intellect level.[3]

There appears to be a fundamental crisis of human values, and the mankind is suffering a psychic pandemic of the most virulent type. It is also called the 'crisis of perception' which aggravates current economic, social and political tensions. Accompanied by raging ecological problems, these tensions tend to push the world even closer to self-destruction or self-annihilation.

What is Conditioning?: The cerebral organ stores the partial experience and fragmentary knowledge (information) coupled with unfulfilled emotions, desires; the brain stores these as frequency and amplitude information and this is called memory or cultural belief structure. The memory is metastable and the disintegrative product is called thought. The brain has been trained, educated over uncountable aeons to repeat these, day after day, year after year, generation after generation, it is a repetitive and mechanical process, and it is called conditioning.

The cerebral organ has been conditioned among the human beings to behave in a particular way. It can receive very subtle matter, thought, ideas, concepts which are all subtle matter. The brain has been conditioned to derive conclusions, analyse, compare, evaluate and arrive at a judgment. The brain is meant for receiving data, processing it, interpreting it and reacting to it. The brain has been conditioned to function within the framework of time and space with the help of causation. The human brain is one of the expressions of the cosmic dance of life.

What is Thought?: The symbolic-dualistic thought is subtle matter. Thought has never nourished happiness, thought has never given peace to man, does not stimulate love or humility and does not stimulate understanding. We are living today where individually and collectively we are far away from the beauty of understanding, communion and relationship with one another, understanding, communion and relationship with nature around us, with living beings around us, and without the act of getting related, there is no life. Life is relationship. To live is to get related harmoniously with the movement of life around you and within you. In relationship movement of the total being is required.

A relationship is something direct, immediate, simple, without any resistance at all. The symbolic-dualistic frame of reference of mind spectrum cannot give any relationship; it is the non-dual and non-conceptual frame of reference of Mind Continuum that has the capacity to bestow relationship. Scientific experience and knowledge is not the content of bondage. Our addiction to the mental, the cerebral pleasure is the content of bondage, the attachment.

The memory of cultural belief structure is the content of culture. This is the movement of the inheritance, the movement of the past within us. Our mind is the time, our mind is the past. A mental, cerebral movement is irrelevant as far as the totality of life, understanding of life is concerned.

This article presents the Nature's evolutionary impulse, which expresses itself as self-unfoldment of man. It discusses science with creativity with special reference to human survival and excellence. Man has a hidden potential to enhance the level of awareness and understand and live the highest quantum energy potential of Consciousness. It discusses a technology for human survival and excellence, and the future of mankind on this planet is assured. This is the consummation of human life.

The Conceptual Crisis of Modern World

The common waking state, or the relative frame of reference, or the symbolic-dualistic frame of reference first cuts itself up into at least one state that *sees*, and at least one other state which is *seen*. In this severed and mutilated condition, whatever it sees is only partially itself. It constructs a time-space-causation matrices, which is called the objective world.

The different steps in observation are: Firstly, the mind perceives the external environments, the fact, the challenge, so the fluctuating energy input is called the challenge; the perception of the fact in philosophical language is called thought-free perception, or pure perception, or non-verbal perception, or factual perception. Secondly, the mind recalls or retrieves the past corresponding memory, which takes up the role of the pseudo-subject with respect to the fact which is the object. To be more precise, the mind severs itself into the subject and the object, and this severance introduces dualism. The subject proceeds to recognition, identification, comparing, naming and storing the object. The whole process implies an exchange of photons (quanta of light), these are 'gentle quantum events', and these bring in a discontinuity at that moment. At the moment of this exchange the distinction between the subject and the object is lost. One flowing web of frequencies (subject) looks at another flowing web of frequencies (object), and then both intermingle losing their identities. Both the subject and the object become continuities of change, so the subject is the object, the thinker is the thought. The interaction may be shown as:

Fact + Recalled Memory → Mutilated Fact + Modified Memory

Thirdly, we perceive the mutilated fact and record the modified memory, where, in principle, the mutilated fact and the modified memory are the same. The interaction is a biochemical interaction or dance; it remembers what the dance was yesterday, so it is always doing the same dance. The perception of the mutilated fact gives us the response, the dualistic action; the will of action is always dualistic.[4]

In the relative frame of reference, the mind-brain equipment is not a frequency analyser but a frequency transformer; in other words, the frequencies of the challenge are transformed to the frequencies of the response. In this process, the mind is said to have severed into the subject and the object dualism. The subject is one flowing web of frequencies which looks at the object, which is another flowing web of frequencies; or in other words, one set of quantum frequencies looks at another set of quantum frequencies. The relative frame of reference brings in a certain order in a world of fluctuation and change, it investigates a universe with 'edges' or processes, and participates in the formulation of its laws.[4]

The Limitations of Science and Technology

About 1600 Kepler and Galileo, simultaneously and independently formulated the principle that the laws of nature are to be discovered by measurement. Huston Smith wrote that '*objective truth*', which is always partial, has bestowed us "with material benefits, but has all erased transcendence from reality map .... and this has produced an identity crisis".[5]

An appraisal of our situation is registered by a Nobel-prize winning biologist, Jacques Monod, in words, "The choice of scientific practice .... has launched the evolution of culture on a one-way path: onto a track which nineteenth-century scientism saw leading infallibly upward to an empyrean noon hour for mankind, whereas what we see opening before us today is an abyss of darkness".[6] George Wald, Nobel Prize in Medicine, 1967, wrote, "We who know where we are going, are now heading rapidly toward self-extinction, toward removing humankind from the cosmic scene, and for the most trivial of reasons: profit, the rivalry of the United States and the Soviet Union, the momentum of the military-industrial complex in both nations. The cosmic drama will go on elsewhere, ignorant of our demise, caring nothing; but we will have no further part in it.... Does that matter? It matters to us".[7] He added, "By now the problem is not transcendence, but survival. If we are to survive there must be a fundamental changes in direction, not only organizational, but in our ways of thinking. We have to think different thoughts and to want different things .... All the mystics through the ages have agreed that to achieve wisdom one must quiet the brain, stop using it as a tool, put aside knowledge and learning, try indeed to free one's consciousness, empty one's mind, and in quiet see what enters". P. Krishna, an eminent scientist, wrote, "We are going towards self-annihilation and not much time is left now".[8]

Science is the search for truth in the objective world, the 'without'. A selfless, unfaltering devotion to truth and the use of knowledge for man's upliftment are the ideals of a scientist. Truth is what all earnest scientists seek. Free enquiry, objectivity, precision, autonomy, freedom, experience are the pillars of the inductive (experimental data) and deductive (theoretical) logic. Discovery is its mission, its perception. It is precise, clear, unprejudiced, which does not condemn, which observes, which sees. It moves from fact to fact. Science is a dialogue between Nature and the universe (man-made cosmos) where questions are asked and Nature responds with the answer, it implies that the insight is born.

A scientific mind takes up "the role of a non-concerned observer", in the words of Schrodinger;[9] it is "unrelated to our beliefs, our ambitions, our hopes", in the words of Prigogine;[10] it must not construct a pseudo-observer, it must see in the present and reject the past remembrances or future projections. The values in science are objective truth, integrity, and honesty.

Science aims at making true and adequate statements about its object. Science and technology mainly focusses attention on the material progress of life and on technical solution to human challenges; it explores a modified use of the known–and this is called invention (not discovery). Although science is a human activity, yet all values are missing and quite particularly meaning and end are missing. Science is an intellectual endeavour, and it rejects all intuition (insight). It is a non-authoritarian approach.

Science makes progress largely by a combination of two aspects: open-mindedness and the following of abstract concepts. Abstract concepts produce narrow-mindedness, so the whole question of moral, spiritual and other dimensions is pushed out of science.

Through knowledge there is no awareness, through knowledge there is no understanding, because experience and knowledge is the past inheritance.

Schrodinger wrote, "Our science–Greek science–is based on objectivation whereby it has cut itself off from an adequate understanding of the Subject of Cognizance, of the mind". Our sensations, perceptions and observation have a strong, personal, subjective tinge and do not convey the nature of the "thing-in-itself", to use Kant's terms. Kant landed us with a complete resignation: "never to know anything at all about his "thing-in-itself",[11] the Supreme Reality, the transcendent quantum energy potential of Consciousness.

The objective science gives knowledge of the object–it is "only an empty shell–a form of symbols. It is knowledge of structural form and not knowledge of content. All through the physical world runs that unknown content, which must surely be the stuff of our Consciousness".[12] Science will only be true to itself if it enters into an enquiry into the unique datum of the subject, or the observer, or the Self, with a view to investigating the reality underlying all events or phenomena.

The answer to this paradox is embedded in educating our physical organism and psychological structure and understand deeply, and this bestows the scientific temper. In a scientific mode of mind, there is no I-consciousness, no thought-structure, no psychological imbalances, but observe 'what is'–which actually is the objective fact. It is not produced by thought.

The Art of Observation: In the art of observation, the attentivity (immanent quantum energy potential of consciousness) takes over as the subject. The attentivity is at a higher quantum energy potential than the cultural belief structure or thought-time. When thought is bombarded with the energy of attention, it results into atom-smashing and thought gets annihilated. Attentivity introduces large fluctuations of energy, which cannot be contained in the thought structure, so thought undergoes disintegration. Attentivity leads the brain from order to higher order.[13] It sees the objective challenge as pure perception, it has the awareness of the inner perceptual image, the values, the significance.

When the system is bombarded by energy of attentivity, it decreases the resistance, the friction, to its flow; the matter content in the consciousness is the source of friction or resistance; and the system undergoes a decrease of matter content which we may call that the system generates inside itself a 'lower level' structure and the system 'escapes into a higher order'. It is an instance of spontaneous higher order appearing out of fluctuations. To remain attentive lays the foundation of a science of spontaneous higher order. Higher order implies higher 'quantum energy potential'.

The Basis of Scientific Method

Erwin Schrodinger, in 1947, put forward two general principles that form the basis of the scientific method–the principle of objectivation and the principle of the understanding of nature.[14] These have been further explored and are discussed as under:

The Principle of Objectivation: Schrodinger wrote, "The physical world picture lacks all the sensual qualities that go to make up the Subject of Cognizance. The model is colourless and soundless and unpalpable. The world of science lacks, or is deprived of, everything that has a meaning only in relation to the consciously, contemplating, perceiving and feeling subject .... The values are missing, and quite particularly meaning and end are missing .... (There) is the absolute silence of all our scientific investigations towards our questions concerning the meaning and scope of the whole display".[15]

Schrodinger wrote, "Mind has erected the objective outside world of the natural philosopher out of its own stuff. Mind could not cope with this gigantic task otherwise than by the simplifying device of excluding itself–withdrawing from its conceptual creation. Hence the latter does not contain its creator".[16] Charles Sherrington wrote, "The material world has only been constructed at the price of taking the self, that is, mind, out of it, removing it; mind is not part of it; obviously, therefore, it can neither act on it nor be acted on by any of its parts".[17] Spinoza and C.J. Jung hold the same opinion. This leads us to a fundamental proposition that: (a) the Subject of Cognizance is at the immanent quantum energy potential of Consciousness; (b) the objective world excludes the Subject from the domain of nature that we endeavour to understand; (c) the objective world is at the lowest quantum energy potential of consciousness; (d) there is no energy exchange between the subject and the object; (e) the subject is "in-here" and the object is "out-there"; (f) the object bestows the *fact*, the objective values; (g) it leads to an awareness of non-dual and non-conceptual frame of reference of mind spectrum; and (h) this leads to invention (and not discovery).

Fritjof Capra wrote, "Rational knowledge and rational activities certainly constitute the major part of scientific research, but are not all there is to it. The rational part of research would, in fact, be useless if it were not complemented by the intuition that gives scientists new insights and makes them creative. These insights tend to come suddenly and, characteristically, not when sitting at a desk working out the equations, but when relaxing in the bath, during a walk in the woods, on the beach, etc. During these periods of relaxation after concentrated intellectual activity, the intuitive mind seems to take over and can produce the sudden clarifying insights which give so much joy and delight to scientific research".[18]

The scientific process that led to its discovery was discussed in an interview with Maurice H. Wilkins, Nobel Prize in Medicine, 1962.[19] The scientist collects all the known data regarding the problem to be investigated. He then formulates the problem based on rational logical way. The scientist puts his whole being into the problem, which implies that the quantum energy potential of the mind enhances, or in other words, he enhances his attentivity to the problems and then stays there. When the mind is at the threshold level (immanent) of potential of consciousness, or the mind is questioned, it provides the answer as insight or intuition. The scientist then plans experiments to verify the intuition in the next few weeks or months. Discoveries come as intuitive flashes. The scientist then writes a paper deliberately as if the intuitive discovery flows from his experimental data. Maurice Wilkins wrote, "I quite agree. A scientific paper is deliberately written in this artificial manner so you can most effectively communicate results to other scientists. Scientific papers are never intended to describe how the work was really done. They simply present the results to other scientists so they can understand what was finally achieved .... The logical and rational is very important element in science. But emphasis on that tends to make people not notice the essential role of intuition". To sum up, a real discovery flows from intuition, but we are in illusion and consider it emerging from intellect in a logical way.

All great discoveries have arisen from the realm of the timelessness, so scientific enquiry is not a cerebral activity and gathering information, but a quest of the Timelessness, the Divinity, the Life Field. A selfless, unfaltering devotion to truth and use of knowledge for man's uplift–higher hierarchical expression of Consciousness–are the only vocation of a scientist.

An objective approach to subjective reactions, subjective feelings gives us objective values, the fact. A simple (pure) perception can result in an objective approach to all the subjective world; this objectivation of the subjective world is a tremendous thing.

The Principle of the Understandability of Nature: The symbolic-dualistic frame of reference of mind spectrum does not have the capacity for understanding. It happens in a non-dual and non-conceptual frame of reference of Mind Continuum. ***Understanding is a movement in the non-duality, a movement of the whole being.*** Understanding comes only when the mind is very quiet, tranquil, silenced.

Understanding is the perfume of a communion. It is not the result of human effort, or human activity, or cerebral activity, but when a human being has the humility to be what he is with nature, with the life around him, then the understanding takes place. We have to step out of mind, out of brain; or in other words, out of the cerebral region. Understanding you cannot acquire. It is a happening when the total being is involved–

from the sensual to the non-sensual, from the conceptual to the non-conceptual, and from the 'successive consciousness' to the 'Simultaneous Consciousness'.

The observation flows to understanding and learning. Understanding and learning are born in non-duality. Intuition (insight) is perception without any doubt. ***Understanding, learning and action are a cyclic process, which results in a spiral going upwards in the vertical dimension; it is a growth in the vertical dimension***. The higher the understanding, the higher the expression of the Consciousness in the human brain-body system.

Recent Discoveries of Modern Science

(a) Many eminent scientists–including Albert Einstein, Werner Heisenberg, Erwin Schrodinger, Arthur Eddington, and so on–have stumbled upon another mode of perception (knowing), which is "understanding of life directly, instead of in the abstract, linear terms of representational thinking".[20] This implies the understanding of the wholeness of life.

(b) A galaxy of scientists–Karl Pribram, Roger Sperry, John Eccles–have opined, "Brain science could no longer afford to shut out that part of the world which we call subjective". We have to "restructure science-education", which takes in its ambient both the objective and the subjective dimension of life and is called the "true-subject"; it observes the whole conditioned and unconditioned psyche which leads to I-consciousness and thought-time going to abeyance; the pure Consciousness (Life Field) bathes the purified brain (neurones) and expresses Itself as order, harmony, nonviolence and peace.

(c) Physicists call the boundary, "the event horizon" ("the frequency barrier") between symbolic-dualistic frame (time) and non-dual frame (timelessness). In the time field, anything that remains is within the speed of light, and in the timeless realm every thing is faster than the speed of light. The speed of light is absolute, it is like a wall that no object can crash through. As we approach the wall, time slows down, mass increases, and space becomes curved.[21]

In a black hole, the photons are devoured in less than a hundred microsecond. Similarly the photons got annihilated when they approach "the event horizon". The time interval is about five thousandths of a second between the cell to signal to the muscle–it corresponds to something moving to and fro two hundred times a second.[22] It is hardly worth noticing anything in such a tiny time scale, yet this is the scale on which our nervous system functions.

(d) In a scientific conference at Moscow in 1996, the Russian scientists "have come up with the idea of a Life Field beyond our physical concepts of time, space and the known electro-magnetic and gravitational fields". In a subsequent Conference at Cambridge University, entitled "Beyond the Brain", it was concluded, "A new scientific approach would include subjective experience as valid information and address all forms of human experience–including intuition, spirituality and mystical encounters".[23] Wills Harman argued that "we need to develop a different form of science to truly understand consciousness". There was a powerful sense that "the transformative possibilities in terms of people across the globe developing an understanding of themselves and each other, and being able to relate in more real and meaningful ways, were tremendous".[23]

Restructuring of Science-Education-Health

(a) ***Restructuring of Science:*** The objective science must restructure itself and consider the subjective and the objective as one harmonious movement. The restructured science deals with the wholeness of life.

(b) ***Restructuring of Education:*** The holistic education is defined as training, purifying the instruments of pure perception. The instruments become a fit channel for self-expression of the Divine–a living of man in the Divine and a Divine living of the Life Field in humanity. The dimension of value education is embedded in the trans-sensual dimension of human personality, the Life Field, the Universal Consciousness.

The holistic education is fundamentally a single dynamic flow of Universal Consciousness and the technologies are (a) ***An Epistemological Revolution Through Scientific Temper***; (b) ***Pilgrimage to the Sacred Temple of Understanding and Learning***; and (c) ***Symbiosis of Science and Spirituality***–are basically one and the same, except a difference of shade. The holistic education embraces both the sensual and the trans-sensual dimensions of life.

(c) ***Restructuring of Medical Education:*** The theme of the Indian Science Congress–2005 is Health Technology. A living in the *present*, the *now* heals, and living in the *past* and duality suppresses man's sensitivity and enhances disease. There is an urgency to restructure medical education which takes in its ambient the psychodynamics of mind-brain-body system and the Unconditioned Energy; or in other words, the wholeness of life.

(d) ***Symbiosis of Science and Spirituality:*** Spirituality is understanding the conditioned mind, the matter content of consciousness, and also to perceive the Unconditioned Energy; so it is the science of the wholeness of life. It aims at self-actualisation of the hidden human potential. Spirituality is fundamental and objective science is a derivative. An integration of science and spirituality is the key to the survival of mankind. It jettisons all pain, misery and travails, and ushers a new era of freedom, peace and bliss. This is the only vocation of the human race. Spirituality is the awareness of the wholeness around you and wholeness within you. In spiritual science the emphasis is on the act of perception, the quality of the instruments for perception, the quality of Consciousness behind the perception. In spirituality, the act of investigation, exploration is conducted on behalf of the whole human race. Spirituality explores what the truth is, what the *fact* is, and what the Reality is behind the truth. Spirituality teaches us to live with the *fact* and transcend the *non-fact*.[24]

(e) ***Intuition:*** Many eminent physicists–Einstein, Schrodinger, Heisenberg, Eddington, and so on–have stumbled upon another mode of knowing, called intimate, or direct, or intuition, or insight, or understanding or non-dual mode of knowing. The "understanding of life directly, instead of in the abstract, linear terms of representational thinking" bestows intuition, spontaneity, sensitivity and creativity. These are metaphysical (quantum logic) insight, falling outside the realm of duality, or the intellectual construction. ***Understanding, learning and action are a cyclic process, which results in a spiral going upwards in a vertical dimension; it is the growth in vertical dimension. The higher the understanding, the higher the expression of consciousness in the human mind-brain-body system***. The higher sensitivity or creativity leads to a perception of pure consciousness.

A non-dual frame of reference of mind spectrum, or understanding of life directly, or intuition does "not submit to codification and analysis" of the psychological mode of mind. It appears that the mystical understanding of the great quantum scientists (or philosophers-mystics or poets) came not from their classical science, but from the quantum logic or pure perception from understanding the wholeness of life.

Mutation or Radical Transformation of the Psyche

Mutation happens in the brain through insight, not through knowledge, not through accumulation. That insight is the ability to see a truth directly, a direct perception of the truth, and education must foster that.

We need restructuring of science-education-health to *observe* truthfully and sincerely the conditioned and the Unconditioned Energy, and this will flow to mutation of the psyche. The different steps in observation, which are expressed to understand and learn, are as under:

(a) ***Ending of I-consciousness:*** If a thought coupled with volitions encounters the true-subject, the I-consciousness is knocked off because it is at the lowest quantum energy potential. This suggests that: (i) the movement of thought-time is independent of I-consciousness; (ii) it is the movement of collective human effort; (iii) both the I-consciousness and thought-structure have a conceptual reality.[25]

(b) ***Ending of Thought-Time:*** When thought-time comes in the realm of true-subject, the photons meet an 'impregnable wall', or "event-horizon", or "frequency-barrier", and are dissipated, which implies that thought-time goes to abeyance and what is left behind is the *fact*, the *true*, the *present*, the *what is*!

Man has to learn through the art of observation to make a quantum jump across the frequency barrier–from lower frequencies (symbolic-dualistic frame of reference) to higher frequencies (non-dual and non-conceptual frame of reference of Mind Continuum). Below the frequency barrier, there is disorder, chaos and disharmony, and this is called the sensual world; and above the frequency barrier there is perfect order, harmony; and this is called the natural world, the Quantum World. Below the frequency barrier is the time field and above the frequency barrier is the timeless realm, the Unknown, the Reality. When Reality bathes the brain cells, there is no pain and misery, and one revels in freedom, harmony, non-violence, peace and bliss. To live in communion with the natural world, Reality, is the consummation of human life.

(c) ***Ending of the Fact:*** If we continue observing or listening to the *fact*, without justification, or condemnation, or motivation, we observe that there is only the *fact* and nothing else. The fact itself is the operator and not you operating on the fact. If you leave the fact alone, it has no time. The fact is free from fear. The fact grows, which implies that there is release of tremendous energy and the fact moves to higher quantum energy potential. This is expressed as Pure Consciousness $\rightarrow$ Fact.

(d) ***Dialogue from within nature:*** We have to initiate a dialogue with nature from within nature, and nature responds to this experimental interrogation. If a scientist, who is aware of "restructured science-education" and lives in that awareness, asks questions addressed to nature, he invariably succeeds in receiving answers directly from nature. Nature is an "open-book" to him.

(e) ***Ending of Violence:*** The violent society is based on laws which are antagonistic to the immutable laws of nature. It is based on callousness and opposition, and not on reverence of life, not on love or tenderness. It is based on acquisition, competition, comparison, exploitation and violence.

The conceptual world is a cultural entertainment of man, collective man, and the concept of identity, individuality, has been sophisticated and refined. What we call ego, the self, the I-consciousness, the "me", has a conceptual reality. Thought structure constructs the ego. There will be violence as long as you live in I-consciousness and thought-time. The ego and thought-structure have to be transcended, it implies a quantum jump from violence to non-violence. The true-subject is engaged in observing the conditioned psyche, which dissolves all psychological and ecological imbalances, terrorism, ethnic conflicts, and so on. It blossoms in a conflict-free society and ushers order, rhythm and peace.

(f) The observation blossoms to freeing the act of perception from the movement of the past, the conditioned energy. When the state of observation is sustained, it changes the quality of your biological structure. The nerves are steady, the chemical system has an equilibrium, equipoise and there is relaxation. There is a growth into a chemically, neurologically relaxed state.

(g) The Universal Consciousness, the Life Field, the Spiritual Energy, the highest quantum energy potential of Consciousness exists throughout the cosmos, and perhaps beyond the cosmos. Emptiness cannot be measured, silence cannot be measured, love cannot be quantified, tenderness and compassion cannot be verbalized. It is the emptiness, or the silence, or the Life Field that heals the psychic pandemic; it ends all violence, terrorism, and so on; and it expresses itself as order and peace. It guarantees human survival and excellence.

The World is Fundamentally a Discontinuous

Nature is not a ramp, but a staircase. Human activities introduce discontinuities in whatever we are observing. These discontinuities are fundamental to the new physics of the twentieth century. Niels Bohr knew that the world was **fundamentally a discontinuous and quantum jumping world**. To Bohr, discontinuity was a fundamental truth.[26]

An event in our nervous systems normally functions in about five thousands of a second. "We are beginning a new age of awareness, the age of quantum consciousness, the age of the conscious atom. By observation within ourselves, we may be able to solve the problems facing on the final frontiers–the frontiers of the human spirit".[27]

The Unmanifest-Manifested

D. S. Kothari wrote, "When an atom makes a transition, or a 'jump', from one stationary state to another the actual process cannot be visualised or even imagined. There are no intermediate stages. We cannot breakdown the process into its components: The entire process of transition from one state to another is a non-visualisable, unanalysable, unity. *It is indivisible.* Its parts cannot even be imagined. It is a 'quantum jump', as we call it".[28] Between any two consecutive orbits, there is the Unmanifest. He added, "In dealing with atomic phenomena we have to recognise that the act of observation is accompanied by an inevitable disturbance which alters the state of the observed system in an unpredictable manner. What is observed is different from what it was before the act of observation. This is inherent in the nature of things. It cannot be eliminated".[29]

There is analogous situation for *thought processes.* As we 'think'– in any sequence of thoughts–there is always a sudden, discontinuous jump from one thought to the next. We are not aware at all of any intermediate stages. If we were so aware, no thinking would be possible. There would be an almost infinite sequence of 'sub-thoughts' between two thoughts, like an infinity of points between the two ends of a line. *Quantum jumps for thought appear to be as much a necessity for the conscious self as these are for the atom.*

The occurrence of observation (seeing) or listening (hearing), smelling or breathing is a movement in the sphere of non-duality. This is expressed in words as:

In the art of observation there is the Unmanifest.

In the art of listening there is the Unmanifest.

In the art of breathing there is the Unmanifest.

In the art of sensual perceptions there is the Unmanifest.[30]

Life begins with breathing in and death begins with breathing out. Each moment when you breathe in, you are reborn, because Unmanifest is going in; each moment when you breathe out you are dead. Love is breathing out, hate is breathing in. Love more–that is breathing out–and your body will gather energy from the whole cosmos. You create the vacuum and the energy comes.[31] A depth understanding of Unmanifest →manifest→Unmanifest breaks down the ego barrier completely, which implies that thought-time has ended. The mind transcends the symbolic-dualistic frame of reference and duality; and makes a quantum jump to non-dual and non-conceptual frame of reference of Mind Continuum.

Nature's Self-Renewal Process

In symbolic-dualistic frame of reference of mind spectrum, breathing-in is inhaling, the Unmanifest; and breathing-out is exhaling, the manifest (the debris). In the non-dual and non-conceptual frame of reference of Mind Continuum, love is breathing-out because then you throw out the Unmanifest for sharing; and hate is breathing-in to take the manifest in for purification. There is discontinuity between breathing-in and breathing-out, and in this discontinuity there is the Unmanifest. Breathing-in and breathing-out are not two opposite things, they are two parts of one process. And these two parts are organic parts, you cannot divide them. Life is a process between breathing-in and breathing-out–you are just a passage, a passer-by to see the great drama of existence.

The natural process is free from any preferences, desires, motives, acquisitions, storing. It is free from any psychological imbalances. It is free from any opinion for or against, no likes or dislikes. You have to understand as to how you have created the mess around you–no body else has created it; it is your mind's disease of preference, of choosing or rejection. Accept life in its wholeness, accept the immutable laws of nature.

Mind and Consciousness

Wilder Penfield concluded that the fact that the mind can survive brain trauma and function under anesthesia points very strongly to the separate existence of the mind. He concluded that, "it is the mind which experiences and it is the brain which records the experience .... our minds and our brains are not at all the same".[32] Brain is a part of the objective world, it can be investigated objectively. Mind is subjective, it is a vibrational self-conscious energy. The control of the mind over the body is an incontrovertible fact of personal experience.

Hideki Yukawa wrote, "It is obvious that unless something rises into the consciousness it cannot become an object of rational thought, of rational consideration. At the same time, everyone will surely agree on the importance of an awareness that living in a world open towards both the exterior and the interior is a special characteristic of man's lot".[33] E.P. Wigner wrote, "The measurement is not completed until its result enters our consciousness .... (this) last step is, at the present state of our knowledge, shrouded in the mystery and no explanation has been given for it so far in terms of quantum mechanics, or in terms of any other theory".[34] He added, "Self-identity demands consciousness. You would not have identity without consciousness. I know that it is my consciousness which knows, which tells me that".[35] Fritjof Capra wrote, "By consciousness I mean the state of mind characterized by self-awareness, where one is aware that he is aware".[36] An explicit involvement of consciousness is an essential factor for any perception.

The nature of consciousness, at its root, is just mirror-like. Erwin Schrodinger wrote, "The world is given but once. Nothing is reflected. The original and the mirror-image are identical .... The world is given to me but once, not one existing and one perceived. Subject and the object are one. The barrier between them cannot be said to have broken down as a result of recent experiences in the physical sciences, for this barrier does not exist".[37] Man has deformed his consciousness, it is now filled with opinions, fragments, interpretations, preferences, judgments, ideals, percepts–this is called conditioned mind, or a broken mirror. Mind (conditioned) distorts the reality and Consciousness reveals it. If scientific observation is continued for a long time, it again becomes a mirror, a pure consciousness.

Mind cannot understand any thing unless the opposite is brought in, because through contrast mind becomes capable of seeing. There is no possibility for the mind to see anything whole. It can only see one half and the other half is inferred. Life cannot be understood if there is no death and happiness is impossible to feel if there is no unhappiness. A scientific observation by restructured science or science with creativity leads to ending of duality.

The States of Consciousness

(a) ***Waking State of Mind:*** Both the subject and the object are at the same quantum energy potential and called successive consciousness. The mind absorbs all your consciousness and transforms into mind stuff. This is at the lowest quantum energy potential of consciousness hence there is interaction between the subject and the object, and one is aware of the distorted object. The whole process is repetitive and mechanical, so it has no understanding and learning.

(b) ***Classical Scientific Mode of Mind:*** The subject is at the immanent quantum energy potential and the object at the successive quantum energy potential of consciousness, hence there is no interaction between the subject and the object. The subject of cognizance is aware of the 'objective fact'–

this is called the no-mind state. The perception gives the "objective knowledge", which is modified use of the existing material; it gives rise to invention, and not discovery.

(c) ***The Restructured Scientific Mode of Mind:*** We have to restructure science-education-health, which takes in its ambient both the subjective and the objective fields. It deals with the wholeness of life, so it is at the maximum (ultimate, or transcendent) quantum energy potential of consciousness. It resolves all psychological imbalances and ecological crisis. It bestows order, rhythm, non-violence and peace.

The Benediction of the Infinite, the Timelessness

All the great saints/sages have exhorted us not to condemn, not to judge, no demand, no hankering for anything, no clinging; which implies transcendence of all psychological imbalances. Some benedictions of nature are as under:

(a) Thinking is a material activity involving brain. We have to learn to transcend I-consciousness and thought-structure. When the mind moves not, time comes to a stop. You relax into a sacred state of non-action, not-knowing, non-experiencing. Relaxation implies silent, vacant, empty mind. Nature expresses itself in a silent mind, so it rejects choice. This takes man to a state of awareness, not in the state of knowledge and memory. Man is born to be free, to live in peace, in imperturbable peace within.

(b) In the ultimate, the goal-oriented mind is a hindrance, the greatest hindrance. You simply *be*! The ultimate will come! Let it be the ultimate's decision and problem, not yours. You leave it to him (Life Field), he knows more. Let it be God's problem, let him worry about it. You don't worry–you simply enjoy life as it moves, while it lasts. You dance and sing and be ecstatic, and let God worry. Why are *you* worried?

(c) When you dance but there is no dancer, when you observe but there is no observer, when you love and there is no lover, it happens! When you walk and there is no walker inside, it happens.

(d) When life happens without you–birth happens, death happens, love happens without you–then why should you be worried.

(e) The truth can only be whole. Between life and death, and death and life there is the Unmanifest and the Unmanifest is the truth. When you see life and death simultaneously, the polarities vanish, and there is only the truth. Life exists in polarities and mind exists in one part of the polarity; that is why mind is always false.

(f) When Intelligence is regenerated, there is only the vibration of pure Consciousness which resolves all our psychological challenges and ecological crisis.

(g) If even one percent of mankind understands this and lives that understanding, this will result in mutation in the human consciousness. Some saints and sages see on the horizon of human consciousness the struggling emergence of a new culture, a new global human culture, a global spirituality–this is the science of life and living. This will flow to order, harmony, non-violence and peace. This guarantees human survival and excellence.

The New Human Being

Let us put aside the whole thought of reform–political, economic, social and religious. We have to be concerned with radical change or mutation of human mind-brain-body system. It happens in a silent mind. The only revolution, is the revolution between man and man, between human beings. That is our only concern. Ilya Prigogine wrote, "It is quite remarkable that we are at a moment both of profound change in the scientific concept of nature and of the structure of human society as a result of the demographic explosion. As a result, there is a need for new relations between man and nature and between man and man. We can no longer accept the old a priori distinction between scientific and ethical values.... Today we know that time is a construction and therefore carries an ethical responsibility".[38] In this revolution there are no blueprints, no ideologies, no conceptual utopias. J. Krishnamurti wrote, "It is *only* the action of will and assertiveness that needs to be changed at all, because the only mischief in relationship is conflict, between individuals or within individuals, and conflict *is* will and assertiveness".[39]

We have to learn to relax from the outward stresses of life and nourish the soul (immanent quantum energy potential of Consciousness). Human mind-brain-body system is a laboratory, an experiment in creating a "New Man"–a human being who lives in harmony with the inner and the outer, with himself and his environment, and who is free from all ideologies and conditionings that now divide humanity.

Intelligence

Intelligence perceives life in its wholeness, and responds to it out of its own wholeness. The perception through intelligence, through sensitivity is a perception in non-duality. In love, beauty there is instantaneous perception. The perception and the response have no time lag between them.

The transcendence of intellect to intelligence; from arrogance of knowledge and experience to the humility of openness and vulnerability; from subject-object duality to non-dual state of mind; from knowledge to intuition, is the quantum jump. When one is born into the realm of intelligence or non-personal sensitivity, then that sensitivity, that intelligence uses the brain and also the physical structure. There is no conflict, no violence, no fear in intelligence.

The communion with the Divine, the Eternal, the Infinite is a happening; it is not the result of my doing. The uncovering of the secret is not a human achievement. It is something that happens, when the human being puts all his conditionings into relaxation, and remains before the mystery of Life in utter humility, in utter nakedness of his psyche. Then the mystery unfurls itself, uncovers itself. It uncovers itself into us.

The consummation of human growth is the manifestation of the Divine, the Self-Unfoldment of man. Life is consummation of human growth.

The Art of Living

As a symbol, we may compare the known (successive consciousness, conditioned psyche, the man-made social cosmos) to a drop of water; and the Unknown to a fathomless and boundless ocean. The known is in the field of time, so it is limited and transient. The Unknown is in the realm of the timelessness, so it is eternal, infinite and immutable.

The arts of observing, listening, understanding, learning, action are direct; and thinking is indirect. The indirect processes are antagonistic to the immutable laws of nature, so the conditioned psyche constructs conflict, pain, and sorrow. The direct happening implies an expression of Cosmic Consciousness in a non-dual and non-conceptual Mind Continuum, so it is beyond the brain and intellect. "Science with creativity" is direct expression of Cosmic Consciousness in the pure mind. David Bohm, an eminent physicist, wrote:

> The ultimate perception does not originate in the brain or any material structure, although a material structure is necessary to manifest it. The subtle mechanism of knowing the truth does not originate in the brain.[40]

The art of living emerges from direct perception or ultimate perception; and this is free from any psychological imbalances, conflict, chaos. The art of "science (restructured science-education-health) with creativity" leads to an expression of the wholeness of life.

Fred Alan Wolf wrote, "We are beginning a new age of awareness, the age of quantum consciousness, the age of the conscious atoms. By looking within ourselves, we may be able to solve the problems facing us on the final frontier–the frontier of the human spirit".[41] It appears that the order of the universe is the order of our minds and reveals a relationship.

An Action Plan or A Paradigm Shift

(a) To educate the educator is to have him understand himself. This is one of the most difficult undertakings, because most of us are already crystallized within a system of thought or a pattern of action. The teachers training programme is *how to think* and not *what to think.*

(b) We have to introduce psychodynamics of mind-brain-body system in science faculty and transpersonal psychology in art faculty as a part of educational curriculum at University/College/School level.

(c) To formulate an Action Plan for global education based on ***Epistemological Revolution Through Scientific Temper***, or pilgrimage to the ***Sacred Temple of Understanding and Learning***, or the symbiosis of ***Science and Spirituality***.

(d) To formulate a global evolutionary policy, to be a co-worker with Nature in its evolutionary impulse.

(e) To construct a new society, which is consistent with the scientific discoveries of harmonious interrelatedness and oneness in Nature. We need a radically different social, economic and material structure–a new architecture of our cultural revolution.

(f) The essence of the masterplan is "Restructuring of Science-Education-Health"–which is called true-subject and deals with the wholeness of life. The true-subject then observes the conditioned psyche and the Unconditioned Energy, which results in I-consciousness and thought-structure going to abeyance, and the transcendent potential of Consciousness is aware of itself. It bestows order, harmony, non-violence and peace.

(g) There will be need to create some infrastructure for conducting courses. There is need to write books for guidance of teachers and students, and for different levels. This is possible if Govt. of India approves of the basic programme. Without Government active support, any action plan will prove to be a failure. And if Government escapes its responsibility, it will jeopardize the future of India and mankind.

Concluding Comment

(a) Under the auspices of the United Nations, an International Conference discussed, "Humanity stands at a critical juncture in history, one that calls for strong moral and spiritual leadership to help set a new direction for society".[42] The challenges facing mankind are not in the external field, but are embedded in the human psyche, and have assumed a global dimension.

(b) Science has now recognized that the whole cosmos (and beyond cosmos) is full of high frequency energy (higher frequency means higher energy) which is the womb of existence. The aim of human life is to perceive and live in that wholeness, which flows into harmony, order, non-violence and peace. Let us work jointly for that consummation of life.

(c) The past disappears, the past is nowhere, just in the memory, the inheritance. The future is nowhere, just in imagination. The past is that which is not now, and the future is that which is not born. The present is the *Now*, the Eternity. Ken Wilber wrote, "This present moment contains all time and is therefore itself timeless, and hence *this timeless present is Eternity itself*, a moment without date or duration, extension or succession, past or future, before or after, "having the whole of its existence simultaneously, which is the nature of Eternity".[43]

(c) There are arts of observation, listening, understanding, learning, acting, and all these are *direct*; but thinking is indirect. Direct implies to live in communion with the immutable laws of nature, and *indirect* means to live antagonistic to the laws of nature. Every *direct* act of living is an act of worship, because it enhances the quantum energy potential of consciousness of the system.

(d) Man does not have anything which is his personal–including brain and memory, which is of humanity and the realm of the timelessness. J. Krishnamurti wrote, "I am the conclusion of all the experience of mankind. The story of all mankind is me .... I am humanity, not the collective".[44] Everything is a grace of nature. We are only dancing dolls, where someone else (Cosmic Consciousness, Life Field) pulls the strings; we are toys in the hands of destiny. A living in communion with nature is free from all psychological imbalances, challenges, strife, conflict, and so on.

(e) The chaos is in our mind-brain-body system–man-made social cosmos. It is a crisis in our consciousness. The transformation/mutation in our consciousness can happen through observation-listening-learning. These acts of observation and listening bestow reaction-free perception, unpolluted perception. This bestows a higher level of awareness that has the capacity to resolve our all challenges and bestow non-violence and peace.

(f) In an oft-quoted statement Schrodinger says: "I consider science an integrating part of our endeavour to answer the one great philosophical question which embraces all others, the one that Plotinus expressed by his brief: *Who are we*? And more than that: I consider this not one of the tasks, but *the* task of science, the only one that really counts".[45] The question "Who am I?" is, on close analysis, no different from the question "What is the abode of Truth?" The search of "Who am I?" is the foundation of all true morality and religion. Erwin Schrodinger again echoed, "Scientific attitudes would have to be rebuilt, science must be made anew. Care is needed".[46]

(g) Jawaharlal Nehru wrote, "It is for the human mind and human spirit to control it (the Buddha or the bomb) and direct it in the right direction. The great path of science is to be tempered by something and that something is spirituality which gives us to some extent the right measure, the right perspective and right direction to look it".[47] Prof. A.P.J. Abdul Kalam, President of India, wrote on 7-10 December, 2003 that we have "to discuss ways in which peace and harmony can be strengthened through developing connectivity between religions and by weaving a beautiful garland of spirituality between various faiths".[48] On September 14, 2004, he said, "You need a new world order system".[49] Recently we published "Science with Creativity".[50] Goverdhan Mehta on July 18, 2000 said, "We have to identify science with creativity". He also emphasised, "the connectivity of minds".[51] Again Jayant Vishnu Narlikar on April 9, 2001, said, "What is needed is a campaign for scientific temper".[52] M.G.K. Menon said, "Unless you are creative, you cannot be innovative .... Commitment and dedication, apart from intellect are required for great scientific discoveries and advancement".[53] A paper has been forwarded to Vedanta, UK.[54]

(h) The mutation in consciousness happens when the true-subject (restructured science-education-health) observes/listens the conditioned psyche and the Unconditioned Energy, or in other words, the wholeness of life. This resolves the age-old tide of I-consciousness, thought-structures, psychological imbalances, ecological crisis, and other human challenges. This guarantees human survival and excellence. It blossoms to compassion; that is, passion for all. Passion bestows love. Love is not different from truth. Love is that state in which the thought process, as time, has completely ceased. Love can be found only in action, which is relationship. Where love is there is transformation. Transformation and love lead to human survival. It is the awareness of the Wholeness, the Oneness of Life that heals the psychic pandemic. It is the Supreme Consciousness/ Intelligence that resolves all the human challenges, and bestows order, harmony, non-violence and peace.

(i) We want a revolution, psychological revolution, in which the whole human race has to participate and every man is an equal partner. This revolution will regenerate or rejuvenate Intelligence so that it perceives the new dimension of an integral and all-inclusive consciousness, that can guarantee human survival along with all fauna and flora.

(j) The "science with creativity" is an experiment of creating a "New Man" – a human being who lives in harmony with the inner and the outer, with himself and his environment, and who is free from all ideologies and conditionings that now divide humanity. The human survival is embedded in this gigantic experiment. And if man escapes his responsibility, he does so at his own peril, of India and of mankind.

References

1. Teilhard de Chardin, in Sampooran Singh, *The Holistic Education*, New Delhi: Siddharth Publications, 1987, p. 109.
2. *The Millennium World Peace Summit of Religions and Spiritual Leaders*, United Nations, 28-31 August 2000; in *Vedanta*, Ramakrishna Vedanta Centre, UK, No 301, p. 224.
3. Sampooran Singh, Dr (Mrs) Kanwaljit Kaur, *Global Education and Human Survival: A Scientific Appraisal*, New Delhi: Sanbun Publishers, March 2002, pp. 46, 35-36.
4. Sampooran Singh, *The Human Paradox (SS: Two)*, Chandigarh: Faith Publishers, 1988, pp. 5-9.
5. Huston Smith, in *Synthesis of Science and Religion*, Mumbai: Bhaktivedanta Institute, June 1988, p. 122.
6. Jacques Monod, *Chance and Necessity*, New York: Vintage Books, 1972, p. 171; in *Synthesis of Science and Religion, ibid.*, p. 127.
7. George Wald, in *The Evolution of Consciousness*, New Delhi: National Publishing House, 1983, pp. 13, 14.
8. P. Krishna, *Education, Science, Spirituality*, USA: Institute for Higher Education, Research and Dialogue, August 1993, p. 12.
9. Erwin Schrodinger, *What is Life? & Mind and Matter*, London: Cambridge University Press, Ed. 1967, p. 128.
10. Ilya Prigogine and Isabella Stengers, *Order Out of Chaos*, Bantam Books, 1984, p. 5.
11. Erwin Schrodinger, *op. cit.*, pp. 140, 136.
12. Arthur Eddington, in Swami Ranganathananda, *Science and Religion*, Calcutta: Advaita Ashrama, 1979, p. 125.
13. Sampooran Singh, *The Self and Its Mind-Brain Equipment*, Chandigarh:

Sanjivini Medical and Educational Trust, 1987, pp. 133-135.

14. Erwin Schrodinger, *op. cit.*, pp. 126-137, 110-125.
15. *ibid.*, p. 148.
16. *ibid.*, p. 131.
17. Charles Sherrington, in Erwin Schrodinger, *op. cit.*, p. 128.
18. Fritjof Capra, *The Tao of Physics*, Bantam Books (Second Edition), 1988, p. 18.
19. Maurice H. Wilkins, in *Synthesis of Science and Religion*, Mumbai: The Bhaktivedanta Institute, June 1988, pp. 31-32.
20. Alan W. Watts, *The Ways of Zen*, New York: Vintage Books, 1957, p. 10.
21. Deepak Chopra, *How to Know God*, London: Rider, 2000, pp. 270-271.
22. Fred Alan Wolf, *Taking a Quantum Leap*, San Francisco: Harper and Row, 1981, pp. 236, 248.
23. Joan Walton, *New Science*, Winter 1996.
24. Sampooran Singh, *A Review on Symbiosis of Science and Spirituality*, Dagshai: The Atam Science Trust, October 7, 2002, pp. 16, 17.
25. Sampooran Singh and Dr (Mrs) Kanwaljit Kaur, *Peace, Security and Survival: A Scientific Quest*, July 5, 2004.
26. Niels Bohr, in Fred Alan Wolf, *Taking the Quantum Leap*, Harper and Row, 1981, pp. 21, 85.
27. Fred Alan Wolf, *ibid.*, pp. 236, 248.
28. D.S. Kothari, *Atom and Self*, in *The Evolution of Consciousness*, New Delhi: National Publishing House, 1983, p. 212.
29. *ibid.*, *Some Thoughts on Science and Religion*, The University of Delhi, 31 October & 3 November 1977, p. 25.
30. Sampooran Singh, *Vedanta*: Ramakrishna Vedanta Centre, Bourne End, Buckinghamshire SL8 5LG UK, No. 315, January-February 2004, p. 15.
31. Osho, *The Book of Nothing*, Pune: Rebel Publishing House Pvt. Ltd., 1975, pp. 15, 17.
32. Wilder Penfield, in Deepak Chopra, *How to Know God*, Rider, 2000, pp. 217, 214.
33. Hideki Yukawa, *Creativity and Intuition*, Tokyo: Kodansha International Ltd., 1973, p. 203.
34. Eugene Wigner, in D.S. Kothari, *Some Thoughts on Science and Religion*, *op. cit.*, p. 26.
35. *ibid.*, in *Synthesis of Science and Religion, op. cit.*, p. 262.
36. Fritjof Capra, in *ibid.*, p. 275.
37. Erwin Schrodinger, *op. cit.*, pp. 146, 137.
38. Ilya Prigogine, *op. cit.*, p. 312.
39. J. Krishnamurti, *The Urgency of Change*, London: Victor Gollancz Ltd., 1977, p. 191.

40. David Bohm, in Gary Zukav, *The Dancing Wu Li Masters*, Fontana/Collins, 1982, p. 327.
41. Fred Alan Wolf, *Taking a Quantum Leap*, San Francisco: Harper and Row, 1981, pp. 236, 248.
42. *The Millennium World Peace Summit of Religious and Spiritual Leaders (United Nations)*, New York: 28-31 August, 2000.
43. Ken Wilber, *The Spectrum of Consciousness*, USA: The Theosophical Publishing House, Quest Book, 1982, p. 98.
44. J. Krishnamurti, *KFI*, 1982, No. 1, p. 40.
45. Erwin Schrodinger, *Science and Humanism*, Cambridge University Press, 1951, pp. 4, 51; in D.S. Kothari, *Atom and Self*, New Delhi: National Publishing House, 1983, p. 208.
46. *Ibid.*, *What is Life*? & *Mind and Matter*, *op. cit.*, p. 132.
47. Jawaharlal Nehru, in *Inauguration of the Prof. D.S. Kothari Centre for Science, Ethics and Education*, Delhi: University of Delhi.
48. Prof. A.P.J. Abdul Kalam, President of India, in *Souvenir*, *Towards a Culture of Harmony and Peace*, December 7-10, 2003.
49. *Ibid.*, *The Tribune*, September 14, 2004.
50. Dr (Mrs) Kanwaljit Kaur, Paramjit Singh and Sampooran Singh, *Science with Creativity*, Vedanta, UK Ramakrishna Vedanta Centre, No. 296, November-December 2000, pp. 256-267.
51. Goverdhan Mehta, in *Global Education & Human Survival*, New Delhi: Sanbun Publishers, March 2002, p. 22.
52. Jayant Vishnu Narlikar, *ibid.*, p. 22.
53. M G K Menon, *The Tribune*, November 28, 2004.
54. Sampooran Singh, *Science With Creativity: Consciousness and Spirituality*, unpublished (submitted to Vedanta, U.K.).

Part II
Project Launched by United Nations on 23 September 2003

Abstract (Chapters 16 – 19)

The UN Foundation, along with partners from around the globe, has launched a major initiative in support of the High-Level Panel appointed by UN Secretary-General Kofi Annan, to assess 21st Century threats to international peace and security. The High-Level Panel will recommend ways in which the international community can reform to effectively address modern-day challenges. [www.unfoundation.org/].

Modern physics has confirmed that psychological imbalances, pollution and environmental disasters, a rising wave of violence and crime, a crisis in health care, an energy crisis, terrorism, corruption, high inflation and unemployment, poverty and hunger in certain parts of the world, are different facets of the fundamental crisis of perception of human mind-brain-body system. The racial conditioned psyche is leading mankind to self-annihilation in a foreseeable period of time. The challenges are not political, nor economic, nor social, but are evolutionary in nature.

The UN is treating the symptoms in the external world through socio-political-economic reforms. These are expedient measures, which are transient, temporary and ephemeral; and do not have the capacity for a permanent and sustainable solution of the human psyche. The United Nations have to initiate "the Global Manhatten Project for Survival of Mankind". If UN escapes its responsibility, it will do so at the peril of the human race.

We have to work here and now for radical revolution, or transformation, or mutation of the human psyche. We have to educate ourselves for a quantum jump from self-knowing through self-observation to self-awareness. Communion with nature is a non-subjective action. It is the integral dimension of the Cosmic Consciousness that leads to the conquest of all human challenges and guarantees survival and peace to the human race. Either we die together, or we live together.

In oneself is embedded the whole world. One must learn to observe the conditioned psyche by the scientific mode of mind; and this leads to global peace and security. The cosmic Consciousness (Nature), out of its benediction, helps to make a quantum jump from psychosocial evolution to spiritual evolution. This ends all human challenges. One revels in freedom, truth, love. This energises a new realm of non-violence, order, harmony, peace and security.

The aims and objects of this monograph is "to open a dialogue with an open mind" especially with scientists, philosophers and social-activists. This sharing leads to self-knowledge of the mind-brain-body system. It flowers to self-awareness of the whole system. The self-awareness or attentivity – in the words of Albert Einstein – opens to "objective observation and understanding", which flows to transcending thought-structure coupled with volitions, and this blossoms to "peace and serenity". This energises Intelligence which resolves all challenges, and man revels in order, harmony, non-violence and peace. This is the only vocation of human life.

It is the moral responsibility of awakened men and Governments to submit this as Agenda for the United Nations. If man escapes his responsibility, he will do so at his own peril and that of Invddia and mankind.

16

The Urgency for Radical Transformation of Human Psyche

Many eminent scientists, philosophers-mystics, political leaders have echoed that man has taken a perilous path; and the psychosocial evolution is leading mankind to self-destruction or self-annihilation. They have suggested healing the diseased human psyche, or to end the psychic pandemic, or to resolve the crisis of perception. Some most spectacular passages are quoted as under:

(a) In 1931, J. Krishnamurti, eminent philosopher-mystic, told Jawaharlal Nehru, that, "if they ignored inner regeneration in the struggle for Independence, India would lose its way".[1] Krishnamurti also remarked, "A general destructive violence, a fragmentation at all levels and a growing lack of sensitivity was permeating the landscape of India".

(b) President Vaclav Havel, Czech Republic, addressing the US Congress in 1990 said, "Without a global revolution in the sphere of human consciousness, nothing will change for the better in our being as human". On July 4, 1994, he spoke at Philadelphia, "The modern age has ended. Today, we are going through a transitional period, when it seems that something is on the way out and something else is painfully being born. It is as if something were crumbling, decaying and exhausting itself, while something else, still indistinct, were arising from the rubble .... The end of the era of rationalism has been catastrophic .... Transcendence as the only real alternative to extinction". In another speech at Stanford University, he suggested to regenerate that: (i) spiritual dimension that connects all cultures and in fact all humanity; (ii) to discover and renew its own transcendental origins; and (iii) modern man has lost: his transcendental anchor".[2]

(c) In 1932 after a World Disarmament Conference in Geneva, Albert Einstein, the greatest physicist, in an unusual bout of anger, exclaimed:

.... they (politicians and statesmen) have cheated us; they have fooled us. Hundreds of millions of people in Europe and in America; billions of people have been and are being cheated, traded and tricked out of their lives, health and well-being.[3]

Einstein wrote, "The significant problems we face cannot be solved at the same level of thinking we used when we created them".

(d) Robert Muller in the Foreword to the Source Book for the Parliament of Religions, Chicago, 1993, wrote:

Nevertheless, one dimension has been missing from this extraordinary journey, a dimension lamented by Secretaries-General Dag Hammarskjold, U Thant and Javier Perez de Cuellar: the spiritual dimension, the highest, deepest, most common, universal and binding dimension of all.... The common heritages and their spirituality can be the greatest single contribution to a better world.[4]

(e) Federico Mayor Zaragoza in an international meet of Nobel Laureates at Paris in 1988 concluded:

Never before, until now, has the tension between science and the human conscience, between technology and ethics, reached a point where it has become a threat to the world as a whole .... We are so dazzled that we do not perceive the threats hanging over our heads, warning us of the pressing need for a radical new and universal ethical outlook on the future of present-day science.[5]

(f) The Committee on Science and Technology, USA, submitted in June 1981 a lengthy report to the House of Representatives, USA, which encouraged serious assessment of further research on "*the physics of consciousness*", and concluded that recent experiments:

.... that there exists an 'interconnectiveness' of the human mind with other minds and with matter .... that the human mind may be able to obtain the information independent of geography and time.[6]

(g) The Union of Concerned Scientists (UCS) issued a "*World Scientists' Warning to Humanity*" in April 1993, signed by over 1670 scientists including 104 Nobel laureates, concluding that :

Human beings and the natural world are on a collision course .... A new ethic is required–a new attitude towards discharging our responsibility for caring for ourselves and for the earth.... This ethic must motivate a great movement, convincing reluctant leaders and reluctant governments and reluctant peoples themselves to effect the needed changes.[7]

(h) Jacques Monod, Nobel Prize winning biologist, wrote in 1972, "No society before ours was ever rent by contradictions so agonising .... What we see opening before us today is an abyss of darkness".[8]

(i) George Wald, Nobel prize in Medicine, 1967, wrote, "Our society has taken a wrong turn .... By now, the problem is not transcendence, but survival".[9]

(j) P. Krishna wrote, "We are going towards self-annihilation and not too much time is left now".[10]

(k) Russian scientists, in 1996, have proposed a Life Field, beyond our physical concepts of time, space and the known concepts of electromagnetic and gravitational fields.[11] This was followed by another scientific conference at Cambridge University, which concluded, "A new scientific approach would include subjective experience as valid information and address all forms of human experience–including intuition, spirituality and mystical encounters".[11] The Life Field appears to be synonymous to Universal Consciousness or *Brahman*.

It appears that our survival is at stake. We cannot escape our responsibility for mutation of our psyche *here* and *now*.

References

1. Pupul Jayakar, *Krishnamurti: A Biography*, Harper and Row, 1986, pp. 397, 314.
2. Vaclav Havel, (a) in *Our Global Neighbourhood: The Report of the Commission on Global Governance*, New York: Oxford University Press, 1995, pp. 353-54; (b) *Speech at Philadelphia, July 4, 1994*; and (c) *Speech at Stanford University, September 29, 1994.*
3. Albert Einstein, in Sampooran Singh, *The Pilgrimage to the Third Millennium*, Chandigarh: Faith Publishers, January 1995, p. 16.
4. Robert Muller, *Foreword to the Source Book for the Parliament of Religions*, Chicago, 1993.
5. Federico Mayor Zaragoza, *A New Ethical Outlook*, The Courier, May 1988, p. 4.
6. *Report to the House of Representatives*, USA: Committee on Science and Technology, June 1981, in R.G. Jahn, February 1982, *Proceedings of the IEEE*, Vol. 70, No. 2, p. 165.
7. Union of Concerned Scientists, *World's Scientists' Warning to Humanity*, USA: 26 Church Street, Cambridge, MA 02238, April 1993.

8. Jacques Monod, in *Synthesis of Science and Religion*, Mumbai: The Bhaktivedanta Institute, June 1988, p. 127.
9. George Wald, in *The Evolution of Consciousness*, New Delhi: National Publishing House, 1983, p. 14.
10. P. Krishna, *Education, Science, Spirituality*, California: Institute for Higher Education, Research and Dialogue, 1993, p. 14.
11. Joan Walton, *Scientists Tune into Consciousness*, New Science, Winter 1996.

17
Symbiosis of Science and Spirituality

Man is an amphibian who lives simultaneously in two worlds–(a) the man-made social cosmos, or time-space-causation matrices, or successive consciousness, or immanent quantum energy potential of consciousness; and (b) the ultimate quantum energy potential of Cosmic Consciousness, or the Simultaneous Consciousness. Our daily living is nothing but a chain of reactions to the compulsions that surrounds us–culturally, socially, economically, politically. The reactions express themselves as thought-structure coupled with I-consciousness, or intellectual-constructions. The Cosmic Consciousness expresses itself as spiritual energy–which expresses itself as order, harmony, non-violence and peace.

The traditional religion is invariably past-oriented and takes you backward, or old thought-structure. ***We see that all knowledge (information), thought-structures, ideals, beliefs, concepts are sterile in transformation of the psyche of man, or in other words, to bring radical transformation in the human psyche.*** We have constructed a society which indicates the collapse of all spiritual values and the glorification of all sensual values–the values of the products of mind and senses, and the values of things made by hand and the machine. The more significance we give to the sensual value of things, the greater the confusion, turmoil and strife.[1-4]

Objective science appears to be an abstract and abstruse collection of data, a repertory of cold and impersonal facts and measurements. It adds to materialism and conditioning of psyche. A triumph of human reason turned into a sad truth. It seems that science debased everything it touched.

A number of movements leading to spiritual awareness, social reformation and political struggle sprang up which manifested the awakening of national soul. Gandhiji through the formula of *Satya* and *Ahimsa* used the spiritual force in the national struggle for political independence against one of the mightiest physical power, the British Empire, and achieved success with glory. Acharya Vinoba conducted another experiment of

Bhoodan Movement (transfer of land). Sri Aurobindo gave birth to entirely a new science of the supermind. With his evolutionary development in the world of spirituality he discovered a new principle of consciousness which has got the potency and promise to radically change the human nature and the world order. The Supermind is the uniting link, the cementing Force, the integrating Factor between the Supreme and the Nature. Swamiji wrote, "The most vital question as to how to employ the conscious force of the supermind, or what techniques to be used in the application of the supermental formula in physical life, remains. .... The scientific formula of the supermind, the dynamic spiritual consciousness has been discovered but the technology for its employment in the service of mankind or its application in the physical life of the world, remains to be developed". These eminent seers/sages basically explored spirituality and lived a spiritual life. But the conditioned human psyche has refused to transform itself.

This article discusses the symbiosis of science and spirituality. The traditional religion and spirituality have failed to radically transform the human psyche. It explores the science of spirituality, or physics of consciousness. The exploration shows a *missing link* in the realm of spirituality, which is "restructuring of science-education", and we call it "true-subject". This is also called the "third alternative" based on spiritual culture. The true-subject has the non-variable awareness, and deals with the wholeness of life. If a thought-structure coupled with volitions (I-consciousness) comes in the field of true-subject, it gets exploded and goes to abeyance. This leads to radical transformation or mutation in the human psyche, which is directed to order, non-violence and peace.

The Universe is False to Itself and Eludes Itself?

As atoms with consciousness are looking at atoms with consciousness, we have the same experience of wonder and mystery whenever we look at the universe. We are looking at ourselves. The universe cannot totally see itself as an object without totally mutilating itself. The attempt to know the universe as an object of knowledge is thus profoundly and inextirpably contradictory. Eddington put it succinctly, "Nature thus provides that knowledge of one-half of the world would ensure ignorance of the other half". And Haldane muttered that "the universe is not only queerer than we suppose, it is queerer than we can suppose".

Spencer Brown, in a most spectacular passage, wrote:

> We cannot escape the fact that the world we know is constructed to see itself.... But in order to do so, evidently it must first cut itself up into at least one state which sees, and at least one other state which is seen. In this severed and mutilated condition, whatever it sees is *only partially* itself.[5]

Biophysicist L.L. Whyte wrote, "Man cannot think where he is, for he has created two worlds from one".[6] Alexander Koyre wrote about the man-made world, "a world, in which, though there is a place for everything, there is no place for man. Thus the world of science–the real world–became estranged and utterly divorced from the world of life". He added, "Two worlds: this means two truths. Or no truth at all. This is the tragedy of the modern mind which "solved the riddle of the universe", but only to replace it by another riddle: the riddle of itself".[7]

Erwin Schrodinger discussed the exclusion of the Subject of Cognizance from the objective world picture and called it the "Principle of Objectivation". He also quoted C.J. Jung, B. Spinoza and Charles Sherrington in support of it.[8] We summarised it as under:

> The human-made social cosmos, or construct of the symbolic-dualistic frame of reference of mind spectrum represents the immanent quantum energy potential, and it is divorced from the ultimate quantum energy potential. ***The construct of the mind is the only "reality" where the transcendent potential has gone to abeyance and its only linkage is the immanent potential. It represents the relative field of consciousness.***[9]

It implies that the subject can never be aware of the true-object, as both the subject and the object are continuities of change and the object has immanent quantum energy potential. This suggests that thought-structure coupled with I-consciousness is always at a lower quantum energy potential.

Arthur Eddington wrote, "The scientific physical body which not only lacks all and every sensual qualities but in addition is riddled with holes; by far the greatest part of it is empty space, just nothingness, interspersed with innumerable tiny specks of something, the electrons and the nuclei whirling around, but always separated by distances at least 100,000 times their own size".[10] He added, "The frank realization that physical science is concerned with a *world of shadows* is one of the most significant of recent advances".[11] It is precisely in the dualism of creating two worlds from one that the universe becomes severed, mutilated, and consequently "false to itself". The dualistic illusion is that the subject is fundamentally separate and distinct from the object. To sum up, ***we do not see things as they are–we see them as we are.***

Modes of Knowing

Many eminent scientists–including Albert Einstein, Werner Heisenberg, Erwin Schrodinger, Arthur Eddington, and so on–have stumbled upon another mode of perception (knowing), which is "understanding of life directly, instead of in the abstract, linear terms of representational thinking".[12-13]

Herman Weyl wrote, "The inner awareness of myself is the basis for understanding of my fellow men". Ilya Prigogine completely agrees with Herman Weyl.[14] Voltaire wrote, ".... everything is governed by immutable laws .... everything is prearranged .... everything is a necessary effect .... we are both toys in the hands of destiny".[15]

The understanding of life directly is an expression of nature in the brain. David Bohm, in a lecture in USA, in April 1977, said:

> The ultimate perception does not originate in the brain or any material structure, although a material structure is necessary to manifest it. The subtle mechanism of knowing the truth does not originate in the brain.[16]

It implies that ultimate perception happens in a trans-sensual dimension, which is timeless (beyond brain). As all knowledge is structured in Consciousness, so ultimate perception is a happening when Universal Consciousness bathes the brain cells. Perception bestows understanding the wholeness of life, which flowers to intuition, spontaneity and right action; it is a happening in the non-dual and non-conceptual frame of reference of Mind Continuum.

Wolfgang Pauli commented upon Bohr's principle of complementarity in words, "Mind and matter are the complementary aspects of the same reality".[17] Bronowski sums up the essential aspects of relativity by asserting that, "Relativity derives essentially from the philosophical analysis which insists that there is not a fact and an observer, but a *joining of the two in an observation .... that event and observer are not separable*".[18] And Erwin Schrodinger puts it bluntly, "Subject and object are only one". "Abandoning dualism" is exactly what the new physics has done. We have to awaken the non-dual frame of reference of Mind Continuum and to perceive the Reality directly.

Restructuring of Science-Education

(a) Many eminent scientists–Erwin Schrodinger, Karl Pribram, Albert Einstein, Hideki Yukawa, Niels Bohr, E.P. Wigner, Roger Sperry, J.C. Eccles, Teilhard de Chardin, Joan Walton, and so on– have advocated that science must take in its ambient the objective and the subjective dimensions of man. This deals with the wholeness of life. Similarly education must take into consideration the sensual and trans-sensual dimension. We call it restructuring of science-education, or scientific mode of mind.

(b) The understanding of life directly, instead of in the abstract, linear terms of representational thinking, implies a direct input of Consciousness in the neurons, and this is supported by

David Bohm. This is written as Pure Consciousness brain.

(c) If a mind sees a sudden danger, or sees something immense (as a snow-covered peak, or a steep precipice, or a deep gorge), the immensity or grandeur possesses the subject momentarily, and there is "an action without idea". If a house is on fire, then one jumps on the ground floor from the first or second floor. This is also an action without idea. It implies that there is a quality of mind where there is no fragmentation. It is active present all the time. It is called the non-dual, or intuition, or insight. It is a state of awareness, which is an expression of the Unmanifest, the Unknown.

(d) D.S. Kothari wrote, "The new theorems, unless trivials, are of course first 'discovered' and then proved. Discovery is a flash of insight. It is not a step by step process, but a sort of quantum jump. A rational account of discovery follows and not precedes the discovery".[19] Ilya Prigogine quoted Kothari in words, "The simple fact is that no measurement, no experiment, or observation is possible without a relevant theoretical framework".[20] The foundation of all scientific discoveries is input from the Unmanifest to the manifest. At a deeper level modern science must accept the subjective dimension of man. The outer (objective) and the inner (subjective) are not two movements. It is a unitary movement, not separate, but one whole. Man has now to treat the outer and the inner as one. We have to restructure science, and it takes in its ambient both the subjective and the objective dimension of life. Similarly, we have to restructure education which deals with the sensual and the trans-sensual dimensions of life. There is an urgency to recognise the "restructuring of science-education".

The March of Modern Science

Deepak Chopra writes, "A nervous system is just a machine for sensing photons".[21] Richard Feynman talked of "Atoms with consciousness, matter with curiosity".[22] Eugene Wigner suggested that our consciousness alters the world by altering us[23]–an example is a quantum jump from symbolic-dualistic frame of reference of mind spectrum to non-dual and non-conceptual frame of reference of Mind Continuum–there is an impregnable wall between the two frames (dualistic frame and non-dual frame). Physicists call this as "event horizon", or "frequency barrier", or "time-barrier", or "quantum frontier". On the dualistic side lies everything that remains within the speed of light; on the non-dual side is anything faster than the speed of light. The speed of light is absolute, it is a like a wall that no object (photon) can crash through. ***As we approach the***

wall, time slows down, mass increases and space becomes curved.[24]

Deepak Chopra wrote:

> The cerebral cortex produces thought by using energy in the form of photons; their interaction takes place on the quantum level, which means that every thought could be traced back to its source at a deeper level. There are no "spiritual" thoughts that stand apart on their own. But ordinary thinking doesn't cross the quantum frontier, even though it could. We are kept on the material level because we pay attention to what the thought means. Our attention is pulled outward rather than inward.

To an experimental physicist, a photon is a quantum of light. Without the quantum level of reality there could be no cosmos. If quantum level of reality (matter content) goes to abeyance, we are left with the *fact*, which blossoms to the highest quantum energy potential of Consciousness.

The role of photons in an exploring mind is analogous to that of black hole in the physical world. Any light that passes too near a black hole gets pulled into its field of gravity. To an outside observer, the photon falls into the black hole forever, frozen in time. Inside the black hole, however, the photon has already been devoured, in less than a hundred microsecond.

Consciousness is what consciousness does. It performs a dual role in the universe. In the world of quantum, it is both the knowledge (information) and the creator of experience. At the non-dual level, it is pure Consciousness or Awareness, and the quantum of matter has gone to abeyance. With the stroke of the twentieth-century quantum eraser, the dividing line between ontology (theory of being) and epistemology (theory of knowing) is rubbed out. The fusion of ontology, epistemology and psychology is beginning to emerge.

We are looking at ourselves. Richard Feynman goes on to say:

> When one discovers how long it takes for the atoms of the brain to be replaced by other atoms, to note that the thing which I call my individuality is only a pattern or dance. The atoms come into my brain, dance a dance, then go out; always new atoms but always doing the same dance, remembering what the dance was yesterday.[25]

The French Chemist, Robert Tournaire says, "Everything that lives conquers space by quantum jumps and realizes duration through quanta".[26] We are living in a dynamic universe of tremendous movement. Roger Godel sums up the whole position of modern science thus:

The vision of the man of science who has reached the farthest point in research melts into a strange world: it is a pure system of energy from which has disappeared–lost, evaporated–the common notion of substance.[27]

The Emptiness or Void is the highest quantum energy potential of Consciousness, or the highest frequency of Consciousness. The common notion of substance is at the lowest quantum energy potential of successive consciousness, there the substance goes to abeyance when Emptiness or Void expresses itself.

Edwin Arnold said, "Measure not with words the Immeasurable".[28] Alan Watts writes, "The modern man cannot tell the difference between the surface and the depth. He seeks the depth by cutting into the surface. But the depth is known only when it reveals itself and ever withdraws from the probing mind".[29] Robert Linssen writes, "The apparent continuity of consciousness stands out against the background of a basic discontinuity". It is quite evident that unless we know this "background of basic discontinuity" the surface phenomenon of continuity will never be seen by us in its true perspective. It is discontinuity which gives perspective to continuity.[30]

The Oneness of Life

Life is a multi-dimensional phenomenon and human beings who are expressions of that phenomenon are themselves multi-dimensional organisms. Life is self-generated, self-sustained, self-perpetuating and self-regulated phenomenon. Life is Infinite, Eternal and Immutable. Life is an expression of Supreme Intelligence.

Life has two dimensions–the successive consciousness (time, known) and the Simultaneous Consciousness (Timelessness, Unknown). As an analogy, we may compare the known to a drop of water, and the Unknown to a fathomless and boundless ocean. The known is in the field of time, so it is limited and transient. The Unknown is in the realm of timelessness, so it is Eternal, Infinite and Immutable. The known deals with knowledge (information) and experience, which are recorded in the brain as a single channel computer. The Unknown transcends the known, so it deals with pure energy at different frequencies, and these are not recorded but bestow a perception from moment to moment.

The known deals with psychological mode and objective scientific mode, so these are pointers to self-destruction and self-annihilation. A scientific theory is always provisional. It is a guide to further development and its own replacement. The known deals with thought-structures and coupled with volitions, so these are static constructions.

Both spiritual and religious approaches bestow the oneness of life. The Upanishads declared, "That thou art", that is, the ultimate supreme Reality and you are one. Swamiji declared, "There is Oneness of cosmos, whether spiritual or physical, are static....". All traditional religious and traditional approaches lead to static concept of oneness of life and as such do not have the potential of dynamic oneness. If oneness is expressed through the objective dimension of consciousness, the spiritual truth of oneness is static. Similarly love which is the potential of living oneness has got extinguished. The heart is the fountain-head of life, the source of love. It appears that to increase the potential of love or heart is a stupendous task, and it requires a tremendous research. And so far whole mankind has failed to find any answer.

An Exploration of the "Missing Link" of Spirituality

So far human consciousness has been moving in the static horizontal dimension, whether it was objective and physical or the subjective and spiritual, whether the time (known) frame or Timelessness (Unknown) frame. It appears that new and dynamic vertical dimension will have to be introduced into human consciousness. The vision is based on recent scientific discoveries which are as under :

(a) Ervin Laszlo, while discussing the theory of the whole, wrote, "It is not an externally related collection of diverse phenomena, but an internally integrated network that, despite its manifest diversity, forms an embracing and unitary totality. We are not just observing it, we are not even just immersed in it: we are integral part of it".[31] It implies that we have to reject the old philosophical concept of "descent from above" and "ascent upwards", but learn about "internally integrated network", or in other words, there is flow of energy from *within* and man attains higher awareness, this is called "man unfolding".

(b) Ilya Prigogine stated, "It is physics that presupposes an observer situated within the observed world. Our dialogue with nature will be successful only if it is carried on from within nature".[32] Obviously experimental interrogation is possible between the "object within" and the "subject within", and not with the "object is out somewhere" and the "subject is within".

(c) We have to restructure science-education which will invariably deal with the wholeness of life. The true-subject is non-variable attentivity, or reaction-free attentivity, or objectless attention.

(d) Mutation does not happen at continuity level (symbolic-dualistic frame of reference); the structure of the mutant may change, which is called adaptability, but its quantum energy potential does not change. Mutation is a happening at the discontinuous level (non-dual and non-conceptual level) and the quantum energy potential of the system enhances.

(e) Modern science has brought man on the fringes of mutation of mind-brain-body system. ***The fundamental breakthrough in the realm of consciousness-research is "restructuring of science-education***". This has basically emerged from the non-dual and non-conceptual frame of reference of Mind Continuum in the vertical dimension. The perceptions are born of non-duality (of Silence) and responses are born of spontaneity. Perception has nothing to do with knowledge (information) and experience, and are not recorded as memory. The perceptions are born from moment to moment. It blossoms to understanding, learning, and action, which is a cyclic process and results in going upwards in a vertical dimension. It is the growth in vertical dimension. The higher the understanding, the higher is the expression of consciousness.

Blossoming the "Missing Link" of Spirituality

The ancient sages/seers gave birth to "spiritual wisdom". This has grown to spiritual science, the physics of Consciousness. We have to initiate an experimental dialogue between true-subject (restructured science-education) and to refine the mind-brain-body system (object) within nature. The atoms with consciousness (true-subject) are looking at atoms with consciousness (object), where both are within nature. Consciousness is the quantum connection between the true-subject and object making up the quantum machine. If this dialogue or observation is sustained for a long chronological time, it expresses as order, harmony, non-violence and peace, and this is called "blossoming of the missing link (restructured science-education) of spirituality.

Ending of I-Consciousness or Ego: If a thought coupled with volition comes in the field of true-subject (restructured science-education), the I-consciousness is knocked off because it is at the lowest quantum energy potential. It implies that the movement of thought structure is independent of my volition, it is independent of the movement of the ego. It is a tremendous discovery that: (a) what I call my volition (I-consciousness) is at a lower quantum energy potential than thought structure; (b) the mental movement has a momentum independent of me so the vanity that these are my thoughts disappears; (c) thought has an independent existence of me, which implies a realisation of the limitations of the activity of volition and the immensity of the thought structure and its movement; or there is nothing like 'I' or 'me' in the movement of thought; and (d) I do not act upon my thoughts, or I do not jump to evaluate or judge them, so this establishes a new relationship of thought structure and myself (I-consciousness).

This observation knocks down the concept that there is a thinker and movement of thought as two separate entities. There is nothing like an independent mind and there is nothing like an independent I-consciousness, and this bestows a sense of great freedom within.[33]

Ending of Thought Structure: When thought structure comes in the field of restructured science, the 'photons' meet an impregnable wall, called 'event horizon', or 'frequency barrier', or 'time barrier'. Deepak Chopra, on the basis of relativistic physics stated, "The speed of light is absolute, it is like a wall that no object can crash through. As we approach the wall, time slows down, mass increases and space becomes curved". He added, "Any place where knowledge stops there is an event horizon". Thought (or photons) cannot cross the 'event horizon', it is bombarded by the non-variable attentivity, and the thought gets annihilated.

At the moment of crossing the 'frequency barrier', the subject-object energy interaction ends, because the photons are knocked down by the energy of attentivity, which is at a higher potential. The object goes to abeyance and dualism ends. The time-space matrices also go to abeyance. The experience and knowledge also stops. All this happens in less than a hundred microseconds.[34]

Vimala Thakar calls the awareness of the outward and the inward movement of life as meditation. If I am simultaneously aware of the objective challenge, the subject reactions and the causes of the reactions, then it results in freedom. Then the momentum of reaction will not carry me over with it, but I will be ahead of the reaction.[35] I will be aware of the objective challenge only. Thought goes to abeyance and there is perception of the *fact*, the *true*, the *present*, the *non-dual*, the *what is*!

Ending of the Fact: If we continue observing or listening to the *fact*, without justification or condemnation or motivation, we observe there is only the fact and nothing else. The fact itself is the operator, not you operating on the fact. If you leave the fact alone, it has no time. The fact is free from fear. The fact grows, which implies that there is release of tremendous energy[36] and the fact moves to higher quantum energy potential. This is expressed as Pure Consciousness → Fact. It helps the fact to make a quantum jump in the vertical dimension of Consciousness. When the fact is left alone, it is operating and you do not have to do a thing about it, it matures and blossoms. Immediacy of perception dissolves the fact, and one revels in Pure Consciousness or Intelligence. Only in Intelligence there is complete security. Intelligence sees the false as the false and ends the false. Mutation happens in the timelessness. To understand Consciousness or an enquiry into the subject is the perception of that immeasurable state.

Understanding and learning are born in non-duality. Intuition (insight) is perception without any doubt. ***Understanding, learning and action***

are a cyclic process, which results in a spiral going upwards in the vertical dimension; it is a growth in the vertical dimension. The higher the understanding, the higher the expression of the Consciousness in the human brain-body system.

Concluding Comment

Man is busy either in horizontally religious or social reforms to radically transformation or mutation of human psyche, but he has totally failed so far.

Our nervous systems are designed to allow us to interact not only with the material level of existence but also with the spiritual levels. A nervous system is just a machine for seeing photons. Everything that lives conquers space by quantum jumps and realises duration through quanta. The energy interaction between the objective and the subjective takes place in less than a few millionth of a second. The objective (outer) and the subjective (inner) are not two separate movements, but one, a unitary movement. We cannot exclude the Subject of Cognizance from the domain of nature, so we have to "restructure science-education" as a single dimension. The "restructured science-education" deals with the wholeness of life, and it is called the "true-subject".

In our nervous system, a neuron can fire after every five thousandths of a second.[37] Human beings have learnt how to live in quantum reality.[37] Fred Alan Wolf wrote, "We are beginning a new age of awareness, the age of quantum consciousness, the age of the conscious atom. By looking within ourselves, we may be able to solve the problems facing us on the final frontier–the frontier of the human spirit.[38]

A photon cannot cross the boundary between symbolic-dualistic frame of mind spectrum and non-dual frame of reference of Mind Continuum, and physicists call the boundary as "the event horizon", or "the frequency barrier", or "the time-barrier", or "the quantum frontier". The quantum jump from symbolic-dualistic frame to non-dual frame is ending of photons or thought-structure. For thought-structure to go to abeyance, it must encounter a realm of higher quantum energy potential, which is provided by the "restructured science-education".

Man's knowledge about himself is less than that of a kindergarten student. We know nothing about: (i) Fear, violence arise through the structure of thought–through thinking about that happened yesterday, or past projected as the future. Thought breeds fear, violence, desire, motive, acquisition and all psychological imbalances; (ii) Creation, or Beauty, or Art (painting, sculptor, poetry, prose) is an expression of non-dual Consciousness. Order, Harmony, Non-violence, Peace, Bliss are not constructs of thought. Ecstasy is not brought about by thought. Bliss is not pleasure; (iii) The quantum consciousness, matter (photons, volitions), values and perception are the greatest miracles.

When true-subject (restructured science-education) observes or experimentally explores the thought-structure coupled with volitions (I-consciousness or ego), which is at a lower quantum energy potential of consciousness, the thought-structure is knocked off and it goes to abeyance. The quantum energy potential of the true-subject gets enhanced. If this technology is sustained over a long chronological time, it blossoms to order, harmony, oneness, non-violence and peace. It is the quantum energy potential of Cosmic Consciousness that governs the realm of spirituality.

Due to human limitation of seeing a time scale (something moving to and fro two hundred times a second) we should understand and learn: (i) to observe or experimental interrogation of the conditioned psyche by "restructured science-education" dimension, which will energise the non-dual frame of mind (supramental dimension in words of Sri Aurobindo); (ii) extend this observation to the fact which results in the fact going to abeyance and energise the Integral Consciousness; and (iii) the Integral Consciousness which knows no frontiers and All-Pervading, Integral Oneness and Perfection upon the earth *here* and *now*, is a technology for the future.

The human survival and excellence is embedded in symbiosis of science and spirituality. And if mankind escapes its responsibility for mutation of human psyche *here* and *now*, it does so at the peril of its own existence.

References

1. Swami Om Poorna Swatantra, *The Eternal Future*, New Delhi: Adarsh Books, 2003, pp. 133, 66, 94.
2. Sampooran Singh, The Atam Science Trust: Dagshai Cantt, *A Symbiosis of Science and Spirituality*, October 7, 2002.
3. Sampooran Singh and Dr (Mrs) Kanwaljit Kaur, *Peace, Security and Survival? : A Scientific Quest*, June 2, 2004.
4. Swami Om Poorna Swatantra, *op. cit.*, pp. 94, 96, 99.
5. Spencer Brown, *Laws of Form*, New York: Julian Press, 1972, pp. 104-05.
6. L.L. Whyte, *The Next Development in Man*, New York: New American Library, Mentor Books, 1950, p. 42.
7. Alexander Koyre, *Newtonian Studies*, Chicago: University of Chicago Press, 1928, pp. 23-24; in Ilya Prigogine and Isabelle Stengers, *Order Out of Chaos*, Bantam Books, pp. 35, 36.
8. Erwin Schrodinger, *What is Life*? & *Mind and Matter*, Cambridge University Press, 1967, pp. 126-131, 137.

9. Sampooran Singh, *The Pilgrimage to the Third Millennium*, Chandigarh: Faith Publishers, January 1995, p. 19.
10. Arthur Eddington, in Erwin Schrodinger, *op. cit.*, p. 130.
11. *ibid.*, p. 130.
12. *ibid.*, in A. Commins and R.N. Linscott, ed. *Man and the Universe, The Philosophers of Science*, New York: Washington Square Press, 1969, p. 384.
13. Alan W. Watts, *The Ways of Zen*, New York: Vintage Books, 1957, p. 10.
14. Herman Weyl, *Philosophy of Mathematics and Natural Science*, Princeton N.J., Princeton University Press, 1949; in Ilya Prigogine and Isabelle Stengers, *op. cit.*, p. 311.
15. Voltaire, *Dictionnaire Philosophique*, Paris, Garnier, 1954; in Ilya Prigogine, *ibid.*, p. 257.
16. David Bohm, in Gary Zukav, *The Dancing Wu Li Masters*, Fontana/Collins, 1982, p. 327.
17. Wolfgang Pauli, in George Wald, *Synthesis of Science and Religion*, Mumbai: The Bhaktivedanta Institute, June 1988, p. 20.
18. J. Bronowski, *The Common Sense of Science*, Cambridge: Harvard University Press, 1955, p. 77; in Ken Wilber, *The Spectrum of Consciousness*, USA: The Theosophical Publishing House, 1982 (Third Quest Book), p. 38.
19. D.S. Kothari, in *The Odyssey of Science, Culture and Consciousness*, New Delhi: Abhinav Publications, 1990, pp. 48-49.
20. *ibid.*, *Some Thoughts on Truth*, New Delhi: Anniversary Address, Indian National Science Academy, 1975, p. 5; in Ilya Prigogine, *op. cit.*, p. 293.
21. Deepak Chopra, *How to Know God*, London: Rider, 2000, p. 172.
22. Richard Feynman, *The Value of Science*, Project Physics Reader 1, Authorised Interim Version, 1968-69, p. 3; in Fred Alan Wolf, *Taking the Quantum Leap*, San Francisco: Harper and Row, 1981, p. 227.
23. Eugene Wigner, in Fred Alan Wolf, *ibid.*, p. 234.
24. Deepak Chopra, *op. cit.*, pp. 271, 94, 206, 270.
25. Richard Feynman, in Fred Alan Wolf, *op. cit.*, p. 228.
26. Robert Tournaire, in Rohit Mehta, *The Eternal Light*, Adyar: The Theosophical Publishing House, 1961, p. 9.
27. Roger Godel, in Rohit Mehta, *ibid.*, p. 15.
28. Sir Edwin Arnold, in Rohit Mehta, *ibid.*, p. 31.
29. Alan Watts, in Rohit Mehta, *ibid.*, p. 31.
30. Robert Linseen, in Rohit Mehta, *ibid.*, p. 32.
31. Ervin Laszlo, in *The Odyssey of Science, Culture and Consciousness*, New Delhi: Abhinav Publications, 1990, p. 237.
32. Ilya Prigogine, *op. cit.*, p. 218.
33. Vimala Thakar, (a) *Through Silence to Meditation*, Ahmedabad: Vimal Prakashan Trust, 1998, pp. 22-27; (b) *ibid.*, *Silence*, Holland: Bookfund,

1989, p. 6; and (c) *ibid.*, *The Invincible*, July-August 1987, Vol. IV, No. 4, p. 14.

34. Sampooran Singh, Dr (Mrs) Kanwaljit Kaur, Paramjit Singh and Amarjit Singh, *March to Peace: The Wisdom of Observation, Listening and the Power of Commitment*, Chandigarh: Faith Publishers, January 20, 2004, pp. 7-8, 20-21.
35. Vimala Thakar, *Mutation of Mind*, Ahmedabad: New Order Book Co., 1972, pp. 122, 171.
36. J. Krishnamurti, *Krishnamurti on Education*, Orient Longman, KFI, 1974, pp. 69, 87, 90.
37. Fred Alan Wolf, *Taking the Quantum Leap*, *op. cit.*, pp. 236, 245.
38. *ibid.*, p. 248

18

Science, Education, Peace and Survival

Man (*Homo sapiens*) has been trying to end conflict, violence, aggression, war in the psyche for the last 10,000 years or so, but all intellectual approaches, thought-structures, beliefs, concepts have proved to be sterile in transforming the human psyche; rather these have added to human conditionings. We have brought the human race to an explosive situation and our life is poised on a razor's edge. From deep within the human psyche, there has developed a terrible power that threatens the extinction of all life-supporting systems within a foreseeable time. The old chasm between knowledge and wisdom has widened dangerously. There has been a fantastic growth in knowledge. Knowledge grows but wisdom atrophies. We are living at one of the great turning points of human history.

Science: We have made accelerative progress in science and technology. Science (objective) appears to be an abstract and abstruse collection of data (information) and experience, a repertory of cold and impersonal facts and measurement. It adds to materialism which is search for power and security. It adds to acquisition, a source of technological innovation with little relevance to human values. The dialogue with nature isolated man from nature instead of bringing him closer to it. A triumph of human reason turned into a sad truth. It seems that science debased everything it touched. Man, in his inner nature, has remained the same as he was thousands of years ago–greedy, envious, aggressive and burdened with sorrow. The psychological growth has been totally arrested. This is lop-sided growth in man. Martin Luther rightly said, "Science has completely finished our spiritual power, we have guided missiles but misguided men".[1]

Education: The educational structure in India, and in the rest of the world, basically cultures the sensate values and totally divorces the inner quantum energy potential of man. Man has learnt to live in the time-space-causation matrices and there is total lack of relevance between the human being and the complex contemporary society. He is in search for inward and outward security, the desire for comfort—this whole process smothers discontetment, puts an end to spontaneity and breeds fear, and fear blockades the intelligent understanding of life. Every activity brings in conflict.

Peace: We are busy in changing the external world, which implies changes in the economic, social, political, ecological, and so on. Wars have never solved human problems and they never will. Resolving international conflicts by means of military solutions, or peace through might of arms, or treaty making perspectives have failed.

In 1932 after a World Disarmament Conference in Geneva, Albert Einstein, in an unusual bout of anger, exclaimed:

> .... they (politicians and statesmen) have cheated us; they have fooled us. Hundreds of millions of people in Europe and in America; billions of people have been and are being cheated, traded and tricked out of their lives, health and well-being.[2]

These remarks are equally valid today. In principle, man is deceiving himself. He has become a puppet, a mechanical golem. He has lost sensitivity, he has lowered his level of perception, he has started living in a synthetic world which is a construct of his mind, and man's world is totally divorced from Reality.

Peace is also related to human psychology. As long as there is inherent violence in the individual psyche, the political leaders of the world and heads of the state shall never be able to end war or create peace in the world. The intellect has the capacity to purchase transient peace between two violent points; but it does not have the capacity to end violence and construct stable peace. Knowledge, concept, and ideal cannot transform the human psyche, and so they cannot bring about a stable peace.

The symbolic-dualistic frame of reference is always agitated, it is always in conflict. The non-dual frame which has the capacity to perceive the whole is always at peace. The awakening of intelligence arises out of observation, self-knowing and compassion. It is the awakening of intelligence or wisdom which is integral to perception, and which alone frees man from duality and from the bondage of time. Freedom bestows stable peace. Mankind has to work for a higher level of perception to achieve stable peace.[3]

We want a psychological revolution, in which the whole human race has to participate and every man is an equal partner. This individual and collective psychological experiment will awaken the integral and all-inclusive dimension of Consciousness and that can guarantee peace on the globe.

The United Nations Foundation, along with partners from around the globe, has launched a major initiative in support of the High-Level

Panel appointed by UN Secretary-General Kofi Annan, to assess 21st Century threats to international peace and security. The High-Level Panel will recommend ways in which the international community can reform to effectively address modern-day challenges. The UN Foundation's initiative will help inform the work of the panel and encourage widespread participation in the debate.[4] Further the UN has initiated a programme for "peace education", in some countries on April 8, 2004.

This article presents a critique on mind-brain-body system, psychological mode of mind, and scientific mode of mind. It also presents ending of I-consciousness and thought-structure and ending of the fact. It explores ending of psychological imbalances–say, violence, fear. It questions the value education. The inner pilgrimage to global peace and security is presented. It explores the benediction of the timeless and action plan to radically transform the human psyche. It resolves all human paradoxes. It blossoms to order, nonviolence and peace.

A Critique on Mind-Brain-Body System

What we call mind (with a lower case 'm') is a conditioned energy, moving through the body, monitored by the brain, operating through the senses. It is a movement of the structured framework of patterns and the dynamics of the behaviour patterns are shared by mankind.[5] We share the consciousness of all humanity, for our sufferings, our pleasures, beliefs, conclusions, opinions, and all the religious dogmas and faiths are shared by all human beings on earth. Philosophers-mystics call it *individualized consciousness*. J. Krishnamurti says, "I am the conclusion of all the experiences of mankind. The story of all mankind is me .... I am neither individual, nor collective. I am humanity".[6]

The mind is at the lowest quantum energy potential or lowest frequencies of consciousness in the brain-body system. We are conditioned cerebrally, neurologically, chemically. It gathers self-knowledge and deals with the *non-fact*, the *past*, the *false*, the *what should be*? It is invariably dualistic, and constructs pain, misery and travails.

What we call Mind (with upper case 'M') is the non-dual frame of reference of Mind Continuum. The Universal Consciousness expresses itself in a non-dual frame as intuition, spontaneity, love and compassion, order and harmony. It is the first-hand personal acquaintance of the quantum jump of the conditioned energy consciousness to Universal Consciousness; or in other words, a quantum jump from fragmentary perception to the perception of the Wholeness. There is oneness and it is shared by the whole mankind. It deals with the *fact*, the *present*, the *true*, the *what is*!

Psychological Mode of Mind

Modern science has shown that "in order to do so (see), evidently it (mind) must first cut itself up into at least one state which sees, and at least one other state which is seen".[7] The mind splits itself into seer and the seen, the thinker and the thought, the subject and the object. There is exchange of energy between the subject and the object, which results in mutilated subject (pseudo-subject) and mutilated object (modified recalled memory); and this energy transduction happens in a few millionth of a second. This results in that both are continuities of change. Eddington puts it succinctly, "Nature thus provides that knowledge of one-half of the world will ensure ignorance of the other half".[8] He added in most spectacular words, "The frank realization that physical science is concerned with a world of shadows is one of the most significant of recent advances .... and that this state of affairs was clearly understood by the great Democritus in the fifth century B.C.".[9]

Alexander Koyre stated that we are living in "a world, in which, though there is a place for everything, there is no place for man. Thus the world of science–the real world–became estranged and utterly divorced from the world of life". He added, "Two worlds: this means two truths, or no truth at all. This is the tragedy of modern mind which "solved the riddle of the universe, but only to replace it by another riddle: the riddle of itself".[10]

In the psychological mode of mind, the universe is severed into a subject and an object, and it becomes mutilated, torn and estranged from itself, and thus rendered false to itself. It is also called the relative frame of reference of mind spectrum, or the time-space-causation matrices, or the *known*, or the *past* memory constructs duality and is repetitive and mechanical. In conflict there is wastage of energy. Every activity leads to increase of entropy, so it is a pointer to death. It has no newness or creativeness, no understanding and no learning. This leads to confusion, memory, contradiction and conflict. The man is groaning with pain and travails, and this is leading to self-annihilation and self-destruction.

Based on the observations of Erwin Schrodinger, C.J. Jung, Charles Sherrington and B. Spinoza, we conclude:

> The human-made social cosmos, or construct of the symbolic-dualistic frame of reference of mind spectrum represents the immanent quantum energy potential, and it is divorced from the ultimate quantum energy potential. ***The construct of the mind is the only "reality" where the transcendent potential has gone to abeyance and its only linkage is the immanent potential. It represents the relative field of consciousness.***[11]

It is evident that any thought-structure is at the immanent quantum energy potential. Further, thought says, "I am the doer, the experiencer", and this brings in the concept of I-consciousness, the ego. So thought-structures and I-consciousness are conceptual constructs, and are illusions.

Scientific Mode of Mind

Many eminent scientists–including Albert Einstein, Werner Heisenberg, Erwin Schrodinger, Arthur Eddington, and so on–have stumbled upon another mode of perception (knowing), which is "understanding of life directly, instead of in the abstract, linear terms of representational thinking".[12] This implies "understanding the wholeness of life". Understanding expresses itself in the non-dual and non-conceptual frame of reference of mind spectrum. ***Understanding is a movement in the non-duality, a movement of the whole being.*** Understanding comes only when the mind is very quiet, tranquil, silenced.

Understanding leads to a perception of the whole. Perception has nothing to do with knowledge (information). ***The perceptions are born of non-duality and responses are born of spontaneity.*** It awakens the awareness, the intelligence, which arises out of observation, self-knowing and compassion.

David Bohm, in a lecture in USA, in April 1977, said:

> The ultimate perception does not originate in the brain or any material structure, although a material structure is necessary to manifest it. The subtle mechanism of knowing the truth does not originate in the brain.[13]

It implies that ultimate perception happens in a trans-sensual dimension, which is timeless (beyond brain). As all knowledge is structured in Consciousness, so ultimate perception is a happening when Universal Consciousness bathes the brain cells. Perception bestows understanding the wholeness of life, which flowers to intuition, spontaneity and right action; it is a happening in the non-dual and non-conceptual frame of reference of Mind Continuum.

Eddington wrote, "The intimate knowledge (intuition or insight) will not submit to codification and analysis". The insight eliminates duality, where you see the subject as the object. This is called the scientific mode of mind, or restructured science which takes the subjective dimension and the objective dimension in its ambient. Similarly we restructure education so that it takes in its fold the sensual and trans-sensual dimension. We couple science and education, it is called "restructured science-education" or true-subject.

The true-subject observes the thought without interfering in its flow, or it does not supply any energy for the sustenance of thought, or there is no energy exchange between the subject and the object; it implies that the pseudo-subject goes to abeyance and non-variable attentivity, or reaction-free attentivity, or objectless attentivity takes over as the true-subject. And the true-subject sees the true-object, the *fact*, the *true*, the *present*, the *what is*!. The perception of the fact eliminates the duality. The very seeing the fact brings an action which is ending of division of mind.

This also bestows a perception that the subjective dimension and the objective dimension are a single dynamic flow, a unitary movement. There is no recording of the perception, as the frequency is above the threshold frequency at the "frequency barrier" or "time barrier".

Ending of I-consciousness and Thought-Structure: If a thought coupled with volition comes in the field of true-subject, the I-consciousness is knocked off. If this observation is continued over a long chronological time, the 'photons' meet an impregnable wall, called "event horizon", or "frequency barrier", or "time-barrier", the thought-structure is also knocked off.[14] We are left with the *fact*, the *true*, the *present*, the *what is*!

The living touch (communion) of a higher order of existence (restructured science-education dimension) influences the lower order of existence (thought-structure and I-consciousness) to undergo mutation and to transcend the limitations of its own dimensions. The Nature's process is a quantum jump from a lower order to a higher order of existence; and the lower order of existence goes to abeyance.

Ending of the Fact: If the observation is continued, there is flow of energy to the fact (Consciousness → Fact) and the fact goes to abeyance. The brain cells are now bathed with the pure Consciousness and it expresses the pure Consciousness.

Ending of Psychological Imbalances

The psychological dependence, imitation, conformity, domination, all that is inward violence. The inward anger, hatred, wanting to dominate people, not only physical domination, but the domination of ideas are psychological violence. We are violent to thought, word and deed. The fact is that we are violent to our inner world. The "cultural belief structure", or the "frequency and amplitude information structure of the past", or the "memory" constructs the human-made cosmos is a synthetic world of violence, fear, envy, anger and psychological imbalances. Violence is an indication of psychological immaturity. Violence is disorder. Every form of escape, distraction, of movement away sustains violence. If one deeply realises this, then the mind is confronted with the "fact", the "what is".

Whenever there is curtailment of freedom, there is exploitation, there is injustice, and psychological violence is curtailment of freedom. When we graft the conceptual on the perceptual, it is called curtailment of freedom.

The fact is that thought-time constructs violent matrices, so the human-made social cosmos is violent. Inwardly there is no duality. There is only "what is", the fact, that is, I am violent. Being violent, I propagate something which I call nonviolence or peace, the non-fact, so there is conflict in the human psyche. Mankind has to learn to jettison non-fact and to live in fact.

Violence: Violence is an indication of psychological immaturity. It is a construct by the symbolic-dualistic frame of reference in the mind spectrum, which is invariably in conflict. All conflict is violence to thought, word and deed. It expresses itself in the human-made social cosmos. All knowledge, concepts, ideologies, will, to become, projections, expectations are at immanent quantum energy potential, these do not have any capacity to bring mutation in the human psyche, hence cannot decrease or end violence in the human mind. On the other hand, every activity in this field constructs violence and adds to societal entropy.

Nonviolence is a percept in the non-dual frame of reference in the mind spectrum.[15] A nonviolent frame or non-dual mind is invariably synergistic to the violent frame or symbolic-dualistic frame of the mind spectrum. The non-dual frame perceives the wholeness, such a perception bestows intuition or insight or understanding of life direct. The insight is totally free from all violence. The non-dual frame is in commune with nature. Nonviolence is the natural law of life.

A quantum jump from violence to nonviolence implies a quantum jump from symbolic-dualistic frame to non-dual frame. This is possible when we deeply understand the psychodynamics and limitations of the mind-brain system. We have to restructure our educational pattern so that dynamics of human mind-brain or transpersonal psychology of man is introduced in our schools/colleges at all levels.

You can't impose the order on top of disorder. You can't impose nonviolence on a consciousness which is violent because that violence has deep-rooted causes in the psyche. Unless those causes are eliminated there is no ending of violence. It is only when violence ends that one can be nonviolent.

To sum up, ***violence is a construct by the symbolic-dualistic frame of reference of mind spectrum and nonviolence is a percept in the non-dual frame of reference of the Mind Continuum.*** Violence is a synthetic construct by the conditioned mind. Living in the synthetic construct leads to destruction or annihilation of the system. The nonviolence is the law of life. Will India initiate a movement for a quantum jump from violence to nonviolence–and this quantum jump "must motivate a great movement, convincing reluctant leaders and reluctant governments and reluctant peoples themselves to effect the needed change".

Fear: When one is afraid–physiologically as well as psychologically–then there is feeling of danger, a feeling of total isolation. We are generally afraid of something, or of a remembrance of something that has happened, or of a projection of a reaction into the future. So psychological fear may be due to recall of past memory or future projection, which that thought is responsible for fear.

The mind, the brain, needs complete security in order to function well, healthily, sanely. Fear energises duality, so it loses security. Fear makes the mind insensitive. A mind that has lost sensitivity, become dull, repetitive. If we observe fear with true-subject (restructured science-education), the thought-structure which has created fear explodes and goes to abeyance, which implies ending fear, or in other words, to regenerate a mind that has no remembrance of something that has caused fear, so that it is completely *whole.* A *whole* mind is without fear. This also applies to other psychological imbalances–say, anger, envy. The art of listening or observation implies to all psychological imbalances–which implies that all psychological imbalances are transcended.

Desire: Freedom from desire means that you are aware of the whole movement of desire. One should not suppress it, or to fulfil it, or identify it, or to condemn it, or justify it, but he observes the movement of desire and then desire goes to abeyance. It is the awareness that ends desire, motive and other psychological imbalances.

Value Education

Recently, many eminent scientists–Werner Heisenberg, Edwin Hubble, Max Planck, G.F. Chew, Bertrand Russell, Lincoln Barnett, Max Born, and so on–have concluded that we cannot impart value education at reason or intellect level.[16]

All ethical values–Freedom, Non-violence, Peace, Harmony, Coherence, Love, Truth–are essentially spiritual values; they proceed from the trans-sensual dimension of human personality, the Life Field, the Universal Consciousness. All ethical-spiritual values self-emerge from the Life Field, the Wholeness of Life. These are eternal and immutable, and shared by mankind. These do not change from society to society, or place to place. These values self-express themselves in a non-dual and non-conceptual frame of reference of the Mind (with an upper case 'M') Continuum. What we need is a quantum jump from symbolic-dualistic frame to non-dual and non-conceptual frame of reference of Mind Continuum. The quantum jump is possible only when there is radical transformation or mutation of the conditioned psyche, or in other

words, the thought-time is transcended. We are on the verge of exploring and perceiving the Reality, and that ensures our survival and excellence.

Our consciousness has two capacities. One is the capacity to accumulate: accumulate wealth, accumulate knowledge. It is the mind that is calculating (symbolic-dualistic frame). The other is the capacity to observe, to explore, to learn and to be aware–which is not accumulation (the non-dual or non-conceptual frame). All value education falls in the capacity to be aware, direct understanding of life.

Education

Understanding comes only through self-knowledge, which is awareness of one's total psychological process. Thus education, in the true sense is: (a) helping the individual to be mature and free, to flower greatly in love and goodness; (b) to understand life is to understand ourselves; (c) intelligence is the capacity to perceive the essential, the *what is*; and to awaken this capacity, in oneself and in others; and (d) education should awaken the capacity to be self-aware and not merely indulge in gratifying self-expression.

The global restructuring of education, or holistic/integral education, or humanistic education, or global value education are synonymous. The global restructuring of education implies ***An Epistemological Revolution Through Scientific Temper***, or the pilgrimage to the ***Sacred Temple of Understanding and Learning***, or the ***Symbiosis of Science and Spirituality*** (science of the wholeness of life). This regenerates intelligence which is born of observation and self-knowing. It jettisons self-assertive tendency of mind, and cultivates and nourishes the self-integrative potential of Mind. It bestows intuition and spontaneity. Discoveries come as intuitive flashes. **Intuition is fundamental and logical reason is a derivative.**

The restructuring of education is basically to perceive the highest quantum energy potential of Life Field, and to live in communion with Nature. It implies to educate human beings in the psychology of cooperation with themselves and others. It bestows a new set of relationships between man and Nature, man and man, man and organisms, and man and environments. It bestows pure perception (pure cognition) of the wholeness of life, or the hidden Nature's evolutionary impulse, or of the nature of Cosmic Life. It is to live in communion with Nature's Cosmic Dance, where all misery, pain and travails are transcended and man revels in freedom, order, harmony, non-violence, peace and bliss. It is the consummation of life.

Any form of education that concerns itself wit[illegible] and not with the whole of ma[illegible] vitably leads to conflict and s[illegible] decrease of sensitivity of mind-brain-body system, and leads in the direction of self-annihilation. The highest function of education is to bring about an integrated individual who is capable of dealing with life as a whole. The Action Plan of the right kind of education is: (a) investigating the flow of conditioned world; (b) exploring the self-expression of Unconditioned Energy, the Life Field; (c) living in the light of that understanding; and (d) introducing this in all colleges and universities. Will India wake up, out of deep slumber, to save itself and mankind from annihilation.

India was once the "Light of Asia". She has now to fulfil her historic role of being the Light of the World. India has been called upon now and here to save Life in the world from extinction. Will she wake up from deep slumber and "***Lead Kindly Light Amid the Encircling Gloom***". We share the privilege and the responsibility.

An Overview of the Web of Life

(a) ***Education:*** The holistic education has two components: (i) investigation of the psychodynamics and limitations of the conditioned psyche, which is called 'self-knowledge'; and (ii) exploring the Unconditioned Energy which implies training and purifying the instruments of perception, which is called self-awareness, or "understanding of life directly", and then that blossoms to intuition, spontaneity and right social action.

(b) ***Technologies for Mutation of Human Psyche:*** (i) Epistemological Revolution Through Scientific Temper; (ii) Pilgrimage to the Sacred Temple of Understanding and Learning; and (iii) Symbiosis of Science and Spirituality.

(c) ***Understanding, Learning and Action:*** These belong to non-dual frame and not to symbolic-dualistic frame of reference of mind spectrum; these are a cyclic process, which results in a spiral going upwards in a vertical dimension; it is a growth in a vertical dimension. The higher the understanding, the higher the expression of the Consciousness in the human mind-brain-body system. It awakens the dimension of the Silence. It establishes a unique relationship between the explorer and the Divine. It is a journey of the alone to the Alone.

Inner Pilgrimage to "Global Peace and Security"

(a) Everything that has been transmitted to our mind through centuries will have to be discarded. When thought-structure and I-consciousness encounter the non-variable awareness of the true-subject, these explode and go to abeyance; and one revels in the *fact*, the *true*, the *present*, the *what is*! The inner pilgrimage is a voyage from self-knowledge through self-observation to self-awareness. It is a journey from "successive consciousness" to "Simultaneous Consciousness" (the dimension of Silence).

(b) The truth has to be lived in the movement of relationship, it cannot be lived in physical isolation. To live is to be related, the truth expresses itself without fear, without ambition, without the desire to assert and dominate. Truth vibrates in the movement of relationship. The perfume of peace can be there when you are with others.

(c) In spirituality, there is nothing to acquire–only to understand the truth and live it. Spirituality is not an acquisitive movement but a movement of understanding, learning and right action.

(d) There cannot be a global peace without a global order. There cannot be a global order without a global ethic. And that global ethic will emerge from a non-dual and non-conceptual frame of reference of Mind Continuum. The world physicists–including Einstein, Schrodinger, Heisenberg, Eddington–have realized that we need the understanding of life directly, instead of in the abstract, linear terms of representational thinking.

(e) We want a psychological revolution, in which the whole human race has to participate and every man is an equal partner. We cannot escape our responsibility to mankind, because any escape is at our own peril.

Peace: It is related to human psychology. As long as there is inherent violence in the individual psyche, the political leaders of the world and heads of the state shall never be able to end war or create peace in the world. The intellect has the capacity to purchase transient peace between two violent points, but it does not have the capacity to end violence and construct sustainable peace.[17]

A quantum jump from the symbolic-dualistic knowledge (the self-interacting state, the successive consciousness) to non-dual and non-conceptual state (the self-referral state, the Simultaneous Consciousness) will bestow lasting global peace and human survival.

Security: The non-dual and non-conceptual frame of reference of Mind Continuum is totally psychologically secure from all challenges of life, which are constructed by man-made social cosmos. It is the construct of the conditioned psyche that adds to psychological insecurity of the system. Global security also encompasses economic and environmental security. The ending of violence in the human psyche bestows harmony, order, peace and global security. The symphony of life forms are free from all psychological insecurity. We have to create a new relationship with Nature through peace and security; and this relationship emerges from the highest quantum energy potential or highest frequency of Cosmic Consciousness.

The Emergence of New Physics

According to David Bohm, an eminent physicist, writes, "We must turn physics around. Instead of starting with parts and showing how they work together (the Cartesian order), we must start with the whole".[18] To understand this, in Bohm's words, we need a new "instrument of thought".[19] We have to base ourselves on the fundamental perception that "intuition is fundamental and rationality is a derivative". Our way of living must be in communion with Nature, and physics (and all sciences and philosophy) and the instrument of thought must have its foundation in intuition (insight).

B.D. Josephson, Nobel Prize in Physics, 1973, writes, "Our nervous systems are designed to allow us to interact not only with the material level of existence but also with the spiritual levels ....".[20] It applies to understand, learn and live with the wholeness of life according to the immutable laws of Nature.

Teaching of Attention/Awareness in the Education Process

In a deep fundamental sense it is not possible to teach anything to anybody. The teacher only points out the fact and it is for the student to analyse, understand and learn depending on the state of his own mind. It has been the misfortune of every great teacher that, while he speaks from his level of consciousness, his students can only receive the message on their levels; and the gulf between the teaching and understanding grows wider with time. Generally the teacher speaks from the level of his non-dual and non-conceptual mind, while the student receives the message at his symbolic-dualistic mind.

We have to educate ourselves with the psychodynamics of the conditioned psyche, to explore the Unconditioned Energy. We have to acquaint ourselves with the art of listening and observation, and living in the light of one's own understanding. A scientific approach is generally preferable to a philosophical approach. Question and answer sessions are also helpful. A dialogue is developed in which each participant is able to put aside his own views and listen to those of others is also useful. A collective process of thought enriches understanding. Some details are also discussed in the Action Plan.

The Benediction of the Timeless

J. Krishnamurti, in 1979, in a dialogue, said :

> India has lived all these centuries on ideas. She has to move from a life based on ideas, which are non-facts, to seeing the fact only.[21]

The benediction of the timeless is waiting, the ground is ready.
Can we create something that is of this benediction.

The "benediction of the timeless" during the last 25 years is "a way of perception, of challenge and response from a state that lay beyond the mind, beyond brain, memory, all responses of consciousness". He added, "A state that comes into being in listening at great depth, where consciousness and its movement do not obstruct. A state where seeing is whole, inclusive, non-fragmented, a state of no movement from or towards; beyond matrix and all racial memories of man". "It was a prophecy that the sacred energy was alive again in the Indian soil".

The scientific discoveries during the last 25 years in the mind of eminent scientists give ample evidence of "the charging the atmosphere with a new energy" which is "benediction of the timeless"; and some of these discoveries are as under:

(a) A nervous system is just a machine for sensing photons. The French Chemist Robert Tourmaire says, "Everything that lives conquers space by quantum jumps and realises duration by quanta".[22] Many eminent scientists have stated that science must take in its ambient the objective and the subjective dimensions of life. The objective (outer) and the subjective (inner) are a single dynamic flow, and not two movements. The energy exchange between the outer and the inner happens in about few millionth of a second. We have to restructure science so that it takes in its ambient both the objective and the subjective dimensions of life. Similarly education must take in its fold the sensual and the trans-sensual dimension of life. So the real-subject is "restructured science-education", which deals with the wholeness of life.

(b) Many eminent scientists–including Albert Einstein, Werner Heisenberg, Erwin Schrodinger, Arthur Eddington, and so on–have stumbled upon another mode of perception (knowing), called intimate, or intuitive, or direct. The direct understanding of life transcends duality. It advocates that the subject and the object are one.

(c) The Committee on Science and Technology, USA, submitted in June 1981 a lengthy report to the House of Representatives, USA, which encouraged serious assessment of further research on "*the physics of consciousness*", and concluded that recent experiments:

> .... that there exists an 'interconnectiveness' of the human mind with other minds and with matter .... that the human mind may be able to obtain the information independent of geography and time.

(d) The Union of Concerned Scientists (UCS) issued a "*World Scientists' Warning to Humanity*" in April 1993, signed by over 1670 scientists including 104 Nobel laureates, concluding that :

> Human beings and the natural world are on a collision course .... A new ethic is required–a new attitude towards discharging our responsibility for caring for ourselves and for the earth.... This ethic must motivate a great movement, convincing reluctant leaders and reluctant governments and reluctant peoples themselves to effect the needed changes.

(e) Russian scientists, in 1996, have proposed a Life Field, beyond our physical concepts of time, space and the known concepts of electromagnetic and gravitational fields.[23] This was followed by another scientific conference at Cambridge University, which concluded, "A new scientific approach would include subjective experience as valid information and address all forms of human experience–including intuition, spirituality and mystical encounters".[23] The Life Field appears to be synonymous to Universal Consciousness or *Brahman*.

(f) We are living in a dynamic universe of tremendous movement. Roger Godel sums up the whole position of modern science thus:

> The vision of the man of science who has reached the farthest point in research melts into a strange world: it is a pure system of energy from which has disappeared–lost, evaporated–the common notion of substance.[24]

The Emptiness or Void is the highest quantum energy potential of Consciousness, or the highest frequency of Consciousness. The common notion of substance is at the lowest quantum energy potential of successive consciousness, there the substance goes to abeyance when Emptiness or Void expresses itself.

(g) We are beginning a new age of awareness, the age of quantum consciousness, the age of the conscious atom.[25]

The age of the "benediction of the timeless" has got initiated due to His Grace. If man takes one step, nature will take one hundred steps to help mankind. Man has to deeply understand and learn that it is the Cosmic Consciousness that governs man, the planet and the cosmos.

Action Plan

It consists of (i) Restructuring of Science [the objective and the subjective dimensions of life are one dynamic flow]; (ii) Restructuring of

Education [a single dynamic flow of the conditioned energy and the Unconditioned Energy, or sensual world and trans-sensual world]; (iii) Awareness of Human Values [these flow from the trans-sensual dimension of life]; and (iv) the Art of Living [living in the wholeness of life, or the oneness of Consciousness].

Mental movement or thought-structure cannot lead to non-duality, as both the subject and the object are at the same quantum energy potential of consciousness. If thought encounters the "restructured science-education", it explodes and is annihilated; so it is an objective approach to the subjective reactions, subjective feelings. It wakes up from the wholeness of life (true-subject).

At the moment of crossing the 'frequency barrier', the subject-object energy interaction ends, because the photons are knocked down by the energy of attentivity, which is at a higher potential. The object goes to abeyance and dualism ends. The time-space matrices also go to abeyance. The experience and knowledge also stops. All this happens in less than a hundred microseconds.

If an entity (thought-structure) at lower quantum energy potential of consciousness comes in the field of higher quantum energy potential (true-subject) of Consciousness, the entity with lower quantum energy potential explodes (cold fission) and is annihilated. When I-consciousness and thought go to abeyance, the fact is left behind.

Herman Weyl wrote, ".... the understanding from within is open to us .... This inner awareness of myself is the basis for the understanding of man".[26] Ilya Prigogine completely agrees with Herman Weyl. He added, "There is a need for new relations between man and nature and between man and man".[27]

In the psychological mode, the subject is "recalled memory" and the object is external time-space matrices, and we deal with partial experience and fragmentary knowledge (information), so we are aware of the *non-fact*, the *false*, the *past*, the *what should be?*. In the scientific mode of mind, the subject is "restructured science-education", which takes in its ambient the subjective and the objective dimensions (the wholeness of life) and object is the *fact*, the *true*, the *present*, the *what is*!, so we deal with the true instruments of perception. So we have to "educate the true subject, the instrument of perception and are aware with the wholeness of life".

Human fulfilment is embedded in understanding of life directly [intuitive vision of non-duality] that ends all dualism, limitations, conditionings, and psychological imbalances; and ushers a new era of order, harmony, non-violence, peace and bliss. This is the consummation of human life.

Concluding Comment

In the present state of mankind–very clever, very developed in one direction, scientifically, technologically, tremendous knowledge–but primitive psychologically, as primitive as the primitive man.

The conditioned psyche is posing a great threat–the humanitarian disaster. There is an urgency to prevent a humanitarian catastrophe of this magnitude as it poses a threat to global stability.

We have to educate ourselves with the psychodynamics of the conditioned psyche (called self-knowledge) and to explore the Unconditioned Energy (called self-awareness). It is an exploration from self-knowledge through self-observation to self-awareness. The restructuring of education also includes to educate the educator. The wisdom of listening and observation is born with the epistemological evolution.

Nature is benevolent so it has bestowed on every man a "new instrument of non-dual and non-conceptual perception". Every man is born with two dimensions–self-knowledge of the *known* and understanding and learning the *known* and the *Unknown*. But the dimension of understanding and learning has to be energized through right kind of education. It implies: (i) Restructuring of Science; (ii) Restructuring of Education; (iii) Awareness of Human Values; and (iv) Living in the Light of that Understanding, Learning and Intelligence.

It is only "restructured science-education" that helps man to grow from knowledge to understanding, from confrontation to cooperation, from rationality to intuition, from intellect to intelligence. Intelligence self-expresses itself in a non-dual frame of Mind Continuum and blossoms to peace and security. The non-dual and non-conceptual frame of reference of Mind Continuum bring in mutation in the brain. Mutation is possible in the brain through insight, not through knowledge, not through accumulation. That insight is the ability to see a truth directly, a direct perception of the truth, and education must foster that.

The truth comes into being when there is direct perception in the consciousness, otherwise what you have is a description of the truth, an idea about it. There is a gap between what you know intellectually as knowledge, which is recorded in the memory, and what you know as direct perception which is your own insight. All education in science or religion or spirituality is what you directly understand–direct perception.

Christ did not become Christ through a church or belief. He came upon that through his own understanding, through his own enquiry. Buddha came upon his consciousness, his understanding, through his own meditation, his own enquiry. The spiritual quest is an enquiry for order in the consciousness of man. A visit to a church or hearing a talk about Christ does not change the consciousness but gives objective knowledge of the consciousness. It is description of the truth, an idea about it. The spiritual quest got arrested. The student has to discover the Consciousness for himself all over again. The spiritual truths are not cumulative. So you cannot teach spirituality.

The aims and objects of this paper is to "initiate a dialogue with an open mind". Such sharing leads to understanding and learning; and this results in intuition (insight), spontaneity and right action. This blossoms to awareness of the Wholeness, which is the consummation of nature's Intelligence.

Will India take a bold step to right kind of education, which implies "***Epistemological Revolution Through Scientific Temper***", or pilgrimage to the "***Sacred Temple of Understanding and Learning***", or "***Symbiosis of Science and Spirituality***"; and all these are the same except a difference of shade. In principle, this is the panacea to resolve all human psychological challenges. To sum up, a "new global security order", "a non-violent peaceful world", cannot emerge from any intellectual approach, but is embedded in the higher hierarchical manifestation of Consciousness in the mind-brain-body system. And this blossoms to "order, harmony, coherence, beauty, non-violence, peace and security".

References

1. Martin Luther, in Sampooran Singh, *The Pilgrimage to the Third Millennium*, Chandigarh: Faith Publishers, January 1995, p. 59.
2. Albert Einstein, in Sampooran Singh, *ibid.*, p. 16.
3. Sampooran Singh, *PsychoScience*, USA, *Stable World Peace and Human Survival*, 1994, Vol. 1, No. 2, pp. 53, 54.
4. *United Nations Foundation:/www.unfoundation.org/.*
5. Sampooran Singh, *A Review on Symbiosis of Science and Spirituality*, Dagshai: The Atam Science Trust, October 7, 2002, p. 2.
6. J. Krishnamurti, 1982, *KFI Bulletin No.* 1, p. 40.
7. G. Spencer Brown, *Laws of Form*, New York: The Julian Press, 1972, pp. 104-105.
8. Arthur Eddington, in Ken Wilber, *The Spectrum of Consciousness*, USA: The Theosophical Publishing House, 1982 (Quest Book), p. 29.
9. *ibid.*, in Erwin Schrodinger, in *What is Life*? & *Mind and Matter*, 1967 Ed., Cambridge University Press, pp. 130, 177.
10. Alexander Koyre, *Newtonian Studies*, Chicago: University of Chicago Press, 1968, pp. 23-24; in Ilya Prigogine, *op. cit.*, pp. 35-36.
11. Sampooran Singh, *The Pilgrimage to the Third Millennium*, Chandigarh: Faith Publishers, January 1995, p. 19.
12. Arthur Eddington, Commins and Linscott, *Man and the Universe*, New York: Washington Square Press, 1969, p. 453; and Alan W. Watts, *The Ways of Zen*, New York: Vintage Books, 1957, p. 10.

19

The States of Mind-Brain-Body System : The Spectrum of Consciousness

The ancient seers/sages of India, about 30,000 years ago (recorded history shows 10,000 years) perceived a state of true illumination. There is One Reality, the Unmanifest-Manifested. The nature of the Unmanifest is 'Deep-Silence', 'Inactivity (Non-Vibration)', 'Passivity', 'Immutability', 'Eternal', and also Activity (Vibration), dynamism and illimitable potency to manifest as many. Activity (Active Reality) expresses which is self-hidden in the Silence (Passive Reality); both are different states of the Supreme Reality, the obverse and converse affirmations; both are Pure Existence and conscious Force, or Self-Existent Bliss and Supreme Intelligence, and are One. It is the Active Reality which manifests as the perfect freedom and omnipotence of an eternal divine activity in innumerable galaxies as inanimate world and plant and animal kingdoms.[1]

The Active Reality is a powerful, highly directional, monochromatic (same frequency) and coherent (the wave is in one phase) beam of energy; or a state of highest frequency (higher frequency means higher energy), or higher quantum energy potential.[2]

The Active Reality has the potential to express itself at different hierarchical expressions of quantum energy potentials of Consciousness, which is termed as One in many. At the level of man, the lowest quantum energy potential of consciousness expresses itself as psychological imbalances, ecological and pollution crises, energy crisis, a crisis in health care, a rising wave of violence and crime, and so on. The crisis is essentially a crisis of perception.

All this suggests a profound imbalance in our culture–in our thoughts and feelings, our values and attitudes, and our social, economic and political structures. The roots of this cultural crisis lies in the imbalance between self-conscious mode of mind and intuitive mode of mind, which have been recognised as characteristic aspects of human nature throughout the ages. They are usually called the rational and intuitive modes, or the pure-scientific and pure religious (spiritual) mode, or the logical and scientific reason and unfettered philosophical reason (quantum logic). The levels of perception have been discussed earlier.[3]

This article discusses: (1) The Psychological Mode of Mind; (2) The Principles of Objectivation and Listening; (3) The Pursuit of Objective Science; (4) The Restructuring of Science-Education; (5) The Principle of Understanding; (6) The Perception of the Fact; and (7) The Total Perception. This is also called the spectrum of consciousness or levels of perception.

The mind-brain-body system is a single dynamic system, a unitary flow. The different states are not separate from one another, but merely as an exegetical convenience, a device to make the complex story of generation of different states of consciousness a little easier to tell. The higher comes *through* the lower, then *rests on* the lower, but does not come *from* the lower.

1. The Psychological Mode of Mind

Man is unique and individual. The common states of mind are waking, dreaming and deep-sleep states. He has the faculty of mind with its powers of reasoning, which include not only the process of analysis and synthesis, but also of memory and imagination. The mind constructs memory, or cultural belief structure, or morphopsychic fields, or causal body plasma.

In order to see itself, the mind first cuts itself up into at least one state (subject) which sees and at least one other state which is seen (object); the subject (memory) and the object are at the same quantum energy potential (immanent potential) but the subject is at a higher momentum; there is transference of energy between the subject and the object, so both the subject and the object are mutilated. The subject and the object are continuities of change, hence the variable subject can never know the variable object completely. In the words of Eddington, "The frank realization that physical science is concerned with a world of shadows is one of the most significant of recent advances".[4] Erwin Schrodinger pointed out that Democritus of Abdera and even before, were aware of the shadowy character of our world in fifth century B.C.[5] Schrodinger also pointed out that "all scientific knowledge is based on sense perception and that nonetheless the scientific views of natural processes found in this way lacks all sensual qualities and therefore cannot account for the latter". He added, "Our world picture is 'colourless, cold, mute' .... so these are lacking in a world model from which we have removed our own mental person".[6]

Fred Alan Wolf wrote:

> Since atoms with consciousness are looking at atoms with consciousness, we have the same experience of wonder and

> the mystery whenever we look at the universe. ***We are looking at ourselves***. It is this process which we call the universe .... Consciousness performs a dual role in the universe. It is both the awareness and the creation of experience. It is the *being* and the *knowing* of experience. With the stroke of the twentieth-century quantum eraser, the dividing line between the ontology (theory of being) and epistemology (theory of knowing) is rubbed out.[7]

The fusion of ontology, epistemology and psychology is beginning to emerge.

2. The Principles of Objectivation and Listening

Objectivation: Erwin Schrodinger wrote:

> Without being aware of it and without being rigorously systematic about it, we exclude the Subject of Cognizance from the domain of nature that we endeavour to understand.... The material world has only been constructed at the price of taking the self, that is, mind, out of it, removing it; mind is not part of it; obviously, therefore, it can neither act on it nor be acted on by any of its parts.... Mind has erected the objective outside world of the natural philosopher out of its own stuff. Mind could not cope with this gigantic task otherwise than by the simplifying device of excluding itself–withdrawing from its conceptual creation. Hence the latter does not contain its creator.[8]

He also quoted J.C. Jung, B. Spinoza and Charles Sherrington. It appears that the objective world is at lower quantum energy potential than the subject of cognizance. Schrodinger wrote:

> We cannot make any factual statement about a given natural object (or physical system) without 'getting in touch' with it. This 'touch' is a real physical interaction. Even if it consists only in our 'looking at the object' the latter must be hit by light-rays and reflect them into the eye, or into some instrument of observation. This means that the object is affected by our observation. You cannot obtain any knowledge about an object while leaving it strictly isolated.[9]

The ancient sages/seers were aware of the art of observation. R. P. Kaushik wrote:

> The first stage prior to recognition and naming is a state of non-verbal or thought-free perception (*nirvikalpa jnana* or pure perception). From this pure perception we proceed to thought, recognition and naming (*savikalpa jnana*). When the observer

> identifies the observed, it classifies and qualifies it. The observer starts either identifying itself with the observed if it is pleasant and desirable, or alienates itself from the observed if it is unpleasant and undesirable. However, in the psychological field, both these processes of identification and alienation are one and the same.[10]

The observer, pseudo-subject is constantly projecting its desires, motives, acquisition, violence, fear, aversions, recognition and knowledge, so it is not observing the observed. It cannot understand the observed. What is observed is different from what was before the act of observation. Kaivalyapada: Patanjal Yoga (23) discussed, "A mind which is dyed with the fusion of the observer and the observed is full of all the riches".[11] Kaivalyapada Patanjal Yoga (25) discussed, "One who sees with this art of pure observation in him ego disappears".[12] We need a psychological fusion of the observer and the observed, and this is observation.

Capra wrote, "Rational knowledge is derived from the sensory experience we have with objects and events in our everyday environment. It belongs to the realm of the intellect, whose function it is to discriminate, divide, compare, measure and categorize. In this way, a world of intellectual distinctions is created; of opposites which can exist oniy in relation to each other, which is why Buddhists call this type of knowledge *relative*".[13]

Some philosophers-mystics call the observed as I-consciousness. Erwin Schrodinger stated that "mind is not part of it (objective world)". He added, "Every man's world picture is and always remains a construct of his mind and cannot be proved to have any other existence, yet the conscious mind itself remains a stranger within that construct, it has no living space in it, you can spot it nowhere in space. It appears that I-consciousness is the objective world, a static structure, a dead matter without any dynamism or consciousness. It is at a lower quantum energy potential than the thought-structure. This is the only structure in the human mind-brain-body system which is not conscious. The Brain has to jettison the static load of I-consciousness and dynamic load of thought-structure before it is free.

Listening: The moment we hear a word, we interpret it and translate it to a synonym to understand it. If the word has a psychological import, the human mind at once loses its equanimity and responds by resistance or identification and psychological pleasure and pain comes into operation. This disturbance distorts listening. The resistance creates a chain of reactions and ultimately destroys our peace and freedom.[14] You listen with ears; then a message (electrical signal transmitted through nervous system) goes from the ear to the inner hearing sensorium. The inner sensorium belongs to the mind, it converts the electrical signal to the message. Eddington wrote:

> The physiologist can trace the nerve mechanism up to the brain (inner sensorium); but ultimately there is a hiatus which no one professes to fill up. Symbolically we can follow the influence of the physical world up to the door of the mind; they ring the bell and then depart.[15]

The mind then observes the message, so the mind transforms the art of listening to the art of observation.

3. The Pursuit of Objective Science

About 1600, Kepler and Galileo simultaneously and independently formulated the principle that laws of nature are to be discovered by measurement. All propositions are confined to that which is objectively measurable and verifiable.

The physical world picture lacks all the sensual qualities (colour and sound, hot and cold) that go to make the subject of cognizance; similarly the objective world of science lacks, or is deprived of, everything that has a meaning only in relation to the conscious subject, which implies all ethical and aesthetical values, everything related to the meaning and scope of the whole display. Schrodinger added, "No personal god can form part of a world model that has only become accessible at the cost of removing everything personal from it".

The objective scientific world (outer) behaves as a particle-aspect of thought, while the inner (subjective) world behaves as a wave-aspect of thought; so in principle, the inner world is at a higher quantum energy potential of consciousness. The objective scientific world can never give us perennial values, or cannot impart value education.

The scientific mode is very factual. It moves from fact to fact. Discovery is its mission, its perception. It is precise, clear, unprejudiced, which does not condemn, which observes, which sees. A scientific mind takes up "the role of a non-concerned observer", in the words of Schrodinger;[16] it is "unrelated to our beliefs, our ambitions, our hopes", in the words of Prigogine[17] it must not construct a pseudo-observer, it must see in the present and reject the past remembrances or future projections. The values in science are objective truth, integrity, and honesty.

In 1929, J. Krishnamurti proclaimed that "truth is a pathless land" and that organised beliefs are an "impediment to inner liberation". The objective scientific world is organised belief, a conceptual model.[18]

Krishnamurti in 1948 said, "If you follow each thought to its completion, you will see that at the end of it there is silence. From that there is renewal. Thought that arises from this silence no longer has desire as its motive force, it emerges from a state that is not clogged with memory .... The new approach is to bring time to an end.

Science is a dialogue with the universe in which questions are asked and insights born. Ilya Prigogine wrote, "It is physics that presupposes an observer situated within the observed world. Our dialogue with nature will be successful only if it is carried on from within nature".[19] If the observer is *within*, and the observed is *somewhere outside*, it gives a mutilated perception–it is the fragmentary perception of the intellect or affair of emotion; and it gives conflict. It is also called the self-interacting dynamics of consciousness, it gives self-knowledge. If both the observer and the observed are *within*, it bestows perception of the objective truth in the objective world.

4. The Restructuring of Science-Education

Many eminent scientists–Erwin Schrodinger, Karl Pribram, Albert Einstein, Hideki Yukawa, Niels Bohr, E.P. Wigner, Roger Sperry, J.C. Eccles, Teilhard de Chardin, John Walton, and so on–have advocated that science must take in its ambient the objective and the subjective dimensions of man. This deals with the wholeness of life. Similarly education must take into consideration the sensual and trans-sensual dimension. We call it restructuring of science-education, or scientific mode of mind.

Many eminent scientists–including Albert Einstein, Werner Heisenberg, Erwin Schrodinger, Arthur Eddington, and so on–have stumbled upon another mode of perception (knowing). Eddington wrote, "The intimate knowledge will not submit to codification and analysis; or rather, when we attempt to analyze it, the intimacy is lost and is replaced by symbolism".[20] Alan W. Watts discussed, "the understanding of life directly, instead of in the abstract terms of representational thinking".[21] The intimate knowledge is called the non-dual knowledge, and it transcends duality. It implies quantum jump from dualistic state to non-dual state, or from objective scientific logic to quantum logic.

The outer and the inner are not two separate movements but a single dynamic flow. The energy exchange between the inner and the outer happens in less than a few millionth of a second. Science must take in its realm both the outer (objective) and the inner (subjective) dimension of life; and this is called restructuring of science. Similarly education must deal with the sensual dimension and trans-sensual dimension of life. The restructured science-education deals with the wholeness of life. The "*subject of cognizance*" is non-variable or reaction-free attentivity, or objectless attention. The restructured science-education is synergistic to thought-structure coupled with volitions.

Ending of I-consciousness or Ego: If a thought coupled with volition comes in the field of true-subject (restructured science-education), the I-consciousness is knocked off because it is at the lowest quantum energy potential. It implies that the movement of thought structure is independent of my volition, it is independent of the movement of the ego. It is a tremendous discovery that: (a) what I call my volition (I-consciousness) is at a lower quantum energy potential than thought structure; (b) the mental movement has a momentum independent of me so the vanity that these are my thoughts disappears; (c) thought has an independent existence of me, which implies a realisation of the limitations of the activity of volition and the immensity of the thought structure and its movement; or there is nothing like 'I' or 'me' in the movement of thought; and (d) I do not act upon my thoughts, or I do not jump to evaluate or judge them, so this establishes a new relationship of thought structure and myself (I-consciousness).

This observation knocks down the concept that there is a thinker and movement of thought as two separate entities. There is nothing like an independent mind and there is nothing like an independent I-consciousness, and this bestows a sense of great freedom within.[22]

Ending of Thought Structure : When thought structure comes in the field of restructured science, the 'photons' meet an impregnable wall, called 'event horizon', or 'frequency barrier', or 'time barrier'. Deepak Chopra, on the basis of relativistic physics stated, "The speed of light is absolute, it is like a wall that no object can crash through. As we approach the wall, time slows down, mass increases and space becomes curved".[23] He added, "Any place where knowledge stops there is an event horizon". Thought (or photons) cannot cross the 'event horizon', it is bombarded by the non-variable attentivity, and the thought gets annihilated.

At the moment of crossing the 'frequency barrier', the subject-object energy interaction ends, because the photons are knocked down by the energy of attentivity, which is at a higher potential. The object goes to abeyance and dualism ends. The time-space matrices also go to abeyance. The experience and knowledge also stops. All this happens in less than a hundred microseconds.[24]

Vimala Thakar calls the awareness of the outward and the inward movement of life as meditation. If I am simultaneously aware of the objective challenge, the subject reactions and the causes of the reactions, then it results in freedom. Then the momentum of reaction will not carry me over with it, but I will be ahead of the reaction.[25] I will be aware of the objective challenge only. Thought goes to abeyance and there is perception of the *fact*, the *true*, the *present*, the *non-dual*, the *what is*!

5. The Principle of Understanding

When thought-structure and I-consciousness go to abeyance, the Intelligence flows to the brain, which bestows intuition (insight), spontaneity and right action. The intelligence is uncluttered by the movement of thought. The dimension of Intelligence, of Unconditioned Energy, of Fundamental Vibration has no past, so it is free from all conditioning and divisive loyalties, etc. It bestows intuition or insight. Insight implies something which you perceive without any logic, without any motive. It is called immediate perception. ***The perceptions are born of non-duality, of silence, and responses are born of spontaneity.***

J. Krishnamurti, in a prophetic message, said:

> Understanding comes into being from the *now*, the *present*, which is always timeless .... Only the truth can liberate the mind from its own ideation; to see the truth the mind must realize the fact that as long as it is agitated, it can have no understanding.... Truth is not cumulative. It is from moment to moment.[26]

Understanding flows in a non-dual mind. Krishnamurti, in 1979, in a dialogue, said:

> India has lived all these centuries on ideas. She has to move from a life based on ideas, which are non-facts, to seeing the fact only.
>
> The benediction of the timeless is waiting, the ground is ready. Can we create something out of this benediction.

Pupul Jayakar commenting on the above wrote, "India was the ground where the seed has been sown .... It is the prophecy that a sacred energy was alive again in the Indian soil". She added.

> Krishnaji conveyed a way of perception, of challenge and response from a state that lay beyond the mind, beyond brain, memory, all responses of consciousness. "A state that comes into being in listening at great depth; where consciousness and its movement do not obstruct. A state where seeing is whole, inclusive, nonfragmented, a state of no movement from or towards; beyond matrix and all racial memories of man".

6. The Perception of the Fact

If we continue observing or listening to the *fact*, without justification or condemnation or motivation, we observe there is only the fact and nothing else. The fact itself is the operator, not you operating on the fact. If you leave the fact alone, it has no time. The fact is free from fear. The fact grows, which implies that there is release of tremendous energy[27] and the fact moves to higher quantum energy potential. This is expressed as Pure Consciousness → Fact. It helps the fact to make a quantum jump in the vertical dimension of Consciousness. When the fact is left alone, it is operating and you do not have to do a thing about it, it matures and blossoms. Immediacy of perception dissolves the fact, and one revels in Pure Consciousness or Intelligence. Only in Intelligence there is complete security. Intelligence sees the false as the false and ends the false. Mutation happens in the timelessness. To understand Consciousness or an enquiry into the subject is the perception of that immeasurable state.

Understanding and learning are born in non-duality. Intuition (insight) is perception without any doubt. ***Understanding, learning and action are a cyclic process, which results in a spiral going upwards in the vertical dimension; it is a growth in the vertical dimension***. The higher the understanding, the higher the expression of the Consciousness in the human brain-body system.[28]

7. The Total Perception

It is perception without the word, which is without thought. It is with the brain (the heart) and with all the senses–it is with the pure mind, it is called the total perception, or the perfect perception, or the holistic perception. Holistic perception dissolves the fact. Perception and understanding are not of time. It is communion with the height and depth of the immense. There is a movement of great ecstasy which is not to be confounded with pleasure. It is this ecstasy which gives to the eyes, to the brain, and to the heart, the quality of innocency. It is born in the state of attention and gets finer and acute in the state of awareness. It is born when the non-dual state of mind is presented as an object to pure consciousness, the subject, and it reveals itself. It is the awareness of the awareness itself, so it can be realised through direct perception of the unified field in the self-referral state of consciousness. Holistic perception implies that the mind is totally free, to be totally unattached to everything that man has put together. It implies to be aware of the wholeness, of the Fundamental Vibration.

Perception in the State of Meditation: In an ocean of Silence, the vibrations of the cosmic energy also end, and this bestows the perception of the one Self of all, the *Brahman*.

Concluding Comment

Every existence is an expression of the consciousness, so it represents a hierarchical expression of the "quantum field of information". The brain is basically the biophysical substrate for the mental processes. The brain is degenerate with regard to mind. Each higher stage is synergistic to its junior components, it includes them but is more than them.

Our crisis is new. No civilisation has previously had to face the challenge of scientific specialisation, and our response must be new. The new response must take its birth from the non-dual frame of reference of the Mind Continuum. It must emerge from the womb of modern science.

Humanity is now poised for the most crucial and the most difficult transition it has ever sought to accomplish. The transition, which man is facing, is energising his own inner potential, or a new mode of consciousness, which can eventually lift the human race above and beyond the violence, fear, ignorance and isolation which beset him today. It is quantum jump from successive consciousness to simultaneous Consciousness (all-inclusive Consciousness). It is self-actualization of the highest quantum energy potential.

The Intelligence uses the brain, so the cerebral become a channel for Its expression. The person is bestowed an inner poise, a tranquil mind. The Intelligence takes up the role of action, the source of perception, the source of response; the Silence or Intelligence has revolutionised the person. The person is reduced to 'nothingness' inside, which the Universal uses for the service of mankind. It is only such person who can create a high-synergy society, create a new civilization and a new society where there is no misery and conflict, and every human being lives in peace, freedom and bliss.

Modern civilisation cannot survive unless it is inspired by the spectrum of Consciousness, or the highest level of perception. One has to understand, learn and live in the symbiosis of science and spirituality. Love and compassion flow from the non-dual frame, the restructured science-education. The spiritual dimension is the innermost truth of the cosmos. This enhances the sensitivity, heightens the level of perception, so these blossom to love. Love flows from the "homogeneous, undifferentiated, dimensionless wholeness" in holovibration. The scientists have to realize that science is a human activity, and all science must deal with the whole. This is the only hope for the world in its present perilous state. Let every scientist see himself as a vehicle of world peace, freedom and bliss. This is the consummation of human life.

References

1. Sampooran Singh, *Dynamic Interplay Between Science and Religion*, Jodhpur: A Jainsons Publication, 1978, pp. 357-386.

2. Sampooran Singh, AVM Manjit Singh (Retd.), Dr (Mrs) Kanwaljit Kaur and Paramjit Singh, *God in Science : Symbiosis of Modern Science and the World's Religions*, Chandigarh: Vishvas Publications Pvt Ltd., July 1999, p. 2.

3. Sampooran Singh, *The Human Paradox* (*SS: Two*), Chandigarh: Faith Publishers, 1988, pp. 35-36; and *ibid.*, *Science of Life*, *ibid.*, October 1994, pp. 44-45.

4. Arthur Eddington, *The Nature of the Physical World*, Cambridge University Press, 1928, Introduction; in Erwin Schrodinger, *What is Life? & Mind and Matter*, Cambridge University Press, 1967, p. 130.

5. Erwin Schrodinger, *ibid.*, p. 177.
6. *ibid.*, p. 128.
7. Fred Alan Wolf, *Taking the Quantum Leap*, Harper and Row, 1981, p. 228-29.
8. Erwin Schrodinger, *op. cit.*. pp. 127, 128, 131.
9. *ibid.*, pp. 135, 132, 148, 150.
10. R. P. Kaushik, *Towards a New Consciousness*, Darshan Yoga Sansthan, 1974 (Ed.), p. 63.
11. *Kaivalyapada: Patanjal Yoga, 23*, in R.P. Kaushik, *ibid.*, p. 65.
12. *ibid.*, 25, p. 66.
13. Fritjof Capra, *The Tao of Physics*, Bantam Books (Second Edition), 1988, p. 14.
14. R. P. Kaushik, *op. cit.*, p. 80.
15. Arthur Eddington, in Sampooran Singh, *The Holistic Education*, New Delhi: Siddharth Publications, 1987, p. 41.
16. Erwin Schrodinger, *op. cit.*, p. 128.
17. Ilya Prigogine and Isabelle Stengers, *Order Out of Chaos*, Bantam Books, 1984, p. 5.
18. J. Krishnamurti, in Pupul Jayakar, *A Biography : Krishnamurti*, Harper and Row, 1986, pp. cover flap, 379, 380, 435.
19. Ilya Prigogine, *op. cit.*, p. 218.
20. Arthur Eddington, in Commins and Linscott, ed., *Man and The Universe, The Philosophers of Science*, New York: Washington Square Press, 1969, p. 453.
21. Alan W. Watts, *The Ways of Zen*, New York: Vintage Books, 1957, p. 10.
22. Vimala Thakar, (a) *Through Silence to Meditation*, Ahmedabad: Vimal Prakashan Trust, 1998, pp. 22-27; (b) *ibid.*, *Silence*, Holland: Bookfund, 1989, p. 6; and (c) *ibid.*, *The Invincible*, July-August 1987, Vol. IV, No. 4, p. 14.
23. Deepak Chopra, *How to Know God*, London: Rider, 2000, pp. 271-72.
24. Sampooran Singh, Dr (Mrs) Kanwaljit Kaur, Paramjit Singh and Amarjit Singh, *March to Peace: The Wisdom of Observation, Listening and the Power of Commitment*, Chandigarh: Faith Publishers, January 20, 2004, pp. 7-8, 20-21.
25. Vimala Thakar, *Mutation of Mind*, Ahmedabad: New Order Book Co., 1972, pp. 122, 171.
26. J. Krishnamurti, *The First and Last Freedom*, London: Victor Gollancz Ltd., 1977, pp. 269, 278, 286.
27. ibid., *Krishnamurti on Education*, Orient Longman, KFI, 1974, pp. 69, 87, 90.
28. Sampooran Singh, *A Review of Symbiosis of Science and Spirituality*, Dagshai: The Atam Science Trust, October 7, 2002, p. 15.

Part III
Health Technology

The theme of the Indian Science Congress – 2005 is Health Technology. All diseases are maladjustment of the mind-brain-body system, or conditioned psyche, or crisis of perception. A living in the present, the now, heals; and living in the past and duality suppresses man's sensitivity and enhances disease. There is an urgency to restructure medical education which takes in its ambient the psychodynamics of the conditioned mind-brain-body system, or Unconditioned Energy; or in other words, the wholeness of life.

Man's psychosocial evolution – over the last one million years, or more – have resulted in conditioning (storing experience and knowledge). Every activity is repetitive and mechanical, it has lost creativity or perceptive sensitivity. Man has started living in a synthetic construct of the mind, and has divorced the Reality. He is living in conflict, duality, pain, suffering, and psychological imbalances. And all this is leading to self-annihilation, self-destruction.

For the last 10,000 years, or more, man has been trying to transform the psyche, but has utterly failed. To resolve our challenges, we have to enhance our level of awareness and live in that quantum energy potential of Consciousness. We have to restructure science-education-health which embraces the wholeness of life. It is synergistic to thought structure and I-consciousness.

When "thought-time and I-consciousness" comes in the field of "restructured science-education-health", the

thought coupled with volition goes to abeyance. What is left behind is the fact, the true, the present, the non-dual, the what is! This energises the Intelligence, which resolves all human challenges and expresses itself as order, rhythm, non-violence, peace and survival.

It is imperative that medical profession and other scientists explore the healing of the psyche or ending psychic pandemic. If man escapes his responsibility, he will do so at his own peril and that of India and mankind.

20

Healing of Conditioned Mind-Brain-Body System

The Ending of Psychic Pandemic

Abstract

The theme of Indian Science Congress–2005 is HEALTH TECHNOLOGY. All diseases are maladjustment of the human mind-brain-body system, or conditioned human psyche, or crisis of perception. Health is a complete physical, mental, psychological and social well-being; it is a dynamic state which is equipoised and balanced. A living in the present, the now heals; and living in the past and duality suppresses man's perceptive sensitivity and enhances disease. The curative functions of medicines have to be supplemented with understanding and living the "symbolic-dualistic frame of reference of mind spectrum (successive consciousness)" and the "non-dual and non-conceptual frame of reference of Mind Continuum (Simultaneous Consciousness)".

There is an urgency to restructure medical education which takes in its ambient the psychodynamics of the mind-brain-body system, or in other words, the wholeness of life. We have to jettison the illusion of the past, and to live in the present, the now. We have to restructure the biomedical model and adopt the holistic ecological perception. The restructured medical education takes in its ambient the wholeness of life.

It is imperative that medical profession and other scientists explore the healing of the psyche or ending psychic pandemic. The secret of healing is not embedded in our mind-brain-body system, but in higher awareness bestowed on us by Cosmic Consciousness or Life Field. And if man escapes his responsibility, he will do so at his own peril and that of India and mankind.

The mechanistic view of life, or Cartesian-Newtonian world view dominated the attitude of physicians towards health and illness. The human body is regarded as a machine that can be analyzed in terms of its parts; disease is seen as the malfunctioning of biological mechanisms which are studied from the point of view of cellular and molecular biology; the doctor's role is to intervene, either physically or chemically, to correct the malfunctioning of a specific mechanism. Three centuries after Descartes, the science of medicine is still based, as George Engel (1977) writes, on "the notion of the body as a machine, of disease as the consequence of breakdown of the machine, and of the doctor's task as repair of the machine". The World Health Organisation in the preamble of its charter wrote, "Health is a state of complete physical, mental and social well-being, and not merely the absence of disease or infirmity". Recently physics brought about a profound change to a holistic and ecological view. The rediscovery of holistic approaches to health and healing have emerged.

Physicists have come to see that all their theories of natural phenomena, including the 'laws' they describe, are creations of the human mind; properties of our conceptual map of reality, rather than of reality itself; or parts of the map, not of the territory. Arthur Eddington wrote:

> The stuff of the world is mind-stuff.... The mind-stuff is not spread in space and time .... Recognizing that the physical world is entirely abstract and without 'actuality' apart from its linkage to consciousness, we restore consciousness to the fundamental position.[1]

We summarize the monumental researches of many eminent scientists in words:

> The human-made social cosmos, or construct of the symbolic-dualistic frame of reference of mind spectrum represents the immanent quantum energy potential, and it is divorced from the ultimate quantum energy potential. ***The construct of the mind is the only "reality" where the transcendent potential has gone to abeyance and its only linkage is the immanent potential. It represents the relative field of consciousness.***[2]

Man's psychosocial evolution–over the last one million years, or more–has resulted in gathering partial experience or fragmentary knowledge (information), and has stored it in the psyche as memory or cultural belief structure–this has resulted in conditioning of the psyche of the whole mankind. The mind splits itself into the seer (subject) and the seen (object). There is energy exchange between the subject and the object (subject object), which happens in a few millionth of a second.

The recalled memory has led to pursuit of materialism, every activity of the mind is repetitive and mechanical, it has lost creativity or perceptive sensitivity.

The whole human race has become a pleasure mongering race. The whole importance is money, security, power, pleasure and the emphasis is on the centre of the ego. The tragedy of human race is that it has lost the elegance of remaining in the wholeness while moving through thought-structure, I-consciousness and psychological imbalances. We started living in a synthetic world and have divorced the reality. We have lost the art of real seeing and real listening. The psychological suffering, pain, conflict, nervous-tensions and chemical-pressures has become a way of living.

The theme of the 92nd Indian Science Congress to be held in Ahmedabad from January 3-7, 2005 is "Health Technology". There is an urgency to reject the biomedical model; and to look at health technology from holistic and ecological view, which basically implies to "heal the conditioned mind-brain-body system", or "to end psychic pandemic". It is an inter-disciplinary exploration and has to be looked into by a team of physicians, neuro-scientists, physicists, philosophers-mystics, and so on.

For the last 10,000 years, or more, man has been trying to transform the conditioned psyche, but all traditional approaches, institutionalised religions, ideals, concepts, thought-structures have failed. The basic cause of failure is that man had been trying to transform the psyche at the same quantum energy potential at which the conditionings were constructed. The psychological imbalances, a rising wave of violence and crime, terrorism, religious fundamentalism, ethnic conflicts, corruption, ecological and pollution crises, increasing unemployment, poverty, hunger, malnutrition, health crisis, are forcing man inevitably to face the realities of the human situation. We have constructed a violent society. All different facets of challenges are one and the same crisis, and that this crisis is essentially a crisis of perception. Jacques Monod, Nobel prize winning biologist, wrote in 1972, "What we see opening before us today is an abyss of darkness".[3] George Wald, Nobel prize in Medicine, 1967, wrote, "Our society has taken a wrong turn.... By now, the problem is not transcendence, but survival".[4]

Man is an amphibian who lives simultaneously in two dimensions– (a) the *known*, the time-space matrices, the successive consciousness, the world of data and symbols, the matter, and (b) the *Unknown,* the timelessness, the simultaneous Consciousness, the Inner World, the Divine. The *known* is at the lowest frequency or hierarchical manifestation of consciousness, it is in the field of time, so it is limited, finite and transitory.

The *Unknown* is at the highest quantum energy potential of simultaneous Consciousness, it is in the realm of the timelessness, so it is immutable, infinite and eternal. As a symbol, we may compare the known to a thimble, and the Unknown to a fathomless and boundless ocean.[5]

To resolve our challenges, we have to enhance our hierarchical level of Consciousness and then live in that quantum energy potential of Consciousness. ***We are beginning a new era of awareness, the age of quantum consciousness, the age of conscious atom.***

This article explores the "healing of the conditioned mind-brain-body system", or in other words, the "ending of the psychic pandemic", which is contagious. It explores the interactions (energy transfer between mind and brain (matter) in the field of the *known*, the time-space matrices, the successive consciousness. This leads to mutilated or deformed perception which flows to strife, pain, misery and travails.

It investigates the *Unknown*, the *Life Field*. It is direct input of the Life Field in the brain without mediation of the sensual world. It is invariably in the realm of the non-dual perception and transcends the I-consciousness. The interaction with matter goes to abeyance. It expresses itself as "understanding of life directly". It bestows pure perception which blossoms to order, harmony, non-violence and peace. It flows to human survival and excellence.

From Biomedical Model to Holistic and Ecological Model

Fritjof Capra wrote, "To go beyond it will require nothing less than a profound cultural revolution. And such a revolution is necessary if we want to improve, or even maintain, our health.... Biomedical research will have to be integrated into a broader system of health care in which the manifestations of all human illness are seen as resulting from the interplay of mind, body, and environment, and are studied and treated accordingly".[6]

Illness is not thought of as an intruding agent, but as due to a pattern of causes leading to disharmony and imbalance. Stress is an imbalance of the organism in response to environmental influences. Stress leads to nervous tension and chemical imbalances. The emotional stress has two principal effects. It suppresses the body's immune system, and, at the same time, leads to normal imbalances that results in an increased production of abnormal cells. Thus optional conditions for cancer growth are created. Once feelings of hope and anticipation are generated, the organism translates them into biological processes and begin to restore balance and revitalize the immune system, using the same pathways that were used in the development of the illness.

The paradigm shift in health care will involve the formulation of new conceptual models, the creation of new institutions, and the implementation of new policies. The physical disease is a manifestation of underlying psychosomatic processes that may be generated by various psychological and social problems. This implies higher hierarchical awareness of Consciousness. The secret of healing does not lie in our physical bodies, but in our Consciousness.

Symbolic-Dualistic Frame of Reference of Mind Spectrum

(a) ***Case One–Physics Model:*** Human beings and the natural world are on a collision course. Humanity is beginning now, to turn its attention to the cause of human suffering and end the suffering. The successive consciousness, or the known field is continually interacting with the recalled memory. R. P. Kaushik wrote, "The first stage prior to recognition and naming is a state of non-verbal or thought-free perception (*nirvikalpa jnana*, or pure perception, or fact, or imageless awareness). From this pure perception, we proceed to thought, recognition and naming (*savikalpa jnana*, mutilated perception, non-fact)".[7] The different steps in perception are: Firstly, the mind perceives the external environments, the fact, the challenge, so the fluctuating energy input is called the challenge; the perception of the fact in philosophical language is called thought-free perception, or pure perception, or non-verbal perception, or factual perception. Secondly, the mind recalls or retrieves the past corresponding memory, which takes up the role of the pseudo-subject with respect to the fact which is the object. To be more precise, the mind severs itself into the subject and the object, and this severance introduces dualism. The subject proceeds to recognition, identification, comparing, naming and storing the object. The whole process implies an exchange of photons (quanta of light), these are 'gentle quantum events', and these bring in a discontinuity at that moment. At the moment of this exchange the distinction between the subject and the object is lost. One flowing web of frequencies (subject) looks at another flowing web of frequencies (object), and then both intermingle losing their identities. Both the subject and the object become continuities of change, so the subject is the object, the thinker is the thought. The interaction may be shown as:

Fact + **Recalled Memory** → **Mutilated Fact** + **Modified Memory**

Thirdly, the mind perceives the mutilated fact and records the modified memory, where, in principle, the mutilated fact and the modified memory are the same. The interaction is a biochemical interaction or dance, it remembers what the dance was yesterday, so it is always doing the same dance. The perception of the mutilated fact gives us the response, the dualistic action; the will of action is always dualistic.[8]

The whole mankind has programmed the mind-brain-body system as a single channel computer. We are engaged in acquisition, storing it in memory, possessing, acquiring and using it. The process is mechanical or repetitive, so there is no newness or creativity. It is this false process which is responsible for all human psychological challenges.

The severance of the universe into a subject and an object, into a knower and a known, "creating of two worlds from one", introduces the primal act of dualism. There is invariably exchange of energy between the environments, object and subject, which results into mutilation of perception. This is a process which is antagonistic to the immutable laws of Nature, so it introduces conflict, contradiction, pain and misery–both individually and collectively.

(b) ***Case Two–Transpersonal Psychology:*** The new thought structures–called cognitive psychology, transpersonal psychology, deep ecology–have emerged recently.[9] In the psychological mode, the mind cuts itself up into a subject (observer, recalled memory, atoms with consciousness) and an object (observed, atoms with consciousness), so mind (thought) is looking itself.

In the language of transpersonal psychology, or deep ecology, we say that: (a) the recording of objective fact as pure perception is by the cognitive part of the being; (b) the recalled memory is by the conative part (sentiments, emotions, feelings) of the being; (c) there is chemical movement between the conation and the cognition which results in grafting or superpositioning the conative part on the cognitive part; (d) this results in mutilation of the cognitive and there is awareness of the mutilated cognition; (e) the modified conative is again recorded; and (f) this is called the code of behaviour (recognition and naming) to monitor the chemical and neurological movements of the mind-brain-body system. The awareness of the mutilated perception is called knowledge which results in sensual behaviour. The whole process may be written as:

$$\text{Bare Cognition} + \text{Conative} \rightarrow \text{Mutilated Cognition} + \text{Modified Conative}$$

The conation is not based upon cognition. The emotive or conative part depends on the science of ethics, or morals, or virtues, which gives a code of conduct of oughts and ought-nots. The emotive or conative is not related to the knowledge part of the being. The sensual behaviour is called action. The cognitive, the conative and the action are developed in our life as water-tight compartments. Religion and ethics control the conative part. The social sciences (knowledge)–economics, politics, sociology–deal with the sensual behaviour. Perhaps there never has been growth of our wholeness in a homogeneous way.

Knowledge does not flow into the chemistry of body, which is governed by conative part of the being, by emotions and feelings. Knowledge prevents the instant comprehension, instant perception, or understanding of life directly.

A brief summary of the transpersonal psychology or deep ecology is as under:

(i) ***Adding to the Conative:*** The mind is in the relative frame of reference, or self-interacting dynamic state at immanent quantum energy potential. There is interaction (energy exchange as photon transfer or chemical movement) between bare cognition and conative. There is transference of psychic energy to physical energy which is recorded as frequency and amplitude information, it adds to the conative part of the being, or matter content of the consciousness. It leads to lowering the level of perceptive sensitivity.

(ii) ***Annihilation of the Conative:*** The mind is in the state of attentiveness. If a thought comes in the field of attentiveness, it is bombarded by the energy of attentiveness and thought gets annihilated. This is basically annihilation of physical energy which leads to decrease of matter content in the consciousness and higher perceptive sensitivity.

(iii) ***Journey Beyond Conative:*** The mind is in the self-referral state or highest quantum energy potential of consciousness. Higher frequency means higher energy. The psychic energy makes a quantum jump beyond a critical frequency ("event horizon", "frequency barrier", "time-barrier") where the psychic energy does not transform itself to matter, so in that state there is no recording of perception as conative. In this state, the original (Simultaneous Consciousness) and the mirror-image (pure perception) are identical.

(iv) ***The Law of Nature:*** For uncounted aeons man has been busy in psychosocial evolution which implies recording and storing conative (partial knowledge and fragmentary experience); he is now trying to embark on ***spiritual evolution which implies to jettison all that he has accumulated and stored***; and this pursuit will bring him in harmony and coherence with nature. The secret of fundamental revolution is man unfolding.

(c) ***Case Three–Time:*** The mind is the background; the mind is the result of psychological time; the mind is the past, the mind is not the future. Thought is the result of time. To become, to acquire, search for security, to aspire for prestige, name and fame, desires, ambitions are time. All psychological imbalances and ecological challenges are time. The mind interacts (energy exchange) with time, and results in mutilated perception, which results in conflict. Conflict leads to pain, misery and suffering.

When one is inattentive, there is energy exchange between mind and the challenge resulting into distortion of perception, because the associations, the images and memories, the time, create distance between the observer and the observed. There is no understanding and learning in the distorted perception. At the moment of attention, all the conditionings disappears, and there is awareness of the *fact*, the *present*. Understanding comes into being from pure perception, awareness of the fact, the now, the present, which is always timeless.

The symbolic-dualistic frame of reference in the mind spectrum is an open system so far as environment is concerned, but it is a closed system so far as Absolute (the Life Field) is concerned. The non-dual frame is a closed system so far as environment is concerned but an open system so far as Absolute is concerned. We have to make a quantum jump from symbolic-dualistic frame (closed system to the Absolute) to non-dual frame (open system to the Absolute); and this brings us in touch with the Reality, the Absolute, the Wholeness. All human psychological problems will vanish when there is perception of the Wholeness.

Non-Dual Frame of Reference of Mind Continuum

If we continue observing or listening to the *fact*, without justification or condemnation or motivation, we observe there is only the fact and nothing else. The fact itself is the operator, not you operating on the fact. If you leave the fact alone, it has no time. The fact is free from fear. The fact grows, which implies that there is release of tremendous energy and the fact moves to higher quantum energy potential. This is expressed as Pure Consciousness → Fact. It helps the fact to make a quantum jump in the vertical dimension of Consciousness. When the fact is left alone, it is operating and you do not have to do a thing about it, it matures and blossoms. Immediacy of perception dissolves the fact, and one revels in Pure Consciousness or Intelligence. Only in Intelligence there is complete security. Intelligence sees the false as the false and ends the false. Mutation happens in the timelessness. To understand Consciousness or an enquiry into the subject is the perception of that immeasurable state.

Schrodinger wrote that, "Consciousness is never expressed in the plural, only in the singular".[10] Similarly, the over-all number of Mind Continuum is just one and the whole mankind, including all other existences, shares it. The observation and listening happens in a non-dual frame of reference of mind continuum.[11]

Understanding of Life Directly

Many eminent scientists –including Albert Einstein, Werner Heisenberg, Erwin Schrodinger, Arthur Eddington, and so on–have stumbled upon another mode of perceptin (knowing), which is "understanding of life directly, instead of in the abstract, linear terms of representational thinking". This is exactly the insight of 300 years of persistent and consistent scientific research. Eddington wrote:

> We have two kinds of knowledge which I call symbolic knowledge and intimate knowledge.... [The] more customary forms of reasoning have been developed for symbolic knowledge only. The intimate knowledge will not submit to codification and analysis; or, rather, when we attempt to analyze it the *intimacy is lost and it is replaced by symbolism.*[12]

This suggests that analysis (or intellectual approach) has to be discarded, or I-consciousness goes to abeyance, and it leads to ending of subject-object dualism.

The subject of cognizance (true-subject) is ***non-variable attentivity, or reaction-free attentivity, or objectless attention***. The true-subject is synergistic to the pseudo-subject (the recalled memory). The pseudo-subject goes to abeyance and true-subject takes over. The true-subject knocks down thought-time, I-consciousness with associated volition which are at a lower quantum energy potential of consciousness.

The quantum jump from pseudo-subject to true subject happens when we deeply understand that objective science takes in its ambient the subjective realm, and the objective field, and this we call ***restructuring*** of science.

The objective and the subjective are inseparable. The notion of Mind Continuum implies both the objective and the subjective worlds. So the mind (one whole movement where "I" has been transcended) cannot "act or be acted" on by environments. *The interaction is possible between the symbolic-dualistic frame of reference, the objective world, the self and the environments.* The new approach of the wholeness of Mind--if observed honestly as an experimental dialogue–ends all subject-object dualism. The realm of the *Unknown* (the wholeness of life) has awareness of the *fact*, the *true*, the *present*, the *what is*!, the *non-dual*, so all interactions between the Mind Continuum with matter are absent. The attributes of Unknown are order, harmony, coherence, non-violence and peace.

By the word 'Life', we imply, every expression of Life Field, or Universal Consciousness, or dynamic creative energy at the highest frequency, in the whole cosmos. Respect for fellow expressions of life generates sensitivity which implies awareness of the Consciousness and love and compassion for every existence. This constructs a just society which implies ending of all conflict, confrontation and violence, and ushering of order, harmony and peace.

Human brain records only violence as memory, or cultural belief structure, or frequency and amplitude information, because it is at the lowest frequency of consciousness. When the frequency of Consciousness is more than the "frequency barrier", or "transient zone", or "event horizon",[13] it does not record any event, or it cannot record the *Silence*.

A depth introspection shows that the outer (objective world) and the inner (subjective world) are one, a unitary movement, not separate, but whole. The perception or awareness of the whole–if observed by honest experiments–ends all subject-object dualism. The ending of "creating of two worlds from one" results in perception of the fact. This results in understanding which blossoms to truth. Krishnamurti said, "India has lived all these centuries on ideas. She has to move from a life based on ideas, which are non-facts, to seeing the fact only".[14]

Ending the Crisis of Mutilated Perception or Healing of the Conditioned Psyche

Consciousness performs a dual role in the universe. In the world of quantum, it is both the awareness and the creation of experience. It is the *being* and the *knowing* of experience. As a *being*, the pure Consciousness expresses itself at the highest hierarchical expression of Consciousness, or the highest quantum energy potential of Consciousness, or the highest frequency of Consciousness. As creation of experience, the successive consciousness expresses itself at the lowest hierarchical expression of consciousness, or lowest frequency of consciousness. Niels Bohr put it "we are both spectators and actors in the great drama of existence".[15] With the stroke of the twentieth-century quantum eraser, the dividing line between the ontology (theory of being) and epistemology (theory of knowing) is rubbed out. The fusion of ontology, epistemology and psychology is beginning to emerge.[16]

Seeing the fact implies that volition or motives drops away, or the movement of thought structure is independent of your volitions. The mentarl movement has a momentum independent of volition or I-consciousness. Thought has a momentum independent of the 'me', so thought is not mine. I look at thought–not to judge, neither to accept nor to reject, not to react upon them, not to change them–I look at the movement of thought in utter freedom. So thought blossoms and withers away. The scientific temper or restructured science sees that there is racial consciousness, a racial momentum of knowledge, experience and thought, and there is nothing like an individual ego, the self, the 'me', then there is a sense of great freedom within. Freedom blossoms to the Silence. Silence is the spontaneous breath of the wholeness of life. This also suggests that non-dual thought is synergistic to 'I' or 'me', so there is discontinuity between 'I' and non-dualistic thought, or in other words there is timelessness.[17]

The scientific mode of mind (restructured science), which is synergistic to psychological mode or thought structure, watches the movement of thought without interfering in its flow, or there is no flow of energy to sustain the thought, or the non-variable energy bombards the thought structure which results in dissipation of the energy of thought. The thought blossoms and withers away, which implies that the I-consciousness goes to abeyance and the *non-fact* transforms itself to *fact*. This is called a Mind with a scientific temper, it is tuned to perceive the *fact*, the *true*, the *present*, the *what is*!, the *non-dual*. The austerity of a scientific approach to everything in life results in purification of the conditioned psyche. The true subject has the awareness to perceive the fact. This leads to mutation of the conditioned psyche.

In the non-dual and non-conceptual frame of reference of mind spectrum, the subject is the non-variable attentivity, it sees the fact as an object. The fact itself is the operator, not you operating on the fact. The spontaneity in the non-dual frame flows to a pure action–action without an idea. The subject (attentivity), the object (the fact) and pure action are one and the same; these flow as a rising spiral in the vertical dimension of Consciousness, of spirituality. In philosophical language, we call it, leave the fact alone because it has no time, or let the fact live and it blossoms instantly. Blossoming implies that attentivity and the fact coalesce, and the whole system makes a quantum jump to a higher level of Consciousness. It is a self-regulated, self-expressing growth. It is a happening.

Concluding Comment

The humanity is poised at a crucial cross-roads in its long and tortuous history on Planet Earth. We stand at a bifurcation where one road is leading to bomb (self-annihilation, self-destruction) and the other road is leading to Buddha (Intelligence, Wisdom).

The road leading to self-annihilation is called psychological mode of mind, or symbolic-dualistic frame of reference of mind spectrum, where the mind, in order to see itself, cuts itself up into a state which sees (subject, the self) and at least another state which is seen (object, matter, atom); there is energy transfer between the subject and the object resulting into duality and deformed perception which expresses itself as conflict, pain and misery. The other road, leading to Buddha, is called non-dual state, or intuition, or insight. As non-dual state has transcended I-consciousness (matter), so there is no energy transfer between Consciousness and matter. In this state there is direct input of the highest potential of Consciousness without mediation of the sensual world, and thus it leads to understanding of life directly. The aim of human life is to perceive and live in this wholeness, which flows into harmony, order, non-violence and peace. Let us work jointly for that consummation of life.

The symbolic-dualistic frame of reference is invariably in disorder and in conflict. Order cannot be imposed on successive consciousness which is disorderly. The disorder in our consciousness has a cause and if that cause is understood by watching it, the disorder is eliminated or ends. And when disorder ends, there is order. Order is there in the non-dual frame of reference.

Life is relationship and to live is to go through these relationships, without causing any scratches or scars or adding subtle matter on the Consciousness and without causing any mutilation to the wholeness of life. It is the integral dimension of Consciousness that can resolve the challenges facing mankind. It is to heal the mind-brain-body system. This is the only guarantee for human survival and excellence.

J. Krishnamurti, in a prophetic wisdom, spoke of the true religious spirit that probed, questioned and negated. He said, "America had not got it. Europe had not got it. In India it had been wiped out and destroyed. Yet it was there in India, waiting in the soil .... The benediction of the timeless is waiting, the ground is ready. Can we create something that is of this benediction".

The future of mankind is open: either we continue the present way of life and destroy ourselves, or we learn to observe the mind in action and resolve the crisis of perception. Let mankind undertake a collective experiment for the mutation of the human psyche, which is the only global prescription to save mankind from annihilation, to heal our diseased mind-brain system, and to heal our planet. We shall surely survive if we understand and prove that we are worthy of survival.[18]

References

1. Arthur Eddington, *Nature of the Physical World*, Cambridge University Press, 1928, pp. 276-277.
2. Sampooran Singh, *The Pilgrimage to the Third Millennium*, Chandigarh: Faith Publishers, 1995, p. 19.
3. Jacques Monod, *Chance and Necessity*, New York: Vintage Books, 1972, p. 171; in *Synthesis of Science and Religion*, India: The Bhaktivedanta Institute, June 1988, p. 127.
4. George Wald, in Kishore Gandhi, *The Evolution of Consciousness*, New Delhi: National Publishing House, 1983, p. 14.
5. Sampooran Singh, *A New Vision of Education and Peace: A Scientific Appraisal*, Chandigarh: Faith Publishers, April 2003, p. 31.
6. Fritjof Capra, *The Turning Point*, London: Wildwood House, 1982, pp. 164-65, 345, 356, 372, 391-94.
7. R.P. Kaushik, *Towards a New Consciousness*, Delhi: Darshan Yoga Sansthan, January 1974, p. 63.
8. Sampooran Singh, *A Review on Symbiosis of Science and Spirituality*, Atam Science, October 7, 2002, pp. 3-4.
9. Sampooran Singh, Dr (Mrs) Kanwaljit Kaur and Paramjit Singh, *The Masterplan Paradigm for Human Survival and Excellence*, Chandigarh: Faith Publishers, 1998, pp. 103-127.
10. Erwin Schrodinger, *What is Life*? & *Mind and Matter*, London: Cambridge University Press, Ed. 1967, pp. 94, 95.
11. Sampooran Singh, *Nature's Evolutionary Impulse*, Vedanta: Ramakrishna Vedanta Center, U.K., November-December 2003, No. 314, pp. 260-265 and January-February 2004, No. 315, pp. 13-19.
12. Arthur Eddington, in Ken Wilber, Commins and Linscott, *Man and the Universe*, *The Philosophers of Science*, New York: Washington Square Press, 1969, p. 453.
13. Deepak Chopra, *How to Know God*, London: Rider, 2000, pp. 270-271.
14. Pupul Jayakar, *J. Krishnamurti: A Biography*, Harper & Row, 1986, pp. 379, 380.
15. Niels Bohr, in Lincoln Barnett, *The Universe and Dr. Einstein*, Mentor Edition, 19, pp. 126-127.
16. Fred Alan Wolf, *Taking the Quantum Leap*, Harper and Row, 1981, p. 229.
17. Vimala Thakar, *Through Silence to Meditation*, Ahmedabad: Vimal Prakashan Trust, 1988, pp. 22-27; and *Silence*, Holland Bookfund, Vimal Thakar 1989, p. 6.
18. Sampooran Singh, *Mutation of Human Psyche: A Paradigm Shift*, in Kishore Gandhi (Ed.), *The Odyssey of Science, Culture and Consciousness*, New Delhi: Abhinav Publications, 1990, p. 170.

21

Science and Society in the Twenty First Century : Quest for Excellence

Abstract

The 91st "Indian Science Congress–2004" declared its aims and objects to be "Science and Society in the Twenty First Century: Quest for Excellence". Many eminent scientists have echoed that the progress of present objective science and present materialistic society is leading mankind to self-annihilation, or self-destruction.

Many Nobel laureates of science–including Albert Einstein, Erwin Schrodinger, Karl Pribram, Hideki Yukawa, Niels Bohr, E. P. Wigner, Roger Sperry and so on–have echoed that objective science must restructure itself to take in its ambient the subjective dimension of human life. We urgently need restructuring of "science-education-values".

The expressions of nature guide us to restructure science-education-values (true-subject), which deals with the wholeness of life. If one observes, or listens, or experimentally interrogates life with true-subject, it will energise the Intelligence which will lead to order, harmony, non-violence, peace; and this will automatically blossom to our survival and excellence.

Understanding is a movement in the non-duality, a movement of the whole being. The perceptions are born of non-duality and responses are born of spontaneity. Perception bestows understanding the wholeness of life, which flowers to intuition (insight), spontaneity and right action. It is pure perception that can lead the human race to survival and excellence.

Science is the search for truth. A selfless, unfaltering devotion to truth and the use of knowledge for man's upliftment are the ideals of a scientist. Modern science is undergoing a profound revolution affecting its very foundation. We are beginning a new age of awareness, the age of quantum consciousness, the age of the conscious atom. Physics studies, "What is an electron?", and there is a reciprocal question from the electron, "Who are you to know me?".

This paper explores the dynamic interplay of science and society. It also explores a technology to resolve the human psychological imbalances, ecological problems and other human challenges. It heals the diseased mind-brain-body system. It leads to a realm of order, non-violence and peace; and is a pointer to human survival and excellence.

The Symbolic-Dualistic Frame of Reference of Mind Spectrum

In an oft-quoted statement, Erwin Schrodinger says:

> I consider science an integrating part of our endeavour to answer the one great philosophical question which embraces all others, the one that Plotinus expressed by his belief: *Who are we?* And more than that: I consider this not one of the tasks, but the task of science, the only one that really counts.[1]

We quote some eminent scientists, who emphasize new dimensions of science:

> Brain science must deal with the awareness of awareness. It could no longer afford to shut out that part of the world which we call subjective.[2]

> Humanity has every reason to place the proclaimers of high moral standards and values above the discoveries of objective truth. What humanity owes to personalities like Buddha, Moses, and Jesus ranks for me higher than all the achievements of the enquiring and the constructive mind.[3]

> .... the importance of an awareness that living in a world open towards both the exterior and the interior is a special characteristic of man's lot.[4]

> We are spectators (objects) and actors (subjects) in the great drama of existence.[5]

> There are two kinds of reality or existence–the existence of my consciousness and the reality or existence of everything else. This latter reality is not absolute, but only relative.[6]

> Sperry emphasised "the importance of a neglected area of science, namely the study of the human subjective experience".[7]

> The unity of conscious experience is provided by the self-conscious mind and not by the neural machinery of the liaison areas of the cerebral hemispheres.[8]

> In a recent (1996) scientific conference at Moscow, the Russian scientists proposed, "A life Field, beyond our physical concepts of time, space and the known electromagnetic and gravitational fields". In another conference at Cambridge, it was proposed, "A new scientific approach would include subjective experience as valid information and address all forms of human experience–including intuition, spirituality and mystical encounters".[9]

Many eminent scientists–including Einstein, Heisenberg, Schrodinger, Eddington, and so on–have stumbled upon another mode of perception (knowing), which is "understanding of life directly". Eddington wrote, "We have two kinds of knowledge which I call symbolic knowledge and intimate knowledge ....The intimate knowledge will not submit to codification and analysis; or, rather, when we attempt to analyze it the *intimacy is lost and it is replaced by symbolism*".[10] Alan W. Watts discussed the second mode of knowing (perception), which is aimed at "the understanding of life directly, instead of in the abstract, linear terms of representational thinking".[11] We have then available to us two basic modes of knowing: (a) the symbolic-dualistic mode, or map, or inferential; and (b) the non-dual and non-conceptual mode of knowing, or intimate, or direct, or understanding the wholeness of life.

Man is an amphibian who lives simultaneously in two dimensions–the subjective (inner) and the objective (outer, time-space-causation matrices). The challenge goes from the objective (outer) to the subjective (inner); the inner responds and results in changing the outer; the modified outer again goes to the inner and there is modified response; and this incessantly goes on and on. The outer and the inner are not two separate movements; these are one, a unitary movement, one whole movement.[12] This movement happens in a few millionth of a second.

The mankind is engaged in "mind looking at mind". Since atoms with consciousness are looking at atoms with consciousness, we are looking at ourselves. Richard Feynman, in prophetic words, wrote, "The atoms come to my brain, dance a dance, then go out, always new atoms but always doing the same dance".[13] A look at the mind–which is often called observation of the conditioned psyche–is only possible when we restructure science, which implies that objective science must restructure itself to take subjective dimension in its fold. The education must restructure itself to embrace both the sensual (outer) and the trans-sensual (inner) dimensions of life. Similarly the perennial values are embedded in the stabilised non-dual frame. We now consider the real-subject as "restructured science-education-values".

Scientific Mode of Mind: A scientific mind takes up "the role of a non-concerned observer", in the words of Schrodinger.[14] "It is unrelated to our beliefs, our ambitions, our hopes", in the words of Prigogine.[15] Bohm called it that "to observe nature with a certain kind of objectivity could be called the germ oi scientific attitude",[16] or scientific temper.

The scientific mode is synergistic to thought and I-consciousness; or in other words, it expresses itself in the non-dual frame. When "thought and I-consciousness" comes in the field of scientific mode the dualistic-thought gets annihilated and goes to abeyance. The true-subject expresses itself as *fact*, which blossoms to Intelligence, which heals the mind-brain-body system. Healing implies ending of symbolic-dualistic frame, and energising Intelligence, which bestows order, harmony, non-violence and peace.[17-19]

Understanding: "Understanding the wholeness of life" is not possible by the symbolic-dualistic frame of reference of mind spectrum, but by the non-dual and non-conceptual frame of reference of Mind Continuum. Understanding is the movement of non-duality, a movement of the whole being.

Understanding comes only when the mind is very quiet, tranquil, silenced. Understanding leads to a perception of the whole. Perception has nothing to do with knowledge (information). The perceptions are born of non-duality and responses are born of spontaneity.

The Non-Dual and Non-Conceptual Frame of Reference of Mind Continuum

The transcendent quantum energy potential expresses itself from *fact* to *fact*; between any two facts there is discontinuity, which we call as void-gap, or stillness-gap, or timeless-gap, and this gap appears to be momentary–as an analogy we say that the gap appears to be less than few millionth of a second. It is interesting that this is the scale in which our nervous system normally functions. The quick transition of one fact to another fact is a discontinuity between two facts. The fact is a state of great depth, stillness in which there is no conflict, no contradiction, no recording as memory. There is no time-space-causation, no object. The fact itself is the operator, not you operating on the fact; let the fact live. There is only the fact and nothing else. If we leave the fact alone, it has no time. The fact is free from fear. When you leave the fact alone, it is operating. The observation of a fact without justification, or condemnation, or motivation releases a tremendous energy. Immediacy of perception, of seeing (observing) dissolves the fact.

When the fact is observed by the true-subject (transcendent potential), there is flow of energy from the true-subject to the fact; this permits the fact to make a quantum jump to the higher state in the vertical dimension of Consciousness. If this observation is continued, the fact also goes to abeyance and the pure Life Field or Universal Consciousness is left behind.[20]

If we deeply observe the complexity of the non-dual and non-conceptual frame of reference of Mind Continuum, we infer that there are many processes at work–(a) the super-luminal (faster-than-light) communion without signals; (b) the mutated psyche regenerates Intelligence and ends all conflict and challenges; (c) all Intelligence or Wisdom is structured in the Unmanifest, the Life Field; and (d) the Life Field can guarantee human survival and it ushers a realm of order, non-violence and peace.

A Society with Values

Any crisis is always new; therefore, to understand it, the mind must be fresh, clear and swift in its pursuit. There must be constant inward revolution. The action of relationship between you and another, between you and me, is society and that relationship must undergo a constant inner revolution, a creative, psychological transformation in man. If our relationship is confused, ego-centric, narrow, limited, we project and bring chaos into our society.[21]

Recently, many eminent scientists–Werner Heisenberg, Edwin Hubble, Max Planck, G.F. Chew, Bertrand Russell, Lincoln Barnett, Max Born, and so on–have concluded that we cannot impart value education at reason or intellect level.[22,23] It is intuition (insight) that can regenerate the mind to be creative.[24] A creative mind bestows perennial values. We bring in another dimensional change which is restructuring science-education-values.

Inculcation of Ethical-Spiritual Values: All ethical values are essentially spiritual values; they proceed from the trans-sensual dimension of human personality, or the depth potential of life, or the Life Field, the Universal Consciousness. All ethical-spiritual values self-emerge from the Life Field, the Reality, the Wholeness of Life. These are eternal and immutable, and shared by mankind. These do not change from society to society, or place to place. These values self-express themselves in a non-dual frame of reference of the Mind (with a higher case 'M') Continuum.

We have to introduce psychodynamics of mind-brain-body system in science faculty and transpersonal psychology in art faculty as a part of educational curriculum at University/College/School levels. The teachers training programme is ***how to think*** and ***not what to think***. There is a need to write books for guidance of teachers and students, and for different levels. Panels of scientists, throughout the globe, will have to explore the wholeness of life, which blossoms to a non-violent and peaceful global society.

Healing the Diseased Mind-Brain-Body System

All traditional approaches, all institutionalised religions, all scriptures–for the last 10,000 years or more–have failed so far to radically transform the human psyche. We see (observe) that all knowledge (information), thought-structures, ideals, beliefs are sterile in the radical transformation or mutation of the psyche, because the traditional approaches were at the same quantum energy potential of consciousness at which the conditionings had happened. The word 'conditionings' implies distortion of our nervous system, chemical system and lowering of sensitivity due to storage of memory in the mind-brain-body system.

We have entered a new era of "health technology", or in other words, the healing of the diseased mind-brain-body system. This is also called the psychic pandemic, which is contagious. The thought-structure coupled with I-consciousness (ego) has constructed all types of somatic diseases (such as AIDS, Heart Stroke) and psychic pandemic, such as psychological imbalances, ecological problems, anger, envy, violence, and so on. The answer is embedded in higher awareness–restructuring of science-education-values coupled with observation and listening–that can heal the diseased system. It is the perception of the Universal Consciousness or Life Field and living in that perception that can heal the human race.

Concluding Comment

The present objective science and the present materialistic society are adding to conditionings of the human psyche, which is leading mankind to self-annihilation.

The human challenges–psychological imbalances, ecological problems and other challenges–can only be resolved through higher hierarchical expression of Consciousness. An exploration of the wholeness of life suggests: (a) ***Restructuring of Science:*** which implies that objective science takes in its fold the subjective dimension of man; (b) ***Restructuring of Education:*** which implies that education in addition to sensual dimension must deal with trans-sensual dimension of man; (c) ***Awareness of Human Values***, which emerges from the ethical-spiritual dimension of man, and (d) ***to live in the light of that understanding.*** To sum up, the true-subject is "restructured science-education-values"; and this dimension observes, or listens, or experimentally interrogates the conditioned psyche; and this leads to ending of all human challenges and ushers a realm of order, non-violence and peace. The "Indian Science Congress" will do a unique and historic service to mankind if it issues a declaration to restructure science-education-values.

The restructured science-education-values is synergistic (higher quantum energy potential) to thought and I-consciousness. It leads to a living in a higher hierarchical expression of Consciousness than that of thought. It is a new perennial value system.

A new ethic, a new attitude, a new value system, towards discharging our responsibility–restructuring of science-education-values–is required.

The ethic–declaration by the scientists–must motivate a great movement, convincing reluctant leaders and reluctant governments and reluctant peoples themselves to effect the needed psychological transformation or mutation of the human mind-brain-body system. This will blossom to human survival and excellence.

If man escapes his responsibility, he will meet the same fate as the dinosaurs. We will be responsible for our own peril, and that of India and mankind.

References

1. Erwin Schrodinger, *Science and Humanism*, London: Cambridge University Press, 1951; in D.S. Kothari. *Atom and Self*, Bharatiya Vidya Bhavan, Bombay, 1983, p. 9.
2. Karl Pribram, in Ken Wilber, *The Holographic Paradigm and Other Paradoxes*, Boulder: Shambhala, 1982, p. 17.
3. Albert Einstein, in Renee Weber, *Dialogues with Scientists and Sages*, London: Routledge & Kegan Paul, 1986, p. 215.
4. Hideki Yukawa, *Creativity and Intuition*, Tokyo: Kodansha International Ltd., 1973, p. 203.
5. Niels Bohr, in Lincoln Barnett, *The Universe and Dr. Einstein*, Mentor ed., pp. 126-27.
6. E.P. Wigner, *Two Kinds of Reality*, 1964, The Monist, Vol. 48, pp. 248-64.
7. Roger Sperry, in *Synthesis of Science and Religion*, Bombay: The Bhaktivedanta Institute, June 1988, p. 199.
8. K.R. Popper and J.C. Eccles, *The Self and Its Brain*, Springer International, 1977, p. 362.
9. Joan Walton, *Scientists Tune into Consciousness*, New Science, Winter 1996.
10. Arthur Eddington, in A. Commins and R.N. Linscott, ed. *The Man and the Universe, The Philosophers of Science*, New York: Washington Square Press, 1969, p. 453.
11. Alan W. Watts, *The Ways of Zen*, New York: Vintage Books, 1957, p. 10.
12. J. Krishnamurti, *Krishnamurti to Himself*, London: Victor Gollancz Ltd., 1987, pp. 129-131.
13. Richard Feynman, in Fred Alan Wolf, *Taking the Quantum Leap*, Harper and Row, 1981, p. 228.
14. Erwin Schrodinger, *What is Life? & Mind and Matter*, London: Cambridge University Press, Ed. 1967, p. 128.
15. Ilya Prigogine and Isabella Stengers, *Order Out of Chaos*, Bantam Books, 1984, p. 5.
16. David Bohm, *New Scientist*, November 11, 1982, p. 364.
17. Sampooran Singh, *Science and "Mind-Brain-Body Interactions*", unpublished.

18. *ibid., The Turning Point: The Ending of Human Suffering*, unpublished.
19. *ibid., March to Peace*: The Wisdom of Observation, Listening and the Power of Commitment, unpublished.
20. J. Krishnamurti, *Within the Mind*, KFI, 1982, p. 148; & *ibid., Krishnamurti on Education*, Orient Longman, 1974, pp. 90, 69.
21. *ibid., The First and Last Freedom*, Victor Gollancz Ltd., 1977, pp. 34-41.
22. Sampooran Singh, Dr (Mrs) Kanwaljit Kaur, Paramjit Singh, *Global Education and Human Survival*, New Delhi: Sanbun Publishers, 2002, pp. 35-36, 46.
23. Sampooran Singh, *A Scientific Vision of Education for a Global Society*, in *Education for a Global Society*, Shipra, 2003, pp. 86-107; & Sampooran Singh, Dr (Mrs) Kanwaljit Kaur, and Paramjit Singh, *Global Values Education*, Chandigarh: Faith Publishers, January 2001, pp. i-xii, 1-116.
24. Dr (Mrs) Kanwaljit Kaur, Paramjit Singh & Sampooran Singh, *Science with Creativity*, Vedanta: Ramakrishna Vedanta Centre, UK, No. 296, November-December 2000, pp. 256-266.

22

Crisis of Subject-Object Dualism

Abstract

The theme of Indian Science Congress–2005 is HEALTH TECHNOLOGY. Disease is seen as the malfunctioning of psychological-biological mechanism of mind-brain-body system. Healing is not primarily a physical process but a mental one. Healing is alive, complex and holistic. All human illness basically results from the interplay of mind, body and environment, so the biomedical model will have to be integrated with ending the psychic pandemic.

We are only aware of a memory-picture of the past, and its future projection; so 'time-space-causation matrices' is an illusion constructed by the successive consciousness. We have to jettison this illusion so that we live in the present, the now. We have to restructure the biomedical model, and adopt the holistic and ecological perception. The restructured medical-education takes in its ambient the wholeness of life.

The theme of "Indian Science Congress–2005" is Health Technology. Present-day objective science has failed so far to resolve psychological imbalances, ecological problems and other challenges, so it is defined in terms of rupture between man and nature. It is adding to the conditioning of the human psyche, so it lowers the perceptive sensitivity. It enhances opposition between man and natural world, which culminates to disease. If you follow a path which is antagonistic to the immutable laws of nature, there is disease.

'Disease' is a maladjustment of the human organism to the environment where there is some psychological-physiological dysfunction. 'Illness' is the subjective state of the person who feels aware of not being well. 'Sickness' is the state of logical social dysfunction.

Three centuries after Descartes, the science of medicine is based on biomedical model. George Engel writes, on "the notion of the body as a machine, of disease as the consequence of breakdown of the machine, and of doctor's task as repair of the machine".[1] The definition of the health given by the World Health Organization in the preamble of the charter may be useful, "Health is a state of complete physical, mental and social well-being and not merely the absence of disease or infirmity". It conveys the holistic, ecological and dynamic nature of health.

The healing represents the coordinated response of the integrated organism to stressful environmental influences which basically flows from thought-structures, I-consciousness and the verbalization. The resolution of psychological imbalances, ecological problems and other challenges, are a part of health care. Many issues that are crucial to health–such as nutrition, employment, population density, and housing–are not sufficiently discussed in medical schools, and thus there is little room for preventive health care in contemporary medicine. John Knowles, President of the Rockfeller Foundation, says bluntly, "The basic biological mechanisms of most of the common diseases are still not well enough known to give clear direction to preventive measures".[2] Illich estimated, "one out of every five patients admitted to a typical research hospital will acquire an iatrogenic illness (illness generated by the medical care process itself), with half of these episodes resulting from complications of drug therapy and a surprising 10 per cent from diagnostic procedures".[3] Victor R. Fuchs wrote, "During the past two decades adverse drug reactions have become a public health problem of alarming proportions producing considerable pain and discomfort for millions each year".[4] Fritjof Capra concludes:

> To go beyond it will require nothing less than a profound cultural revolution. And such a revolution is necessary if we want to improve, or even maintain, our health.... Biomedical research will have to be integrated into a broader system of health care in which the manifestations of all human illness are seen as resulting from the interplay of mind, body, and environment, and are studied and treated accordingly.[5]

The United Nations Children's Fund stated, "the day will come when the progress of nations will be judged, not by their military or economic strength, not by the splendour of their capital cities and public buildings, but by the well being of their people, by their level of health, nutrition and education".

This paper deals with health technology and healing of the conditioned psyche. It discussed the subject-object duality. It explores the mystery of sensual qualities and human emotions. It discusses restructuring of medical-education so that there is ending of dualistic thought-structure and I-consciousness.

The Crisis of Subject-Object Dualism

Modern physics has confirmed that all the concepts we use to describe nature are limited, that they are not features of reality, but creations of the mind; parts of the map, not of the territory. The world extended in space and time is but our representation. Spencer Brown, in a most spectacular passage, wrote that in order to see itself, the mind "first cuts itself up into at least one state which sees, and at least one other state which is seen. In this severed and mutilated condition, whatever it sees is only partially itself".[6] There is energy exchange (photon exchange) between the seer and the seen, or the subject and the object; and this energy exchange happens in a few millionth of a second. In technical parlance, this is written as subject ⇋ object; we are not aware of the real subject or real object, but aware of the distorted subject and distorted object.

The *homo sapiens* emerged at about 2.5 million years ago. Man had been observing, comparing and seeking to classify his observations, and storing these in the brain as frequency and amplitude information (experience and knowledge), and called it memory or cultural belief structure. The memory is meta-stable, it spontaneously disintegrates and the by-product is called thought entangled with volition, emotion, desire, and so on. Thought-time constructs chemical pressures and nervous tensions. All your relationships are adjustments within these pressures and tensions. We live in these conflicts–anger, jealousy, fear, violence–neurological and chemical imbalances. These construct pain, misery and travails.

Erwin Schrodinger wrote, "Subject and object are only one. The barrier between them cannot be said to have broken down as a result of recent experience in the physical sciences, *for this barrier does not exist*".[7] Werner Heisenberg concluded, "From the very start we are involved in the argument between nature and man in which science plays only a part, so that the common division of the world into subject and object, inner world and outer world, body and soul, is no longer adequate and leads us into difficulties".[8] Erwin Schrodinger heartily concurs, and states simply, "These shortcomings can hardly be avoided except by abandoning dualism".[9]

The error of dualism forms the roots of intellection and is therefore next to impossible to uproot by intellection. ***Symbolic knowledge is dualistic knowledge.*** "Abandoning dualism" is exactly what the new physics had done. Besides relinquishing the illusory division between subject and object, wave and particle, mind and body, mental and material, the new physics–with the brilliant help of Albert Einstein–abandoned the dualism of space and time, energy and matter, and even space and objects.

Many eminent scientists–including Einstein, Schrodinger, Heisenberg, Eddington, and so on–have stumbled upon *another mode of knowing*, in words:

> We have two kinds of knowledge which I call symbolic knowledge and intimate knowledge.... [The] more customary forms of

> reasoning have been developed for symbolic knowledge only. The intimate knowledge will not submit to codification and analysis; or, rather, when we attempt to analyse it the *intimacy is lost and it is replaced by symbolism.*[10]

This mode of knowing is called *intimate*, or *direct*, or *non-dual perception.* Alan Watts added that non-dual mode of perception leads to the "understanding of life directly", instead of in the abstract, linear terms of representational thinking.[11]

The recall of memory has introduced a subtle illusion which was first spotted by St Augustine and recently confirmed by Schrodinger and Watts. Bertrand Russell summarised St. Augustine's viewpoint in words, "the past and future can only be thought of as present: past must be identified with memory, and future with expectation, memory and expectation being both present facts".[12] Schrodinger states, "Mind is always *now*. There is really no before and after for Mind. There is only a now that includes memories and expectations".[13] Alan Watts wrote, "From memories you infer that there have been past events. But you are not aware of any past events. You know the past only in the present and as part of the present".[14]

The mind first perceives the *present*, the *now*, the *fact*, then it constructs the sensations of the 'past', which is identified with memory and the 'future' which is expectation. The past and the future is *non-fact*. The whole process takes less than 1/10,000 of a second. The fact is an expression of Simultaneous Consciousness and non-fact is that of successive consciousness. If this is understood, not intellectually apprehended, then the past and future are knocked off and one lives in the present. The time-space matrices go to abeyance. Nature's expression is the *fact* and the time-space construct is the non-fact, the illusion; and illusion constructs pain, misery and travails.

The present is the fact and the sensation transforms the fact to non-fact, from true to false, from present to the mutilated present. Ancient sages also realised this characteristics of mind.[15] Living in non-fact enhances disease. And living in the fact ends the disease, or heals the psyche. Living in fact bestows order, rhythm, non-violence and peace.

Location of the Memory or Cultural Belief Structure: Pribram believes that memories are encoded not in neurons, or small groupings of neurons, but in patterns of nerve impulses that crisscross the entire brain. The human brain has the capacity to memorize something on the order of 10 million bits of information during the average human lifetime. It has been demonstrated that one cubic centimeter of film can hold as many as 10 billion bits of information. Pribram's belief that our brains mathematically construct "hard" reality by relying on input from a "frequency domain" has also received a good deal of experimental support.

The Mystery of Sensual Qualities

Schrödinger concluded, "All scientific knowledge is based on sense perception, and that none the less scientific views of natural processes formed in this way lack all sensual qualities and therefore cannot account for the latter".[16] He added:

> Our world picture (is) 'colourless, cold, mute'. Colour and sound, hot and cold are our immediate sensations; small wonder that they are lacking in a world model from which we have removed our own mental person.... The material world has only been constructed at the price of taking the self, that is, mind, out of it, removing it; mind is not part of it; obviously, therefore, it can neither act on it nor be acted on by any of its parts.... the physical world picture lacks all the sensual qualities that go to make up the Subject of Cognizance. The model is colourless and soundless and unpalpable.

He added that "the world extended in space and time is but our representation".[17]

John Eccles pierces the sensory illusion with one startling but irrefutable assertion, "I want you to realize that there is no colour in the natural world and no sound–nothing of this kind; no textures, no patterns, no beauty, no scent....".[18]

It suggests, none of the objective facts upon which we usually base our reality is fundamentally valid. The synthetic world in which we live is divorced from the reality. The construct of the mind is an illusion. The illusory world is bound to give us pain, sorrow and travails.

The observer's colourful impression of the phenomenon vouchsafes not the slightest clue to its physical nature, although this is known for the last 2,500 years. It appears that: (a) the successive or sensual consciousness first makes a "colourless, cold and mute" picture in the brain sensoriums and in this picture there is latent (or unmanifest) colour and sound, hot and cold sensations; (b) the sensual image in the brain is then scanned by the Simultaneous Consciousness, and our colourful impression of the phenomenon is regenerated; (c) all this happens in less than a few millionth of a second; (d) the above happens as a thought-structure is absent in this process; and (e) it is a transformation from the non-fact (absence of colour and sound, and hot and cold) to the fact (regeneration of colourful impression). It appears that in this process, this is the first experimental evidence when any thought-structure coupled with volition is totally absent; and once thought-structure is absent, nature restores the balance. Every man repeats this experience many times a day.

The Human Emotions

A basic emotion such as fear can be described as an abstract feeling or a tangible molecule of the hormone adrenaline.[19] And wherever thought goes, a chemical goes with it. The awareness expresses itself as the biochemistry of the body. The whole dynamic profile–neurotransmitters, hormones, receptors and other vital biochemicals will alter with the change of perception.

With every breath, you inhale hundreds of millions of atom of air exhaled yesterday by someone. The ancient sages of India declared:

As is the microcosm, so is the macrocosm.
As is the atom, so is the universe.
As is the human body, so is the cosmic body.
As is the human mind, so is the cosmic mind.[19]

Hideki Yukawa wrote:

> The human emotions have their origins deep in the human heart. In most cases, their beginnings lie in regions beyond the reach of human consciousness and moral reflection..... man has things in him that are unknown even to himself. He still retains within him many things that he possessed before man became man. He has them whether he realizes it or not. The human emotions are closely related to these.... Every individual has in him things that cannot be simply defined. Thus human emotions, and human happiness in turn, are closely bound up with these indefinables.[20]

Yukawa added that we have to explore "by letting all the things that lie hidden deep at the bottom of consciousness rise to the surface" through observation of our perceptions. He strongly suggested that "our humanity in the world of the future must (explore) from now on". Victor F. Weisskopf quoted, "Man divorced from nature could not be happy and man's power to resist nature is hopelessly punny.... There is the large gap between the superhuman task and the frailties of human endeavour....".[21] He added that we must realize that "the task of turning the age-old tide of human ambition and aggression" is a difficult one. We need a new way of thinking about human values".

Restructuring of Medical-Education

The old paradigm is biomedical model and it is defined as the image of the body as a mindless machine; and this machine has to be repaired. Larry Dossey pointed out, "The inherent biology of the disease is overwhelmingly important and that feelings, emotions, and attitudes are simply along for the ride".[22] The new paradigm teaches us that emotions are not fleeting events isolated in mental space; they are expressions of awareness, the fundamental stuff of life.

Healing cannot be understood unless one observes violence, anger, envy, fear, belief, assumptions, expectations, and so on. The restructuring of medical-education implies "psychodynamics of mind-brain-body system" as a part of medical-education and the present model of making a quantum jump from symbolic-dualistic frame of reference of mind spectrum to non-dual and non-conceptual frame of reference of Mind Continuum; or in other words, ending the crisis of perception. The fundamental is that biochemistry of the body is a product of awareness.

The restructuring of medical-education takes in its ambient the wholeness of life and is the key to health technology. It is a pointer towards the emergence of a new human race, with a new culture and a new dynamics, a new foundation of human relationship. This is the consummation of human life.

Concluding Comment

The psychosocial evolution of man, over uncountable aeons, has led to conditioning of the human psyche. There is a crisis in health care, pollution and other environmental disasters; a rising wave of violence and crime; there is a crisis of hunger, malnutrition, unemployment in certain parts of the globe, and all these are different facets of one and the same crisis, and it is called crisis of perception or psychic pandemic.

We have to educate our physical organism and psychological structure. The restructured medical-education implies to understand, to learn so that one jettisons the man-made social cosmos, and lives in communion with the immutable laws of nature.

The Mind is only the *present*, the *now*, the *fact*, the *non-dual*, the *what is*! This ends the crisis of perception and crisis of mind-brain-body dualism; and regenerates it to its natural state. This understanding knocks down the *non-fact*, the *false*, the *duality*, the *past*, the *what should be*? The perceptive sensitivity heals the mind-brain-body system. The human destiny is embedded in restructuring the medical-education. It is the Cosmic Consciousness that governs the "Health Technology".

References

1. George L. Engel, *The Need for a New Medical Model: A Challenge for Biomedicine*, Science, April 8, 1977.
2. John Knowless, ed., *The Responsibility of the Individual, Doing Better and Feeling Worse*, New York: Norton, 1977.
3. Ivan Illich, *Medical Nemesis*, New York: Bantam, 1977, p. 23.
4. Victor R. Fuchs, *Who Shall Live*?, New York: Basic Books, 1974, p. 120.

5. Fritjof Capra, *The Turning Point*, London: Wildwood House, 1982, pp. 164-165.
6. Spencer Brown, *Laws of Form*, New York: Julian Press, 1972, pp. 104-105.
7. Erwin Schrodinger, *What is Life? & Mind and Matter*, London: Cambridge University Press, 1969, p. 137.
8. Werner Heisenberg, *The Physicist's Conception of Nature*, Harcourt, Brace, 1958, p. 24.
9. Erwin Schrodinger, *My View of the World*, London: Cambridge University Press, 1964, p. 62.
10. Arthur Eddington, in A. Commins and R.N. Linscott, ed. *Man and the Universe, The Philosophers of Science*, New York: Washington Square press, 1969, p. 453.
11. Alan W. Watts, *The Ways of Zen*, New York: Vintage Books, 1957, p. 10.
12. Bertrand Russell, *A History of Western Philosophy*, New York: Simon and Schuster, 1945.
13. Erwin Schrodinger, *op. cit.*, p. 145.
14. Alan W. Watts, *The Wisdom of Insecurity*, New York: Vintage, 1968, p. 82.
15. R.P. Kaushik, in *Healing of Mind-Brain-Body System, The Ending of Psychic Pandemic*, p. 16.
16. Erwin Schrodinger, *What is Life? & Mind and Matter*, Cambridge University Press, 1967 Ed., p. 177.
17. *ibid.*, pp. 128, 148, 146.
18. John Eccles, in Deepak Chopra, *op. cit.*, p. 12.
19. Deepak Chopra, *ibid.*, pp. 16, 27.
20. Hideki Yukawa, *Creativity and Intuition*, Tokyo: Kodansha International Ltd., 1973, pp. 205-206.
21. Victor F. Weisskopf, in Hideki Yukawa, *ibid.*, Introduction, pp. 9, 13.
22. Larry Dossey, *Medicine and Meaning*, in Deepak Chopra, *Ageless Body, Timeless Mind*, New York: Three Rivers Press, 1993, p. 21.

23
Crisis of Perception

Abstract

The theme of Indian Science Congress–2005 is HEALTH TECHNOLOGY. All diseases are maladjustment of the human mind-brain-body system, or conditioned human psyche, or crisis of perception. The curative functions of medicines have to be supplemented with understanding and living the "symbolic-dualistic frame of reference of mind spectrum (successive consciousness)" and the "non-dual and non-conceptual frame of reference of Mind Continuum (Simultaneous Consciousness)".

Man lives simultaneously in two dimensions–the "outer, the time-space-causation matrices" and the "inner, the timelessness". An awareness of the wholeness of life heals. Healing implies ending the crisis of perception. We have to restructure our science-education and observe and listen the conditioned psyche. This will flow to intuition (insight), spontaneity and right action. This regenerates Intelligence which flows to healing the psyche.

There is an urgency to restructure medical education which takes in its ambient the psychodynamics of the mind-brain-body system, or in other words, the wholeness of life.

The secret of healing is not embedded in our brain-body system, but in higher awareness bestowed on us by Cosmic Consciousness or Life Field.

Man's psychosocial evolution–for a million years or more–has developed in us that remarkable ability of the body to withstand a host of infectious diseases. This immune barrier did not allow even such powerful carriers of fatal epidemics as the plague bacillus and the cholera vibrio to exterminate mankind in the past. Recently Acquired Immunodeficiency Syndrome (AIDS) has emerged–it, rather than penetrating the immune barrier, speedily tears it down.

Askold Silin, a USSR scientist, says, ".... this puts the entire system of immunity, as broadly understood, catastrophically at risk. In other words, our civilisation has obviously entered a period of dangerous instability".[1] Mary Alan Fletcher and Marvin Stein state, "A person's mental state affects this immunity". They have also discussed the role of the mind in improving a patient's immune system. This has given birth to a new discipline, called psychoimmunology, which is based on the fact that there is considerable evidence of an interaction between the central nervous system and immune system; or to be more precise, between the mind and the body, and between morpho-psychic fields and morpho-somatic fields. The true cause of disease is "the conditioning of the human psyche" and the true cause of healing is "the mutation of the human psyche".[2]

Fritjof Capra wrote, "We have high inflation and unemployment, we have an energy crisis, a crisis in health care, pollution and other environmental disasters, a rising wave of violence and crime, and crime, and so on .... All different facets of one and the same crisis, and this crisis is essentially a crisis of perception".[3]

Mankind is caught in an unprecedented "crisis of perception", which has global dimensions. It is leading mankind to schizophrenic attitudes. It results in decreasing the level of rationality and in lowering the level of sensitivity. It makes the mind-brain-body system as mechanistic and repetitive. The system cannot perceive the values. It has lost the faculty to have holistic perception and it constructs pain, misery and travails. The gravity and the global extent of the crisis suggests that the present state represents a severe psychic disease of mankind.

We have built a society which is violent. Throughout existence, human beings have been violent and are violent. The violence in the human psyche (as also the fear and the consequent search of security) has compelled man to construct doomsday machines (nuclear weapons, chemical and bacteriological weapons). The whole mankind stands at the edge of an abyss of total annihilation. The extinction of life is at the very core of man's anxiety.

The socio-economic-political systems, the institutionalized religions and the reforms in the external world have so far failed to transform man–to transform human motivation. Human problems are constructs of the human mind, and all problems are interrelated and interpenetrated psychologically. The biochemistry of the body is a product of awareness, and the body governs health/disease. The known, the external world has failed us completely.

Something dramatic is happening at the psycho-biological level. P.P. Venugopalan at the India Science Congress 2004 said:

> Current scenario in health care industry indicates undue prominence to physical component of health, with scant regard to mental and social components of health and with total neglect towards spiritual component of health. There is a need to change the health care paradigm purely from curative medicine to basic health care services.[4]

The theme of the 92nd "Indian Science Congress–2005" is Health Technology. We explore health technology from a holistic and ecological view point. It explores ending of dualistic thought-time and I-consciousness. It also explores the realm of the Unknown, the timelessness–it explores the deeper levels of mind-brain-body system. It leads to healing the conditioned psyche, or ending the crisis of perception. It also explores the spiritual component of health.

Physics of Consciousness?

The Universal Consciousness or Life Field expresses Itself in two dominant modes: (a) It expresses itself in the symbolic-dualistic frame of reference in the mind spectrum, any event or entity is materialistic and remains within the velocity of light–this is called "successive consciousness"; and (b) It expresses itself in the non-dual and non-conceptual frame of reference of Mind Continuum; it transcends all time-space-causation matrices; any event or entity is encoded in the superluminal (faster-than-light) channel, and everything is interconnected and in communion–and this is called "Simultaneous Consciousness". The successive consciousness is at the lowest frequencies, or in other words, it is at the immanent quantum energy potential of consciousness, or the lowest expression of quantum energy potential of Life Field. The Simultaneous Consciousness is at the highest frequency, or in other words, the transcendent quantum energy potential of Consciousness, or the highest expression of Life Field.[5]

Recently many eminent scientists–Einstein, Schrodinger, Pribram, Yukawa, Wigner, Bohr, Sperry, Eccles, and so on have opined that objective science must take in its ambient the subjective dimension of man–and this is called restructuring of science. Similarly education must restructure itself to deal with the sensual and trans-sensual dimension of life. The restructured science-education deals with the wholeness of life, and true subject–non-variable attentivity, or reaction-free attentivity, or objectless attention.[6]

Mind-Brain-Body System

What we call mind (with a lower case 'm') is a conditioned energy, moving through the body, monitored by brain, operating through the

can have is to realize that it is limited and conditioned therefore it is incapable of seeing (or perceiving) the truth. This is the supreme realization for the intellect and realizing this it becomes silent and still. The subject and the object coalesce and both vanish. The unconditioned energy, the Fundamental vibration gets energised and bathes the brain. Total silencing of the intellect is the flowering of love, of truth, which implies ending of the crisis of perception.

If during observation, thought-time and I-consciousness comes in the field of true-subject, the thought coupled with its volitions explodes (cold fission) and is annihilated. What is left behind is the *fact*, the *true*, the *present*, the *non-dual*, the *what is*! Observation implies: (a) to remain with the question such that no thought interferes; (b) to be aware of inattention and the awareness of inattention flowers itself into attention; and (c) an attentive mind bestows answer to the challenge. An attentive mind is at a higher quantum energy potential, higher level of sensitivity, higher level of perception. The pure perception is always new. It is in the present. It is complete ending of psychological time. It is understanding of life directly. The pure perception is free from any conflict, so all inner psychological problems and also external problems such as mad armament race, fear of nuclear holocaust, completely vanish. This offers a total solution for human problems. The mind revels in peace, freedom and bliss.

Observation of the Non-Dual Frame of Mind Continuum

If we continue observing or listening to the *fact*, without justification or condemnation or motivation, we observe there is only the fact and nothing else. The fact itself is the operator, not you operating on the fact. If you leave the fact alone, it has no time. The fact is free from fear. The fact grows, which implies that there is release of tremendous energy and the fact moves to higher quantum energy potential. This is expressed as Pure Consciousness → Fact. It helps the fact to make a quantum jump in the vertical dimension of Consciousness. When the fact is left alone, it is operating and you do not have to do a thing about it, it matures and blossoms. Immediacy of perception dissolves the fact, and one revels in Pure Consciousness or Intelligence. Only in Intelligence there is complete security. Intelligence sees the false as the false and ends the false. Mutation happens in the timelessness. To understand Consciousness or an enquiry into the subject is the perception of that immeasurable state.

Schrodinger wrote that, "Consciousness is never expressed in the plural, only in the singular".[16] Similarly, the over-all number of Mind Continuum is just one and the whole mankind, including all other existences, shares it. The observation and listening happens in a non-dual frame of reference of mind continuum.[17]

Quantum Healing

Deepak Chopra wrote, "Healing is not primarily a physical process but a mental one.... Healing is alive, complex and holistic.... the mind can go deep enough to change the very patterns that design the body. It can wipe mistakes off the blue print, so to speak, to destroy any disease–cancer, diabetes, coronary heart disease–that has disturbed the design". He added, "Many cures (of cancer, tumor) that shares mysterious origins–faith healing, spontaneous remissions and the effective use of placebos, or 'dummy drugs'–also point toward a quantum leap, which is the faculty of inner awareness seems to have promoted a drastic jump–a quantum leap–in the healing mechanism".[18]

Chopra says, "Cancer, or any other disease, is nothing more than the sequence of fleeting moments (thought-time), each with its own emotions, its own mind-body chemistry". If one gives in to helplessness and fear, then one sends neuro-peptides associated with negative emotions, these latch into the immune cells, and the immune response loses its efficiency. An estimated 6 billion reactions are taking place in each cell every second". The individual chemical reaction takes less than 1/10,000th of a second.

Quantum healing is defined as the ability of one mode of Consciousness (Simultaneous Consciousness) to spontaneously correct the mistakes in another mode of consciousness (successive consciousness); it is often called a "quantum leap" or "***spontaneous remissions***". It is the higher quantum energy potential of Consciousness, at the perceptual level, that heals; and is free of side effects. Quantum healing is not for personal gain, but it is on behalf of the whole human race, or behalf of the whole human family.

Chopra says, "Quantum healing moves away from external, high technology methods towards the deepest core of mind–(brain)–body system. This core is where healing begins". This is a journey that breaks down barriers of thought-structures, I-consciousness, and verbalization, and ignores cultural fences. Quantum healing is *spontaneous remission* and "that behaviour is completely unpredictable", because it happens in a timeless and non-dual realm. Quantum healing is defined to explore *spontaneous remission* and to enhance its happenings.

The secret of cure–say cancer, tumor, and so on–is embedded in: (a) the doctor must make an inner journey, taking his understanding beyond the limits of his psychological-physiological system into higher awareness; (b) impart these lessons to his patients; and (c) the spontaneous remission is a function of the level of awareness which the patient understands and lives. This solution is beckoning over the horizon with an urgency. Leaping across the time-space boundary, surviving the waves of destruction that swallows up mankind, man marches ahead to quantum healing of mankind. The immutable laws of nature are embedded in quantum healing.

Nature invariably expresses itself in a non-dual and non-conceptual frame of reference of Mind Continuum; it is in the realm of the timelessness; hence nature's activity is a deep mystery. One has to understand the timeless realm and non-dual realm and live in that understanding, and this provides the key to quantum healing and health technology. However the exploration is fundamentally based on the arts of observation and listening, or experimental interrogation of nature, and the Nature responds and provides an answer to the challenges.

Symbiosis of Health Technology and Spirituality

Spirituality is the realm for understanding the wholeness of life and living what you understand. There is no scope for any psychological imbalances. Similarly health technology also takes in its ambient the wholeness of life. The health technology and spirituality are synonyms except a difference of shade.

The scientific mode of mind is the stepping stone both for health technology and spirituality. All these entities are non-authoritarian mode of non-dual and non-conceptual frame of reference and leads the thought-structure and I-consciousness going to abeyance. It leads to non-chattering of the mind, or the silence, or the equipoised mind. A silent mind has the capacity to heal all illness, it ends all dysfunction of brain-body system.

Concluding Comment

When "thought-time and I-consciousness" goes to abeyance, there is the non-dual and non-conceptual Mind Continuum–this is often called "no-mind" state or "timeless mind". When no-mind state is stabilised, the Intelligence is energised which heals the human psyche or ending of the psychic pandemic. There is the new realm of order, rhythm, non-violence and peace.

Once 'self' (thought-structures and I-consciousness, or past memory) dissolves, we have true freedom, freedom from time, freedom from all our suffering. This freedom alone will lead to a silent mind, a mind that no longer chatters, a mind that is deep and tranquil, a mind that does not live in the knowledge of yesterdays and tomorrows, a mind that lives in the Now, a mind that does not live in the knowledge of Now but in the feeling of Now. Such a mind is the source of all energy, source of all knowledge, the mind in which thought has no movement in time, the mind in which thought finds its own place, the mind that is the source of all creation, the ***mind that is supreme love and compassion***, the mind that does not know any divisions, the mind that pervades the entire human consciousness.[19]

Ervin Laszlo concludes, "Thanks to the convergence of science with intuitive insight, we now possess the critical mass of essential concepts and ideas to fulfil the dream. We can be more than conscious parts in an evolving totality; we can be parts that truly fulfil their potentials and become conscious of the totality–and come to live in harmony with it".[20]

It is the Cosmic Consciousness or Life Field that governs the healing of the psyche, and this is called the real health technology.

Fritjof Capra wrote, "The rational part of research would in fact, be useless, if it were not complemented by the intuition that gives scientists new insights and make them creative".[21] Intuition is fundamental and intellect is a derivative. We intuit that any curative medicine will have a marginal efficiency unless it is complemented by the intuitive non-dual thought to end physiological and psychological dysfunction. If a patient has an awareness of his own psychological imbalances (or he is attentive), this will go a long way in his healing.

References

1. Askold Silin, *Soviet Review*, 1988, Vol. xxv, No. 5, pp. 48-52.
2. Dr Mary Alan Fletcher and Dr Marvin Stein, in Kanwaljit and Sampooran Singh, *The Tribune*, July 16, 1989.
3. Fritjof Capra, *The Turning Point*, London: Wildwood House, 1982, Preface.
4. P.P. Venugopalan, *91st Indian Science Congress–2004*, p. 9.
5. Sampooran Singh, Dr (Mrs) Kanwaljit Kaur, Paramjit Singh and Amarjit Singh, *March to Peace: The Wisdom of Observation, Listening and the Power of Commitment*, Chandigarh: Faith Publishers, January 2004, pp. 14-15.
6. *ibid.*, pp. 21-22.
7. Sampooran Singh, *A Review on Symbiosis of Science and Spirituality*, Dagshai: The Atam Science Trust, October 7, 2002, p. 2.
8. J. Krishnamurti, *KFI*, 1982, Bulletin No. 1, pp. 40, 27-28.
9. D.S. Kothari, *Atom and Self*, in *The Evolution of Consciousness*, New Delhi: National Publishing House, 1983, pp. 177, 178.
10. Wilder Penfield, in Deepak Chopra, *How to Know God*, London: Rider, 2000, pp. 215, 217.
11. David Bohm, in Gary Zukav, *The Dancing Wu Li Masters*, Fontana/Collins, 1982, p. 327.
12. Candace Pert, in Fritjof Capra, *The Web of Life*, Flamingo, 1997, p. 277.
13. Blaise Pascal, in Brij B. Khare, *J. Krishnamurti: Things of the Mind*, Motilal Banarsidass, Delhi, 1988, p. 148.

14. Arthur Eddington, Ed. Commins and Linscott, *Man and the Universe, The Philosophers of Science*, New York: Washington Square Press, 1969, p. 453.
15. Sampooran Singh, Dr (Mrs) Kanwaljit Kaur and Paramjit Singh, *Global Education and Human Survival*, Sanbun Publishers, March 2002, pp. 35-36, 46.
16. Erwin Schrodinger, *What is Life*? & *Mind and Matter*, London: Cambridge University Press, Ed. 1967, pp. 94, 95.
17. Sampooran Singh, *Nature's Evolutionary Impulse*, Vedanta: Ramakrishna Vedanta Center, U.K., November-December 2003, No. 314, pp. 260-265 and January-February 2004, No. 315, pp. 13-19.
18. Deepak Chopra, *Quantum Healing*, Bantam Books, 1989, pp. 2, 18, 20, 267.
19. B.M. Khanna, in *The Odyssey of Science, Culture and Consciousness*, New Delhi: Abhinav Publications, 1990, p. 165.
20. Ervin Laszlo, in *ibid*., p. 238.
21. Fritjof Capra, *The Tao of Physics*, Bantam Books (Second Edition), 1988, p. 18.

24
Symbiosis of Science and Spirituality

Abstract

During the last 5-7 decades, many eminent scientists have started exploration of Cosmic Consciousness or Life Field, and have concluded that consciousness manifests in two dominant dimensions–(a) "successive consciousness", which is not mine, the brain is not mine, and the I-consciousness is not mine. I am the conclusion of the experience and knowledge (information) of mankind. The story of mankind is me. I am neither the individual nor the collective. I am humanity; and (b) "Simultaneous Consciousness", which is the substratum of all existences; it is at the highest quantum energy potential of Consciousness. It is shared by whole mankind. Erwin Schrodinger also emphasised, "The over-all number of minds is just one. The mind is always now", the present.

The Consciousness expresses itself at different hierarchical levels. If a lower state (lower quantum energy potential, or lower frequencies of consciousness) come in the field of higher state, the lower state is bombarded by attentivity and gets dissipated. This results in I-consciousness and thought-structure going to abeyance, and man rises in the vertical dimension of Consciousness. This state is often called no-mind or state of silence or emptiness. The emptiness enhances the perceptive sensitivity, the alertness. This view is almost identical to that of Gregory Bateson and Kurt Godel.

Spirituality is the science of life and living. It has the potential to rectify the "inner structural crisis" or the "crisis of perception". We need urgently symbiosis of science and spirituality. This is a pointer to grow into the dimensions of non-violence, fearlessness, love and peace.

Science is the search for truth. A selfless, unfaltering devotion to truth and the use of knowledge for man's upliftment are the ideals of a scientist. Modern science is undergoing a profound revolution affecting its very foundation. We are beginning a new age of awareness, the age of quantum consciousness, the age of the conscious atom. Physics studies, "What is an electron?", and there is a reciprocal question from the electron, "Who are you to know me?". Modern physics has confirmed that "all the basic concepts we use to describe nature are limited, that they are not features of reality, but creations of the mind; parts of the map, not of the territory".[1] Capra explored parallels between modern physics and Eastern mysticism. He wrote, "Quantum theory and relativity theory– both force us to see the world very much in the way a Hindu, Buddhist, or Taoist sees it, and how this similarity strengthens when we look at the recent attempts to combine these two theories in order to describe the phenomena of the submicroscopic world; the properties and interactions of the subatomic particles of which all matter is made". He added, "The patterns scientists observe in nature are intimately connected with the patterns of their minds–with their concepts, thoughts and values .... Scientists therefore are responsible for their research not only intellectually but also morally".[2]

Julius Robert Oppenheimer wrote, ".... the general notions about human understanding which are illustrated by discoveries in atomic physics are not in the nature of things wholly unfamiliar, wholly unheard of, or new. Even in our own culture they have a history and in Buddhist and Hindu thought a more considerable and central place. What we shall find is an examplification, an encouragement, and a refinement of old wisdom".[3] Niels Bohr wrote, "For a parallel to the lesson of atomic theory .... (We must turn) to those kinds of epistemological problems with which already thinkers like the Buddha and Lao Tzu have been confronted, when trying to harmonize our position as spectators and actors in the great drama of existence".[4] Albert Einstein stated, "Humanity has every reason to place the proclaimers of high moral standards and values above the discoveries of objective truth. What humanity owes to personalities like Buddha, Moses, and Jesus ranks for me higher than all the achievements of the enquiring and the constructive mind".[5]

Hideki Yukawa wrote, "The development of science (objective), far from encouraging the formation and development of an integrated view of man in his many different aspects, has tended rather to split and destroy that view". He added:

> We should of course be grateful to the machine for taking over, expanding, and stepping up all kinds of processes hitherto performed by men, but when it begins gradually to usurp even the functions of the human brain one cannot but wonder where it will all end.... The danger that all these trends will combine

> to destroy the unity of man's various aspects and lead eventually to the loss even of his humanity cannot be denied. It is equally undeniable, I believe, that such a split would deprive man of his happiness.

He suggested, "To save ourselves, by such efforts, from the danger of a loss of, or a split in, our humanity in the world of the future–this, I believe, is the course that man must take from now on. This, it is my personal conviction, is true wisdom for modern man".[6]

In a recent scientific conference at Moscow, the Russian scientists proposed, "A life Field, beyond our physical concepts of time, space and the known electromagnetic and gravitational fields". In another conference at Cambridge, it was proposed, "A new scientific approach would include subjective experience as valid information and address all forms of human experience–including intuition, spirituality and mystical encounters".[7]

Many distinguished scientists have emphasised about the need for convergence of science and mystical insights (exploration of non-dual and non-conceptual state), which is the need of the hour, for the sheer survival of biological life in this planet and also for another adventure for higher hierarchical expression of consciousness. Only a quantum jump in this area will enable the human being to live in harmony with himself, community, laws of nature and the cosmos.

What is Consciousness?

The Universal Consciousness or Life Field expresses Itself in two dominant modes: (a) It expresses itself in the symbolic-dualistic frame of reference in the mind spectrum, any event or entity is materialistic and remains within the velocity of light–this is called "successive consciousness"; and (b) It expresses itself in the non-dual and non-conceptual frame of reference of Mind Continuum; it transcends all time-space-causation matrices; any event or entity is encoded in the superluminal (faster-than-light) channel, and everything is interconnected and in communion–and this is called "Simultaneous Consciousness". The successive consciousness is at the lowest frequencies, or in other words, it is at the immanent quantum energy potential of consciousness, or the lowest expression of quantum energy potential of Life Field. The Simultaneous Consciousness is at the highest frequency, or in other words, the transcendent quantum energy potential of Consciousness, or the highest expression of Life Field.

Eugene Wigner stated, "There are two kinds of reality or existence–the existence of my consciousness (Simultaneous Consciousness) and the reality or existence of everything else (successive consciousness).

The latter reality is not absolute, but only relative".[8] And to quote Cyril Hinshelwood, "To deny the reality of the inner world is a flat negation of all that is immediate in existence and to minimize its existence is to depreciate the very purpose of living and to explain away as a product of natural selection is a plain fallacy".[9]

Eugene Wigner stated, "Self-identity demands consciousness. You would not have identity without consciousness. Yes, consciousness creates identity. I know that I am I. And it is my consciousness which knows, which tells me that".[10] Edwin Hubble wrote, "The world of pure values, that world which science cannot enter, has no concern whatsoever with probable knowledge. There finality–eternal, ultimate truth–is earnestly sought".[11] Recently many eminent scientists–Werner Heisenberg, Edwin Hubble, Max Planck, G.F. Chew, Bertrand Russell, Lincoln Barnett, Max Born, and so on–have concluded that we cannot impart value education at reason or intellect level.[12]

Yukawa wrote, "It is obvious that unless something rises into the consciousness it cannot become an object of rational thought, of rational consideration. At the same time, everyone will surely agree on the importance of an awareness that living in a world open towards both the exterior and the interior is a special characteristic of man's lot".[13] Eugene Wigner wrote, "The measurement is not completed until its result enters our consciousness.... (this) last step is, at the present state of our knowledge, shrouded in the mystery and no explanation has been given for it so far in terms of quantum mechanics, or in terms of any other theory".[14] Fritjof Capra wrote, "By consciousness, I mean the state of mind characterized by self-awareness, where one is aware that he is aware".[15] He added that we know.... But science, at present, does not know how to describe the nature of consciousness".

Mind-Brain-Body System

D.S. Kothari, in prophetic words, wrote, "The external world is *public* and *objective*, and the internal world is *private* and *subjective*.... Atom or brain belongs to the external objective world of space-time and matter-energy. Self or mind belongs to the internal subjective world. It is not describable in terms of space-time and matter-energy concepts. Self or mind, therefore, lies outside natural science".[16] Wilder Penfield concluded, "Our minds and our brains are not at all the same.... It is the mind which experiences and it is the brain that records the experience".[17] David Bohm stated:

> The ultimate perception does not originate in the brain or any material structure, although a material structure is necessary to manifest it. The subtle mechanism of knowing the truth does not originate in the brain.[18]

What we call mind (with a lower case 'm') is a conditioned energy, moving through the body, monitored by brain, operating through the senses. It is a movement of the structured framework of patterns and the dynamics of behaviour patterns are shared by all human beings. The time-space matrices represent the relative field of consciousness. It constructs pain, misery, suffering and travails. All knowledge, concepts, ideals, intellectual approaches are sterile in transforming the conditioned psyche, or to bring in radical revolution in man.

The mind is a conditioned conscious energy, conditioned by the total human race through untold centuries. It generally deals with thought structures which are invariably entangled with volitions, emotions, sentiments, desires, and so on. Conditioning implies the lowest hierarchical expression of consciousness, or the lowest quantum energy potential of consciousness in the mind-brain-body system.[19]

Man is an amphibian, who lives simultaneously in two dimensions:

(a) The ***known***, the time-space-causation matrices, the time, the immanent potential of successive consciousness, the differentiated individuated expression of that cosmic unity at the biological level, the physical level and psychological level; the immanence means the totality of *what is*, it is immanent in matter. The known constructs chemical pressures, nervous tension and conflict, and constructs disease.

(b) The ***Unknown***, the Life Field, the Universal Consciousness, the transcendent potential, the timelessness. It is the undifferentiated, unindividuated complexity of Life, the homogeneous wholeness of life, but it is beyond matter. The immanence offers no guidance, in regard to the much more fundamental problems of the relationship of man in his transcendence.[20,21] The Unknown is fundamental; it bestows quantum healing and health technology.

The Cosmic Consciousness expresses itself at different hierarchical levels. Each higher state (higher quantum energy potential of consciousness) is synergistic to its junior components; it includes them but is more than them. If a lower state comes in the field of the higher state, it is bombarded by the higher awareness and the lower gets dissipated or annihilated.

The brain is basically the biophysical substrate for the mental processes. The brain is degenerate with regard to the mind. We have to investigate the degenerate relationships between mind (successive consciousness) and brain, and explore the relationships between spirit (Life Field) and brain. Candace Pert wrote, "White blood cells are bits of the brain floating around the body"[22] and "the entire body is alive with thought".[23]

The Non-Dual and Non-Conceptual Frame of Reference of Mind Continuum

What we call Mind (with upper case 'M') is the non-dual frame of reference of Mind spectrum. The Universal Consciousness expresses Itself in a non-dual frame as intuition, spontaneity, love and compassion, order and harmony. It is the first-hand personal acquaintance of the quantum jump of the conditioned energy consciousness to Universal Consciousness; or in other words, a quantum jump fiom fragmentary perception to the perception of the Wholeness.

The emptiness, the point of zero vibration of matter, is not a void, but the starting point of everything that exists. Quantum physics has discovered that the empty space is mysteriously rich in energy. Modern science has brought man on the fringes of mutation of mind-brain-body system. Now we are on the verge of extending this richness into the human dimension.

Gregory Baterson wrote, "Mind is the essence of being alive".[24] He added:

> The individual mind is immanent but not only in the body. It is immanent also in pathways and messages outside the body; and there is a larger Mind of which the individual mind is only a subsystem. This larger Mind is comparable to God and is perhaps what some people mean by "God", but it is still immanent in the total interconnected social system and planetary ecology.[25]

To the views of Bateson and Schrodinger, Kurt Godel added, "There is a single mind behind all the various appearances and activities of the world". Larry Dossey stated that the mind is omnipresent, infinite and eternal. It is immaterial and non-local. He added, "Man contains the spark of the Divine; *Atman* and *Brahman* are one".

It is a non-subjective and non-objective state. It is non-cerebral, non-psychological exploration of the Reality. The non-dual and non-conceptual frame of reference of Mind Continuum and Life Field are synonymous.

The Systems View of Life

Mind is a dynamics of self-organisation and brain is the biological structure through which this dynamics is carried out. It implies that these are open systems, which means that they have to maintain a continuous exchange of energy and matter with their environment to stay alive. The psychosocial evolution of man is governed by self-organising system–metabolism, self-renewal, self-healing, self-regeneration–it maintains a continuous environment to stay alive. The system has a hidden potential of self-transcendence.[26]

The non-dual frame of reference is independent of the environments, and depends on two complementary tendencies of self-organising system–self-organising system and self-transcendence–and depends on the Unmanifest, the Life Field, the Cosmic Consciousness.

Spirituality

We find ourselves in a universe that breeds life and possesses the very particular properties that make that possible. Life is a multi-dimensional phenomenon and human beings are expressions of that phenomenon are themselves multi-dimensional organisms. Life is self-generated, self-sustained, self-controlled, self-regulated phenomenon. Life seems to be an energy of Intelligence, that has been unfolding, unwinding, uncovering, manifesting itself for billions of years and yet has remained ever virgin and ever fresh. We call Life Eternal, Infinite, Immutable.

Spirituality is the science of life and living. Its dimensions are homogeneous, undifferentiated and non-dimensional, so there is spontaneous organic inter-relatedness of all that exists. Spirituality is homogeneous wholeness. In spiritual science, the emphasis is upon the act of perception, the quality of the instruments employed for perception, the quality of consciousness behind the perception. In spirituality we proceed from the whole and with the awareness of the whole we observe the parts.

Spirituality is an experimental science and as precise as mathematics. It is verifiable by another explorer; but this *wisdom* or *truth* cannot be passed by one experimenter to another (non-communicable truth). So every body is all alone to undertake this exploration. Man is only a conduit for expression of nature's evolutionary impulse.

Spirituality rejects the man-made social cosmos; it rejects subject and object split, which is called subject-object dualism; it rejects all processes of evaluations and comparisons by reason or intellect; it rejects all grafting of conceptual reality on the perceptual reality; and it rejects all pain, misery and conflict. It imbibes the immutable laws of nature, the true expression of nature, so it goads man to live in pure perception–the *fact*, the *true*, the *present*, the *non-dual*, the *what is*! Spirituality is exploring nature *here* and *now*, where the brain-body is used as a mirror to reflect nature's expression. In principle, we explore nature's expression or manifestation at different hierarchical levels of expressions of Consciousness.

The whole mankind is unknowingly caught in an "inner structural crisis" at symbolic-dualistic frame of reference of mind spectrum. Spirituality has the potential to rectify the inner crisis, and understand and live according to the immutable laws of nature. This is a pointer to persuade the human beings to grow into the maturity of love, friendship and peace.

Concluding Comment

For the last 10,000 years or more, man has been trying to transform the conditioned psyche, but all traditional approaches, institutionalized religions, ideals, concepts, thought-structures have failed. The "inner crisis of perception" is leading man to self-annihilation to self-destruction. Jacques Monod, Nobel prize winning biologist, wrote in 1972, "What we see opening before us today is an abyss of darkness".[27] George Wald, Nobel prize in Medicine, 1967, wrote, "Our society has taken a wrong turn.... By now, the problem is not transcendence, but survival".[28]

Fritjof Capra suggested, "We need a new paradigm, a new vision of reality–a fundamental change in our thoughts, perceptions and values.... This is likely to result in a transformation of unprecedented dimensions, a turning point for the planet as a whole".[29]

We have to restructure our science-education and observe and listen to the conditioned psyche. This will flow to intuition (insight), spontaneity and right action. This regenerates Intelligence which resolves all crises of psychological imbalances, ecological problems and all human challenges.

The evolutionary transformation of this magnitude–the transformation from psychosocial to spiritual evolution–cannot be prevented by short-term socio-political-economic activity, and this provides the strongest security and faith for the future. We urgently need symbiosis of science and spirituality *here* and *now*. Spirituality is fundamental and science is a derivative, where science takes in its ambient both the objective and the subjective dimensions of man.

References

1. Fritjof Capra, *The Tao of Physics*, Second Edition, Bantam Books, 1988, pp. 147, 277.
2. *ibid.*, pp. 5, xvii (Preface).
3. Julius Robert Oppenheimer, in Kishore Gandhi (Ed.), *The Evolution of Consciousness*, New Delhi: National Publishing House, 1983, pp. vii-viii (preface).
4. Niels Bohr, in *ibid.*, p. viii (Preface).
5. Albert Einstein, in Renee Weber, *Dialogue With Scientists and Sages*, London: Routledge & Kegan Paul, 1986, p. 215.
6. Hideki Yukawa, *Creativity and Intuition*, Kodansha International Ltd., 1973, pp. 204, 205, 206.
7. Joan Walton, *Scientists Tune into Consciousness*, New Science, Winter 1996.
8. Eugene Wigner, in D.S. Kothari, *Some Thoughts on Science and Religion*, The University of Delhi, 31st Oct and 3rd Nov. 1977, p. 3.

9. Cyril Hinshelwood, in D.S. Kothari, *ibid.*, p. 3.
10. Eugene Wigner, in *Synthesis of Science and Religion*, Mumbai: The Bhaktivedanta Institute, June 1988, p. 262.
11. Edwin Hubble, in *ibid.*, p. 119.
12. Sampooran Singh, Dr (Mrs) Kanwaljit Kaur and Paramjit Singh, in *Global Education and Human Survival*, New Delhi: Sanbun Publishers, March 2002, pp. 46, 35-36.
13. Hideki Yukawa, *Creativity and Intuition*, *op. cit.*, p. 203.
14. Eugene Wigner, in D.S. Kothari, *op. cit.*, p. 26.
15. Fritjof Capra, in *Synthesis of Science and Religion*, *op. cit.*, p. 275.
16. D.S. Kothari, *Atom and Self*, in *The Evolution of Consciousness*, New Delhi: National Publishing House, 1983, pp. 209, 211.
17. Wilder Penfield, in Deepak Chopra, *How to Know God*, London: Rider, 2000, pp. 215, 217.
18. David Bohm, in Gary Zukav, *The Dancing Wu Li Masters*, Fontana/Collins, 1982, p. 327.
19. Sampooran Singh, *Atam Science*, Dagshai Cantt: The Atam Science Trust, October 7, 2002, p. 2.
20. Sampooran Singh, Dr (Mrs) Kanwaljit Kaur and Paramjit Singh, *Pathways to Peace: The Wisdom of Listening and the Power of Commitment*, Chandigarh: Faith Publishers, 1.1.2004, pp. 1-42.
21. Sampooran Singh, Dr (Mrs) Kanwaljit Kaur, Paramjit Singh and Amarjit Singh., *March to Peace*: *The Wisdom of Observation, Listening and the Power of Commitment*, *ibid.*, 20.1.2004, pp. 1-24.
22. Candace Pert, in Fritjof Capra, *The Web of Life*, Flamingo, 1996, p. 277.
23. Larry Dossey, *Medical Science and Non-Violence*, New Delhi: Gandhi Peace Foundation, 1988, pp. 12-13, 14.
24. Gregory Baterson, in Fritjof Capra, *The Evolution of Consciousness*, New Delhi: National Publishing House, 1983, p. 247.
25. *ibid.*, in Larry Dossey, *Medical Science and Non-Violence*, *op. cit.*, pp. 12-13.
26. Fritjof Capra, *ibid.*, p. 247.
27. Jacques Monod, *Chance and Necessity*, New York: Vintage Books, 1972, p. 171; in *Synthesis of Science and Religion*, Mumbai: The Bhaktivedanta Institute, June 1988, p. 127.
28. George Wald, in Kishore Gandhi, *The Evolution of Consciousness*, *op. cit.*, p. 14.
29. Fritjof Capra, in *The Evolution of Consciousness*, *ibid.*, p. 243.

25
Interface of "Real Science" and "Real Religion"

Abstract

The recent scientific discoveries indicate that man lives simultaneously in two dimensions–the objective and the subjective, and both are a unitary dynamic flow. So we have to restructure science which takes in its ambient both the dimensions, the wholeness of life–and this is called "real science".

The ancient Indian thought discussed two dimensions to every religion–religion as historically conditioned socio-political expression; and religion as a spiritual dimension which is eternal, infinite and immutable, and the pursuit of spiritual dimension is called "real religion".

Both real science (restructured Science-Education) and real religion (restructured Religion-Faith-Values) are in search of truth and both approaches are non-authoritarian, non-dualistic and non-causation. And these help to transcend all psychological imbalances, ecological challenges and end all human sufferings and conflicts. These grow to order, harmony, non-violence and peace. These are two complementary disciplines and thus help to evolve a complete human civilisation for which the world is ripe and waiting.

We urgently need a symbiosis of real science and real religion, which are the dimensions of the wholeness of life, and as such are synonymous. These lead to human survival and excellence.

Humanity's ethical and spiritual development has not kept pace with the accelerative progress of science and technology, and this imbalance threatens to destabilize and even destroy human civilization. There appears to be a fundamental crisis of values which aggravates current economic, social and political tensions. Accompanied by raging psychological and ecological problems, these tensions tend to push the world even closer to self-destruction.

Both science and religion have their origin in man's basic urge and his deepest aspirations. Science provides an understanding of nature. It tells us what is possible in the world of nature and what is not, but it does not and cannot tell us what we *should* or *ought* to do. Science deals with "is", religion with "ought". India with its unique heritage and potential, now entering a new renaissance, has a special obligation to explore the challenge.

This article is a serious and sustained look at the interface of "real science" (e.g., physics and physiology) and "real religion" (e.g., mysticism and transcendence), a topic that more than one scholar has termed "epochal". The exploration of consciousness is the meeting ground for real science and real religion.

Real Science

Science is the search for truth. A selfless, unfaltering devotion to truth and the use of knowledge for man's upliftment are the ideals of a scientist. Truth is what all earnest scientists seek. The aim of classical science is to study nature and human experience and knowledge (information) objectively. Objectivity and precision, both as to thought and its verbal formulation, are two important characteristics of the scientific method.

D.S. Kothari, in prophetic words, wrote, "The external world is *public* and *objective*, and the internal world is *private* and *subjective*.... Atom or brain belongs to the external objective world of space-time and matter-energy. Self or mind belongs to the internal subjective world. It is not describable in terms of space-time and matter-energy concepts. Self or mind, therefore, lies outside natural science".[1] Wilder Penfield concluded, "Our minds and our brains are not at all the same.... It is the mind which experiences and it is the brain that records the experience".[2] David Bohm stated:

The ultimate perception does not originate in the brain or any material structure, although a material structure is necessary to manifest it. The subtle mechanism of knowing the truth does not originate in the brain.[3]

It implies that the Self, or Life Field expresses itself as *fact* (mirror-image) in the brain, there is no interaction between the Self and brain, but brain mediates as body sensations and mental world (thoughts with volitions).

The brain is basically the biophysical substrate for the mental processes. The brain is degenerate with regard to the mind. We have to investigate the degenerate relationships between mind (successive consciousness) and brain, and explore the relationships between spirit (Life Field) and brain. Candace Pert wrote, "White blood cells are bits of the brain floating around the body"[4] and "the entire body is alive with thought".[5] We have to understand mind-brain-body as one whole system.

Kothari discussed that objective communicable statements become possible about pairs of sense impressions and never about single sense impression. It is this which eliminates subjectivity from science, eliminates "I" and is the basis of the objectivity of science.[6]

Rationality gives us minor inventions. The new theorems, unless trivial, are of course first "discovered" and then "proved". Discoveries come as intuitive flashes. A rational account of a discovery, the proof, follows and not precedes the discovery. Fundamental discoveries which go deep into the nature of things are the result of uncommon intuition and faith, not cold logic. Intuition is fundamental and rationality is a derivative. A symbolic-dualistic frame is repetitive and mechanical and does not have the capacity to bestow intuition. Intuition flows from non-dual and non-conceptual frame of reference of Mind Continuum. We have to educate ourselves to make a quantum jump from symbolic-dualistic frame to non-dual frame of Mind Continuum.

It is important to recognise that in *quantum mechanics, Consciousness or Self, has a significance which has no counterpart in classical physics.* This was emphasised by von Neumann and further developed by many others, notably Wigner. We cannot observe the course of nature without disturbing it; observation means interference with what we are observing; observation disturbs reality. The very crux of twentieth-century physics is the recognition that the observer cannot be excluded from his observations; he is an intrinsic participant in them. We have seen that an act of measurement, even an ideal one, inevitably an unpredictably disturbs the state of the dynamic system under observation.[7]

Many eminent scientists have discussed that man lives simultaneously in two dimension–the objective (outer) and the subjective (inner). The outer and the inner are one, a unitary movement, one whole movement. Science must transform its dimensions to take in its ambient both the outer and the inner dimensions, the objective and the subjective dimensions of life. Further education is the sensual and the trans-sensual dimension. The new dimension of restructured science is science-education, and this we call the "real science", or real scientific mode of mind. The restructured scientific mind is precise, clear, unprejudiced, which does not condemn, which observes, which sees. The real science deals with the wholeness of life, so it is synergistic to thought-structures coupled with the volitions.

Consciousness is always the subject and never the object. ***Consciousness cannot perceive its own coming into being (birth) nor its own extinction.***[8] Schrodinger wrote, "Consciousness is never experienced in the plural, only in singular.... the consciousness is a singular of which the plural is unknown". He added, "Mind is by its very nature a *singulare tantum*. I should say: the over-all number of minds is just one. I venture to call it indestructible since it has a peculiar time-table, namely mind is always *now*. There is really no before and after for mind. There is only a now that includes memories and expectations".[9] Consciousness is shared by whole mankind.

Real Religion

Swami Ranganathananda discussed two dimensions to every religion: (a) a historically conditioned socio-political expression of religion, which is local, parochial and temporary in application; and (b) it consists of the truly spiritual dimension, which is eternal, infinite and immutable; with its emphasis on personal morality, and disciplines designed to ensure the spiritual growth in man.[10] Swami Vivekananda wrote:

You must bear in mind that religion does not consist in talk, or doctrines, or books, but in realisation; it is not learning but being.[11]

Religion is the manifestation of the divinity already in man.[12]

> Each soul is potentially divine.... This is the whole of religion. Doctrines, or dogmas, or rituals, or books, or temples, or forms, are but secondary details.[13]

Religion is the cultivation of freedom in the search of truth. Religious education, in the true sense, is to encourage the child to understand his own relationships to people. Man has an in-built faculty of *self-awareness* and *understanding*. That understanding which is not knowing has a perceptive sensitivity.

A real religion is perception of the order behind the visible disorder. All activity or all events in the symbolic-dualistic frame in our lives–indeed all happenings in the entire universe are illusions. Rather, the usual investigation of life and time is seen as fairly insignificant, and the usual personal struggle leads to pain, misery and travails. It is the non-dual, non-conceptual frame of reference of Mind Continuum that bestows on us a real religion.

A non-subjective perception is the foundation of real religion. A religious mind is beyond duality, beyond causation, beyond time, beyond limitation. It is the non-dual frame that bestows the religious mind, or real religion. The essence of religion is freedom; it means to have no conflict, psychologically, inwardly. The characteristics of restructured science (real science) are identical to that of restructured real religion.

To sum up, the perception of the *fact*, the *true*, the *present*, the *non-dual*, the *what is*! is real science and real religion. Both real science and real religion are synonymous, because both are in search of the truth that sustains man and that the truth of the universe. Both investigate the life field domain, or "holistic frequency realm" that transcends spatial and temporal boundaries. The true religious mind and true scientific mind are non-authoritative, non-dualistic, and both deal with pure perception. Both encourage intuition (insight), spontaneity and right action. Both move from *fact* to *fact*.

Albert Einstein stated, "I cannot conceive of a genuine scientist without profound faith.... Science without religion is lame, religion without science is blind".[14] Schumacher wrote, "The modern experiment to live without religion has failed, and once we have understood this we know what our 'post-modern' talks really are?"[15] A.N. Whitehead said, "The future of civilisation depends on the degree to which we can balance the forces of science and religion". He added that the essence of education is "it is religion.... which inculcates duty and reverence".[16] It is evident that both real science and real religion depend on faith in the Unmanifest, the Life Field, the Wholeness of Life, the Holistic Frequency Realm. We define the restructuring of religion as Religion-Faith-Values. The dimensions of restructured science is Science-Education.

The Principle of Understanding

The human-made social cosmos, or construct of the symbolic-dualistic frame of reference of mind spectrum represents the immanent quantum energy potential, and it is divorced from the ultimate quantum energy potential. ***The construct of the mind is the only "reality" where the transcendent potential has gone to abeyance and its only linkage is the immanent potential. It represents the relative field of consciousness.*** The symbolic-dualistic frame of reference has not the capacity to understand nature, because its functioning is repetitive and mechanistic, it has no creativity, no understanding and no learning. As long as the mind is agitated, it can have no understanding.

The non-dual and non-conceptual frame of reference observes the fact and understand the truth lying behind the fact. In stillness of mind, there is no projection of thought. Understanding comes only when the mind is quiet.

Understanding happens when the frequency of Consciousness is more than the velocity of light. Understanding flows to learning. Understanding and learning awakens Intelligence, which resolves all human challenges.

Non-Dual and Non-Conceptual Mode of Mind

There is only the *fact*, which is the mirror-image of the wholeness of life. The fact itself is the operator, not you operating on the fact. There is only the fact and nothing else. If you leave it alone, it has no time. The fact is free from fear. The fact grows and matures. When the fact is left alone it blossoms. Let the fact live.[17]

When you observe or listen deeply the fact, it creates its own movement. It implies that when fact is listened, there is flow of energy from the Unmanifest to the fact and its quantum energy potential goes on increasing. Life is a process of learning in non-duality. To look at the fact is the only thing that matters. ***The observation of a fact without justification or condemnation releases tremendous energy.***[18] Observation of a fact implies that pure consciousness sees itself as fact, and this permits a flow of energy from pure consciousness to the fact. The energy release is expressed as Pure Consciousness → Fact. It helps the fact to make a quantum jump in the vertical dimension of Consciousness.

Perception and understanding are not of time. Immediacy of perception, of observing (seeing), dissolves the fact. And one revels in pure Consciousness, the Bliss. The subject in the non-dual frame of reference is pure Consciousness and fact is the mirror-image–we call it Mind Continuum. The whole mankind shares the Mind Continuum. It invariably expresses itself in the non-dual frame and expresses itself as the fact. The fact flows to understanding and learning. Everything is governed by immutable laws. Everything is a necessary effect. It is the causeless cause; it expresses itself out of its free will. To understand Consciousness, or an enquiry into a subject is the perception of that immeasurable state, the Life Field.

The quantum jump of the conditioned mind to non-dual mind suggests that there is nothing like an individual mind, that there is nothing like an I-consciousness. Thought is the product of collective human effort through uncountable aeons, but it is stored in the brain individually. I am neither individual, nor collective, but humanity.[19] In a non-dual frame, nature expresses itself as fact, so the whole mankind shares the Consciousness, and the Mind Continuum is just one.

Erwin Schrodinger raised the baffling questions–'Who are we really?', 'Where I have come from?', and 'Where I am going?'. Nachiketa in the *Katha Upanishad* raised the question, 'Who am I?'. The identical questions are, 'What is the abode of Truth?', 'Does Truth reside in space and time, or is it outside both space and time?'.[20] Answer to these questions can only come from observation of non-dual and non-conceptual frame of reference of Mind Continuum, and these approaches are the same of 'real science' and 'real religion'.

Intellect and Intuition

The symbolic-dualistic frame of reference constructs time-space-causation matrices at the lowest frequencies of consciousness–called successive consciousness; there is interaction between the observer and the observed; there is an awareness of the mutilated observed and the mutilated observer, which is analysis, which is correction, the altering and the adding. Knowledge and the activity of knowing is a cerebral activity of having many built-in limitations in it. Intellect gives us experience and knowledge, which is always limited.

Many eminent scientists–Einstein, Schrodinger, Heisenberg, Eddington and so on–have stumbled upon another mode of knowing, called intimate, or non-dual, or intuition (insight). The intuition emerges from the non-dual frame of reference, and one is aware of the *fact*. It is insight alone that can decondition the brain. Insight emerges from the wholeness of life; there can be logical, sane, rational action. Only then there can be flowering of the brain, which implies complete relationship with the mind.

Spirituality

It is a science of Life and Living. It explores the conditioned psyche and Unconditioned realm through observation by restructured science-education dimension. Observation implies non-identification, non-evaluation, non-judgment and non-comparison. It does not graft the conceptual over the perceptual. It is a dance of energy without matter, so it is emanation out of emptiness, which is unanalysable, indefinable. Perception is always direct, a non-cerebral, non-psychological exploration of the Reality.

Knowledge is always indirect and therefore partial and limited. Perception bestows the wholeness of life. Perception leads to unconditional relaxation, which is tension-free state of the nervous system and a pressure-free state of the chemical system of the being. Spirituality is the inner transformation in the quality and content of consciousness. It is a mutation. It is a dimensional transformation. Mutation happens in the non-duality. It is a non-subjective and non-objective state.

Love is a principle of Life. Love, which is uncontaminated, unpolluted, is Intelligence. Love is a perceptive sensitivity. Love is understanding without the help of verbalization. Love is the energy which fills the emptiness of the Cosmos.

The real science and real religion will lead to an alternative culture. It bestows inner relaxation, inner peace, inner equipoise. The quality of perception is transformed, and therefore the quality of relationship also changes.

The Turning Point

Fritjof Capra wrote, "We need a new paradigm, a new vision of reality–a fundamental change in our thoughts, perceptions and values.... The current changes are likely to result in a transformation of unprecedenfed dimension, a turning point for the planet as a whole". Ilya Prigogine wrote, "Every living organism is a self-organizing system, which means that its order and function is not imposed by the environment but is established by the system itself". The two complementary tendencies of self-organizing system–self-maintenance and self-transcendence–are in continual dynamic interplay, and both contribute to the phenomenon of evolutionary adaptation. Capra defined "mind is the dynamics of self-organisation, and the brain is the biological structure through which this dynamics is carried out".[21]

The observation of the mind-brain-body system leads to a self-organizing and self-transcendence system. And this results in a quantum jump from psychosocial evolution to spiritual evolution. The non-dual frame is closed to the environments and open to the Unmanifest, so mutation is not imposed by the environment but it happens in the system itself. It implies that the radical transformation or mutation is governed by the Unmanifest, the Life Field. The cultural renaissance is a turning point for the planet as a whole.

Concluding Comment

Many eminent scientists have stated that "real science" must take in its ambient the objective and the subjective dimensions of life; or in other words, it deals with the wholeness of life. Similarly 'real religion' takes into consideration the sensual and trans-sensual dimensions of life; or in other words, the real religion deals with the spiritual dimension of life, which is eternal, infinite and immutable. Both real science and real religion have non-authoritarian and non-dualistic approach and are in search of truth. In principle, real science (restructured Science-Education), real religion (restructured Religion-Faith-Values) and Spirituality are synonymous and are one.

The occurrence of seeing (observing) or hearing (listening), breathing or smelling is a movement in the sphere of non-duality. Similarly understanding, learning, intuition (insight), spontaneity and right action are in the realm of non-duality. All perennial values, including spiritual values are a product of human subjectivity, or human inner potential, or Life Field. The dimension of Awareness, which is an energy born of the emptiness of silence, is in the realm of non-authoritarian, non-dualistic and non-causation.[22]

Every existence (physical, biological and psychological)–atom, event, happening–is a cosmic dance of the play of the Unmanifest and the manifest. All this suggests a oneness and interrelatedness, or Mind only. This energises Intelligence which ends all psychological imbalances, ecological problems and other challenges, and man revels in order, rhythm, non-violence and peace.

The restructured science-education and real religion will regenerate and rejuvenate human mind so that it perceives the wholeness of life, which is the new dimension of an integral and all-inclusive Consciousness, that can guarantee human survival along with all fauna and flora.

Man is born: (a) to transcend the structural crisis, or the cultural belief structure, or the memory, or the self-knowledge of the conditioned psyche; and (b) to live in the dimension of self-awareness, understanding and learning. It involves a quantum jump from symbolic-dualistic frame to non-dual frame, or from intellect to intuition, or the lowest frequencies of consciousness to the Supreme Highest Frequency of Consciousness. It is the greatest vocation in the world.

References

1. D.S. Kothari, *Atom and Self*, in *The Evolution of Consciousness*, New Delhi: National Publishing House, 1983, p. 211.
2. Wilder Penfield, in Deepak Chopra, *How to Know God*, London: Rider, 2000, pp. 215, 217.
3. David Bohm, in Gary Zukav, *The Dancing Wu Li Masters*, Fontana/Collins, 1982, p. 327.
4. Candace Pert, in Fritjof Capra, *The Web of Life*, Flamingo, 1996, p. 277.
5. Larry Dossey, *Medical Science and Non-Violence*, New Delhi: Gandhi Peace Foundation, 1988, pp. 12-13, 14.
6. D.S. Kothari, *Some Thoughts on Science and Religion*, University of Delhi, October 31 and November 3, 1977, p. 44.
7. Von Neumann, in D.S. Kothari, *Atom and Self, op. cit.*, p. 230.
8. D.S. Kothari, *The Perception of Truth in Science and Philosophy*, in *The Odyssey of Science, Culture and Consciousness*, New Delhi: Abhinav Publications, 1990, p. 46.
9. Erwin Schrodinger, *What is Life? & Mind and Matter*, Cambridge University Press, 1967 (Edition), pp. 94, 95, 145, 152.
10. Swami Ranganathananda, *Science and Religion*, Calcutta: Advaita Ashrama, 1979, p. 65.
11. Swami Vivekananda, *Complete Works*, Vol. IV, eighth edition, p. 35, in *ibid.*, p. 85.
12. *ibid.*, p. 358, in *ibid.*, p. 86.
13. *ibid.*, in *Vedanta*, Ramakrishna Vedanta Centre, UK, November-December, 2003, No. 314, Back Cover Page.
14. Albert Einstein, in D.S. Kothari, *Atom and Self, op. cit.*, pp. 218-219
15. E.F. Schumacher, *ibid.*, p. 209.
16. A.N. Whitehead, *ibid.*, p. 209.
17. J. Krishnamurti, *Within the Mind*, KFI, 1982, p. 148.

18. *ibid.*, *Krishnamurti on Education*, Orient Longman, KFI, 1974, pp. 90, 87, 69.

19. *ibid.*, KFI Bulletin, 1982, No. 1, p. 40.

20. D.S. Kothari, *Atom and Self, op. cit.*, p. 208.

21. Fritjof Capra, *The Turning Point*, in *The Evolution of Consciousness, op. cit.*, pp. 243, 246, 247.

22. Sampooran Singh, *Nature's Evolutionary Impulse*, Vedanta: Ramakrishna Vedanta Centre, UK, November-December 2003, No. 314, pp. 260-265, and January-February 2004, No. 315, pp. 13-19.

26
Questions and Answers

Q. 1 ***Please discuss I-consciousness or Ego?***

A. Living is a movement of acquisition, storing it in memory, possessing, acquiring, owning and using it. There is comparison, competition, jealousy, the desire to dominate, the necessity to depend upon aggression, violence. The emergence of the ego is a psychophysical process, taking place in the realm of duality, so it is an *indirect* process. It is a cerebral process which requires the help of knowledge, experience and memory. It is in the field of symbolic-dualistic frame of reference of mind spectrum. It is an indirect (distorted) contact with truth.

The "I" feels alive only in movement–movement of acquiring or movement of reacting. The movement is a living, because when a thought travels in the body, it consumes nervous energy. When emotions travel in the body, it affects chemical system, it affects the health. Every activity of I-consciousness and thought structure leads to enhancing entropy–nervous tension and chemical pressure–of the system, which is an indication that the system is leading us to self-destruction, to self-annihilation, to death. The basic challenge facing mankind is not to add toxins and to wash out the old toxins accumulated in the system.

Many eminent neuro-scientists, neuro-physiologists and neuro-surgeons have suggested that the "Brain science .... could no longer afford to shut out that part of the world which we call subjective". It is evident that the subjective (inner) dimension and the objective (outer) dimensions of man are a unitary movement, one whole. The energy exchange between the subjective and the objective happens in a few millionth of a second. Similarly education must take in its realm the sensory world and the trans-sensual world. It is evident that we will have to "restructure science-education" which deals with the wholeness of life–and this we call as true-subject. Putting it in philosophical language, there is physical reaction, the observed world is situated within the observer's world, our dialogue with nature is from within nature, there is steady flame of attention which is non-subjective and non-objective.[1] Observation leads to withering of the *fact*, and there just remains a flame of alertness, of sensitivity–this is what we call silence.

I-consciousness does not have any factual reality, it is a conceptual structure. When I-consciousness goes to abeyance or non-action, it is called silence. Silence is the non-action of the ego. Silence is the total relaxation of the ego, the "self", the "me". Discontinuity of the movement of knowledge, experience and inheritance is silence.

1. Vimala Thakar, *What is Meditation?*, India: Vimal Prakashan Trust, 1998, p. 18

Q. 2 ***May we discuss Health Technology and the technique of healing?***

A. When thought does not move, when emotions do not move, when there is no pressure on the nervous system or the chemical system, when there is that holistic relaxation, then the curative and the healing energies in the body begin to move. It is the relaxation that has healing energies. It is the relaxation that activises the creative energies. The highest quantum energy potential or the highest frequency of the Consciousness is the creative energy, or the healing energy. The inhaling and exhaling breathing in relaxation becomes rhythmical, so this happens in the dimension of silence.

Meditation is a way of life in which you never lose your balance. It is an inner equipoise. We will have to educate ourselves for dimensional mutation or dimensional transformation.

Education teaches the techniques of motion, movement, speech, and so on. But the parents or the schools never educate the child to the science of solitude, stillness and silence. There is an urgency to initiate the "restructured curriculum of education"–investigating the psychodynamics of conditioned psyche, exploring Unconditioned Energy, exploring the silence and this leads to energising the creative energy or the healing energy. We will have to restructure medical education.

The silence activises the Intelligence or perceptive sensitivity. The content in the emptiness of silence is full of Intelligence–in India they call it *Atman*. Intelligence is an energy born of the emptiness of silence, of the space of silence.

Thought is intellect which is a cerebral energy. Thought is an energy created by the past inheritance. Impulse is a biological energy. Intelligence is an energy born of emptiness of silence. It is only in the state of meditation that love can flower. You become an expression of love, as a drop of water is the expression of the ocean. They have the same quality.

Q. 3 ***What is meditation? What is its relationship to the emergence of a new human race?***

A. Meditation is the essence of spirituality. We have to educate our physical organism and psychological structure to move into non-action gracefully and voluntarily. The Cosmic Intelligence takes over the charge of our being. A new balanced human being who has no imbalances, and therefore no impurities, but who has a grandeur of inner equipoise and a majesty of outer sensual balance comes into our life.

The meditation, or no-mind state, or non-dual frame of reference of mind spectrum is a state of consciousness in which there is no centre as the "I" or the "me" or the "self"; in which the thought structure has gone to abeyance; in which the mind does not divide itself to subject and object and as such it is free from duality; and there is holistic awareness or perceptive sensitivity. It regenerates Intelligence and manifests as unity of life.

Meditation is a by-product of being in the dimension of silence. It leads to inner mutation. It regenerates Intelligence. The Intelligence controls the intellect, and the intellectual understanding controls the behaviour of the sense organs–the intellectual understanding is non-dual, and the behaviour of the sense organs is non-dual. There is no fear, no acquisitveness, no desire for ownership and possession, no desire to dominate over others. A new human race, with a new human culture and a new dynamics, a new foundation for human relationship, will be there.

Meditation is a dimensional transformation–it is the silencing of thought structure coupled with volitions. It is a dimensional transformation from thought structure (successive consciousness) to the dimension of life (Simultaneous Consciousness). It is the awareness of the wholeness of life–an awareness without division, without fragmentation. It is a revolution in the content of consciousness. It is a revolution in the texture of our perception and our response.

Q. 4 What is self-education?

A. Enquiry is a kind of self-education. Observation is the perception without psychological involvement, without any kind of reaction. Reaction implies evaluation, judgement, condemnation, comparison. Education implies unlearning the incorrect (false) and learning the correct (true) way of living. Self-education implies to find out the truth and jettison the false. Observation is personal encounter with the fact. So the knowledge about the fact gets converted into understanding of fact.

Silence is effortless alertness. The alertness is the subject and it sees the fact. Observation without the observer is the state of the wholeness of perception and wholeness of responses. So observation as a dimension of your whole life becomes a movement of the spontaneity, of that wholeness.

We have to educate our physical organism and psychological structure. We have to observe, or enquire, or explore, or experimentally interrogate the conditioned mind (psyche) and Unconditioned Energy by true-subject (restructured science-education); and this flows from action of conditioned mind to non-action of mind, from dualistic activity of mind to non-dual state gracefully and voluntarily. Understanding is a movement in the non-duality, a movement of the whole being. The perceptions are born of non-duality and responses are born of spontaneity. The state of no-mind blossoms into regeneration of Supreme Intelligence which takes into its fold the being, or in other words, the Cosmic Intelligence takes over the charge of our being and things happen by themselves.

Q. 5 *Is it possible to end violence and aggression from the planet? Is it possible to end terrorism?*

A. The recent challenges are terrorism, corruption, religious fundamentalism, ethnic conflicts, drug trafficking have erupted during the last few decades. The root of all challenges–psychological imbalances, ecological crisis, terrorism, corruption and so on–is embedded in the conditioned psyche; and all these challenges are some form of violence and aggression. Obviously it is only higher quantum energy potential of Cosmic Consciousness that can end these challenges.

Every world leader talks of tackling (say terrorism) at the international level. We opine that brute force available with Governments will temporarily suppress the terrorism, which means that terrorism at the conscious level of human mind will be suppressed, but the seeds of terrorism will go from conscious level to deep subconscious level; and terrorism may erupt at any time any where in the world.

The world will have to tackle these challenges at two levels:

(a) The challenges are not political, nor economic, nor social; but are evolutionary in nature. Man is treating the symptoms in the external field through socio-political-economic reforms. These may lead to postponement of crisis, but it has no capacity to end the crisis. Expedient measures to meet the present challenges are intellectual constructions. These may partially ameliorate human suffering. These measures will be transient and temporary and ephemeral.

Seventeen Asian countries, including India, met on October 22, 2004, and adopted a declaration saying that "the threats posed by terrorism, separatism and extremism 'undermine the very foundation of international peace and security' and stressed that the fight against these should be global, comprehensive and sustained and not selective or discriminatory and should avoid applying double standards";–these are fundamentally ***expedient*** measures, which are transient, temporary and local. The expedient measures cannot resolve violence and terrorism stored at the subconscious level of the conditioned mind.

(b) Permanent measures are to heal the diseased human psyche, or to work for radical transformation of human psyche. D.S. Kothari, an eminent physicist, quoted Buddha in words, "What the Buddha proclaimed about the imperative need to ***know*** the mind, to ***shape*** the mind, and to ***liberate*** the mind has never been more true than in the Age of the Atom". Permanent measures bring mutation in the human psyche. These lead to quantum jump from symbolic-dualistic frame to non-dual frame of Mind Continuum; and it bestows intuition and spontaneity. It is the non-dual and non-conceptual frame of reference of Mind Continuum that has the capacity to end violence, terrorism and corruption.

It is unfortunate that mankind is not investigating the conditioned psyche and exploring the Unconditioned Energy; or in other words, exploring the symbiosis of science and spirituality, which is evident from the following:

(a) The Committee on Science and Technology, USA, submitted in June 1981 a lengthy report to the House of Representatives, USA, which encouraged serious assessment of further research on "*the physics of consciousness*", and concluded that recent experiments:

> .... that there exists an 'interconnectiveness' of the human mind with other minds and with matter; .... that the human mind may be able to obtain the information independent of geography and time.

(b) Richard Lamm, Former Governor of Colorado, quoted Stuart Udall, and said, "The whole human enterprise is a machine without brakes, for there are no indications that the world's political leaders will deal with the realities until catastrophes occur .... We have already passed the point of no return, and tragic convulsions are at hand".

(c) The Union of Concerned Scientists–over 1670 scientists, including 104 Nobel laureates–sent "*World Scientists' Warning to Humanity*" in April 1993; which concluded:

A new ethic is required–a new attitude towards discharging our responsibility for caring for ourselves and for the earth. We must recognize the earth's limited capacity to provide for us. We must recognize its fragility. We must no longer allow it to be ravaged. This ethic must motivate a great movement, convincing reluctant leaders and reluctant governments and reluctant peoples themselves to effect the needed changes.

Every one agrees on the urgency to eradicate the cancer of global terrorism and violence, and corruption and organised crime. If man fails the total responsibility to end this cancer, the evolutionary impulse of Nature is bound to act and end the cancer (mankind) through some catastrophes; so we are doomed to disaster. The answer to the paradox is that it is the Cosmic Consciousness that has the capacity to end all psychological challenges including terrorism. This is the only hope for mankind's survival. This is the only vocation of mankind.

Sri Aurobindo, an eminent philosopher-mystic predicted, "The East alone has some knowledge of the truth, the East alone can teach the West, the East alone can save mankind.... the initiative can come from India and although the scope must be universal, the central movement may be hers .... A catastrophe may intervene and interrupt and destroy what is being done, but even then the final result is sure". This highlights India's responsibility and a grim warning to the world.

Q. 6 ***May we discuss Nature's Evolutionary Impulse?***

A. J. Krishnamurti, in prophetic words, wrote, "I am the conclusion of all the experiences of mankind. The story of all mankind is me .... I question the whole concept that I am an individual, not that I am the collective. I am humanity, not the collective".[1] He again added, "We are the history of mankind. We are the story of mankind. If we don't know how to read the book with clarity, without any interpretation, then we are going to destroy ourselves".[2] We inherit the brain, total human knowledge (information) and experience, and store it in our psyche. Man has nothing of his own, it is all (brain and memory) inheritance.

The symbolic-dualistic frame of reference is repetitive and mechanical, so it is the past. It does not have any understanding. Krishnamurti stated, "An ancient race, three to five thousand years of certain culture has been wiped out overnight".[2] ***The crisis is conditioned human psyche, "not wars or nuclear war"***. Karan Singh concluded, "Today, after billions of years of prebiological evolution and metabiological evolution, mankind is at an evolutionary crossroads. We stand at a juncture wherein we are in supreme peril–not a peril from another species, not a peril from outer space, but a peril from ourselves. From deep within the human psyche, there has developed the terrible power that threatens not only our generation but generations yet to be born, and not only our race, but all species of life on this planet".[3] The inward world is vast, immense, incalculably deep. And this is leading us to self-destruction, or self-annihilation, or collective genocide. We need exploration of the whole psyche.

We start with the enquiry or observation of the cause, dynamics and limitations of objective science, value education and health technology in the light of discoveries of modern science. We have to "restructure science" which implies that the objective and the subjective dimensions of life are a single dynamic flow; "restructure education", which takes in its fold both the sensual and the trans-sensual dimensions; and "restructure health" which takes in its ambient the physical, environmental and thought, and are a part of self-education. In principle, we consider to "restructure science-education-health" which is called true-subject.

The symbolic-dualistic frame of reference of mind spectrum is repetitive and mechanical, so it cannot give us understanding. The non-dual and non-conceptual frame of reference of Mind Continuum bestows understanding. Understanding flows to learning. During observation, thought structure coupled with its volitions comes in the field of true-subject, thought goes to abeyance and only Intelligence bathing the neurons is left behind.

The evolutionary impulse is leading mankind to regeneration of Intelligence which is, in principle, Nature's Grace. It is the Cosmic Consciousness that governs Nature's evolutionary impulse. This will flow into emergence of a new human species when all psychological imbalances have gone to abeyance and man revels in order, harmony, non-violence and peace. This only is the social, psychological and even the political revolution. The only vocation of mankind is to resolve this paradox *here* and *now*. This is the consummation of human life. This is the new human being.

References

1. KFI, 1982, No. 1, p. 40.
2. KFI, 1983, No. 3, pp. 27-28.
3. Karan Singh, in *Synthesis of Science and Religion*, Mumbai: The Bhaktivedanta Institute, June 1988, p. 23.

Index

H

I

J

K

L

M

S

T